THE RISE OF VIRTUAL REALITY

It is All in Your Head

Anthony Napoleon, Ph.D.

Graphics and video references included in this book are part of the public domain and are included herein solely for the purpose of commentary, criticism and/or documentation. Copyrighted material cited herein falls under the Fair Use exemption to U.S. Copyright laws.

"The Rise of Virtual Reality: It is All in Your Head," by Dr. Anthony Napoleon, Ph.D. 978-1-63868-023-9 (softcover); 978-1-63868-024-6 (hardcover); 978-1-63868-025-3 (eBook).

Published 2021 by Virtualbookworm.com Publishing Inc., P.O. Box 9949, College Station, TX 77842, US.

Aspiration

Discover the better version of your objectively real-world self, then be that real person. Even better, be the real-world person your real-world dog thinks you are.

Dedication

You know who you are, and I have already expressed my appreciation. In the real world, that is how we do things.

TABLE OF CONTENTS

Preface

Imagine what it would be like to stroll along the Pacific Ocean on a starlit summer evening. You'd find your senses immersed in the rhythmic sounds of breaking waves, warm sea breezes, the smell of salt air, and the feel of cool sand under your feet. You couldn't help but look up at the heavens at which point you'd be awestruck by the spectacle of an infinite number of stars and other celestial bodies sparkling in the night sky. If by chance you are feeling the least bit envious, consider this—that smart phone you have in your pocket or sitting on its charger has proven to be a viable competitor to the sensory portrait I just drew for you. Not only have I seen smart phone screens compete with and win the battle for people's attention on those summer starlit nights along the Pacific Ocean, but also, I've seen screens win the battle for people's attention in the presence of wonderful and loving people. The battle for your attention is serious business, and for the first time in human history, vested interests have found ways to capture every last drop of it. What they do not capture, you give away—and in so doing, you give away your soul.

PART I

CHAPTER I

PRESTIDIGITATION: Magic in a Real Bottle

FIRST AXIOM OF VIRTUAL REALITY

Human beings find virtual presentations, modifications, replications, and/or augmentations of objective reality to be extremely pleasurable.

At the outset it may be helpful to provide some cursory definitions of alternative realities in common usage as of the writing of this book, one of which is commonly referred to as virtual reality. Keep in mind the following working definitions in common usage are not demarcated from one another with clear lines of delineation.

VR: Virtual Reality - As the name implies, "virtual" connotes a manmade reality or presentation of it that is, in varying degrees, a likeness of objective reality. Taken to its ultimate technological end point, virtual reality would be indistinguishable from objective reality. The current author includes displays of objective reality as a type of VR. These may be drawings of real things or digital device screens, which transmit places, things, or language in varying contexts, including screen coverage of an objectively real event as in live sports broadcasts. As of 2020, developers' efforts along the path toward a more perfect—that is, overlapping—virtual reality experience includes the following technological conduits, including but not limited to the Oculus Rift, HTC Vive, Google Cardboard, and the VR Walker Sports Virtual Reality Unit, just to name a few.[1]

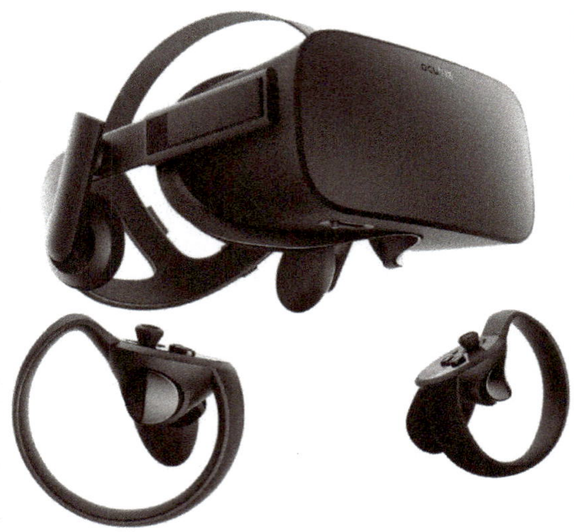

Oculus Rift by Facebook, Inc.

AR: Augmented Reality - This flavor of alternative reality keeps all or major parts of a transmitted objective reality as its canvas/context, upon which a virtual component is introduced onto/into that canvas/context. Historians will undoubtedly mention *Pokemon Go* as one of the first popular AR experiences.

Pokemon Go by Niantic, Inc.

[1] The reader should be cognizant of the primitive nature of our current VR technology - a fact that if not recognized today, will be patently evident in the not-too-distant future.

MR: Mixed Reality – This term is in common usage, but the current author considers it to lack sufficient precision to have scientific meaning. MR is a mélange of objective, AR, and VR in various combinations that create an experience that maintains objective reality as a backdrop, but adds to that canvas of VR worlds and AR components in the user's sensory field, with an emphasis upon the visual. A very early version of what we might label MR as of 2020 is Microsoft's HoloLens 2.

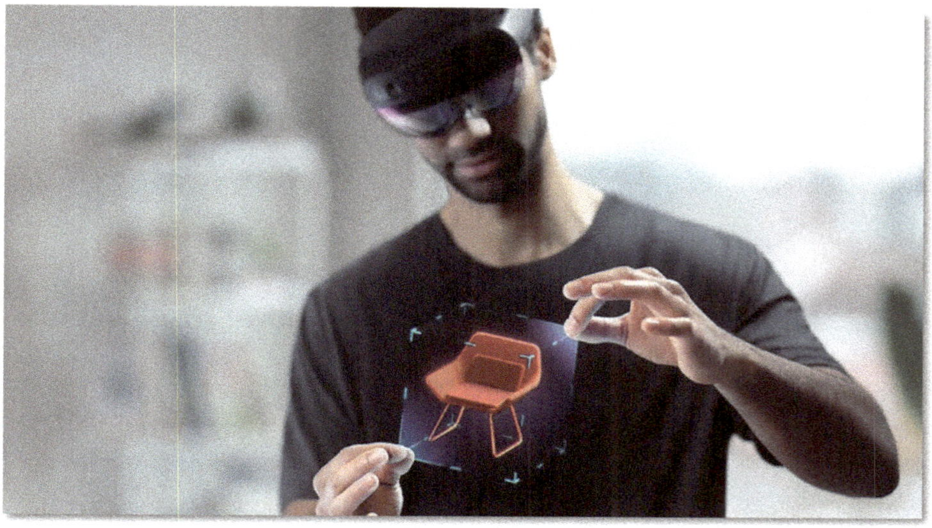

HoloLens 2 by Microsoft Corporation

ER: Extended Reality – Again, we include this term only because it may be one that is familiar to the reader, but we consider it to be void of scientific meaning. We surmise its originators recognized that at some point in the future, the various and sundry iterations of OR, VR, AR, et al. will come together to create yet another subjective experience that combines the best of each world. Later we will be adding dimension and contour to the various forms of reality we humans have created, but before we move on, here is our definition of objective reality.

OR: Objective Reality – When we use the term "alternative realities," our reference point for what constitutes "alternate" is OR. In keeping with the old adage "a picture is worth a thousand words":

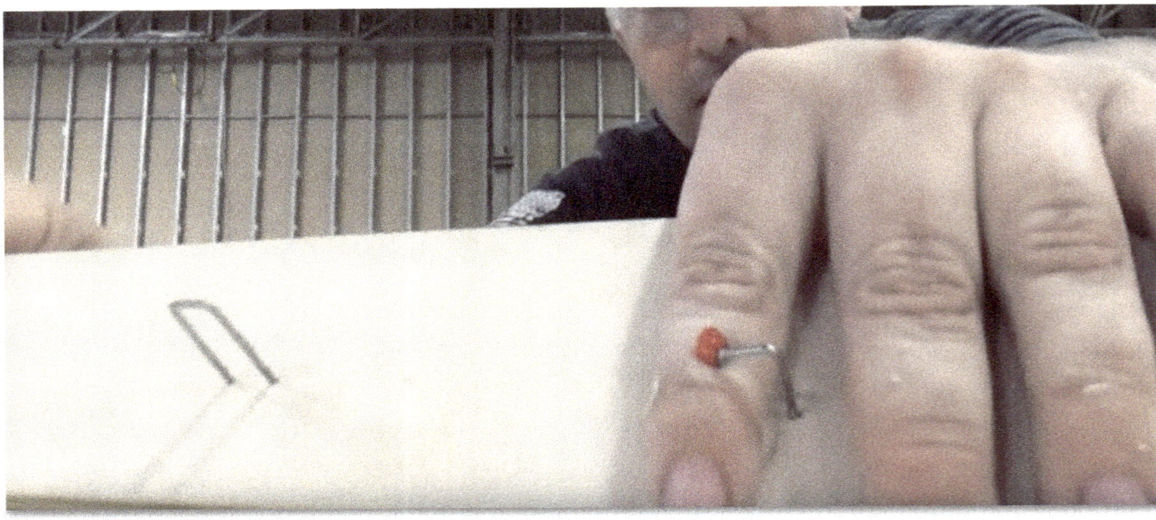

OR: Objective Reality

At the outset I offer these additional terms and their definitions for the reader's reference, keeping in mind I will add dimension and contour to them as we move forward.

The Tesseract Dimension – Also known as the fourth dimension, it is that relationship state of virtual and objective reality when they merge so perfectly, they become one and the same. Tesseract is that alternative reality moment of singularity that consists of a reality functionally autonomous from its component parts. This moment of singularity will occur at some time in the future and will require transformational technology that is as of yet theoretical.

V the Reality – Vested interests have concluded that virtual renditions of objective reality serve their interests, and that individual's free choice interactions with objective reality do not. Virtual the Reality—operationally defined as, **Virtual IS the Reality**—is being both sold and surreptitiously forced upon the global community as I pen this book. It is being sold using various social engineering strategies that make use of the selling points of convenience and safety, while tapping into social conformity trendiness, among others. It is being forced upon global populations by systematically removing the ability of individuals to have easy access to, or sometimes obviating, objective interactions with personally controllable means of objective interactions and transactions, e.g., cash, the operation of motor vehicles, in-person education, and bank accounts with OR money.

Activities that are currently cumbersome thanks to V the Reality will become impossible to do at some point in the future. Your personal, business, civic, and recreational lives without big tech and government's digital creations, infrastructure, and ethos will be impossible in the future. Importantly, tech and government's ethos will be enforced using revocable access to social media, cancel culture group enforcement, strict enforcement of politically correct speech, and removing privacy protections. When V the Reality consumes OR reality, then what is real will be synonymous with truth, what is right, and anyone who dares question these distortions will suffer the wrath of those who promote and have been consumed by V the Reality. With these terms and definitions in mind, let's begin.

Human beings are objectively real entities that live in an objectively real world, where the laws of physics/biophysics regulate how our physical bodies interact with the objective and virtual world and its contents. And as you may have already ascertained, mistakenly stapling your finger instead of a piece of wood will immediately convince you of the validity of my last assertion. Virtual reality, on the other hand, is like magic because its claim to fame is, at least in part, that it can defy the laws of physics, e.g., first-person virtual shooters can "kill" and be "killed" without consideration of real-world consequences, and commercial pilots practicing on flight simulators can crash into the side of a mountain and everyone walks away—and yes, if a VR game involving stapling wood were to be made, you wouldn't have to stop everything and go to the ER if you mistook your finger for a piece of wood. Nevertheless, VR and OR are inextricably connected to one another.

The 1960s TV series *I Dream of Jeannie* serves as both a literal and metaphoric example of this fusion. By simply blinking while crossing her arms, Barbara Eden's character could send her enemies to the North Pole or join her astronaut husband in space.

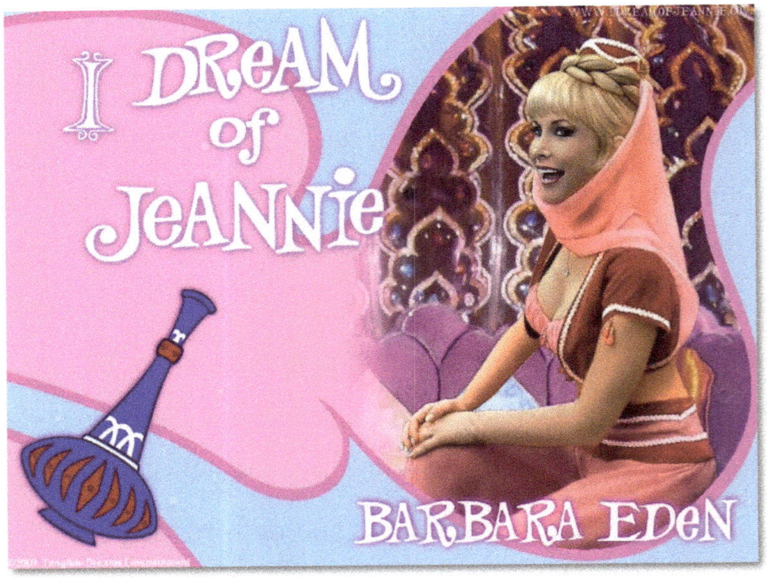

Barbara Eden as Jeannie and Her Magic Bottle Getaway Home from *I Dream of Jeannie* TV Series Circa 1960s (Courtesy of Tangible Dreams Entertainment)

But just like all virtual reality, a lot of real-world set design had to be constructed to make Jeannie's virtual reality come to life, to wit:

Barbara Eden Climbing into Her "Magic Bottle Set" from the Soundstage of *I Dream of Jeannie* TV Series Circa 1960s

"Magic Bottle Set" from the Soundstage of I Dream of Jeannie TV Series Circa 1960s

And just like the magic created on *I Dream of Jeannie*, the vessels within which this thing we call virtual reality is stored, played back, and interacted with are always objectively real entities that are governed by the laws of physics.

VR can be as straightforward as a screen upon which images of objectively real or fabricated people, things, or contexts are displayed, streamed, or live casted— or it may one day be defined as where OR and VR fuse so seamlessly that it will create a fourth dimension of reality, e.g., the Tesseract Dimension.

Postproduction Still from the Movie The Matrix Four-Scheduled Release Date December 2021

(NPV Entertainment)

Virtual reality can also be interactive with OR, as we find in augmented reality. Augmented reality's claim to fame is that objective reality becomes even more meaningful when we add a complementary virtual component to it. This claim is born out in the real world. Take, for example, the AR cockpit of the F35 Fighter Jet. Real-life dogfights are simultaneously played out virtually on screens as well as in the air. When AR and OR are combined in modern fighter aircraft, augmented reality heightens a pilot's visuomotor skill set and provides a greater chance of splashing your adversary while living to tell about it.

F-35 Cockpit/ Virtual Reality and Objective Reality Augmented

F-35 Cockpit Demonstrator

Our love affair with alternative realities may be something wired into us. What is it about human beings that motivate us to modify objective reality?

CHAPTER II

HOMO SAPIENS: Man as a Virtual Reality Developer

What is absolutely fascinating about the human experience is that although we are objective creatures living in an objective world, we are also genetically programmed to automatically and without awareness transform our perceptions of the objective world into symbolic, or virtual, representations of it. In that sense, we are all virtual reality developers whether we can code or not. [2]

We also possess the ability to fabricate virtual worlds out of whole cloth and store these fantasy worlds in our central nervous system (CNS). We are wired to transform our perceptions and summary neuro-processing of objective reality and fabrications into real-world CNS structures and chemistry that we can store and "play back." Think of "playing back" as similar to streaming a movie. The movie serves as a virtual reality experience where the objective laws of physics don't necessarily impose their regulations upon the story or its characters, e.g., think about the maneuvers of the Millennium Falcon. Nevertheless, the laws of physics/biophysics do impose their governance upon the biological vessel and its contents that stores and plays back those stories. When we play back some of our

---

[2] Başar E and Düzgün A (2016) Links of Consciousness, Perception, and Memory by Means of Delta Oscillations of Brain. Front. Psychol. 7:275. doi: 10.3389/fpsyg.2016.00275.

stored virtual realities while sleeping, we call it *dreaming*. If we let our minds wander during the day, some call it daydreaming. Both are versions of intrinsic VR.

The recall and playback of the virtual symbols in the objectively real storage device we label the CNS comprises a virtual reality play in the theater of our mind. Our virtual reality theatrical productions, whether we are dreaming, imagining or fanaticizing, allows us to perform feats of time travel, fly, jump, perform Herculean feats of strength, and almost anything else imaginable that defies the laws of physics.

Movie Poster for the 1985 Film Brazil

A good way to discern the experiential differences between VR and OR worlds is to think about *driving* a car on an interstate or freeway versus *operating* a driving simulator/video driving game. In the external objective world, the laws of physics set parameters for how you, a real-world biological entity in a physical vehicle, moves through time and space, navigating manmade and natural terrain features, other vehicles, and other external world objects. As you drive down the road, your sensory system perceives stimuli from traffic signs and lights and other objects, both stationary and kinetic. All five senses are involved in the act of driving, including somatosensory stimuli that involve vibrations transmitted through the suspension of your vehicle through your car's seat and steering wheel. Even smell can be involved in real-world driving, e.g., fuel odors, burning materials, etc. But even in external world driving, the internal virtual world is ever present.

As you drive a vehicle, various and sundry external world stimuli, e.g., landmarks, topography, and the like, comprise data that are seamlessly transformed into symbolic representations from which an internal virtual driving world is simultaneously constructed. This virtual world includes things like cognitive maps. Cognitive maps are virtual world representations of external world stimuli. You, as a real-world driver, have a cognitive map for every location you can navigate to without any outside assistance. Now, let's compare the experiences of real-world driving to virtual-world "driving," beginning with some of the more subtle psychological considerations of the people who make VR "driving" possible.

Consider for a moment the ironic world of fabricators of virtual reality experiences, including driving games and simulators. The designers, coders, and fabricators make objectively real and tangible things, things that are inextricably governed by the laws of objective world physics, but which provide an internal virtual world experience unshackled from those same laws of physics. Your central nervous system, where your virtual world experience takes place, is most certainly an objectively real conglomeration of biological matter. But it is the experience that makes it possible for a person sitting in their game room to race in the Indy 500—that is, the VR version of the Indy 500.

Suspending the laws of real-world physics and replacing them with virtual-world physics, as we find in simulators and games, creates some fascinating experiential phenomena. For example, a user operating a driving simulator can

VIRTUALLY strike a VIRTUAL pedestrian with such VIRTUAL force that in the OR world, a REAL pedestrian would be killed or severely injured. Driving simulators often take the real-life consequences of such horrific events, and our response to them, and turn them on their heads.

A real-world driver about to slam into a tree going 100 mph/160.93 km/h would naturally have a look of terror on her face and experience impending doom. Pilots' last words on flight recorders just before they know they will die are heart-wrenching when their words are paired with their vocal affect, e.g. Air France flight 447: "Fuck, we're dead" or Alaska Airlines Flight 261: "Ma, I love ya." Compare those heart-wrenching expressions of terror and resignation to the reactions of some operators of driving/pilot simulators who smile or laugh as they careen through the air in the virtual world of the simulator. In the virtual world, even the most horrific event becomes death-defying and void of life-changing consequences in the objective world.

The driving/flight simulator's claim to fame is that the laws of external world physics do not necessarily regulate the SYMBOLS of real-world objects and terrain, including us, as they do objective world objects and terrain—but at the same time, they replicate the objectively real world. And even though the best driving/flight simulators/games replicate vehicle dynamics, the fact of the matter is the operator will not literally die, nor will she literally kill anyone or anything in the virtual world, if she happens to be involved in a "fatal" accident. Nevertheless, the simulator, as the name implies, encourages the suspension of a conscious awareness of reality by carefully recreating it so that the operator can act AS IF he or she is navigating a vehicle in the objective world. In fact, the measure of the quality and sophistication of a driving simulator is how easy it is for the operator to suspend her real world for a virtual-world experience. So, think about that nifty legerdemain your brain pulls off where an objective world entity (you) suspends his/her cognitive awareness of reality in favor of focusing upon the virtual world. We know what we are doing is not real, but we pretend that it is. And the better we are at suspending our sense of reality, the more we enjoy the process of creating our virtual world.

One other measure of the quality of any simulator is worth noting here, and it involves whether the cognitive maps and visuomotor skills learned from driving simulators can be generalized to external world driving. It also illustrates how human beings conflate virtual and objective reality—but not completely, if the person in question is mentally stable, and you will soon learn why.

Gran Turismo is one of the, if not the, premier driving game/simulators for the mass market as of the writing of this book. On January 18, 2018, CNBC published the following promotional tease for an upcoming episode of automobile aficionado *Jay Leno's Garage* TV Series:

> *"GT Academy winner Ricardo Sanchez has virtually driven the Willow Springs Racetrack hundreds of times. He meets up with Jay Leno at the racetrack to compare reality and virtual reality. Will his virtual skills transfer over to real world driving? All New Jay Leno's Garage Thursdays 10P ET/PT."*

Mr. Sanchez had "driven" *Gran Turismo's* virtual rendition of the Willow Springs International Motorsports Park's road racing course hundreds of times. In fact, Mr. Sanchez competed against thousands of other virtual world racers to earn the right to become an objectively real-world racing car driver.

During the episode, Mr. Sanchez drove a Nissan GT-R Nismo GT3 Racer around the objective world's Willow Spring's racing course for the first time with Mr. Leno. Mr. Sanchez was immediately familiar with the track's layout, curves, terrain, etc., which helped him navigate the course like a seasoned pro. Jay Leno asked Mr. Sanchez the operant question from the author's perspective:

> *Jay Leno: "Do you ever push a car in real life as you do in the game?"*
>
> *Mr. Sanchez: "In real life you go a bit under, especially because if you do make a mistake it is going to be a hot one. There is no reset button or anything, you just hit the wall and that is it."*

At the end of the interview Mr. Leno said the following to Mr. Sanchez: "You're lucky you were playing *Gran Turismo*, imagine if you had been playing Donkey Kong...how much different your career would be now." I'll have a lot more to say about how human beings navigate the objective and virtual worlds throughout this book.

CHAPTER III

THE MAGIC TRICK: Is it Ella or Memorex?

Let's refer back to *Gran Turismo* champ Mr. Sanchez for a moment. The operator of the driving simulator intellectually KNOWS, as we learned in the case of Mr. Sanchez, that what he sees, hears, and sometimes feels in his virtual world (depending upon the sophistication of the simulator itself) is NOT objectively real—or does he?

This question and its answers are, in part, both philosophical and scientific in nature. In the case of Mr. Sanchez, he told us that he is acutely aware of the difference between VR and OR. However, as technology becomes more sophisticated and the chasm between objective reality and its virtual world facsimile become indistinguishable, these questions, though philosophical and scientific in nature, may also become academic.

Were it not for the deadly consequences of allowing his conscious mind to completely succumb to the siren song of virtual reality, would Mr. Sanchez or any of the millions of *Gran Turismo* gamers retain their objective awareness of the differences between objective and virtual world driving? I can certainly envision technological advances in the not-too-distant future where even the most astute and well-adjusted person will no longer be able to answer the question posed by the Memorex Tape Corporation in one of its 1980s television advertisements: "Is it live, or is it Memorex?"

Memorex Recording Tape Print Ad, Circa 1980s with Jazz Singer Ella Fitzgerald

Even in the days when music was recorded on the physical medium of wax, virtual world innovators tried to convert the objective into a virtual world facsimile so that their creations would blur the difference between the two in the minds of their customers. Not a week goes by where some clever virtual world developers push the envelope toward conflation between VR and OR. For example, on August 30, 2018 Acer announced what it called "The Immersive Predator Thronos Gaming Chair." Endgadget's review of the chair included the following narrative:

> *"[T]he game was as immersive as you'd expect. The Thronos's rumbling synced up with the action on screen -- it was particularly impressive as rocks tumbled around me as I was trying to escape an underground tomb."* [3]

Acer's Predator Thronos Gaming Chair

The old saying, "be careful what you wish for" could not be truer for virtual world developers. Do VR developers really want to make objective and virtual worlds

[3] Endgadget (2018) Acer's Predator Thronos is a cockpit masquerading as gaming chair, by Devindra Hardawar.

indistinguishable? Have developers, users or lawmakers for that matter thought through the unintended consequences when VR and OR become indistinguishable? [4] Mr. Sanchez would probably feel very uncomfortable if technology advances to the point where he could no longer tell the difference in his mind between a virtual racetrack and the real thing, because in the real world there will always be a difference between virtual and real-world experiences—and sometimes that difference is the delta between life and death. But technology is advancing at record speed, and in the not-too-distant future we may have to attach warning labels to our virtual world technology and virtual reality developers may hit a brick wall, no pun intended, that is analogous to the limits of silicon miniaturization, smaller than an atom. Quarks or neutrinos, perhaps?

I can assure the reader that social engineers and the people who hire them have already made plans, no matter how far into the future they may be implemented, for how to exploit the inevitable creation of this fourth dimensional reality—that is, Tesseract reality—and it does not bode well for personal freedom. As you will learn as you continue reading, social engineers are well on their way to achieving their ultimate goals.

The fourth dimension becomes even more of a threat to personal freedom when we take into consideration that the cortical areas of our brains, where our awareness of objective reality resides, may inform its owner that a virtual reality experience is not objectively real, but the user's affective centers located in their brainstem may not only be unable to make the distinction, but may not WANT to make such distinctions.

As biotechnology advances, unless we are told that what we are experiencing is not objectively real, we will most certainly not be able to ascertain the difference using our senses. Even with the current state of our technology, our brainstems often conflate objective and virtual world reality to the point where the differences

---

[4] The author anticipates thoughtful reader's questions regarding the delta between "indistinguishable" and V the Reality. The former simply means that the delta becomes imperceptible to users, and/or VR is so pleasurable to experience users will be hesitant to make the distinction.

are blurred. Who hasn't been fooled by a cleverly Photoshopped image? Add to that the fact that our conscious minds enjoy the obviation of objective world physics; it is a foregone conclusion that in the not-too-distant future, it will only require a slight nudge to make it impossible to make the distinction between an objective and a virtual-world experience. And even if your sensory analysis of a virtual-world experience can independently ascertain that what you are experiencing is not objectively real, will you want to make such distinctions? Will you pay for experiences so "real" that unless you were told, and then believed they were VR, you could not tell the difference using your senses and reasoning acumen? Would you want to make the distinction?

Roy Orbison's Hologram Australian Tour 2018

One of the main attractions of the virtual world is the fact that the vast majority of human beings experience the laws of physics, and the regulators of the objective world can be maddeningly frustrating, with sexual frustrations/rejection right at the top of the list—especially for men. The intensity of these frustrations have been exacerbated, if not socially engineered, by inculcating artificially high self-esteem and the mindset of entitlement into global populations, especially digital native populations. Remember this last point, because ameliorating the maddening frustration that comes with living in the objective world as a normal person is the primary *emotional* motivation for people who are pushing the boundaries of virtual world technology. Sure, you can probably find a virtual world developer/ entrepreneur who will tell you that he is *only* motivated by giving the "market" what it wants—i.e., making money—but truth be told, I have to wonder if the objective world were as forgiving and gracious as the virtual world they create, whether anyone walking along the ocean on a starlit night would be staring down at their smartphone.

It is my clinical opinion that the programming and engineering geniuses who are busy creating, for example, life-like sex cyborgs, super-powerful warriors, or magical worlds where you, too, can be the winner/hero, are motivated by primal forces to create a virtual reality that social engineers have convinced them they are entitled to, but the OR world has denied them.

And speaking of virtual-world sex partners, before the reader attaches a negative label to virtual-world developers whose focus is upon creating ideal sexual partners: If the standard for evaluating sexual partners is the "world class" standard, then it is not only the stereotypical programming "nerd" who is motivated to engineer the world-class sexual ideal. It is virtually everyone who is sexually active. And to revisit a common thread in this book, keep in mind when the time comes that when virtual world sex partners become so close to the real thing—and it will happen—that it will take an expert to tell the difference, if even they can make the distinction, then the term "sexually active" and "sex partner" will have a totally new meaning from what it means for today's readers. For those among my readers who already have a serious case of future shock, you may wish to tighten your real and virtual seatbelts, because turbulence lies ahead, or as a virtual-world experience named *Pirates of the Caribbean* informs guests:

> *"If ye come seeking adventure and salty old pirates, eh? Sure, you come to the proper place. But keep a weather eye open mates and hold on*

tight—with both hands, if you please. There be squalls ahead! And Davy Jones waiting for them what don't obey." [5]

Entrance to Pirates of the Caribbean Virtual Experience, Disneyland, Anaheim, California

Now is a good time to draw a distinction between subsets of virtual experiences using *Pirates of the Caribbean* VR and the now-retired *Star Tours VR* experiences created by Disney engineers (Imagineers) as our examples. The distinction in flavors of VR has to do with quantum mechanics, believe it or not. Virtual experiences that transport humans objectively in time and space, while immersing them in a fabricated but objectively real environment, is what the current author calls VR + Time and Space Vector Manipulation, or VR + TSVM. In Pirates, we are physically moved in time and space using boats on rails through a fabricated world. Parts of that world include animatronic renditions of sentient beings, e.g., humans, cats, dogs, and pigs in various created sets. Compare VR + TSVM to the AR experience of Disney's *Star Tours,* where guests remain seated while 3D space is

[5] Official Disneyland Pirates of the Caribbean Script.

shifted in a non-linear fashion so as to trick our vestibulo-ocular reflex system into creating a virtual experience. We'll cover this in more detail later, but first let's talk a little bit about neuropsychology and virtual experiences.

CHAPTER IV

THE VESSEL OF HUMAN EXPERIENCES: The Brain

As touched upon earlier, virtual reality is only made possible because humans are capable of transforming sensory data from the objective world into tangible structural and neuro-chemical entities and circuit patterns that reside within our CNS. These brain-based structures and chemical imprints, along with the patterns they produce, have been referred to as engrams. Engrams and their related neurotransmitter conduction patterns in residence comprise neurological ecosystems where experiences reside.

Engrams are the neuro-chemical facsimiles of the objective world created from our perceptions, and represent symbols of the external world. Symbols of the objective world become unshackled from the immutable laws of physics that control the objective world when we manipulate them in the virtual world. Just like an animation time and space become as malleable as a soft piece of clay—that is, unless the real-world entity of the engram is defective and/or the supporting CNS anatomy and physiology are dysfunctional, or the engram(s) are damaged.

Virtual-world analogies to the content/medium parallel are woefully inadequate because of dynamics part and parcel to the Tesseract dimension, along with the fact that it is impossible to do justice to the complex dynamics of neurobiology in a single chapter. With those apologies made, comparing objective and virtual world deltas to animation art may help some readers to better discern some important precepts about virtual reality. Let me illustrate this referring to a couple of classic cartoon characters.

When Wile E. Coyote chased the ever-so-clever Road Runner over the edge of a cliff, he defied the laws of gravity and numerous other laws of physics, including his death-defying crash to the bottom of the canyon floor. That classic Looney Tunes scene is pure virtual reality; but these characters and their exploits can ONLY exist as long as the medium upon which these characters were drawn and the projection apparatus used to make these characters come to life remain OR would be functional. Even if functional, however, none of Wile E. Coyote's death-defying feats can or would take place from your perspective, unless your CNS vessel and its various physiological functions also remain intact and biologically viable. Thus, the technology that functions as an external storage device/console and our CNS need to stay intact, or our virtual experiences disappear. Gaming consoles can break down and flight simulators can go dark and people can lose consciousness.

SECOND AXIOM OF VIRTUAL REALITY

Virtual reality experiences live in and are totally dependent upon an objective entity named the CNS, and its various parts and supportive structures and systems.

"Our consciousness is a brain-generated neurologic illusion. Our brain creates representations of reality, self, other people, objects, set designs, and landscape, which correspond quite accurately to reality. It is, however, not reality, but simulations. Our consciousness also encompasses the entire scope of the human narrative, developing step by step as our experience is mapped into memory from our beginnings as a fetus until death. Through our experience, the brain links together neuronal maps from all its areas. It builds higher and higher levels of cortical order into our memory. The most fundamental mappings include the amygdala and limbic system. The function of the early fetal amygdala and limbic system was to map our survival interactions with our maternal environment. This begins early in utero. This brain

circuitry links the body, hormones, subcortical brain, and the cortex—the amygdala for impulses of fear and pleasure; the hippocampus for gluing memories; the cingulate gyrus for attention and autonomic functions, such as heart rate and blood pressure; the hypothalamus for regulating the autonomic nervous system; and the thalamus, the relay station from the subcortex. The morphogenesis of the limbic system is progressive and ongoing throughout fetal/newborn development. By the time we are born, these limbic circuits have matured and are sufficiently organized for the foundational appetites and rudimentary emotions of fear, anger, alarm, sadness, satisfaction, pleasure, hunger, and thirst. We have mapped our maternal attachment, responsiveness, and provision experience through the limbic system since early in fetal life. These mappings continue to build higher and higher levels of cortical order." [6]

Wile E. Coyote and Road Runner. Loony Tunes Character Creators: Chuck Jones and Michael Maltese

---

[6] Robert A. Berezin, MD: On Consciousness: Explaining the Brain's Beautiful Illusion. Medscape Psychiatry Commentary, April 5, 2019.

No better proof of the neuropsychological VR in our head can be found than as evidenced by the parallels of defective or dysfunctional media to human disease processes. Although too numerous to list in their entirety, one example includes how memories of real-world events may no longer be accessible to Alzheimer's patients because of the disruptive effects of plaque formations located, in part, in the substantia nigra of the afflicted patient's CNS. For now, look at the following graphic images of your brain and some of its structures, and realize this is the vessel without which VR, OR, AR, MR, ER, et al. *experiences* would not and could not exist.

Motor and Sensory Regions of the Cerebral Cortex

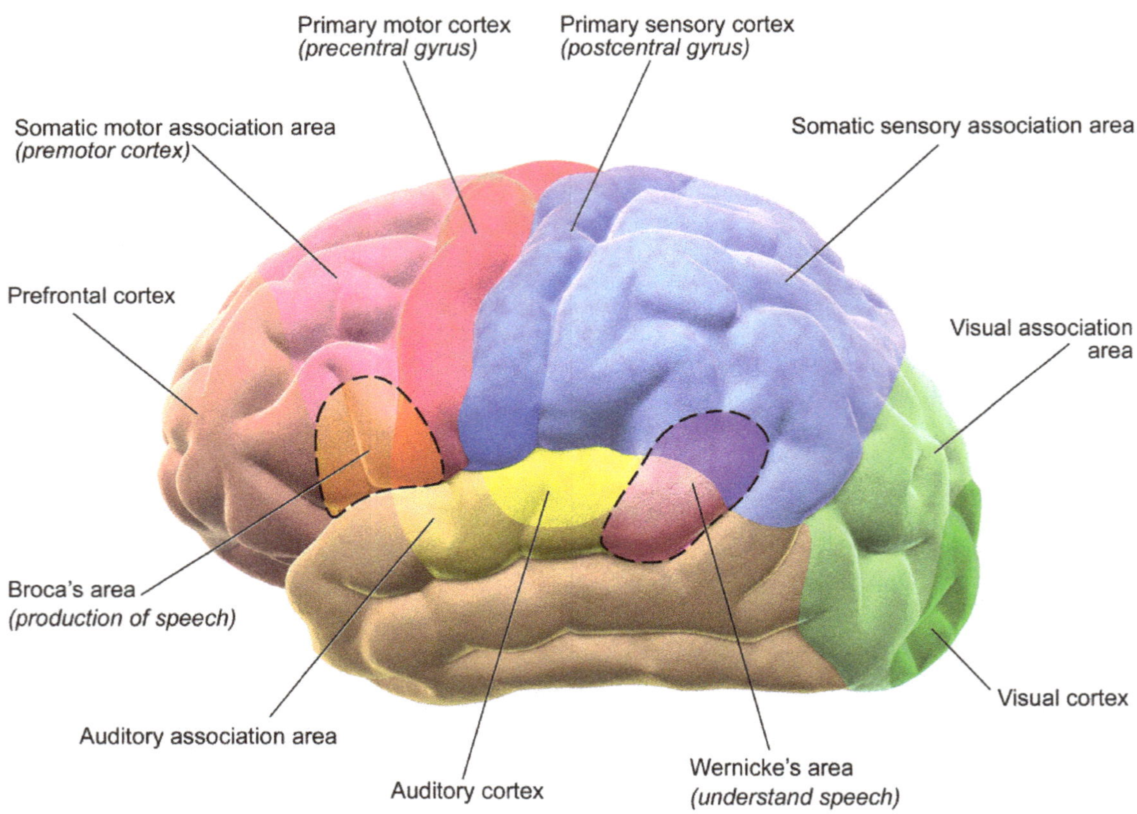

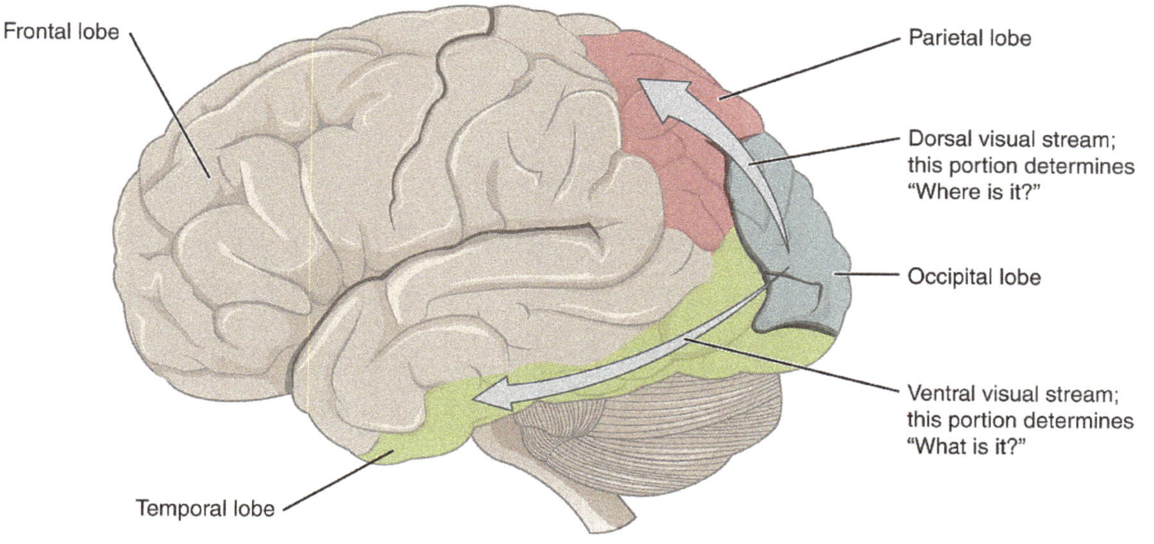

Earlier we discussed sophisticated virtual reality-inducing simulators that tilt operators/guests/participants on a 3D axis. When participants are tilted on a 3D axis, dramatic changes occur in their inner ear's vestibular system. The inner ear and its various structures and functions are fundamental to how human beings orient themselves in space.

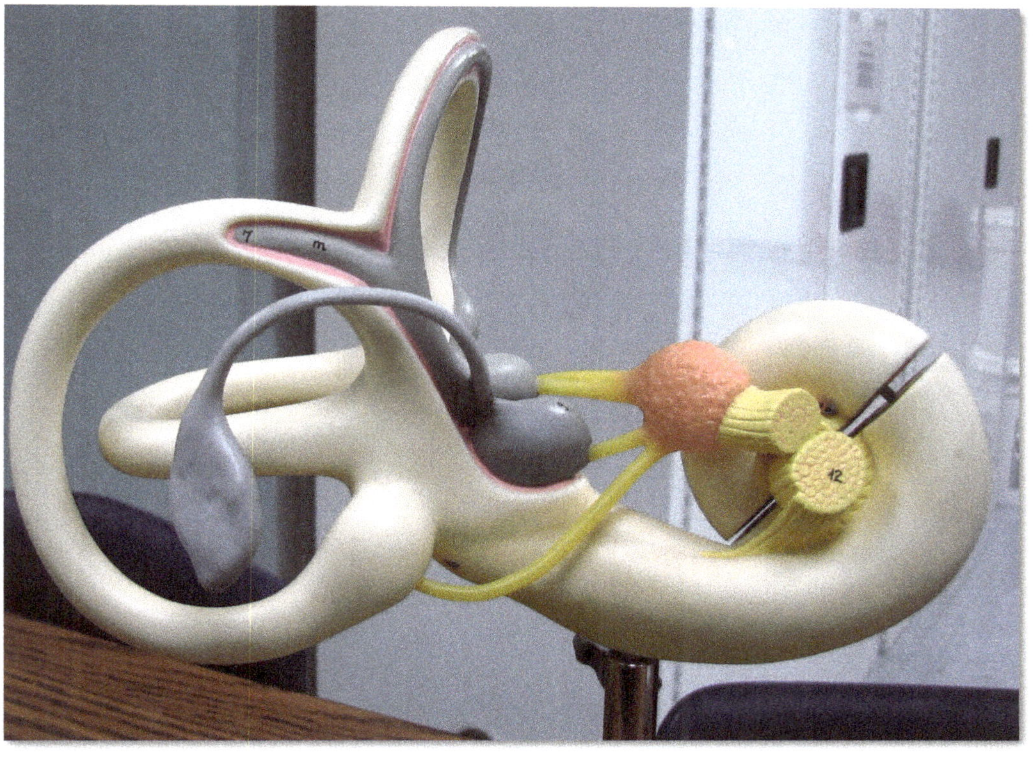

The Inner Ear Component to the Vestibulo-Ocular Reflex

If you study the immediately preceding image of your inner ear, you'll notice three curvilinear chambers or canals. These are called semicircular canals. Each of your canals registers movement along the X, Y or Z-axes. For example, one canal senses up-and-down movement. The second canal registers side-to-side movement, while the third canal senses tilting movements. The ability to register movements simultaneously on 3D axes is made possible because each chamber is filled with a dynamic fluid we call endolymph, and each canal is lined with nerve endings we call hair cells. Any change in your 3D orientation creates movement(s) of the endolymph, which in turn changes the amount and pattern of hair cell excitation. Hair cells communicate with your brain vis-à-vis the acoustic nerve. Your brain processes nerve impulses from your inner ear and compares them to visual input and other somatosensory data to "tell" you "where you are in space"—or in the instance of immersive VR, where you *think* you are in space and time.

A human being's changing orientation on 3D axes can have many dramatic effects. Consider that a virtual reality simulator moves the operator/user/guest along the X, Y and/or Z-axes, even though he is strapped into an otherwise stationary seat and has a conscious awareness that he/she is not actually taking a trip to Endor. When objective-world 3D movements are synchronized with visual cues, the sense of actually moving through time and space is made eerily "real." The virtual reality participant feels changes in acceleration, braking, dropping, elevation, and other movements along the x, y and z axes. One of the more dramatic effects is related to what we term the vestibulo-ocular reflex (VOR), and occurs when we tilt our heads, or may occur when operating a simulator that reorients us on 3D axes. The VOR is responsible in large measure for the feeling of motion sickness that causes some guests to vomit. As an aside, treatments for motion sickness often include medications that dull the sensitivity of hair cells in our inner ear, e.g., Meclizine. [7]

---

[7] Meclizine hydrochloride controls the activity of hair cells present within the inner ear. Therefore, it helps to treat vertigo symptoms, such as spinning and dizziness.

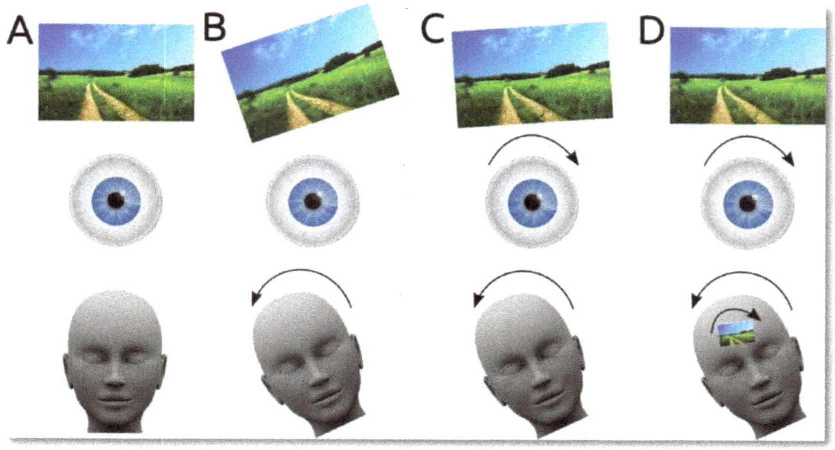

***Vestibulo-Ocular Reflex and Head Tilts**: (Courtesy of Cold Sprint Harbor Institute)*

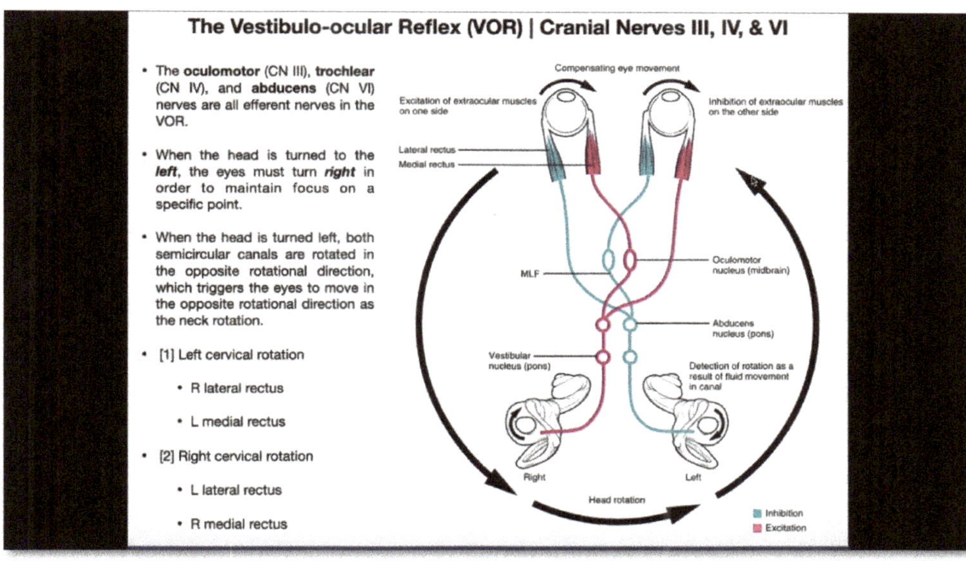

Vestibulo-Ocular Reflex

8

Backstage Star Tours Flight Simulator with 3D Servos Disneyland Parks circa 2010

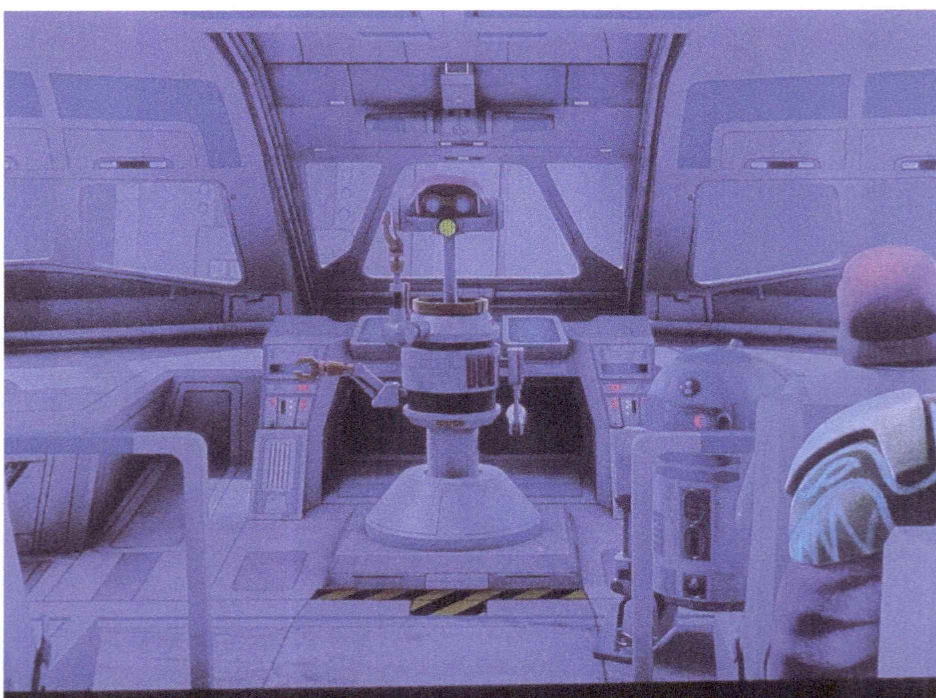

Star Tours Attraction Still: Disneyland Theme Parks circa 2010

[8] Disneyland Theme Parks HD video of Star Tours Attraction. https://youtu.be/nED36n2lVO0

"The vestibulo-ocular reflex (VOR) is generated by sensory signals from the labyrinth canals and otoliths, relayed through the vestibular nuclei where the signals are modulated by the cerebellum, then fed to the extraocular muscle motoneurons in the oculomotor, trochlear, and abducens nucleus via the medial longitudinal fasciculus (mlf) or the brachium conjunctivum (Büttner-Ennever 1992b; Büttner-Ennever 2000). This reflex is a slow compensatory eye movement, and during a period of continuous stimulation it is interrupted by fast resetting saccades, giving rise to the typical fast and slow phases of vestibular nystagmus (Leigh and Zee, 2006)." [9]

"When a patron enters a movie theater, she knows with absolute certainty that the images she sees and the dialogue and sound track she hears are merely recreations of real things or fabricated from whole cloth. She knows that she is not looking at an actual person on the movie screen but a projected image of a real person. Nevertheless, as she sits comfortably in her movie theater seat, knowing full well that what she is seeing and hearing is not objective reality, she responds as though she is immersed in an objectively real environment. [10] *For example, if a movie patron is shown a first-person point of view roller coaster scene, she will likely experience vestibular disequilibrium and may, in fact, become sick to her stomach and could vomit. Her CNS has reacted to virtual reality and in turn modifies any number of somatic processes existent in the objective world. She feels almost exactly as if she is actually riding on a real roller coaster. Flight simulators cue sensory systems using changes in orientation, gravity and movement that*

[9] Anja K.E. Horn, Christopher Adamczyk, (2012). The Human Nervous System. Academic Press, 3rd Edition.

[10] To visualize this phenomenon, access this YouTube video of children emotionally reacting to a puppet show: https://www.youtube.com/watch?v=HR5IJ7XRpRQ

mirrors the visual and auditory images displayed to the pilot or patron. When somatic and sensory cues are synchronized with sounds and images, the effect can be a virtual reality that rivals the real thing." [11]

It is one thing to create futuristic starships and space travel, but quite another to create out of whole cloth a version of reality that becomes V the Reality in the world of pop music idols. As a preface, I'd like to remind readers of a pop music scandal that occurred when 1990s Grammy Award winning singing duo Fab Morvan and Rob Pilatus, aka Milli Vanilli, were discovered to be lip-syncing their songs. Jodie Rocco, Linda Rocco, John Davis, and Brad Howel performed the vocals in reality. Mind you, lip-syncing in the pop music business had been going on in one form or another for decades before Milli Vanilli, but it took the duo to bring it to the forefront. The duo's career ended in shame and eventually led to the death of Rob Pilatus from alcohol and prescription drugs in 1998. Moran's career today includes doing D.J. work in Europe for the Heineken beer company. Fast-forward twenty years, and we have pop diva Hatsune Miku—or should I write "virtual" pop diva?

[11] Napoleon, Anthony (2015) Shadow Men: An encyclopedia of mind control (page 6, ¶ 5-6) VBW Publishing, College Station, Texas.

Virtual Pop Diva Hatsune Miku

Here we see Hatsune at one of her many sold-out concerts that have raked in hundreds of millions of dollars.

Holograph Pop Diva Hatsune Miku Singing to a Standing Room Only Crowd of REAL people at the Hammerstein Ballroom in New York City

"Hatsune Miku, one of Japan's most famous pop stars, has been 16 for the past seven years. She wears her cascading aquamarine hair in

> *pigtails that skim the ground when she dances, and according to stats offered up on her record company's website,* ***she stands five-two and weighs about 93 pounds.*** *She has opened for Lady Gaga, collaborated with Pharrell, and sung more than 100,000 songs, dabbling quite literally in every genre imaginable. If you've heard of her, you've probably heard her described as a "hologram";* ***maybe you've also heard people say she doesn't exist. But both of these are the kind of misnomers that are liable to send her legions of die-hard fans — and there are 2.5 million of them on Facebook — into cardiac arrest.*** *(Don't even think about calling her a cartoon.) She is, depending on whom you ask, a harbinger of a radically collaborative future in pop music or a holographic horsewoman of the apocalypse. Indeed, last month, shortly after she made her much-discussed American-network debut on The Late Show With David Letterman and shortly before her two headlining shows at the Hammerstein Ballroom, a New York Times headline wondered, "Does Hatsune Miku's Ascent Mean the End of Music As We Know It?"*[12]

I want to make it clear that the allure of Hatsune Miku is not that holographic shows are entertaining and fun—it is that the virtual character Hatsune Miku elicits feelings of sexual attraction and idolization from real-world beings that are indistinguishable from sexual attraction and idolization directed at real people. Her adoring fans were raised in a sea of virtual reality, where objective reality is relegated to the back seat. To her millions of fans, she is as real as Taylor Swift, or the most current flesh-and-blood pop idol, for those reading this in the future. If you are reading this in the distant future, there may no longer be flesh-and-blood pop

---

[12] Vulture: Hatsune Miku Is a Piece of Software. She May Also Be the Future of Music. Article by: Lindsay Zoladz, November 19, 2014.

idols. Readers in the future may be tempted to ask, "What was that like when so-called real people performed?" By the way, Hitsune's voice is machine-generated. [13]

Vocaloid fans spelling out "Miku"

What is it about our neuropsychology that allows us to experience the thrill of piloting a star ship to the moon of Endor, when we know as a matter of fact we're at Disneyland, or project feelings of idolization reserved for other sentient beings onto software-sourced virtual reality? Well, one specialized neuron may help to explain how that is possible. And while the entire story is much more complex and nuanced, a good place to start is what neuroscientists have labeled the mirror neuron.

"A mirror neuron is a neuron that fires both when an animal acts and when the animal observes the same action performed by another. Thus, the neuron "mirrors" the behavior of the other, as though the observer was engaged in the

---

[13] Vocaloid is a singing voice synthesizer software product. Its signal processing part was developed through a joint research project led by Kenmochi Hideki at the Pompeu Fabra University in Barcelona, Spain, in 2000, is financed by the Yamaha Corporation, that developed the software into the commercial product "Vocaloid" released in 2004. See Hatsune Miku in concert: https://youtu.be/rL5YKZ9ecpg

action himself. Such neurons have been directly observed in primate species. Birds have been shown to have imitative resonance behaviors, and neurological evidence suggests the presence of some form of mirroring system. In humans, brain activity consistent with that of mirror neurons has been found in the premotor cortex, the supplementary motor area, the primary somatosensory cortex, and the inferior parietal cortex." [14]

Let us focus upon this sentence written by Dr. Rizzolatti: "A mirror neuron is a neuron that fires both when an animal acts and when the animal ***observes*** the same action performed by another." Think about how most of us observe others doing this or that on any given day, using a brief jaunt down memory lane. Early man simply gazed upon the object of his attention. He or she gazed openly, or from behind some object so as to remain anonymous. Later, man developed spyglasses, then cameras. Today he uses spy satellites and similar clandestine apparatuses that, again, permit the observer to remain anonymous.

But far and away the most popular and ubiquitous tool we use to observe others is the digital device. We use screens to observe others while most often hidden behind a veil of secrecy, whether those screens are attached to the various and sundry devices we label tablets, phones, televisions or whatever means or device will exist tomorrow. Our digital devices are the means by which virtual reality is delivered to our front doorstep. And when we observe others on screens, our mirror neuronal system kicks into high gear.

---

[14] 2 Rizzolatti, Giacomo; Craighero, Laila (2004), "The mirror-neuron system" (PDF). Annual Review of Neuroscience 27 (1): 169–192. doi:10.1146/annurev.neuro.27.070203.144230. PMID 15217330.
-Keysers, Christian (2010), "Mirror Neurons" (PDF). Current Biology 19 (21): R971–973. doi:10.1016/j.cub.2009.08.026. PMID 19922849.
- Keysers, Christian (2011-06-23), The Empathic Brain. Kindle.
- Rizzolatti, Giacomo; Fadiga, Luciano (1999), "Resonance Behaviors and Mirror Neurons". Italiennes de Biologie 137: 85–100.
-Akins, Chana; Klein, Edward (2002), "Imitative Learning in Japanese Quail using Bidirectional Control Procedure". Animal Learning and Behavior 30 (3): 275–281. doi:10.3758/bf03192836. PMID 12391793.
- Molenberghs P, Cunnington R, Mattingley J (July 2009), "Is the mirror neuron system involved in imitation?
A short review and meta-analysis." Neuroscience & Biobehavioral Reviews 33 (1): 975–980. doi:10.1016/j.neubiorev.2009.03.010.

The mirror neuronal system is not isolated from other parts of the brain. It tethers to almost every other sensory, cognitive, and affective centers in our brain. What we see, hear, or feel in the virtual world can create the same phenomenological experiences found in the objective world. The interconnectedness of our stored CNS experiences can be analogized to a row of dominoes. All it takes is to knock one domino down in the OR world, and all the dominoes stored in our CNS may fall as well.

For example, sometimes listening to a song first heard during your adolescent years may transport you back to that time in your life, as encoded in your virtual world. Those songs may trigger our memories of things long lost in the caverns of our minds, including the mental images of friends, sweethearts, and places. Watching a movie, we saw with our first love may initiate a cascade of feelings and thoughts and transport us back in time not only to that exact location, but also, you may relive all the sensory experiences of that time. Something very similar may occur in the virtual world, where an objective-world originated engram that took up residence in the VR world of our mind may be triggered by an objective- or virtual-world stimuli years later, and again we may relive thoughts and emotions not felt since they were originally experienced. Classics media stations exist because of these early neurobiology fingerprints and their attached affective memories.

What may account for much of the attraction of screens is exactly what we have been describing that goes on in your CNS. Starlit summer night walks along the Pacific Ocean are relatively static sets of stimuli that must first be encoded into their virtual representations, whereas virtual reality screens bombard CNS virtual reality encoder, which can create a forest fire of CNS activation that feels good, in part because the participant in the virtual reality of the screen can simply sit back and react and interact with thoughts, feelings, and behaviors that reside in our heads.

CHAPTER V

EPISTEMOLOGY: In The Beginning There Were Philosophers

A running theme we will revisit time and time again, because it is so important, is that virtual worlds are capable of defying the laws of objective world physics but dependent on it—e.g., guaranteed resurrection when shot dead is completely dependent upon the functionality of the objective world vessel it calls its home, i.e., the human brain and the anatomical and physiological structures and functions that maintain the CNS. If the home of virtual reality suffers a fatal gunshot wound, then everything in the virtual world disappears. On the other hand, if a virtual world person suffers a fatal gunshot wound, a resurrection is all but guaranteed.

What about the inverse analog to this notion—that is, what is the relationship between the real-world encoder of objective reality, and the objective reality separate from the real encoder? Will objective reality cease to exist if the encoder of that objective reality dies, in the same way that virtual reality dies when its human vessel dies? These questions are pertinent to our quest to better understand virtual reality experiences, as well as where future technological advances will take us.

Our philosophy students will be reminded of an analogous question first addressed by an Anglican bishop and Irish philosopher in 1709 by the name of

George Berkeley. His original question will be familiar to many of you: "If a tree falls in a forest and no one is around to hear it, does it make a sound?" The Anglican bishop took the position that objective reality is the *sine qua non* of subjective reality—or as we more properly refer to it, a version of virtual reality. He argued that, for instance, tables and chairs only exist in our minds once we perceive them, and that they do not exist in the real world without our perception of them. Incongruously, however, Berkeley concluded that the tree would make a sound because God heard it. How he knew that to be the case, given that his tree would not exist accordingly to his immaterialism thesis unless he had perceived the tree, suggests to this author that as an Anglican bishop who took a classic secular humanist philosophical perspective needed to pay homage to God—if not for God's sake, then for the Anglican church's need to be validated, lest he become excommunicated. [15]

In that same century, another man named Rene Descartes contemplated the relationship between virtual and objective worlds, though no professor I was honored to study under or read has ever made the connection. Descartes' declaration, "*Je pense, donc je suis,*" (I think, therefore I am) is just another iteration of Berkeley's immaterialism thesis, but instead of focusing upon perception of the real world, Descartes focused upon his awareness of his own cognitive function as proving an objective fact—that is, his material existence. [16] Descartes wrote:

> *"I have convinced myself that there is absolutely nothing in the world, no sky, no earth, no minds, no bodies. Does it now follow that I, too, do not exist? No. If I convinced myself of something [or thought anything at all], then I certainly existed. But there is a deceiver of supreme power*

---

[15] Berkeley, George (1709-Original Publication Date) An Essay Toward a New Theory of Vision. Echo Library, Paperback Shop, Limited. Cockrup Farm House, Colin St. Aldwyn, Cirencester GL75AZ.
[16] Descarte's declaration was known as the Cogito Ergo Sum argument in the English speaking world.
[16] Descartes. Meditationes de prima philosophia, (Meditations on First Philosophy). éd. de Amstelodami, ex typographia Blavania, 1685, Vicifons. AT.

> *and cunning who deliberately and constantly deceives me. In that case, I, too, undoubtedly exist, if he deceives me; and let him deceive me as much as he can, he will never bring it about that I am nothing, so long as I think that I am something. So, after considering everything very thoroughly, I must finally conclude that the proposition, I am, I exist, is necessarily true whenever it is put forward by me or conceived in my mind.* [17]

This author takes into consideration the fourth or Tesseract dimension when contemplating this interesting philosophical question by interjecting a fact of virtual reality: The virtual world interacts with and is tethered to the objective world. Both worlds exist in the sense that the real world and the vessel within which virtual reality resides must adhere to the laws of physics, while the virtual world Berkeley addressed as the subjective and Descartes identified by the existence of his thinking do not, necessarily, have to adhere to the laws of physics. Is the subjective world of virtual reality real? You bet it is—but more tenuously than its objective world relatives.

As to Berkeley's and Descartes' queries—objective reality is functionally autonomous from the perceiver and encoder of it. This is why the perceiver of objective reality died when he/she suffered a mortal gunshot wound, and his/her perceptions of that objective reality died right along with the perceiver—but not objective reality itself. Think of this analogy to objective world motor sports. When NASCAR champion Dale Earnhardt died at the 2001 Daytona 500, his cognitive maps of the track residing in countless engrams within his CNS died right along with him, but the objective world race track called the Daytona 500 remains to this day, and so does the Daytona 500 race. When virtual reality's home is diseased or has suffered an injury, objective world shackles once again attach themselves to everything living in our virtual world.

As we learned in Animal Farm, "some animals are more equal than others." I bring this subject up because virtual reality being dependent upon the machinery of the mind must take into consideration that not all minds are created equally—and this is true when it comes to the experiences associated with virtual reality—so we must never forget that when we talk about the experiences of VR, et al., even though the OR world technology may be the same, the experiences are not necessarily the same. Not only cognitive, but also affective centers of the brain are not equal between people; that is, some brains are more discerning and reactive than others.

We have known for a long time that daredevils as a rule are not necessarily brave when they engage in death-defying feats. It takes a much higher threshold of external stimuli to make daredevils feel exhilaration when compared to most people. A person with a more reactive brainstem may feel exhilaration when he experiences a beautiful view from atop a hill. My own clinical experience with daredevils is that one of the primary reasons they take risks and engage in death-defying stunts is so they can experience the subjective feeling of exhilaration. The term "adrenaline junkie" misses a key point in that it is not, necessarily, the adrenaline rush that becomes addictive, but the feeling of being alive that is missing in these people at baseline. I recall one daredevil who told me "I skydive so I can feel normal."

The reader may also think of differences between people as not unlike the differences between a computer's central processor—e.g., number of cores, clock speed, bus characteristics, etc. Differences between people can also be analogized to the delta between horsepower and torque ratings of various automobiles. While both analogies are flawed because our brains don't really work like computers and our various intelligence/functionality measures cannot be literally compared to horsepower ratings, the central tenet of the analogies are accurate. Thus:

THIRD AXIOM OF VIRTUAL REALITY

Some brains are more powerful, efficient, and reactive than other brains. The ability to encode the real world into the OR world residing engrams, then

manipulate those engrams within that OR world, varies greatly between people in terms of creativity, efficiency, reactivity, and discernment.

Soap Box Derby Racers

Lewis Hamilton Formula One Champ Pictured with His F-1 Race Car

If man's perceptions and information processing of OR physics comport with reality, then his cognitive map-driven navigation of the real world is likely to be smooth sailing. If, on the other hand, man's perceptions and information processing are asynchronous with OR physics, then her cognitive map-driven navigation of the real world becomes fraught with difficulty and will, sooner or later, end in any number of problems, frustrations, or outright disaster. I'll provide the reader with just one example of the consequences that may occur when a simple error occurs in rendering our perception of objective reality into a virtual-world cognitive map. For illustration purposes, I will use an objective and virtual-world problem not infrequently confronted by world-class mountain climbers.

A climber who perceives then processes sensory input data related to the distance between two points over a deep crevasse will invariably construct a virtual-world cognitive map that will guide her jumping maneuver over the crevasse. For the jump to be successful, her CNS must function efficiently, and most important, accurately as it executes a hundred or more discrete visuomotor behaviors. For any of this to happen, tens of thousands of biological maintenance functions must do their job in the background. If all goes well, our climber's virtual-world cognitive map will serve as the blueprint for her objective-world maneuver, and she will make it safely over the crevasse.

If our mountain climber attempts to traverse the crevasse in the objective world, and her objective-world CNS failed in constructing an accurate cognitive map of the objective world, she may very well die; and if she does, her cognitive map of the crevasse, along with everything else in her virtual world, will die right along with her. We do not have to go to the top of Mount McKinley to make the point about how your CNS perceives then processes real-world stimuli—you are engaged in this process right at this very moment.

CHAPTER VI

THE EMERGENCE: Nonverbal Then Words Then Technology

I will now briefly discuss what you are doing right at this very moment in order to take you into the foyer of the virtual reality monument I am constructing that you call a book. Reading is an act of navigating both objective and virtual reality. The reader visualizes[18] letters, which comprise words, clauses, phrases and sentences, paragraphs, etc. It is the reader's CNS language centers that imbue meaning to the words and syntax I am creating for you.

Words can be symbols or proxies for tangible things like cars, or any other real-world entity or object. They can also be symbols or proxies for abstract ideas, concepts or imaginary objects, or entities. Words can also represent other symbols. For example, synonyms are words that may be interchangeable with other words. Words and the sentences, paragraphs, and books they make up may reference abstract things like ideas, notions, concepts, and philosophical constructs. Keep in mind that reading begins as a series of discrete perceptual behaviors (visualization

---

[18] I have chosen to not address Braille readers, because to do justice to the somatosensory neuropsychology of reading using Braille would require that I digress into a rather complex discussion of CNS behavior. I have also chosen not to delve into the world of audio books. Regardless, the distinctions between the objective and virtual world are similar for both sighted and sightless people and audio book "readers."

of marks/letters, or in some cases tactile recognition of designs, i.e., Braille). The resultant meanings of these tangible acts exist exclusively within the virtual world of neurochemistry located in the language centers of the reader's brain, where they may tether and then spread to other parts of the reader's CNS, not unlike the way a wildfire fans out. A master among wordsmiths will illustrate:

Juliet:
O Romeo, Romeo! wherefore art thou Romeo?
Deny thy father and refuse thy name;
Or, if thou wilt not, be but sworn my love,
And I'll no longer be a Capulet.
Romeo:
[Aside] Shall I hear more, or shall I speak at this?
Juliet:
'Tis but thy name that is my enemy;
Thou art thyself, though not a Montague.
What's Montague? It is nor hand, nor foot,
Nor arm, nor face, nor any other part
Belonging to a man. O, be some other name!
What's in a name? That which we call a rose
By any other name would smell as sweet;
So Romeo would, were he not Romeo call'd,
Retain that dear perfection which he owes
Without that title. Romeo, doff thy name,
And for that name which is no part of thee
Take all myself.
Romeo:
I take thee at thy word:
Call me but love, and I'll be new baptized;

Henceforth I never will be Romeo. [19]

Shakespeare's words originated in the creative centers of his mind. Now contemplate the virtual reality of words used to convey an objective reality IF one believes those words to be literally true, to wit:

Orthodox Jewish Bible: Bereshis 1:1 (OJB) In the beginning Elohim created hashomayim (the heavens, Himel) and haaretz (the earth). The year of original publication: 1200 to 100 Before Christ, B.C. or Before the Common Era B.C.E.

New King James Version: Genesis 1:1 (NKJV) In the beginning God created the heavens and the earth. The year of publication: 1611.

The words and their syntax as quoted from the beginning parts of the Christian Bible, regardless of translation, are virtual representations of an objective world creation of the earth—but only if the reader believes the virtual world of language in his head comports with objective reality. Take note that **any** after-the-fact communication of an OR world event, transmitted either by spoken, written words, or non-verbal artifacts, ***can only be achieved*** using virtual reality symbols. This is not true for creative fabrications using words, however. Why is this true? How else could an event that took place in the past (The Creation of the World) be communicated at some future time, unless the content creators used the tools of virtual reality? After all:

Only virtual reality and the symbols that reside there can violate the laws of objective world physics and time travel to the future.[20]

The symbols used by the writers of the Bible, with particular reference to the Book of Genesis—or more accurately Bereishit or fundamentally בראשית—utilized a

---

[19] William Shakespeare: *Romeo and Juliet*, Act II, Scene I.

[20] The current author is well aware of any number of theoretical physicists who have postulated that time travel is not only possible but fits squarely within doctrinaire physics. I choose not to turn this book into a class on quantum/theoretical physics for what should be obvious reasons. Nevertheless, as it stands today, time travel in the OR world is just that - theoretical.

coherent framework of symbols, i.e., the language known as Hebrew. Reflect upon the Spanish idiom *de la mano a la boca se pierde la sopa*; that is, "many a slip betwixt cup and lip," as we might say in English. With that idiom in mind, this is what the first few lines of Genesis looked like after they were originally transformed into virtual reality symbols from a mental portrait that existed in some person or person's mind. If you are a Biblical scholar or taught the precepts of the Christian or Jewish religions, the English word you use to label that person is Moses—or more fundamentally, the symbol that people of that era would have used to identify Moses is: משה רבנו.

בְּרֵאשִׁית בָּרָא אֱלֹהִים אֵת הַשָּׁמַיִם וְאֵת הָאָרֶץ׃
וְהָאָרֶץ הָיְתָה תֹהוּ וָבֹהוּ וְחֹשֶׁךְ עַל־פְּנֵי תְהוֹם וְרוּחַ
אֱלֹהִים מְרַחֶפֶת עַל־פְּנֵי הַמָּיִם׃ וַיֹּאמֶר אֱלֹהִים יְהִי־
אוֹר וַיְהִי־אוֹר׃

GENESIS 1:1

Text Analysis

Go to Parallel Hebrew

Strong's	Hebrew	English	Morphology
7225 [e]	בְּרֵאשִׁית bə-rê-šîṯ	In the beginning	Prep-b | N-fs
1254 [e]	בָּרָא bā-rā	created	V-Qal-Perf-3ms
430 [e]	אֱלֹהִים 'ĕ-lō-hîm;	God	N-mp
853 [e]	אֵת 'êṯ	-	DirObjM
8064 [e]	הַשָּׁמַיִם haš-šā-ma-yim	the heavens	Art | N-mp

853 [e]	וְאֵת wə-’êṯ	and	Conj-w | DirObjM
776 [e]	הָאָֽרֶץ׃ hā-’ā-reṣ.	the earth	Art | N-fs

[21]

Now let me add historical proof that words and their various combinations constitute a form of virtual reality—virtual because words and their combinations possess the ability to time travel, something that can only be done in the VR, et al. world. In our instant example, time travel is evinced by the timeline of various translations of the first virtual reality explication of objective reality—that is, if you believe this virtual world replicates the object world, to wit:

Biblical Translation History (earliest to most recent)

- 1,400 BC: The first written Word of God: The Ten Commandments delivered to Moses.
- 500 BC: Completion of All Original Hebrew Manuscripts, which make up The 39 Books of the Old Testament.
- 200 BC: Completion of the Septuagint Greek Manuscripts, which contain The 39 Old Testament Books AND 14 Apocrypha Books.
- 1st Century AD: Completion of All Original Greek Manuscripts, which make up The 27 Books of the New Testament.
- 315 AD: Athenasius, the Bishop of Alexandria, identifies the 27 books of the New Testament, which are today recognized as the canon of scripture.
- 382 AD: Jerome's Latin Vulgate Manuscripts Produced, which contain All 80 Books (39 Old Test. + 14 Apocrypha + 27 New Test.).
- 500 AD: Scriptures have been Translated into Over 500 Languages. 600 AD: LATIN was the Only Language Allowed for Scripture.

[21] https://biblehub.com/text/genesis/1-1.htm

- 995 AD: Anglo-Saxon (Early Roots of English Language) Translations of The New Testament Produced.
- 1384 AD: Wycliffe is the First Person to Produce a (Hand-Written) manuscript Copy of the Complete Bible; All 80 Books.
- 1455 AD: Gutenberg Invents the Printing Press; Books May Now be mass-Produced Instead of Individually Hand-Written. The First Book Ever Printed is Gutenberg's Bible in Latin.
- 1516 AD: Erasmus Produces a Greek/Latin Parallel New Testament. 1522 AD: Martin Luther's German New Testament.
- 1526 AD: William Tyndale's New Testament; The First New Testament printed in the English Language.
- 1535 AD: Myles Coverdale's Bible; The First Complete Bible printed in the English Language (80 Books: O.T. & N.T. & Apocrypha).
- 1537 AD: Tyndale-Matthews Bible; The Second Complete Bible printed in English. Done by John "Thomas Matthew" Rogers (80 Books).
- 1539 AD: The "Great Bible" Printed; The First English Language Bible Authorized for Public Use (80 Books).
- 1560 AD: The Geneva Bible Printed; The First English Language Bible to add Numbered Verses to Each Chapter (80 Books).
- 1568 AD: The Bishops Bible Printed; The Bible of which the King James was a Revision (80 Books).
- 1609 AD: The Douay Old Testament is added to the Rheims New Testament (of 1582) Making the First Complete English Catholic Bible; Translated from the Latin Vulgate (80 Books).
- 1611 AD: The King James Bible Printed; Originally with All 80 Books. The Apocrypha was Officially Removed in 1885, Leaving Only 66 Books.
- 1782 AD: Robert Aitken's Bible; The First English Language Bible (KJV) Printed in America.

- 1791 AD: Isaac Collins and Isaiah Thomas Respectively Produce the First Family Bible and First Illustrated Bible Printed in America. Both were King James Versions, with All 80 Books.
- 1808 AD: Jane Aitken's Bible (Daughter of Robert Aitken); The First Bible to be Printed by a Woman.
- 1833 AD: Noah Webster's Bible; After Producing his Famous Dictionary, Webster Printed his Own Revision of the King James Bible.
- 1841 AD: English Hexapla New Testament; an Early Textual Comparison showing the Greek and 6 Famous English Translations in Parallel Columns.
- 1846 AD: The Illuminated Bible; The Most Lavishly Illustrated Bible printed in America. A King James Version, with All 80 Books.
- 1885 AD: The "English Revised Version" Bible; The First Major English Revision of the KJV.
- 1901 AD: The "American Standard Version"; The First Major American Revision of the KJV.
- 1971 AD: The "New American Standard Bible" (NASB) is Published as a "Modern and Accurate Word for Word English Translation" of the Bible.
- 1973 AD: The "New International Version" (NIV) is Published as a "Modern and Accurate Phrase for Phrase English Translation" of the Bible.
- 1982 AD: The "New King James Version" (NKJV) is Published as a "Modern English Version Maintaining the Original Style of the King James."

- 2002 AD: The English Standard Version (ESV) is published as a translation to bridge the gap between the accuracy of the NASB and the readability of the NIV. [22]

All of us are so used to conflating our CNS virtual world representations of objective reality, in our most recent example the use of words, that most of the time we have no conscious awareness that this clever sleight of hand trick is no different than when a modern-day virtual reality coder attempts to replicate a walkthrough of an objectively real museum—for example, the Louvre[23], or a fantastical world created out of thin air, e.g., James Cameron's Avatar. [24]

Musee du Louvre Paris, France

[22] 316 Antique Bibles. Specialists in fine antiquarian Holy Bibles, Works in Theology, Bible Leaves and Prints from 1380 A.D. through 1899 A.D.

[23] https://www.youvisit.com/tour/louvremuseum

[24] James Cameron (2009) Avatar.

Scene from James Cameron's Avatar-3 (Image courtesy of 20th Century Studios)

Egocentrism along with ethnocentrism exercise their distortion dynamics in the virtual world. Referencing the languages of the Bible as they were first transformed into symbols makes the point. English speakers forget that their virtual-world symbols and the meanings of those symbols are very different when compared to those people who spoke and wrote in their native tongue/language that English speakers/writers refer to as Hebrew.

I have no doubt that early man was motivated to communicate with other humans using any means possible. Humans felt the need to communicate thoughts, ideas, emotions, and memories encoded in our engrams that were created by our interactions with the objective world. Think of engrams as footprints in the snow, made by anything that is no longer in the same time frame as the observer. These footprints are NOT the shoe, nor are they the person or other being that walked in the snow. Nevertheless, the footprints serve as symbols that are presumed to be one and the same as OR world feet in a person's mind.

Before language and drawings were used as symbols of what humans had experienced in the objective world, early man engaged in pantomime, in particular, the act of pointing. Animals other than man appear to have a genome-based pantomime ability to use non-verbal behavior to communicate some real-world events to another sentient being.

English Pointer

Imagine that you are an early human who went out from your lair to forage for food. On this day you come upon a large and ferocious animal that you had never seen, heard or smelled before. As you experienced this animal, your CNS encodes your sensory input into engrams and/or transient patterns of potentiated neurotransmitters that remain after you and the animal parted ways. As you make your way back to your lair, your heart still racing, what do you think that early human was motivated to do when he joined his family, friends, or group?

Man's need to convey at times one, two, et seq. what he had experienced at time zero is **only made possible by virtual reality**. The objective reality experience of both ancient and modern man is transient by definition. But by the very nature of how man's CNS works, that fleeting objective reality becomes encoded into our CNS, where the laws of physics that regulate time and space no longer apply.

Our early ancestors were undoubtedly motivated to communicate their most exciting experiences BECAUSE they were memorized. And thanks to an interesting quality of our CNS, the memory of exciting events creates a cascading effect where the thoughts, emotions, and feelings, including all the physical reactions experienced in the objective world at time zero, are recreated— and thus experienced again—during time one.

We must conclude that our early ancestors communicated their exciting adventures to their peers. And thanks to another nifty artifact of homo sapiens' CNS, e.g., mirror neurons, those peers could relive the exciting adventures of others, even though they had not experienced them in the objective world, while sitting in relative comfort and safety around the fire pit. Who amongst us has not experienced an animated recantation of a past event from someone excited to tell us, e.g., "You won't believe what just happened?" What follows is a photograph of one of man's earliest ventures into the world of virtual reality, and the imprints of the media he used to communicate his experiences:

Lascaux Cave Painting-One of the Earliest Recorded Examples of Virtual Reality [25]

FOURTH AXIOM OF VIRTUAL REALITY

Virtual reality is a multidimensional state of reality that exists separate from, yet inextricably linked to, objective reality.

Virtual reality can be a facsimile of objective reality as replicated by objective representations, e.g., the cave paintings at Lascaux, France. The source of this virtual reality developer's cave paintings is a constant in almost all of virtual reality's forms, and it existed in the CNS of the developer. Paintings can be realistic depictions of objective reality—that is, mirror objective images—or they may be abstract depictions of objective reality. The more abstract, the more separate is this particular virtual reality from the objective world, and more closely sourced from the CNS of the developer and not objective reality itself. Our modern-day classifications of painting styles reflect the degree to which OR is translated then communicated using graphic media, e.g., realist, impressionist, modern, etc.

Virtual reality can be separated by the laws of physics, as in the above referenced example of artistic representation, or they may be interactive, as in video games or social media. Virtual reality can be supplemental to objective reality, as in augmented virtual reality; or in some more complex iterations, virtual reality can be separated initially, and then reconnected to reality. Sometimes virtual reality can be so alienated from objective reality that the relationship can only be ascertained when the immutable laws that govern objective reality reestablish their control over the intermediary virtual worlds created by man. Virtual reality that is completely disjointed and separated from objective reality by definition is not technically speaking a virtual reality, but a reality unto itself. But make no mistake—VR and OR are joined at the hip. What better proof than the stock market to make that point?

---

[25] Lascaux Cave is a rock shelter in the Dordogne Valley of France replete with virtual representations of the objective realities of the period as encoded by the inhabitants of the region who perceived them then encoded them into CNS engrams. They were painted between 15,000 and 17,000 years ago.

CHAPTER VII

MONEY: Stocks, Currencies, and Investments

By now readers understand that the hallmark characteristic of virtual reality is that its storyline and content are unshackled by real-world governance. Those regulators include the laws of physics, societal laws, regulations, moral and social conformity constraints, and interpersonal dynamics, among other OR world governors. Many people find shedding these limits to be entertaining, fun, and liberating, hence our first Axiom of Virtual Reality.

When it comes to the immutable laws of OR physics, the punishment for violating them is evinced in cause of death data and, of course, ER visits for stapled fingers. Engaging in OR world moral turpitude not infrequently results in being labeled a sex offender for the rest of your life. On the other hand, engaging anonymously in the VR versions of such felonious behaviors results in no legal repercussions, e.g., *Rape Day* and *Grand Theft Auto*.

Anonymous Gamer "Playing" *Rape Day* by Valve

Nevertheless, for all the innocent AND felonious pleasures associated with shedding the shackles of the real world when the virtual and real world spheres come into conflict, just like Mr. Sanchez taught us, hitting the wall on a real-world racetrack restores a proper perspective of the relationship between OR and VR.

FIFTH AXIOM OF VIRTUAL REALITY

If human beings use VR tools and interfaces within an OR context, then great danger exists if people forget for one moment that OR world governance rules supreme. It is only a matter of time as to when OR asserts itself.

It is not just cops and robbers where alternative realities have had their disruptive influences on OR human behavior and societal norms—white-collar crime and its socially acceptable cousins in the gaming business have been greatly influenced by VR, et al. Take, for instance, stock trading.

Stock exchanges are markets of real-world businesses and their buyers of stakes or shares in the company. Businesses in the OR world have profits and losses, employees, products and/or services, and their prospects are tied to supply and demand for their goods and/or services in addition to any number of other real-world governors. Publicly traded companies' market value and viability may be assessed using any number of OR metrics, in addition to all the things we just mentioned, like price to earnings ratio, price to sales ratio, book value per share, price to book ratio, earnings before interest, taxes, and amortization (EBITA) as well as more qualitative real-world shackles like customer satisfaction, industry trajectories, management acumen, etc. So, what would a VR stock market game look like? Would it be something like a digital version of the board game Monopoly?

A stock market VR game could unshackle itself from reality like first-person shooter games unshackle players from the OR world of life and death. Players could buy fictional companies with fake money and would compete against other buyers and sellers and anything else that goes along with buying and selling stocks. Gamers could take out a mortgage on their home and invest it in a company, and if it goes bust—hit reset. However, if you play this stock market game in the OR world, sooner or later you might do what lots of people did in the stock market crash of 1929: you'd think about killing yourself.

What if a hybrid version of the OR and VR stock market game existed? What if the OR world stock market consisted of various manmade VR/AR cogs temporarily disconnected from the shackles of the real world, and what if those virtual world parts could be used to manipulate cogs in the OR world of the stock market? In this hybrid reality, could the virtual world of stock market machinations wreak havoc on the real world of publicly traded companies? Could stock trades become disconnected from real-world governance and the fundamental measures of what constitutes a viable business? You bet—at least for a time.

In January of 2021, a gamer and virtual-OR world stock trading aficionado by the name of Keith Gill set about to commandeer one particular virtual world part of the machinery of OR Wall Street stock trading. That part involved exploiting the shorting of publicly traded companies in order to create a short squeeze. Shorting stocks has been a strategy talked about at OR world restaurants for decades in New York City that trade in steak tartare and veal. To be sure, Wall Street insiders long ago mastered any number of permutations they created and then interposed between buying and selling stocks, e.g., options, short selling, arbitrage, collateralized debt obligations, etc. We'll define these terms of art and say more about other virtual-world machinations that are part of Wall Street later in this chapter, but for now I want to lay the groundwork for our discussion of how the VR/AR/OR world hybrids distort the OR world of buying and selling stocks.

Keith Gill aka RoaringKitty - DeepFuckingValue

The 34-year-old Gill accessed a virtual world chat room named Reddit. Reddit describes itself as a "social news aggregation, web content rating, and discussion website." How popular is Reddit, and who uses it? These data were compiled at the end of 2020:

> There were 49.2 billion upvotes on Reddit as of October 2020. There are 52 million daily active Reddit users. Reddit had over 2.5 million different subreddits in December 2020. 23% of Reddit users are of the 25-29 age group.

Besides the virtual world of Reddit, we have to bring into our discussion the stock trading app Robinhood if we want to fully understand hybrid realities and how they impact real-world businesses. This app democratized virtual manipulation of the real world of stock trading—case in point, the Gamestop (NYSE: GME) stock market drama of early 2021.

GME is a brick and mortar business that sells video games and related paraphernalia. Like a lot of brick-and-mortar businesses that trade in a commodity that long ago became digitized—that is, streamed—GME was on its last legs—or so it seemed. The 2021 GME stock drama was only made possible by AR-hybrid tools used in the OR world of trading stocks. For those who may not be familiar with the GME drama of 2021, take a look at the price action of GME in January of 2021:

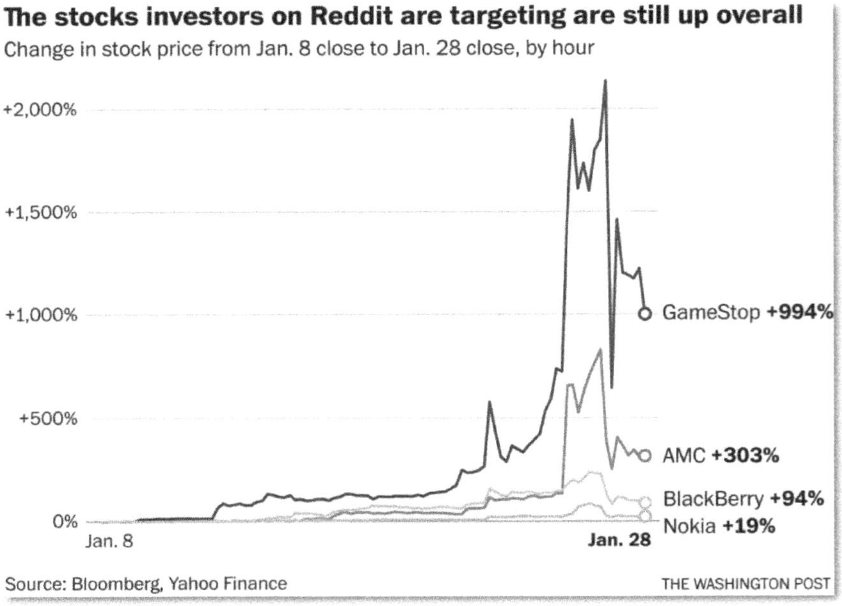

Price Action Over a 20-Day Period for 3 Publicly Traded Stocks

Now, you might ask, how does the value of a brick-and-mortar retail operation that sells video games increase 1000% in a few days when NOTHING about the fundamentals, i.e., OR world of the business, changed? During a 20-day period in January of 2021, a brick-and-mortar game business struggling to make ends meet in a digital world was "gamed" by an army of individuals sitting behind personal computer screens who used virtual-OR world reality distortion tools to squeeze short sellers—one of which was a mega-rich hedge fund that had used their own versions of virtual-OR world tools to make money from a bet that GME would plummet to near zero, and along the way their hedge fund would become the beneficiary of a windfall profit.

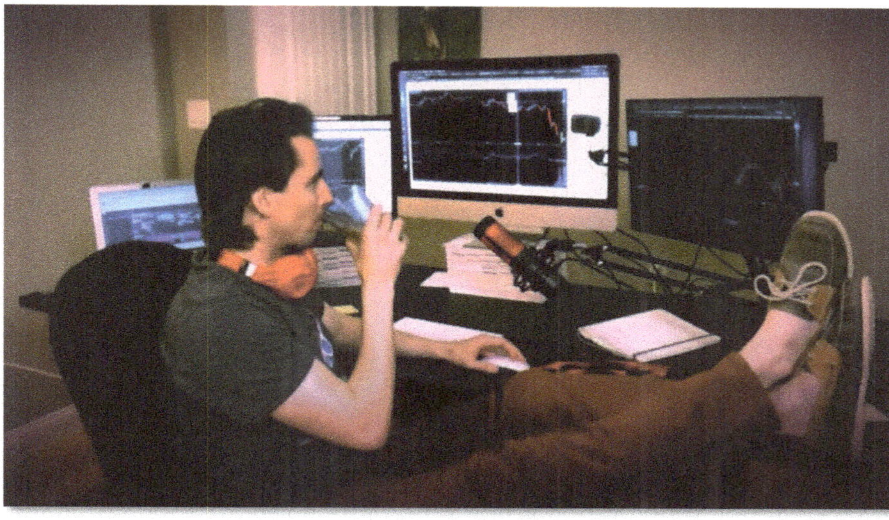

Keith Gill Trading Stocks from Home

We didn't always have VR-OR stock trading hybrid tools. As recently as 1987, human beings gathered in "trading pits" located in brick-and-mortar buildings, where buyers and sellers that dealt in futures stood face-to-face, using hand signals and yelling at and over one another to arrive at a price that was limited in scope by group psychology and the laws of real-world physics. Look at these two New York Stock Exchange photos, one from 1987 and the other from 1950:

Futures Trading Pit Circa 1987 (Closed 2015)

1950s Stock Trader (ticker tape and blackboard)

Objective reality limited the number of trades that could be made in one day simply because of how and where buyers and sellers carried out the trades, i.e., in the OR world. Realize that in 2021, virtual reality platforms can execute millions of stock trades per SECOND as directed by a computer that uses algorithms to game price action. No human being living in the OR world could do that, but in the AR world of modern-day stock trading, millisecond huge volume trades is just how the "whales" do it.

As we delve into stock trading and its relationship to and with VR and AR, keep this question in the back of your minds. Could the things I am going to teach you about stock trading move global markets without AR and VR? The AR-enabled legal, illegal, and borderline structural additions that Wall Street traders have added to their stock trading armamentarium are a sight to behold and provide a window into the world of how VR and AR can be interlaced with the OR world—and when used for nefarious and targeted purposes, can and do move global markets.

Spoofing – AR gamers trick OR and other AR players involved in trading stocks by feigning interest in certain stocks through the creation of a VR-based illusion that a demand for, or lack thereof, a particular stock exists in the OR world. VR gamers may bid a large number of limit orders to buy or sell a stock, to make other VR gamers believe there is pressure to sell or buy the stock in question.

Spoofers pull off their scam by canceling their orders just before they are filled. Spoofers never intend for their orders to be filled, because their only purpose is to induce other gamers to use their VR world screens to bid up or sell the stock being spoofed. Once the price of the targeted stock is manipulated to the spoofer's buy or sell point, the scam artist pounces and executes an immediate buy or sell trade. In the case of AR-assisted driven trading, all of this can take place in the blink of an eye.

Imagine trying to spoof buyers and sellers in the OR world of a trading pit. How long do you think it would take in the OR world before one trader would look the manipulative trader in the eye and say, "What are you up to?" Under the Dodd-Frank Act of 2010, spoofing was made illegal—but then again, so is stealing cars, sexual assault, and war crimes.

Short Selling – I should begin by stating that short selling is legal as of 2021, although at times it has been prohibited during periods of market upheaval, e.g., in 2008, short selling financial stocks was temporarily prohibited. Here is the official press release from the Securities and Exchange Commission (SEC) doing just that on September 19, 2008:

> *FOR IMMEDIATE RELEASE*
>
> *2008-211*
>
> *Washington, D.C., Sept. 19, 2008 — The Securities and Exchange Commission, acting in concert with the U.K. Financial Services Authority, took temporary emergency action to prohibit short selling in financial companies to protect the integrity and quality of the securities market and strengthen investor confidence. The U.K. FSA took similar action yesterday.*

So, what is short selling? Here is how Mint Global Markets, Inc.'s Speed Trader Division defines it:

> *"Short selling is essentially the opposite of purchasing a stock and allows traders to profit when the stock price drops. Rather than directly*

buying a stock, short sellers borrow a stock from their broker and then immediately sell the borrowed shares at the current price. If the stock price drops, as the short sellers predicted, they can then purchase shares at the new, lower price in order to return the shares they borrowed from their broker. On the other hand, if the stock price increases, the short sellers take a loss because they have to re-purchase shares at a now higher price in order to pay back the shares they borrowed from their broker."

So, imagine what would be involved in the OR world when it came to borrowing shares to be able to "short" a stock? If you are the lender, you would insist upon meeting the person to whom you are lending shares, and if you are the buyer, you certainly want to make sure the borrower will make good on your gamble—with "gambling" being the operant word.

In the VR world, can you imagine what havoc gamblers would be able to inflict upon markets when shorting stocks without real-world limitations? You don't have to imagine, because we have an ample data bank full of real-world examples of that havoc. Here are some of the SEC's efforts to regulate short sales, which again, can only have global market influence when joined at the hip with AR.

The first SEC effort is termed The Uptick Rule. This was implemented in 1938, although it was first introduced on paper as part of the Securities Exchange Act of 1934. For short sellers to execute a trade, they must wait for the stock in question to tick up from its previous price. Why would the SEC implement this rule? Because without it, stock gamblers could sit behind their VR terminals and incessantly drive down stock prices. Why would people sell when they see prices going down? Because in times of panic, emotions take over, and short-selling gamers could take advantage of and actually exacerbate other traders' panic. This actually happened and was no small part of what triggered the Great Depression of 1929—even without the advent of VR. It is the difference between an atomic bomb (representing the OR world, or fission) and a hydrogen bomb (representing the VR world, or fusion) The reader may find it interesting that the uptick rule was repealed by the SEC in 2007, just one year before the great crash of 2008 that was made worse by short sellers executing trades from their VR terminals. In 2008, the uptick rule was reinstituted for a short time and took shorting off the table. After 2008, the SEC focused on other regulations designed to mitigate the ease with which unscrupulous traders could game a system made possible on a grand scale by VR—case in point, *naked* short sales.

What is a naked short sale? Recall that short sellers must borrow shares from a broker in order to sell them to a buyer. But what if a short seller never borrowed the shares—that is, didn't have in her possession the actual stocks she promised to sell? That is called naked short selling, and it is not unheard of for naked short sellers to fail to deliver on their promise. In 2005, the SEC passed Regulation SHO. Further changes to Regulation SHO came in 2010. One of the issues the SEC was trying to control was the use of short selling to artificially force down the price of a security like GME. It specifically dealt with this problem via the modification of Rule 201, aka *The Alternative Uptick Rule*. This rule was designed to replace some of the protections lost by the repeal of the 1938 uptick rule, by imposing the uptick rule for any stock that has lost more than 10% of its value in a single day. It is designed to prevent extreme selling pressure that results when VR traders exploit economic instability to create what is called a "short squeeze." A "squeeze" occurs when buyers jump in to move the price up in a stock that has been heavily shorted. Realize that with each tick up in price, the short seller, knowing that he is obligated to buy the stock, is faced with the specter that he will have to buy it back at a premium. Since there are no limits to how much he can lose, because a stock can continue to rise but only go so low in price, he will at some point act to preserve his capital, i.e., "cover his short" position(s).

Short squeezes have many inglorious kindred games, but two are particularly noteworthy because of their relationship to virtual reality—the Pump and Dump, and the Short and Distort.

Pump and Dump: Pump and Dump is self-explanatory. A person, or typically a cabal of conspirators, talks up a stock to trigger the public's greed motivation. Pumping up a stock might sound something like this: "This under-the-radar stock has a proprietary battery technology that will revolutionize the EV market" or "rumor has it that Warren Buffet is about to buy 500 million shares of XYZ security." Once the greed-frenzied public jumps into the stock en masse, the schemers sell the artificially inflated priced stock to the remaining dupes among the retail investors who believe the jam is still on.

Short and Distort: The Short and Distort is the other side of the same scheming coin as pump and dump, only this time a short seller—or again, usually a cabal of agents for short sellers—take to various media outlets to expose an alleged fatal flaw in either products, services, or company management.

The reason that pump and dump/short and distort works is because the public can be stampeded to engage in all sorts of self-destructive behaviors if their fear and greed instincts are triggered. VR is integral to stock manipulation these days. Pumpers and distorters often use screen names and email addresses that imply they are associated with reputable entities, such as the SEC or Financial Industry Regulatory Authority (FINRA).

These master prevaricators who use VR to manipulate stock prices flood message boards behind a veil of anonymity, which makes it very difficult for an investor to verify the claims. "Get out now!" or "Lawyers are looking into a class action lawsuit" are just a couple of VR messages used to stampede a fearful, greed-frenzied public. As with almost all VR, anonymity and role-playing are de rigueur. Want to verify this for yourself? Do an address search for some Fortune 500 looking websites and service providers. I conducted one the other day for a continuing education outfit whose website would force a visitor to conclude it was a mini-Harvard medical school. Turns out the address took me to a strip mall, specifically a Postal Annex address. You see, websites are VR—and as we all know, in the VR world Spiderman is "real." Anonymity comes into play in stock manipulation because anyone who questions the veracity of the pump and dump/short and distort schemers becomes the target of coordinated VR attacks on social media. Again, imagine trying to pull off a global pump and dump/short and distort scheme without the VR cog in OR world stock trading.

Now, back to VR master Keith Gill, who allegedly used Reddit and Robinhood to pump up GME. Out of a desire to be perfectly fair to Mr. Gill, Keith's mother asserted that her son is a true believer in the *fundamental* (OR world) valuation metrics of this particular brick-and-mortar video game store in a world of digitally downloaded games and that the wild moves in GME had nothing to do with her son's behavior related to pumping the stock on social media. Mrs. Gill's defense of her son is one of the reasons we celebrate Mother's Day.

Mr. Gill, cohorts, and their kindred spirits use/used publicly traded company's 13F disclosures to ascertain the source of huge short positions that the OR Wall Street shorts had taken. Think of a heavily shorted stock by a hedge fund as a loaded gun that, if the stock price dramatically increases, goes off, killing the hedge fund operator and the collateral casualty minnows that had also shorted the stock. In the case of GME, Melvin Capital had taken a huge short position in the stock. Now this is where VR comes into play, because absent the ability to sit anonymously behind a screen coordinating/encouraging or pumping up a stock in order to force Melvin Capital into a short squeeze box, the scale of the short squeeze would be significantly less—if it would occur at all. How can one person coordinate the stock buying behavior of so many people that he can bring a gigantic hedge fund to its knees?

Ever hear of flash mobs? Flash mobs are an artifact of VR, in the same way that Reddit message boards encourage en masse stock buying or selling a stock whose fundamental value has not changed. VR stock talk and trading is the common person's answer to Wall Street's power lunch or steakhouse dinners, where people in the know, some of them insiders, divvy up the spoils of stock trading—which sometimes includes exploiting a retail investor's fear and greed emotions. But if the reader is thinking that the VR parts of stock trading have evened the playing field between Wall Street insiders and the common folk, think again.

The stock-trading app Robinhood is free to the user. And we all know what we have learned: when an app is free, that means the user is the product—and despite more recent reconsiderations of that old saw, it is certainly true in the case of Robinhood. You see, Robinhood sells its users' trading activity to Wall Street traders, who pay a pretty penny to buy the data so that they can turn around and program their VR mega workstations' algorithms in order to exploit the price action of the retail investors using their app. I am also informed that Wall Street insiders take up residence on places like Reddit, where they can play the crowd. I am reminded of the Wisdom of Solomon when it comes to the players who trade in greed and fear:

> *"The thing that hath been, it is that which shall be, and that which is done is that which shall be done and there is no new thing under the sun."*

CHAPTER VIII

NON FUNGIBLE TOKENS: Embracing Things You Cannot Hold

In March of 2021, Jack Dorsey, CEO of Twitter, put up for auction his first tweet "just setting up my twttr" on the digital auction site "Valuables." The winning bid was $2.9 million. You might ask: How does a person buy a tweet? Well, you can't buy the tweet, per se, but you can buy a non-fungible token (NFT) of Mr. Dorsey's first tweet memorialized within block/blockchain technology, the same VR technology behind Bitcoin.

The "non fungible" part of the NFT label means the computer code is unique—that is, one of a kind—and the "token" part is comprised of a VR digital code that resides somewhere on a server(s) in memory. The OR world human who will own Mr. Dorsey's first tweet that lives in the ether will be provided a digital certificate, "signed" and "verified" by Mr. Dorsey.

> "In its FAQ section, the Valuables auction site explains that a tweet purchased continues to live on the social media site, but the purchaser

gets a digital certificate of the tweet that's "unique because it has been signed and verified by the creator." [26]

The VR digital certificate of the VR tweet, stored in the VR world of the block/blockchain and housed in some OR world device, could be printed onto cellulose or a derivative OR medium to show to others. But then again, without Mr. Dorsey's OR signature, would anyone believe the certificate to be authentic? VR-azzi who buy such VR tokens have been provided an online forum wherein they can display their non-fungible tokens, which is a forger's dream come true. VR-azzi's love of NFT collecting is one measure of the value some human beings ascribe to VR in an OR world.

To get a comparative sense of the value human beings ascribe to VR vs. OR, I find it helpful to compare NFT valuations to OR world collecting. Using Mr. Dorsey's $2.9 million dollar "just setting up my twttr" block/blockchain source code as a standard of comparison, what value would a collection of William Shakespeare's plays in original book form warrant? Here is a description from the auction house Christies of one such auction:

> *"No one in history has had such a colossal impact on English literature and language as William Shakespeare. Oft-quoted, imitated, and voiced on stages throughout the world, the words of Shakespeare could have been lost for ever had it not been for John Heminge and Henry Condell, the writer's friends and fellow actors who compiled Mr. William Shakespeare's Comedies, Histories, & Tragedies, often referred to as the 'First Folio'.*
>
> *Published in 1623, seven years after Shakespeare's death, the First Folio brought together the author's collected plays for the first time. The folio edition contains 36 plays, including 17 that were printed during his*

---

[26] New York Post. *Bids for Jack Dorsey's first tweet reach $2M in online auction.* Story by: Eileen AJ Connelly, March 6, 2021.

lifetime, one that was printed after his death, and 18 that might have otherwise been lost — among them Macbeth, Twelfth Night, Measure for Measure and Julius Caesar." [27]

The winning bidder was physically provided the OR world book, containing what is arguably the greatest plays ever penned. The winning bid—slightly less than $10 million. Or to put this OR world value in context, only 3.4 times more valuable than Mr. Dorsey's brilliantly crafted tweet consisting of five words, one of which is an abbreviation (twttr).

---

[27] Christies Auction House: The first complete copy of Shakespeare's 'First Folio' to come to market in a generation. October, 2020

Jack Dorsey, author of the $2.9 million dollar block/blockchain NFT "just setting up my twttr."

Let's draw another comparative value to an OR world creation by a couple of famous tech personalities you may have heard of: Steve Jobs and Steve Wozniak. Most of you are familiar with the story of how Apple, then known as Apple Computer, got started in the Jobs' family garage.

Steve Jobs' Family Home Showing the First Home of Apple Computer—The Jobs' Family's Garage

So what do you think one of the first Apple computers is worth? We know what Mr. Dorsey's five-word NFT is worth—what do you think?

Steve Jobs, chief executive officer of Apple Inc., and Apple co-founder Steve Wozniak (Getty Images)

Apple 1

Well, if you guessed this OR world piece of history actually touched by Jobs and Wozniak, and oozing with the provenance of everything inside your Mac or iPhone, sold for a little over $470,000, you would be correct. Just think, your OR hands holding an OR Apple 1, briefcase, and supporting documents touched by Woz and

Jobs is worth a mere fraction of Mr. Dorsey's brilliant five-word VR NFT "just setting up my twttr."

If you are beginning to catch on that we are in the midst of a tsunami of a moral and economic valuation revolution brought to you by digital natives steeped in the VR world since birth, you would be correct.

I think it is important to drive home the point which may have escaped the attention of the reader—VR devalues that which is valued in the OR world, because the OR world demands real-world performance, whereas the VR world enables a virtual performance without the strictures of talent, skills and functionality. To put it in economic terms, VR performance has a much bigger market than OR world performance, which may help to explain why an NFT of a five-word fragmented sentence that any 4-year-old could create is worth millions, while sonnets penned by William Shakespeare don't even come close. The reader may have noticed that Wall Street and their media outlets and animating personalities are "all in" on this NFT craze. As a longtime analyst of the media entertainment complex, I think of NFTs as "new blood" to keep digital native viewers tuning in and the profiteers raking in the moolah. Let me share another VR vs. OR world valuation exemplar:

How many people can become guitar virtuosos like the late Stevie Ray Vaughn or the legendary Jeff Beck, versus becoming a Guitar Hero champ? Leave it to the brilliant creators of South Park, Matt Stone and Trey Parker, to make this point perhaps first and better than anyone else when they focused upon the kids' devaluation of real-world guitar playing in favor of VR guitar "playing", to wit:

Scene: The Marsh Household Kitchen with guitar riffs heard in the background

Randy: What are the boys doing?

Sharon: Oh, Stan and Kyle bought a new video game together.

Randy: They can play guitar now?

Sharon: Oh no, they're just little plastic controllers. You hit the colored buttons and it makes the guitar track on the game play.

Randy: Oh.

Sharon: If they spent half the time learning a real instrument as they do playing that game, who knows what they could accomplish.

Randy: Hey yeah.

The kids are seen playing Guitar Hero

Stan: Listen to that video crowd, they love us.

Randy: So you boys like this music, huh?

Kyle: Yea dude it's Guitar Hero.

Butters: Stan and Kyle are really good at it.

Randy: Well, you kids want to see something that's really cool? Check this out.

Randy leaves to get his electric guitar. He is seen plugging in his guitar to an amp and begins to play an almost perfect rendition of the band Kansas' hit, Carry on Wayward Son. After a few bars Stan interrupts:

Stan: *Dad....Dad! What are you doing?*

Randy: **I can actually play** a lot of these songs on a **real guitar**. You want me to teach you boys how?

The boys react to Randy's question with dumbfounded silence—then Cartman speaks:

Cartman: Uh, that's gay, Mr. Marsh.

Stan: Yeah, that's stupid, Dad.

Randy: **But...but this is real.**

Cartman: **Real guitars are for old people.**

Clyde: Do you mind, sir? We want to watch Stan and Kyle play.

Randy takes off his guitar and leaves the room in shock. Next scene shows Stan and Kyle with their guitar controllers when Stan says:

Stan: *Alright, let's try to score 60,000 points this time.*

Guitar Hero was released in 2005. Since that time, and until January of 2021, the Guitar Hero series has sold more than 25 million units, raking in more than $2 billion dollars in sales.

You must be wondering if Cartman's admonition to Randy that "real guitars are for old people" is true. VR guitar virtuosity is far easier to achieve than OR world guitar playing virtuosity. Digital natives actually attend contests called "air guitar" competitions where the winners are paid tens of thousands of dollars. Perhaps the unsolvable chasm between generations can be understood by the fact that most people over the age of 50 would never even consider putting the VR world of Guitar Hero into the same category as OR world guitar playing. But the overarching point is crystal clear: if a person grows up in the VR world of Guitar Hero, then just like Mr. Dorsey's five-word NFT is worth more on the open market than is a collection of William Shakespeare's sonnets, or letters penned by Thomas Jefferson or Mahatma Gandhi, then VR would be expected to be more valuable than OR to people socially engineered to devalue the OR world. But there is more to the story.

The overlap between VR and OR when it comes to collectibles raises some fascinating questions, the answers to which shed light on our analysis of the biopsychosocial ramifications of alternative realities. Let's go back to Jack Dorsey's five-word tweet that sold for $2.9 million at auction. Now, the NFT of that tweet is encoded in the block/blockchain. The VR of the Dorsey looks like a random group of letters and numbers, and is the blockchain code for whatever it is that is to be encoded. So let's take a look at the SHA-256 HASH [28] for Mr. Dorsey's multi-million dollar tweet:

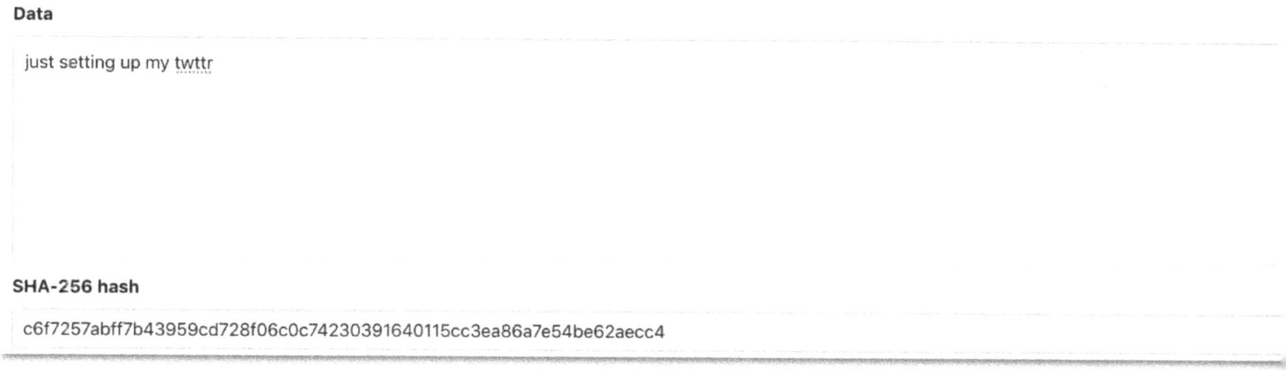

The blockchain code that sold for $2.9 million looks like this:

c6f7257abff7b43959cd728f06c0c74230391640115cc3ea86a7e54be62aecc4

Does the bidder *own* the storage device(s) where the above code resides in memory? Am I plagiarizing Mr. Dorsey's brilliant tweet worth multiple millions of dollars by providing to my readers its exact SHA-256 hash code? Have I just forged Mr. Dorsey's $2.9 million NFT by writing it down in this book?

I dare say my forgery is an exact forgery that would rival the greatest grand master painter forgers the world has ever known—except I wasn't first to transform Mr. Dorsey's tweet into blockchain code. So what? Isn't the temporal issue faced by all OR world forgery experts? Isn't this why forgery detectives examine paint using electron microscopy to determine its chemical composition, in order to compare it to paint available during the time frame of original master painter compared to the paint available to a modern-day forger?

The collector who purchased one of the other first editions of Shakespeare's collective works in 2014 for $6 million can hold it in her OR world hands. Will the winning bidder for Mr. Dorsey's brilliant literary tour de force hold the blockchain

---

[28] The SHA (Secure Hash Algorithm) is one of a number of cryptographic hash functions. A cryptographic hash is like a signature for a data set. If you would like to compare two sets of raw data (source of the file, text, or similar) it is always better to hash it and compare SHA256 values. It is like the fingerprints of the data. Even if only one symbol is changed, the algorithm will produce a different hash value. SHA256 algorithm generates an almost unique, fixed-size 256-bit (32-byte) hash. Hash is so called a one-way function. This makes it suitable for checking the integrity of your data, challenge hash authentication, anti-tamper, digital signatures, and blockchain.

code in her hand? Could she hold the code in her hand? Will she, if she so desires, lay claim to the original server(s) that stored the first SHA-256 HASH of her Dorsey, so she can hold it in her hands like an art collector would hold her original Picasso?

> ***She devalues her hands because they are objectively real, just as she is real. She has no meaningful awareness that her behavior mirrors that which she has been socially engineered to be—a real person who believes she is a virtual entity.***

How many people have actually seen the engrams and neurotransmitters where VR resides? And if you were to see them, you would only visualize blobs of varying shades, contour, and histological terrain. This is also true for SHA-256 HASH codes. Digital natives live in their heads, and "ownership" has, itself, become a VR concept. Will she display her NFT certificate in a frame on her wall, or will she digitally convert the OR world cellulose or derivative material upon which her original Dorsey certificate exists into a TIFF, PICT, or JPG and store that on her personal computer, or in the cloud?

> **She can display it using any one of her digital devices, but so can I, with the only difference between *my* display of her Dorsey and *her* version is that the one she says she "owns" exists in her head, and the minds of other members of her VR temple.**

In fact, she could choose to have her OR world certificate of the blockchain itself converted into its SHA-256 HASH version. Wouldn't that be more in keeping with her valuation metric? Here is a perfect copy of the brilliant Dorsey tweet worth $2.9 million—plus, as an added bonus, the tweet commemorating the auction of this literary tour du force:

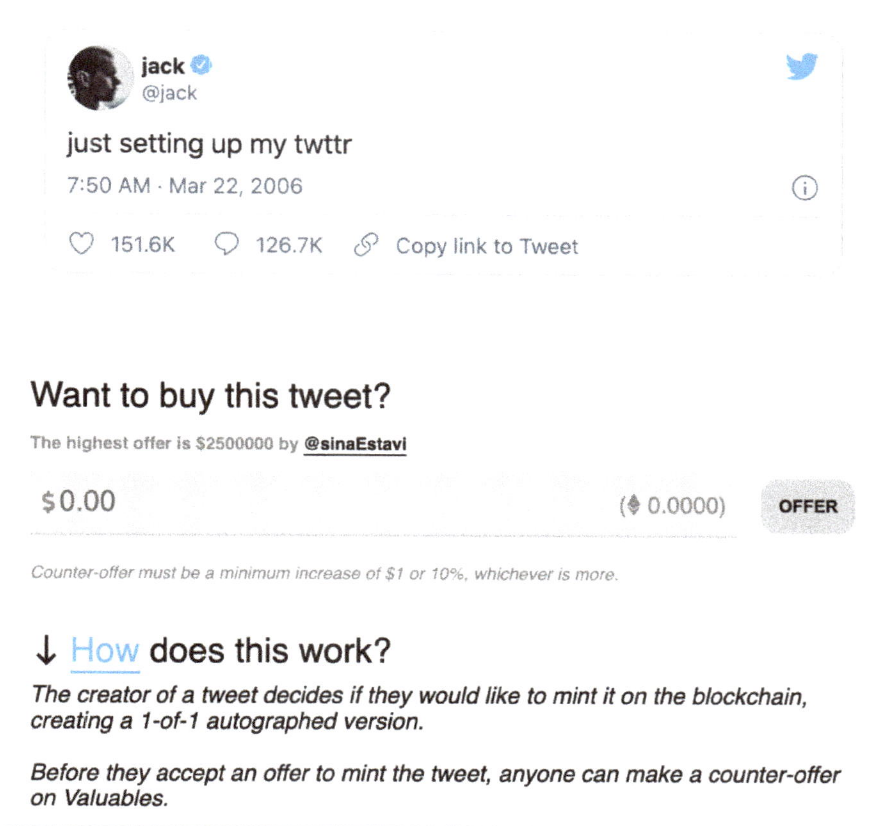

If only there was a way to compare the value of an artist's OR world prints to his other works of art encapsulated in the blockchain. Perhaps that would give us an empirical measure of the value of VR without the confounding variable of the underlying OR art.

We are in luck, because we can do just that. Enter one Mike Winklemann, aka Beeple. To quote Jacob Kastrenakes:

> *"Until October, the most Mike Winkelmann — the digital artist known as Beeple —* ***had ever sold a print for was $100****. Today, an NFT of his work sold for $69 million at Christie's. The sale positions him "among the* ***top three most valuable living artists****," according to the auction house. The record-smashing NFT sale comes after months of increasingly valuable auctions. In October, Winkelmann sold his first series of NFTs, with a pair going for $66,666.66 each. In December, he sold a series of works for $3.5 million total. And last month, one of the NFTs that originally sold for $66,666.66 was resold for $6.6 million.*

[The] auction's winner doesn't get much: a digital file, mostly, plus some vague rights to present the image. But Winkelmann expects to work with the buyer to find various ways to display the piece physically, whether that's on a TV in their house or projected onto "the side of a fucking building" at Art Basel. *There's already been pushback against the rise of NFTs. Plenty of works of questionable artistic value are being sold at hype-driven auctions. Artists' works have allegedly been stolen and auctioned off as authentic. And many artists are concerned about the climate impact of art sales that rely on blockchain technology, which is notoriously inefficient by design. (Winkelmann said he plans to buy carbon offset for all his NFTs going forward so that their impact is a net positive.)"* (Emphasis Added) [29]

The rise of NFTs brings us to our next Axiom of Virtual Reality—and in keeping with this axiom, I will not display an OR photo of the $69 million Beeple, because:

SIXTH AXIOM OF VIRTUAL REALITY

Backstage vested interests, not serendipity, is the driving force behind the push to make V the Reality synonymous with the truth.

We live in a time where explicit moral judgment is frowned upon. The reasons for this are beyond the scope of this book. However, the explanations, were they to be offered, have less to do with the pernicious character of some suspect ulteriorly motivated critique than they do with the imprimatur enforced against anyone who would dare criticize a social ethos where money can be made, no matter how inane and misguided it may be. Moral judgment aside, why a person would choose to pay 28 times more for this—**c6f7257abff7b43959cd728f06c0c74230391640115cc3ea86a7e54be62aecc4**—than a signed letter penned by President John F. Kenney to one of his alleged paramours, just one month before he would be gunned down by assassins, that sold for a mere

[29] The Verge. *Beeple sold an NFT for $69 million*, story by: Jacob Kastrenakas. March 11, 2021.

$88,970.53 in 2016, directs this author to answer that question in more detail in our upcoming chapters, to wit:

ALS as president signed "J.," four pages, 5 x 6.5, no date but circa October 1963. Letter to Mary Pinchot Meyer, a family friend and one of JFK's alleged lovers. In full:

> *"Why don't you leave suburbia for once—come and see me—either here—or at the Cape next week or in Boston the 19th. I know it is unwise, irrational, and that you may hate it—on the other hand you may not—and I will love it. You say that it is good for me not to get what I want. After all of these years—you should give me a more loving answer than that. Why don't you just say yes."*

In fine condition, with the tops of the White House stationery clipped off by Evelyn Lincoln; the faded presidential seal watermarks are visible under bright light. Accompanied by a full and unused sheet of White House stationery. Provenance: Estate of Robert White. [30]

Would President Kennedy's OR world letter have been worth as much as the Dorsey or Beeple if it, too, had been encoded into the blockchain? Take a look at the SHA-156 HASH JFK letter, and you tell me:

c8db2c7e1146d37331e15ceb01c3e796a1b031df4fdfee713c587280c3b32937

Someone willing to spend $2.9 million on a five-word SHA-256 HASH could have also purchased this OR world Ferrari for less than $500,000—but then again, it is **only** a **real** world tangible piece of machinery designed, fabricated, owned, and driven by Enzo Ferrari himself. You can touch, smell, see, hear, and somatically experience it:

---

[30] RR Auction: Item 8021 - John F. Kennedy Handwritten Letter to Mary Pinchot Meyer Catalog 478 (Jun 2016).

1962 Ferrari 330 GT 2+2 Coupe Owned and Driven by Enzo Ferrari (Photo by Daniel Schmitt & Company)

If you are willing to pocket an extra $900,000.00 and spend only $2 million on the following home, you could forego "buying" the Dorsey SHA-256 HASH and instead own this OR world home in Jacksonville, Florida—remember, food, shelter, and clothing are the necessities of life, and for a fraction of Jack's tweet, you could own the most expensive of those three necessities:

Cape Home for sale on Zillow • Price: $2,000,000 • 7,953 square feet •

5 Bed / 9 Bath • Lot Size: 1 acre

Before we move on, I'll leave you with yet another artwork to be auctioned at Christies in London in 2021. It seems only fitting to sum up this section in our book with this particular work of art, because its title suggests to me that it would be a perfect fit for any NFT auction:

Bansky: "I can't believe you morons actually buy this sh*t." [31]

The only thing I can add that would constitute the cherry on top of this Billy Mays genre TV commercial fake sundae is a quote from Paris Hilton. In an interview with CNBC's Sarah Eisen on April Fool's Day, 2021 (you can't make this stuff up), when asked why she is involved with NFTs, this is what she said: "I've always been an innovator." Yes indeed, an innovator, Miss Hilton.

As we continue our journey to better discern alternative realities' hold on mankind and the V part of VR's burgeoning economic value, perhaps we can decipher this replacement reality, even if we are not won over by its Siren song. For now, keep in mind our sixth axiom—because if VR becomes V the Reality, then all bets are off, and like changing the base 10 reference point for the arithmetic we all learned and use on a daily basis, nothing, and I mean nothing, will add up correctly again.

---

[31] Note: Yes, this IS the actual title of this work of art.

CHAPTER IX

V THE REALITY: Control is the End Game

SEVENTH AXIOM OF VIRTUAL REALITY

V the Reality is being sold as the dominant and superseding norm by a consortium of people who want more money, power, and control over life on earth.

It is no secret that people can be conditioned from birth to prefer the cognitive, affective, and behavioral modalities to which they were first and repeatedly exposed to growing up. We certainly see this phenomenon play out when it comes to languages, accents, music, art, food, and even stress levels. But more important than all of these cultural acclimation preferences, the developing brain can not only be psychologically but structurally modified to prefer and interact more efficiently with distinct interactive modalities, including sensory, cortical, and behavioral. Our neural structural designs take on added significance when one appreciates that human beings tend to become enamored with those cognitive, affective and behavioral tasks that are familiar to them, and that we have learned to both like and master. I am going to explore what I think is an intriguing hypothesis: that VR became **V the Reality** in the same way that the robot Hal in *2001: A Space Odyssey* took dominion over the people he was designed to serve.

The Hal 9000 from the Movie 2001: A Space Odyssey (Stanley Kubrick and Arthur C. Clarke)

We certainly see the interactive nature/nurture pattern demonstrated in the case of child prodigies. Children with innate musical abilities often demonstrate their penchant for music before the age of five years. In most instances, those same musical prodigies seek out music and musical instruments. These interactive exposures to various sensory musical modalities often manifest as a replicable pattern of not only a great love for, but also skill sets at playing, singing, dancing, or composing. Even in cases where special innate talent is not present, children who repeatedly interact with this or that sensory modality come to prefer their familiar modalities to those to which they have had less exposure.

Digital native is a label that describes a person whose earliest sensory exposures were to computers, the web, video games, smart phones, social media, and various other technological devices that serve as conveyances for virtual and augmented realities. Here are some of the labels used to describe digital natives:

Generation 2020, Internet Generation (I-Gen), Screensters, and Zeds.[32] Digital acumen as a generational characteristic was applied first to the millennial generation[33], and with each succeeding generation, e.g., Gen-Z and Gen-Alpha, the term proved to be a better fit. When it comes to Gens Z and Alpha, these children were so completely immersed in and acculturated to VR and AR realities that some authors have referred to them as neo-digital natives, true digital natives, or digital integrators. [34] Regardless of the label, the early neuropsychological conditioning to VR and AR realities is the digital native's distinguishing acculturation fingerprint.

Generation Z Circa 2015

---

[32] Rothman, Darla, PhD (2020) A Tsunami of Learners Called Generation Z.

[33] Re: Millennials - Researchers and popular media use the early 1980s as starting birth years and the mid-1990s to early 2000s as ending birth years, with 1981 to 1996 being a widely accepted defining range for the generation. Please see: Rauch, Jonathan (November 2018). "Generation next, Millennials will outnumber baby-boomers in 2019". The Economist. Archived from the original on 13 March 2019.

[34] C.f. Prensky, Marc (September 2001). "Digital Natives, Digital Immigrants Part 1." On the Horizon. 9 (5): 1–6. doi:10.1108/10748120110424816. ISSN 1074-8121.
Thomas, Michael (April 2011). Deconstructing Digital Natives: Young People, Technology, and the New Literacies. Taylor & Francis. ISBN 978-1-136-73900-2.
Takahashi, Toshie T. "Japanese Youth and Mobile Media". (May 2016) Rikkyo University.

Digital Integrators at Play Circa 2021

Non-Digital, Future Digital Immigrants at Play Circa 1950s

The scientific data on how early exposure to the VR world of digital devices and content affects biopsychosocial factors and function are fascinating. I have personally taken note of the fact that prolonged and early exposure to screen stimuli in all of its various forms has modified the neuropsychological fingerprint of digital natives in my own clinical and forensic practice.

I was tasked with diagnosing, and then treating a 12-year-old digital native boy who had been diagnosed as suffering from a non-specific attention deficit disorder. His attention span was flighty, and the minute anyone asked him to focus on a discrete task or spoken interaction, it was only a matter of seconds before his visual, auditory, and positional focus disconnected. I soon learned that unless I entertained him with impressions, funny voices, or gymnastic tricks, his attention vaporized.

In addition to my traditional library of assessment, diagnostic, and treatment modalities I added a Nintendo Entertainment System (NES) and a bevy of games—eventually adding an AR dimensional Wii video game console. I could sit my patient in front of my NES, pop in Mario Brothers, and he would sit for hours as if a tractor beam was holding his attention. The first and only time he ever connected with another human being occurred when we were playing side by side. He was pro-proficient at most video games until he had mastered them, and then the tractor beam holding his attention was seemingly turned off, and his attention would once again wander.

Besides being an avid pro-proficient video gamer, my patient was also a reckless skateboarder. He was a reasonably skilled, fair to middling skateboarder, but he was also reckless and hung around other skateboarders who were skateboarding risk takers. It was the risk taking that came from being reckless that captured his attention—that is, surviving a risky skateboard stunt made him feel alive and connected to other survivors, in addition to feeling superior to those injured. Learning a complex skateboard trick, as Tony Hawk may have made famous, was beyond my patient's capabilities, because it required a tenacious focus and frustration tolerance to repeated failures as practice led to performance success **in the OR world.** Mastery of complex skateboard tricks required of him physicality above and beyond his digits manipulating a controller and the need for instant gratification from discovering the secret to moving to the next game level.

My clinical analysis and successful treatment of this young man is not the subject of this section. However, this one patient's case does provide a good introduction to this thing we call VR and how it impacts your brain, personality, behavioral choices, and values. My experience in treating, studying, and researching digital natives' cognitive and emotional functions informs me that while their brains may have been bioengineered, that is, "re-wired" to accommodate the skill sets required to interface with the world of VR, their verbal and non-verbal motor skill sets do not necessarily translate 1:1 in the OR world. This is especially true when it comes to a digital native's personality and emotional conditioning. In fact, VR world conditioning may be deleterious to OR world functioning. Let me hasten to add before we proceed, I certainly recognize the confounds that are part and parcel to using prolific action gamers as subjects to measure changes in CNS structure and function. Nevertheless, this population does provide researchers a good starting point to get to the bottom of the biopsychosocial impact of immersing ourselves in the VR, et al. worlds for prolonged periods of time, or having been acculturated by a VR-focused environment since birth.

VR technologies are sensory stimulators, whether we are talking about web pages, social media content, or certainly action video games. A digital native gamer, for example, is bombarded with left and right visual channel stimuli comprised of movements, colors, patterns, faces, backgrounds, and contexts. VR objects and backgrounds appear, disappear, move, and morph. Even when we redact CNS involvement separated from dedicated visual perception pathways, a lot is going on:

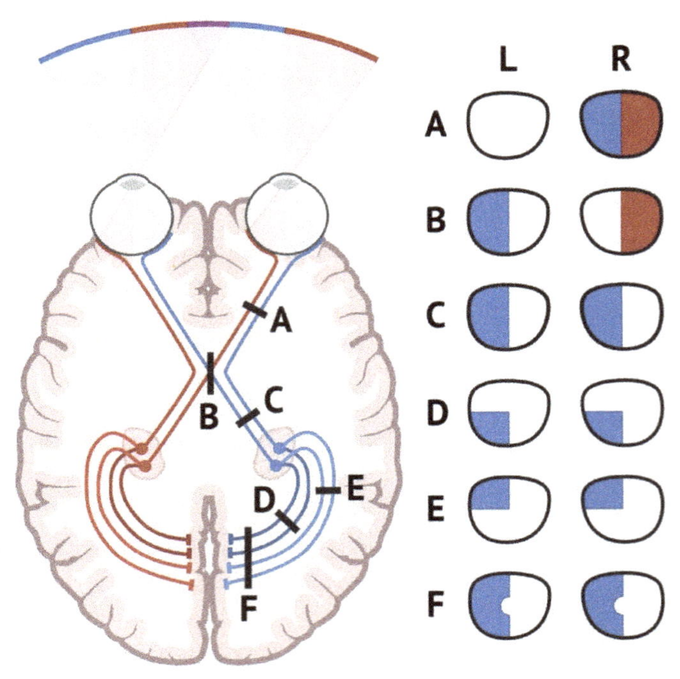

Simplified Depiction of Human Visual Pathways

CNS involvement with the sensory stimuli bombarding a video gamer's sensory system disproportionately involves processes related to motor responses to the game's contextual rules that instruct the strategies which, when implemented by motor responses, will help the gamer achieve his goal. What I just described is not static or one-and-done. The sensory motor interactivity is dynamic and changes from second to second. In neuropsychology, we often refer to visuomotor structures and function when we measure such things.

While it may appear that video gaming singularly hones various and sundry sensory motor systems involved with mastering the game, it also creates an artificiality construct where VR/AR sensory stimuli and expected motor responses create their own world, within which the gamer has a specialized set of visuomotor, personality, and affective conditioning characteristics that may not be complementary or even applicable to much of the OR world. As a reference point for my readers, it is clear that structural changes to the CNS are a fact in the CNS of long-term and prolific gamers and have been empirically visualized, to wit:

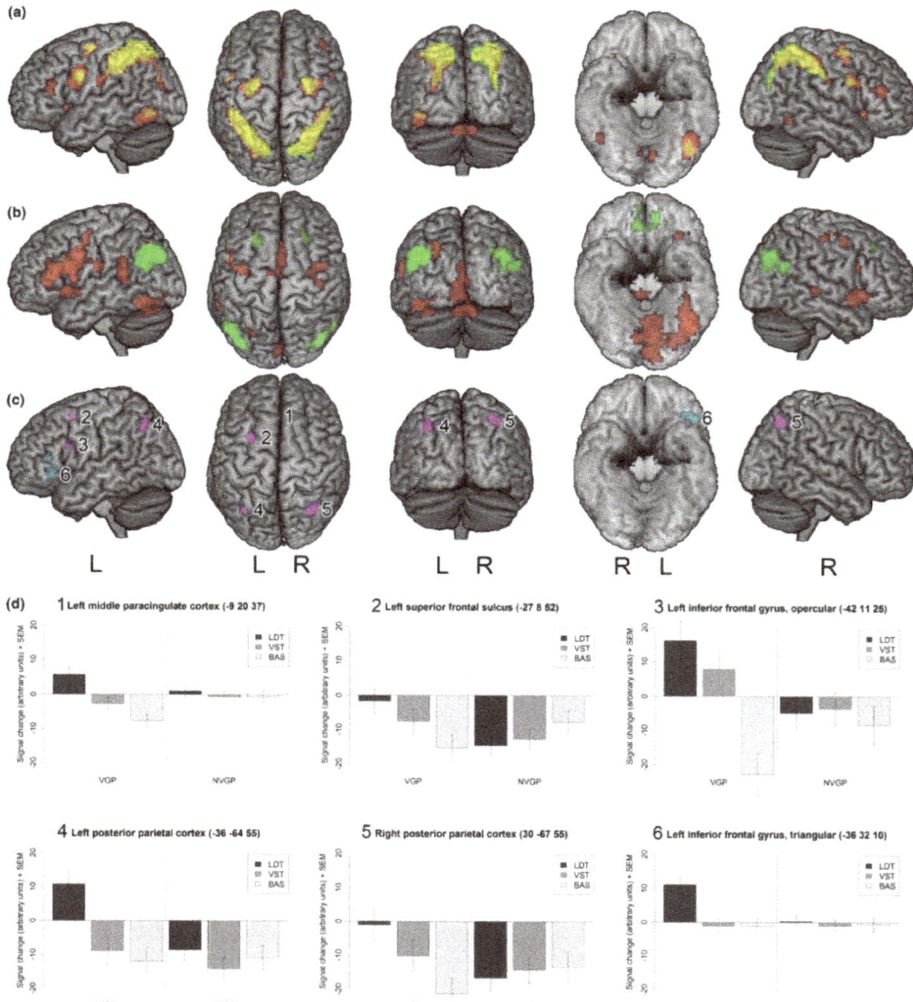

(a) Activation for the letter detection task (LDT, red) and the visuospatial task (VST, green) compared with the baseline task (BAS, overlapping regions are shown in yellow). (b) Activation for the letter detection task compared with the visuospatial task (red) and vice versa (green). (c) Activation for video gamers (VGP) compared with nonvideo gamers (NVGP) for the letter detection task compared with the baseline task (violet) and compared with the visuospatial task (blue). (d) BOLD signal change estimates for all tasks in regions with significant group differences.

The authors of this 2017 study examined the neurological changes of action video gamers' brains and compared them to OR world cognitive assessment measures. Their conclusions are consistent with my clinical experiences:

> *"We compared task performance and brain activation in a visuospatial task (VST) and a letter detection task (LDT) between action video gamers (VGP) and nongamers (NVGP) in order to investigate the effects*

of longtime gaming on cognitive and brain functions. There were no statistically significant differences in performance between VGP and NVGP. Regarding brain activation, we found a significantly different increase in the BOLD signal from a baseline task to the LDT in VGP compared with NVGP in the left middle paracingulate cortex, the left superior frontal sulcus, the opercular part of the left inferior frontal gyrus, and the left and right posterior parietal cortex. Furthermore, we identified increased activation in the triangular part of the left inferior frontal gyrus in VGP relative to NVGP when activation during the LDT was compared with activation during the VST. In sum, longtime action video gaming had no influence on accuracy rate or reaction time in our VST or LDT. Despite their comparable task performance, however, VGP and NVGP exhibited clear-cut differences in brain activation patterns presumably reflecting differences in neural engagement, especially during verbal cognitive tasks. [35]

One of the most critical but often overlooked distinguishing features of most VR, AR, et al. gaming systems is the controller itself. Video controllers are actuated using de minimis motor movements that are timed and reactionary in nature. Jess Grey, writing for WIRED, shared the magazine's top controller picks for Switch, Xbox, PS4, and PC.

[35] Fabio Richlan, Juliane Schubert, Rebecca Mayer, Florian Hutzler, Martin Kronbichler. (December, 2017): Action video gaming and the brain: fMRI effects without behavioral effects in visual and verbal cognitive tasks. Brain and Behavior

[36]

WIRED Magazines Top Controller Picks for Switch, Xbox, PS4, and PC.

The CNS visuomotor- sensory areas of the brain bio-engineered by long-term and prolific action video gamers do not translate to the OR world 1:1 because of, in part, the de minimis motor movements of an action gamer's wrists and digits, e.g.,

---

[36] WIRED Magazine, Story by Jess Grey: Top Controller Picks for Switch, Xbox, PS4, and PC, March 4, 2021.

tapping, swiping, toggling, pushing, etc. In other words, as was found in the Richlan, et al. study, unless interaction with OR world objects, people, and their social systems and culture adhere to the same skill sets, neuropsychological substrates, experiential interactive rules, and governance found in action video gaming behavior as the neurological hard wired functionality advantages of rapid sensory perception-responses, the VR version of multi-tasking and making choices on the fly will not generalize effectively 1:1 to the real world, if at all.

Digital immigrants born in the 1940s and '50s, including the remaining few digital isolates living in the 21st century, had a built-in advantage when it came to their childhood cognitive, emotional, and behavior conditioning relationship with the OR world, because their brains were bioengineered to reflect a nearly 1:1 relationship with the OR world's biopsychosocial genome. Let me make it clear that the advantages of digital immigrants' OR rooted experiences that benefited them later in life are not a cultural time in space phenomenon—that is, I am not engaging in a form of nostalgic "good old days" confirmation bias. My analysis is scientifically informed by empirically derived and replicable data. The dynamic between digital immigrants and digital natives finds:

> **It is easier for digital immigrants to adapt to and learn the rules of the VR world than it is for digital natives to learn skill sets unique to the OR world. One of the reasons this dynamic is true has to do with the fact that immigrants can find innumerable opportunities, including didactic contexts, to experience first-hand VR worlds, whereas digital natives have few learning opportunities to retool their biopsychosocial skill sets, especially given the fact that their peers are just like them.**

Human beings are OR beings living in an OR world, governed by OR physics. The advantages of having been acculturated in an OR world transcend generational differences or culture, per se. What skill sets digital immigrants lack when it comes to VR world devices are related to their unfamiliarity with those skills, but to a greater degree their emotional rejection of them, e.g., "I'd rather talk to someone on the phone and hear their voice than text them." Texting seems impersonal is a complaint I often hear from digital immigrants—not that they don't know how or find it hard to text.

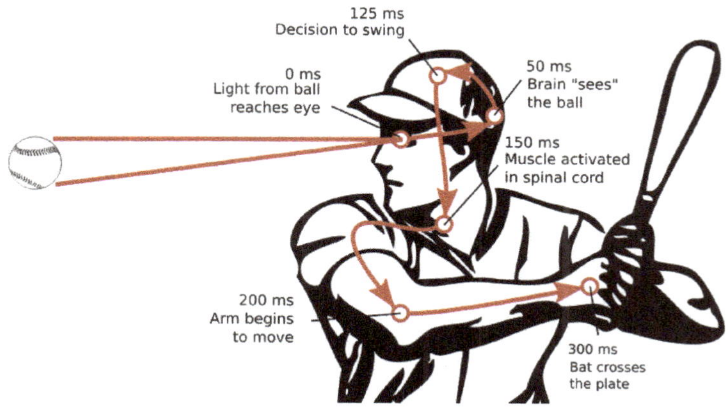

CNS and Peripheral Motor Skill Sets Employed by OR World Baseball Batter

Running, pivoting, stopping, throwing, catching, and manipulating OR world objects in 3D space, and interacting with and adapting to human beings in an OR contextual world where each person has their own unique personality, personal and group motivations, fears, hopes, and feelings, are important things to learn early in life. Knowing the name of the person with whom you interact, actually looking them in the eye and in person, conveys authenticity, and perhaps most importantly:

> ***In the OR world, no reset button exists. In the real world, pain, injury, errors, poor sportsmanship and hurt feelings are personal, not anonymous. Red flagging a race means waiting, crashes may mean a trip to the hospital or the end of your career or life. Real-world costs for failure far exceed the cost of a new gaming system. In the real world, performance means the difference between eating and starving, being hero or villain, and adapting to the fact that betrayal is part of life. Taken in whole, these factors are a reasonably good operational definition of life itself in the OR world.***

OR World CNS Bioengineering Circa 1960s

OR World CNS Bioengineering Circa 1950s

OR World CNS Bioengineering Circa 1940s

OR World CNS Bioengineering Circa 1930s

Recall our discussion of *Gran Turismo* champion Ricardo Sanchez. His familiarity with *Gran Turismo's* Willow Springs International Motorsports Park translated almost perfectly to the OR world track, ***but only when he was all alone on the track***. Here is why parts of *Gran Turismo's* game translated well to the OR world—but first, look at the *Gran Turismo's* first licensed controller:

The First Official "*Gran Turismo* Sport" Steering Controller [37]

The controller itself is a step above a handheld, digit-actuated controller. Secondly, realize that the photorealistic topography in the game is, by definition, a close VR version of the OR track.

> **But this is where the translation from the VR to the OR world of racing failed. OR racing against other OR racers requires the acquisition of an entirely new set of skills and mastery of personal and group psychodynamics.**

Recall what Mr. Sanchez shared with us during his Q&A with Jay Leno:

> *"Jay Leno: "Do you ever push a car in real life as you do in the game?*
>
> *Mr. Sanchez: "In real life you go a bit under, especially because if you do make a mistake it is going to be a hot one. There is no reset button or anything, you just hit the wall and that is it."*

---

[37] The Thrustmaster T300RS GT Edition, officially licensed by Gran Tursimo, is the next big thing in driving-game controllers. The virtual steering wheel—created for Gran Turismo Sport, the driving game exclusive to PlayStation®4—features cutting-edge technology that includes an industrial brushless motor with full Force Feedback and 1080-degrees of rotation. It's also compatible with PlayStation®3 and PCs.

Who has "the line" going into a turn, who allows or does not allow drifting behind them, changing track conditions, avoiding crashes, knowing who to trust or not trust on the track, are just a few of a myriad of things you must learn and master. Jealousy between drivers and vying for team membership with egoistic car owners are variables you simply can't pick up in a VR version of an OR world activity. OR world racers find it remarkably easy to move to VR versions of actual tracks they've competed on—but it is a step down for them.

It is not just learning, but also unlearning that is required to make the transition from VR to OR world racing. Mr. Sanchez had to UNLEARN the ever-present conditioning of any action video game that is part and parcel to the reset button. Since we know that VR and OR relationships are a function of how well VR mimics its OR world reference, the closer the fit, the greater the VR skill set application to the OR world. Had Mr. Sanchez been driving a 1950s Indy roadster instead of a 21st century Nissan GT-R Nismo GT3 Racer:

Nissan GT-R Nismo GT3 Racer

Roger Ward Sitting in His Leader Card, Offenhauser Indy 500 Roadster (Courtesy of Motor Sport Magazine)

Can you imagine the VR rendition of this minimally aerodynamic, zero digital, 60-plus-year-old technology? Can you imagine what it would be like to drive one of these old-time racing machines for 500 miles when the only feedback you received about the car's functions came from an analog speedometer, fuel, oil pressure, and RPM gauges? The only way Ward's pit crew could communicate with him was by holding up a chalkboard as the driver sped past at 160mph/257.5kmh on the front straightaway, or when he pulled into the pits. These cars had no power steering, ABS, or driver modifiable aerodynamics, and the steering wheel linkage required drivers to turn a shuttering steering wheel as much as 90 degrees using their own brute strength, absent power steering. Driver skill sets included heat tolerance, seeing through oil-splattered windshields and a seat of your pants—literally—ability to feel what was going on with the car's mechanical systems, as well as the condition of the tires and roadway. Drivers knew and overcame the fear from knowing they were in a life-and-death career driving these cars. No crumple zones, no crash-forgiving raceway walls, no fireproof suits, no scientifically designed crash helmets, and the list goes on.

The current author spoke with Roger Ward over lunch in 1990 about his battle with winner Jim Rathman during the1960 Indianapolis 500 when he came in second place. Roger shared with me his exhaustion near the end of the race. He told me he could *feel* his tire's tread wearing with each passing lap during the last 25 miles of the race: "I expected a horrific blowout at any moment." He said his arms were so worn out from fighting the unwieldy racer the last few laps, they began to quiver with muscle fatigue. Would a VR action video game version of racing during Roger Ward's era even sell, even if it could be manufactured? Drivers back then reported being exhausted and feeling "beaten up" after one of those races. Would today's digital natives pay to play *that* game?

Oil-Splattered Winner of the 1959 and 1962 Indianapolis 500 Roger Ward (Courtesy of Motor Sport Magazine)

I want to make it crystal clear that I make a distinction between video gaming and related iterations of VR that are designed to immerse the participant into an alternative reality or AR of a known reality. As I stated in the beginning, one of the purposes of our work here is to refine current definitions of alternative realities. VR– participant observer (VR – PO) subsumes video gaming, most of our screen time, and social media. When a gamer plays *Grand Theft Auto,* he participates but also observes, not unlike a puppeteer. VR – immersion (VR – I) or AR – I describes experiences where the participant enters a world as if he were actually there. 2021 technology never totally removes the observer part of the equation, whether we are talking about VR – PO or VR/AR – I, but one day it will.

So this begs the question: what modifications, if any, do VR and AR-immersive experiences have on the brain? Our reference point is OR world structure and function:

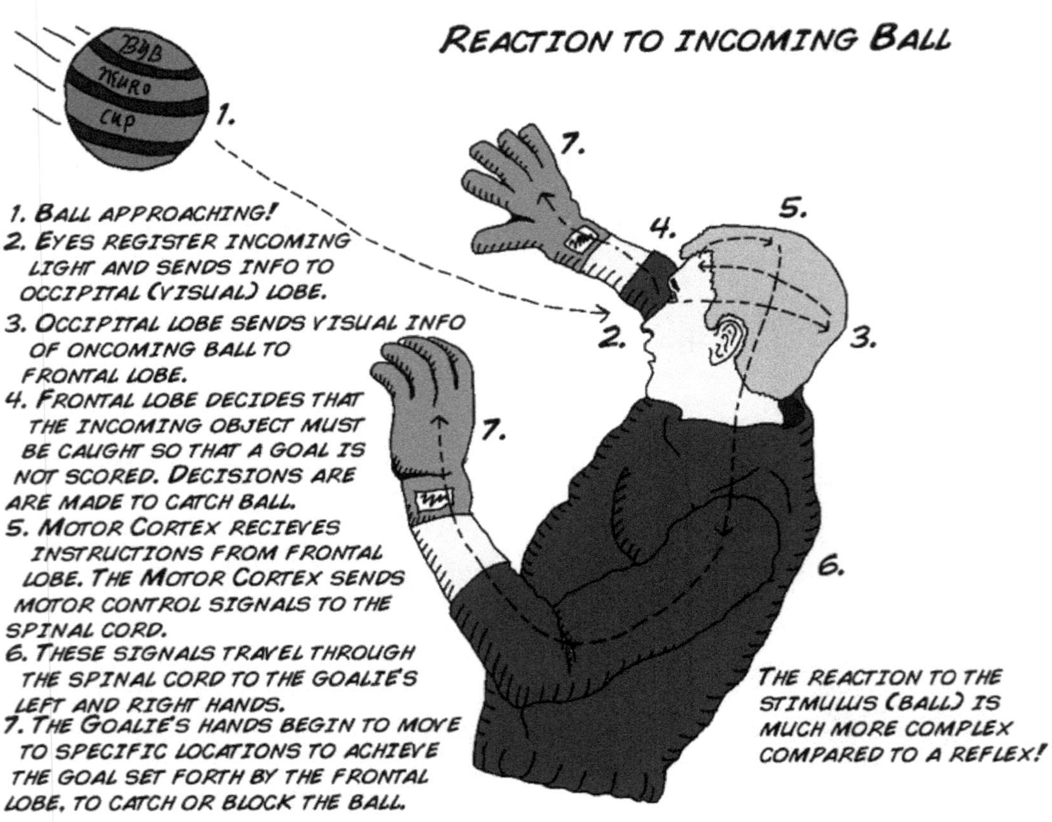

OR World Soccer Goalie's CNS Activation While Defending the Net

PES2020 European Football Video Game

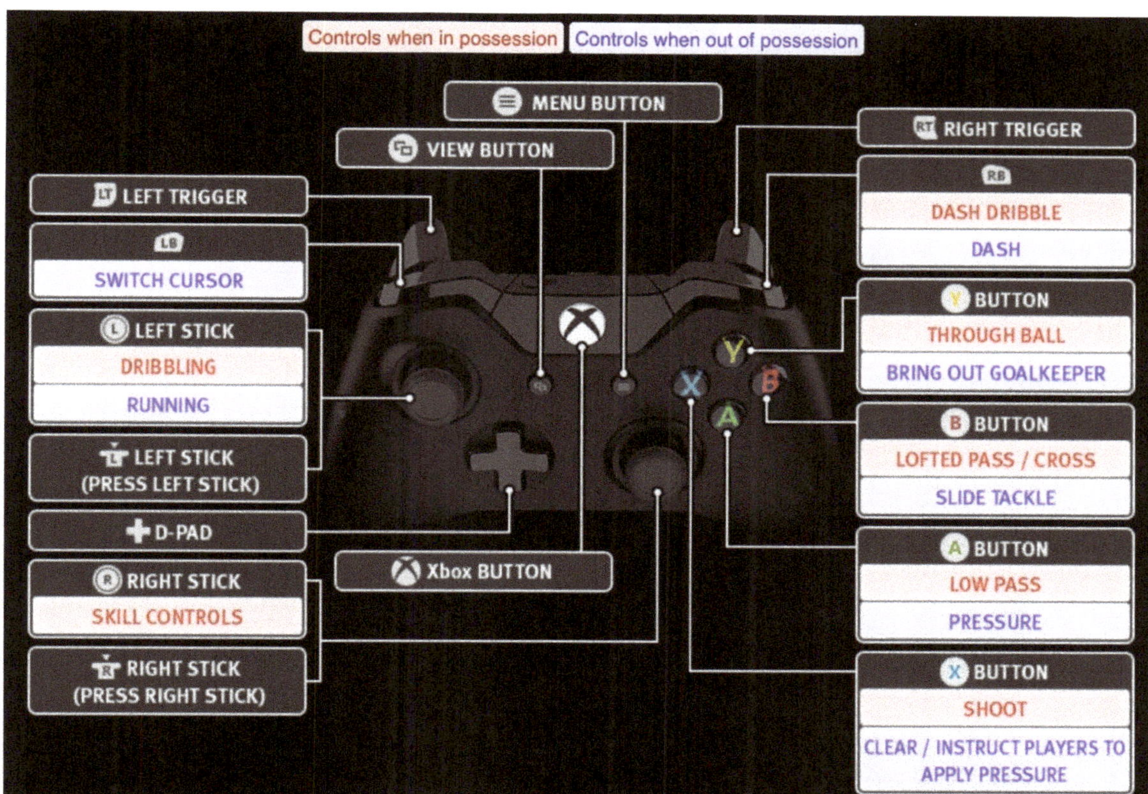

PES2020 European Football Video Game Controller

It should not come as a surprise that, given the plasticity of CNS neurological structures and chemistry in response to long-term and prolific sensory interactive stimuli, VR that takes the form of 2D and 3D video gaming results in structural and functional changes to parts of the brain, in addition to neuropsychological modifications.

In 2018, Dr. Greg West and colleagues at the University of Montreal established a causal link between prolific video gaming behavior and deleterious changes in the hippocampus. [38] The hippocampus is a complex brain structure located deep within the temporal lobe of our brains. It has a major role in learning and memory, among other related cognitive and affective functions.

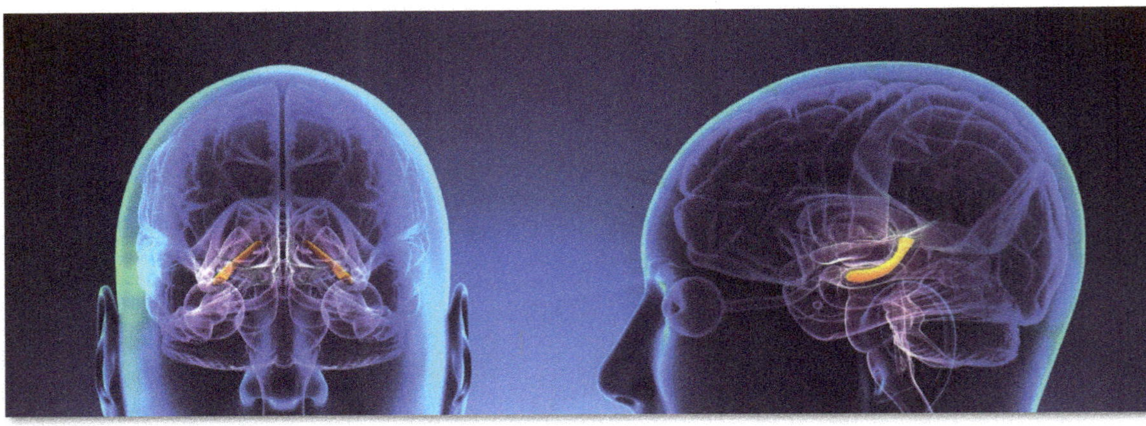

Hippocampus

Researchers exposed subjects on two gaming platforms for 90 hours: On 3D games, e.g., *Super Mario Brothers*, and on first person shooter games, e.g., *Call of Duty*. Subjects in both the experimental and control groups had their brains scanned before and after their 90 hours of gaming. What is most enlightening about this study is that depending upon the gamer's strategy used to interact with the games, the experimental group's hippocampuses were structurally remodeled—and not necessarily for the better. Players who used a response strategy when playing first-person shooter games experienced a diminution in the gray matter that comprises their hippocampus. Depletion of gray matter in the hippocampus has been causally linked to PTSD, young person's depressive syndromes, and when older being at risk for various dementias including Alzheimer's disease. 3D games that encourage a

[38] G L West, K Konishi, M Diarra, J Benady-Chorney, B L Drisdelle, L Dahmani, D J Sodums, F Lepore, P Jolicoeur, V D Bohbot. Impact of video games on plasticity of the hippocampus. Molecular Psychiatry, 2017; DOI: 10.1038/mp.2017.155.

more conceptual and spatial strategy to navigate the game had a positive cognitive impact. Regardless, the generalizability of certain skill sets learned while engaged in VR – participant observer is not 1:1 to the OR world and, as we will learn, may make living in the OR world more problematic—not only for the digital natives, but for those who must interact with them.

Since birth, Gen-Z people have had their brains bioengineered by continual exposure to a sensory smorgasbord show comprised of complex digital visual stimuli with accentuating soundtracks and darting bite sized accompanying content. And just like a body builder who focuses upon his biceps while neglecting other parts of his body, Gen-Z's visual processing and attention centers have been so thoroughly bioengineered they are noticeably different when compared to digital immigrants brains as visualized by fMRI as well as other brain imaging modalities.

One consequence of the bioengineering of visual processing centers is that Gen-Z people often prefer visual saturated learning modalities, because those areas of their brain were molded by digital technology. This reminds me of the bug receptors located in frog retinas. Frog's visual processing centers, beginning with their retinas, are attuned to rapidly moving small images in their field of vision. If you want to get a frog's attention, take a pea-sized object, about the size of a fly, and make it fly around in the frog's field of vision. That will capture the frog's attention, and I am sure if the frog could talk, he would tell you that he prefers that type of stimuli because his brain and peripheral visual processing structures were made for those stimuli. Human beings also have areas of our CNS dedicated to processing certain modalities of stimuli.

Two such neuronal bundles are labeled Broca's and Wernicke's areas. Think of Broca's area as an expressive speech bundle of neurons, and Wernicke's area as a receptive speech center. I don't want the reader to think of your CNS as having discrete modules that only do one thing. That is not the way our brains work—even though at one time, early neurologists may have considered that to be truer than not. As our understanding of the neurobiology of language has evolved, we have expanded our understanding of Broca's and Wernicke's areas to include multiple interconnections and pathways in these and other language centers. [39] Regardless, bioengineering through long term and prolific exposure to VR participant – observer—immersion sensory stimuli results in hyper-development and potentiating of the areas of our brains designed to process those stimuli while rerouting neuronal exercising from other areas—again demonstrate overlap and boundary crossing, not distinct areas of demarcation. I'm not just talking about video game exposure; I am including being exposed to the virtual world since birth.

My clinical experience in treating and analyzing digital integrators, most of whom are tethered to their screens most of the day and night, display changes in receptive speech skills, both in terms of discernment and attention span. That experience finds that screensters even dream within VR contexts, i.e., dreaming is by its very nature VR—but when dreams' storylines involve VR, then we have entered unchartered territory.

The apologist's myth designed to explain away attention span deficits, namely that Gen-Z people are good at executing and processing data from more than one source at a time, that is, they are good at multitasking is simply not true. They may *appear* to do more than one thing at once, but upon careful analysis, what I have found is that what looks like multitasking is more appropriately called rapid sequencing from one stream or sensory source to another. Think of surfing the web only to be interrupted with a message, which is interrupted by a new "friend" notification on their social media account to their dog barking. Gen Z'ers bounce around sensory stimuli like a gluttonous patron at a buffet. What is really going on is Gen Z'ers don't multitask, they bounce. They abandon one stream of content only to bounce to another stream without bookmarking where they left off. When they return to their abandoned stream, if they return, they focus upon whatever is on their screen at their new session, not necessarily the older session. Changes in

---

[39] Pascale Tremblay, Anthony Steven Dick (2016) *Broca and Wernicke are dead, or moving past the classic model of language neurobiology.* Volume 162, November 2016, Pages 60-71.

information processing have profound implications for how we learn and interact with one another, and our culture's zeitgeist.

Content makers and providers are aware of their Gen Z audience's unique cognitive processing patterns. In an attempt to keep what limited focus their Gen Z audiences have at their disposal to take in their content, narrative content producers have taken to letting their audience know that it won't take long to read their abbreviated article—abbreviated because the non-Cliff's Notes articles digital immigrants read in the New York Times, for example, overtax Gen Z's frustration tolerance and are slowly disappearing right along with cellulose newspapers.

by **Emily Baker**
13th March 2021

The advert secured millions of views on social media alone Credit: Supplied to Plant Based News

Reading Time: 2 minutes

A vegan advert that first went viral in Israel garnered over 15 million views in the UK since its debut two months ago. Vegan Friendly created the ad. They are a non-profit organization that seeks to end animal suffering by promoting plant-based food.

Given what we know about what VR and its various iterations have done to digital native's brains, prefacing a story with the promise that it will take only 120 seconds to read is smart, sadly necessary, and a harbinger for what is to come (See immediately preceding image).

> *"[O]ur constant bombardment of small bits of information from Twitter, Facebook or TV with its six second patterns of imaging is rewiring the brain to expect information to be delivered in short, rapid bursts. Among instructors there is some consensus that the attention span of this generation is more limited when compared to earlier generations. Continued interactions with a fast-paced, sensory-laden, multimedia environment predispose/influence brains to adopt a shorter attention span. In the classroom, the average student's attention span* ***is seven to ten minutes****; but online, it is now* ***eight seconds****. That has a lot to do with* ***hypertext****, which encourages learners to point or click on a link to get the information they need without reading all of the text.* ***"Keyword spotting"*** *is a preferred strategy to locate needed information. Otherwise, the average person only spends* ***two seconds per web site*** *while searching. When learners are shown online text and content, they generally want to look at color images and read* ***less than 20% of text****. That calculates* ***to 4.4 seconds for every 100 words on the page. Forty-three percent of teenagers*** *want to learn on the Internet and not use paper-based materials. Thirty-eight percent prefer blended learning and* ***16% prefer using books to learn****."* [40]

To illustrate how we are moving full speed ahead into a **V the Reality** world, I want to circle back to NFTs for a moment. Recall Mr. Dorsey's brilliant 5-word tweet "setting up my twittr" coded as a NFT that sold at auction for $2.9 million, and the Beeple NFT digital art collage that sold for $69 million? Well, in March of 2021, Krista Kim sold a NFT of a 3-D digital home she calls the "Mars House." A couple of things are noteworthy here. First, I want the reader to study how the story of this

---

[40] Ibid 27

NFT sale was presented in written form, keeping in mind that digital natives have flighty and short attention spans:

Creator who sold NFT house for $500,000: We'll be 'living in an augmented reality lifestyle' soon

PUBLISHED WED, MAR 17 2021·2:56 PM EDT

Kevin Stankiewicz
@KEVIN_STANK

KEY POINTS

- Contemporary artist Krista Kim told CNBC she sees NFTs playing a key role in an augmented reality future.
- I actually foresee that we will be living in an augmented reality lifestyle within a very short period," added Kim.
- Kim recently sold an NFT digital house in a transaction valued at more than $500,000.

Notice something? Just like the previous article on vegan food that informed their digital native readers the article would only take 2 minutes to read, the Krista Kim article gave the Cliff's Notes version right at the top. Publishers these days know their digital native audience, and the fact of the matter is the KEY POINTS are all most digital natives will take the time to read. For those who may have a somewhat more resilient attention span, the article and Kim herself made some fascinating observations that both confirm our analysis thus far and capture what our **V the Reality** world has become:

> *"Right now, a lot of the [NFT] art that's currently available on platforms, it's a very limited parameter of how you can present the art," Kim said Wednesday. "It's presented, basically, as a digital file, a beautiful drawing or video on your screen, but my intention was to look beyond that." The new owner of Mars House, she said, will be able to upload the file into various metaverses — 3D immersive worlds — and experience the digital real estate there. She said Mars House represents*

> *the "next generation of NFT art." "For me, I actually foresee that we will be living in an augmented reality lifestyle within a very short period," Kim said, predicting it could happen in "a couple years."* [41]

Miss Kim described her home in an earlier interview this way:

> ***"I see it as a weekend home, like a villa," Kim told The Post. "It's perfect for a couple."***

If you will pardon my OR world perspective on this, I make this observation: "Okay, but there is one big problem I see with this perfect home for a couple.

> **YOU CAN'T ACTUALLY LIVE IN IT BECAUSE IT DOES NOT EXIST IN THE REAL WORLD!"**

I can imagine this colloquy between an OR world buyer and a digital native real estate agent:

BUYER: Are the bathrooms equipped with bidets?

REAL ESTATE AGENT: Why does that matter? How old are you?

Here is a photograph of Krista Kim. For the record, Ms. Kim is reposing on an OR world satin sheet. She is adorned with OR world earrings, wristwatch, and makeup. And while I readily admit that my next declaration is purely speculative, she lives inside an OR world home where she created her MARS HOME. One final observation—if Ms. Kim was able to create a $500,000 NFT she described as constituting "the perfect home for a couple," perhaps she could create an entire community of NFT homes that would be "the perfect homes for people living on the streets." Do you think that would help solve the homeless problem?

---

[41] CNBC, *Creator who sold NFT house for $500,000: We'll be 'living in an augmented reality lifestyle' soon.* Story by: Kevin Stankiewicz, March 17, 2021.

0eefcf5915857351c2dd4f6a592f8d7a3f262bd87358830e34f6978172822ae8

CHAPTER X

TURNING INWARD: The Rise of Alternative Realities

Tectonic shifts in a culture's zeitgeist never occur in a vacuum. It was World War II that catapulted American women into the workforce, as memorialized with the iconic *Rosie the Riveter.* The great pandemic of 1918, which began on a farm in Kansas, would likely have never become the worldwide plague that it turned into without World War I.

It is difficult to imagine the rise of VR, et al., without the advent of the silicon chip or the worldwide web. The inventors of theses technological underpinnings of VR in all of its various forms were and are digital immigrants—whether it was German engineer Werner Jacobi, who patented the first integrated transistor amplifier in 1949; British engineer Geoffrey Dummer, who integrated a variety of standard electronic components into a unitary semiconductor crystal in 1952; or miniaturization chip innovators Harwick Johnson, Sidney Darlington and Yasuo Tarui. Steve Jobs and Steve Wozniak, who started Apple Computer and popularized digital devices in use today that provide VR and AR interfaces for hundreds of millions of digital natives, were/are digital explorers. But those technological advances and their innovators alone can't account for the tsunami overtaking our culture marked by the rise of virtual reality and the diminution of objective reality values and ethos.

Other psychosocial factors, in addition to the biological changes in neuropsychology we have documented, had to preexist the modification of mindsets and values that led to our current world. All of these factors acting synergistically have created a VR zeitgeist where people walking along the Pacific Ocean on a warm starlit evening, accompanied by the sounds of waves, sea gulls and the smell of salt air, appear to be held captive by a digital tractor beam. This tractor beam force field emanates from digital devices. People under the influence act as if they are in a sensory isolation chamber that forces them to turn inward, where the only sensory stimuli they have access to comes from an OLED or the latest-greatest screen technology. Life sentence prisoners do something eerily similar—i.e., turn inward.

THE EIGHTH AXIOM OF VIRTUAL REALITY

The only value OR world objects and experiences have is that value imbued to them by sentient beings. When real world objects and experiences are no longer valued, sentient beings will invariably turn their attention to alternative realities—that means they will turn inward.

The first generation of human beings literally bioengineered to adopt **V the Reality** is Gen Z. They were born between the years 1997 and 2015. Their valuation of OR objects and experiences is determined by how well OR objects and experiences provide a service and/or function to them—and not infrequently, how OR world objects facilitate their addiction to VR. Let's take automobiles and driving, for example. Z's use other people's cars, i.e., ride sharing as a first choice more so than any other generation. It is not a coincidence that Uber and Lyft came into existence when Gen Z was coming of age. When they do buy cars, they are focused on how the car interfaces with the digital technology they rely upon, e.g., whether the car features Apple or Android Car Play, produces its own WiFi hot spot and how well its infotainment system interfaces with their existing digital fingerprint.

Past generations, especially the baby boomers' fascination with horsepower, torque, wheels, and exhaust sounds, seldom show up on Gen Z's radar. Since functionality is key, Z'ers want reliability, good gas mileage, and practicality. It is hard to sell them on some of the decorative flash that was so popular with boomer and millennial generations. That decorative flash costs money, and digital integrators saw their Gen X parents suffer economic hardship as the result of the 2008 stock market crash. Some lost their childhood homes and witnessed family fights over money during that time. Driving skill pride is a thing of the past, as AI and autonomous driving technology has obviated or minimized the value of those skill sets. You can forget pride of ownership—that ethos belongs to older people.

While we are examining digital natives' relationship with OR world objects, it is important to take note of Gen Z's cultural history:

- The 9/11 World Trade Center and Pentagon attacks is a historical event, something they learned about at school or from their parents or grandparents.
- Z'ers have been biopsychosocially molded by and exposed to digital VR from birth. It IS the norm for them.
- The internet just is. It is a given, like TV was a given for Gen X'ers.
- President Obama is not an anomaly in politics because of his race, nor is women in positions of power.
- This generation witnessed or personally experienced financial hardship.
- If Gen Z'ers are U.S. citizens, they have never known a time when their country was not at war or in a foreign conflict.
- Sexuality is ubiquitous and not delineated by inflexible gender boundaries.
- LGBTQ+ issues are part of their normal worldview.
- Traditional marriage between a man and a woman seems old-fashioned.
- Z'ers tend to feel lonely and isolated, more so than previous generations.
- Dating is naturally mediated by digital technology. "Swiping left" has a similar meaning to this generation as getting the brush-off had to boomers, millennials and Gen X.
- Brand loyalty is important but tenuous and is greatly impacted by value judgments about the social behavior of the company.
- They are more money-conscious than their immediately preceding generations.

Gen Z is the first generation to have been completely immersed in alternative realties since birth. Nevertheless, prior generations served to make the transition from OR world to VR immersion possible for Gen Z. The transition over the past 75 years was marked by earlier generations' ever-growing relationship with technology that made virtual reality, et al., what it is today. Here is a brief overview of some of the milestones along the path to **V the Reality** over the past 75 years:

BABY BOOMERS: (Also known as Boomers)

Birth years: 1946 to 1964

Age range: 57 to 75 (as of 2021)

Population size: 71.6 million

Virtual fingerprint: This generation comprises the last generation that consumes non-digital media, albeit that consumption is waning e.g., cellulose printed newspapers, magazines, and linearly broadcast television. They do use digital devices, and some are quite proficient at interfacing with them. When they fully embrace VR technologies, they are often called "digital immigrants." Most boomers have immigrated to social media, e.g., ninety percent or so have Facebook accounts. Still, their preferred emotional reference reality is OR.

Communication preferences: Face to face and/or telephones are their favored way of communicating, with email use commonplace. FaceTime, Zoom, et al., have become more ubiquitous due to COVID-19 restrictions and technological advances. This generation remains ambivalent about texting more so than any other generation, because they view it as impersonal and a step backwards.

Relationship with OR world objects and experiences: This is the last generation to have the ethos "pride of ownership." This generation collects objects, including muscle cars that were popular during their youth. They own homes and intend to pass down to their children material objects and things they have cared for. They value driving skills and many have rejected self-driving cars because of the loss of control that goes along with them. To this generation, giving outside parties control over their car is tantamount to giving away a cherished personal freedom: driving.

…………………………………….

GEN X (Also known as Latchkey Kids or the MTV Generation)

Birth years: 1965 to 1980

Age Range: 41 to 56 years-old (as of 2021)

Population size: 65.2 million

Virtual fingerprint: Of all the generations not immersed in alternative realities as children, Gen X'ers are the most likely to be digital immigrants. The youngest members of this group were exposed as children to what was then the new world of digital media and devices. Their nickname "latchkey" comes from the fact that huge numbers of them returned home from school to an empty house.

Communication preferences: Almost all of this generation has immigrated to VR devices. While still not totally committed to texting and online dating, the youngest in this generation have accepted and use many of the same communication modalities as younger generations.

Relationship with OR world objects and experiences: The average Gen X'er has $140,000-plus in debt. This has put a damper on their pleasurable relationship they may have had with OR world objects and experiences growing up. The oldest in this group have pride of ownership, and the youngest among them no longer value owning things outright, as did their predecessor generation. Still, OR world experiences are preferred over those constructed in the VR world. When traveling, unlike Gen Z travelers, the experience is not necessarily planned and prepped for VR sharing in real time.

....

Millennial Generation: (Also known as Gen Y, Gen Me, Gen We, Echo Boomers).

Birth years: 1981 to 1996.

Age range: 25 to 40 years-old (as of 2021).

Population size: 72 million.

Virtual fingerprint: Millennials view VR as a means to an end, with that end as a way to get what they want in the OR world. Much of their attraction to smart phones is related to their meaning as a status symbol. Their generation popularized many of the online shopping and travel tools in widespread use today. This generation flocked to online stock trading and saw their parents go bust in the 2008 market and housing crash.

Communication preferences: Their consumer focus found a happy home when it came to online shopping. This generation was first to adopt Facebook's predecessors, e.g., SixDegrees in 1997, Blogger in 1999, Friendster in 2002 and Myspace in 2003. COVID-19 sped up their adoption of virtual meetings.

Relationship with OR world objects and experiences: Gen Me lived through 9/11 and watched in real time the internet become what it is today. Co-founder of America Online (AOL) Steve Case noted recently that in 1985, people spent one hour per week on the net. Compare this to Gen Z'ers, who virtually live on the net or stay connected in one form or another through notifications 24/7.

....

Now that we have reviewed the predecessors to the most VR-immersed generation to have ever lived, let's return to our analysis of Gen Z.

Gen Z (Also known as: iGeneration, Post-Millennials, Homeland Generation).

Birth Years: 1997 to 2015.

Age Range: 6 to 24 (as of 2021).

Population size: 68 million.

Virtual fingerprint: The average Gen Z'er received their first mobile phone at age ten. Before that, they were provided access to their parent's smart phones. Not only did they witness their parents' use of digital devices, many were taught by their parents to use them as a rite of passage. They have grown up in a virtually connected world, and their smart phones have become like supernumerary virtual appendages.

Relationship with OR world objects and experiences: Debt fear has made this generation aware of what can happen when a person loses touch with the OR world's governing realities. They learned this, in part, by watching their parents' financial ups and downs. They also have learned that "all that glitters is not gold" when it comes to VR technologies. Prior generations were so bedazzled with this new thing called VR that they adopted it without question. This generation knows nothing but the VR world, so for them the dark side of VR—whether it is being VR bullied, exposed to online predators or feeling isolated by living their lives online—is their *reality,* and many of them are taking a second look. Keep in mind that Gen

Z'ers never knew a world without smart phones, a country not at war (If residents of the USA), online dating, trolling, selfies, Photoshopped images and online porn.

With regard to Gen Z feeling isolated and lonely, these findings may seem counterintuitive given the number of social media "friends" and connectedness to others vis-à-vis VR, but a closer clinical analysis may shed light on this. First, here are data regarding Gen Z's emotional fingerprint:

> *"Gen Z spends less time with their friends face-to-face and more time online and on social media. As we know from decades of research, people who interact with others face-to-face are less likely to be lonely. Recent research suggests that those who spend more time on social media, in contrast, are more likely to be lonely."* [42]

Cigna Health data shed light on some of the psychodynamics of Gen Z:

> *"Unfortunately, it seems that the younger generations are feeling this (loneliness) the most. The study found that Loneliness scores rose among the younger generations, with the youngest generation, Gen Z, feeling the loneliest. Gen Z, individuals born between the 1997 and the early 2000s, scored a 48.3 overall. Millennials, those born between the years 1981 and 1996, then scored a 45.3 on the Loneliness scale. Gen X scored a dreary 45.1 and Baby Boomers scored a 42.4. Those of grandparenting or great-grandparenting age, the Greatest Generation, were the least lonely, with a score of 38.6. Cigna's findings not only identified Gen Z (adults 18-22) as the loneliest generation, but also the generation that claims to be in the worst health compared to other age demographics. 'While we know that this is a group that's coming of age and making life transitions, these findings give us a clear and surprising picture of how this generation perceives themselves,' says Nemecek. 'It's important the communities that these young people are a part of take*

[42] Jean Twenge, Professor of Psychology at San Diego University, in: Addiction Center, *Study Reveals Gen Z As The Loneliest Generation In America*, by: Jena Hilliard | August 14, 2019.

> *note and explore solutions. It's critical that they have spaces where young people can connect face-to-face to form meaningful relationships.'"* [43]

To understand the loneliness of Gen Z, we must first realize that up until Gen Z, the ratio between OR human-to-human interaction, though moving in the direction of VR human-to-human interaction with each succeeding generation, included a significant OR component, with the World War II generation having a nearly 100:0 percent ratio between OR human-to-human vs. VR human-to-human. Today's (2021) Gen Z generation have ratios that are at least 50:50, and in some cases 10:90 percent ratios between OR human-to-human and VR human-to-human interactions. It is not a coincidence that the World War II generation is the least lonely of all generations spanning over the past 100 years despite the fact that as people get older, they lose family members, friends, and because of health issues can become socially isolated. How is it that people in their teens and early twenties in the prime of their lives are suffering from any number of health issues secondary to loneliness and social isolation, given a sea of "friends" and continual VR contact with many people? Insight into the answers to this question can be found in this question: how dangerous can OR world isolation in a sea of social connectivity be to your overall health?

> "Research has found that loneliness has the same impact on mortality as smoking 15 cigarettes a day, making it even more dangerous than obesity." [44]

A couple of old saws come to mind that capture the experience of Gen Z. From a man adrift on the ocean dying of thirst: "Water, water everywhere, and not a drop to drink" and "No greater loneliness exists than a person alone in a crowd."

The existential experience of being connected vis-à-vis social media and smart phone access, and yet feeling isolated, is much worse than simply being alone,

---

[43] - Douglas Nemecek, MD, Chief Medical Officer for Behavioral Health at Cigna, in: Addiction Center, *Study Reveals Gen Z As The Loneliest Generation In America*, by: Jena Hilliard | August 14, 2019
[44] Ibid.

as was the case for older generations without access to VR social media and smart phones. We all know the meaning of "friend" as it relates to Facebook, but what does it really mean? Well, such distinctions between OR world friends and VR world friends is the difference between sitting down and enjoying a piece of apple pie, and smelling an apple pie baking in the oven. Both sources of sensory stimuli are unmistakably apple pie, but one is consumable and the other is a reminder of what you don't have but exists somewhere. Not only is VR connectedness not satisfying, it makes things worse.

This is the dynamic in play: Social media deludes its participants into believing they are socially connected, but what it really does is make the contrast between OR human-to-human contact and VR human-to-human contact only starker and more dramatic. Ultimately, the problem is fundamental in nature. And when it comes to fundamental, nothing is more fundamental in nature than sex.

CHAPTER XI

SEX: Your Brain As A Sex Toy

> *"Several billion-dollar businesses rely upon your brain's responses to symbolic displays of real things. [P]hone sex is nothing more than the manipulation of sexual arousal using auditory symbols, i.e., words and sexual arousal sounds. Speech is comprised of these symbols we have named words. Your brain responds to words similarly to the way it responds to the physical entities and acts that are represented by those same words. Your brain, in turn, regulates your body. It regulates such things as heart rate, vasodilatation/vasoconstriction, breathing rate, adrenaline and testosterone levels, pupil size and hundreds of thousands of other central and peripheral somatic processes, including the sexual arousal response. The fact that human beings can be sexually aroused and have a sexual experience by merely talking on the phone is proof positive of how the brain confuses symbolic displays of sex with the real thing."* [45]

Phone sex is the predecessor to sexting, with the former still a viable business raking in tens of millions of dollars each year across the globe. Make no mistake,

---

[45] Napoleon, Anthony (2015). Shadow Men: An encyclopedia of mind control. VBW Publishing, College Station, Texas.

however, both written and spoken words trigger human beings to replay the virtual sexual dramas that reside in our CNS. The classic rock band Aerosmith's music video *Sweet Emotion* captured the OR vs. VR discordance we've discussed throughout this book, when they portrayed the VR women that men envision during phone sex versus those who actually exist in the OR world on the other end of the phone, or smart phone. Instead of the nubile sex kittens imagined in the virtual world of male phone sex patrons, the video depicted relatively unattractive OR world women working from home.

From the Aerosmith Music Video Sweet Emotion – VR

From the Aerosmith Music Video Sweet Emotion – OR

The sexual experiences had by phone and sexting participants are objectively real. In fact, not only is the sexual response real, but sometimes the emotions of connectedness and what some people have described as love can also be experienced in the virtual world of sex. Sometimes virtual sex is so pleasurable that it becomes addictive.

I reflect upon a patient (Mr. Y) addicted to phone sex who sought help at our hospital during my clinical residency years. He had a six-month sexual and emotional relationship with a phone sex worker. When he arrived at our service, he was spending, in today's dollars, $5,000 per month. When he was unable to connect with his VR love interest he would become sad, sometimes becoming extremely anxious over her absence.

Mr. Y was intent upon meeting her in the OR world. Recognizing the discordant nature of VR vs. OR, I was ambivalent about his desire to turn a VR relationship into an OR world version of the same. However, I wanted to stop the bleeding of not only the $5,000 per month, but also, the emotional toll his addiction to VR sex was having upon him.

At some point, my patient's VR world play streaming live in his head reached critical mass, and he persuaded the phone sex worker to meet him face to face. She was reluctant until my patient offered to pay her a one lump sum of $5,000—C.O.D. I arranged for the meeting to take place at the hospital in hopes of managing what I recognized as an inherently problematic transition from VR to OR. I'll never forget the call from the nurses' station that a young woman was here to see me for her 3:00 P.M. joint session appointment. We both waited with bated breath.

You are probably wondering what she looked like, right? Ponder why you are interested in the answer before I answer it in the next sentence. She was a beautiful girl in her early twenties. She proved to be everything and more that my patient had described to me from the VR images in his mind. She was beautiful, smart, and sophisticated. During the hour-long session I could sense that all was not well on her end, while my patient was ecstatic that he had finally met the love of his life.

A few weeks later, a very depressed Mr. Y told me that Miss X and he had broken up. He told me that he was convinced that she really liked him and that they had a connection, but she had broken off their VR relationship. When he called the phone sex service, he was routed to another woman and not the object of his affection. I asked him if he refused to pay her. He said not only had he not refused to pay her, but he offered to pay her double to continue to talk with him.

A week or so later, I got a call from Miss X. What do you think she told me? She was gracious, charming and told me that my patient was a very nice person, but that in person he wasn't her cup of tea. She went on to say that she could never have actual sex with him (her words) because he didn't turn her on and that she was looking for someone/something else. I shared this story with you because it is illustrative of the oftentimes subtle and counterintuitive nature of alternative reality experiences that are transformed into their OR world versions. Undoubtedly countless online daters know what I am talking about—and believe me, you are not alone.

What if VR and OR world experiences could be melded into a hybrid version "reality" where human beings could easily pretend they were having a once-in-a-lifetime OR world sexual experience that had all the positive aspects of a VR experience but few, if any, of the negatives associated with a particular OR world experience? Are we there yet? A burgeoning artificial intelligence, VR and cyborg consortium is betting on the fact that they have the magic formula for the perfect melding of VR and OR sexual experiences: Enter the sex cyborg. [46]

Imagine the perfect sexual partner as defined by a majority of people polled—attractive, willing, isn't judgmental, no performance pressure. Those characteristics happen to describe sexual cyborgs to a tee. In addition to these behavioral characteristics, imagine your cyborg is as beautiful to look at as the most beautiful model or movie star to have ever lived. Imagine she has the figure, hair color, ethnicity and sexual responsiveness of your dream sexual partner. Would something like that interest you? Well, if you are a male living in many parts of the civilized world the answer is, for an ever-growing number of men, yes. [47] Like all technological inventions, sex dolls have evolved over the years. Sex dolls have evolved from this:

---

[46] cyborg | ˈsīˌbôrg |noun. a fictional or hypothetical person whose physical abilities are extended beyond normal human limitations by mechanical elements built into the body.

[47] Females are not being ignored, nor is the author being male centric. The fact of the matter is women are not a financially viable market for male sex cyborgs for reasons far beyond the scope of this book. Gay men comprise the almost exclusive market for male sex dolls. Suffice to say, for women a sexual partner you keep around needs to be more human that droid – not so with an ever-growing number of men.

Sex Doll from the 1970s

To this:

Twenty First Century Sex Cyborg (Doll)

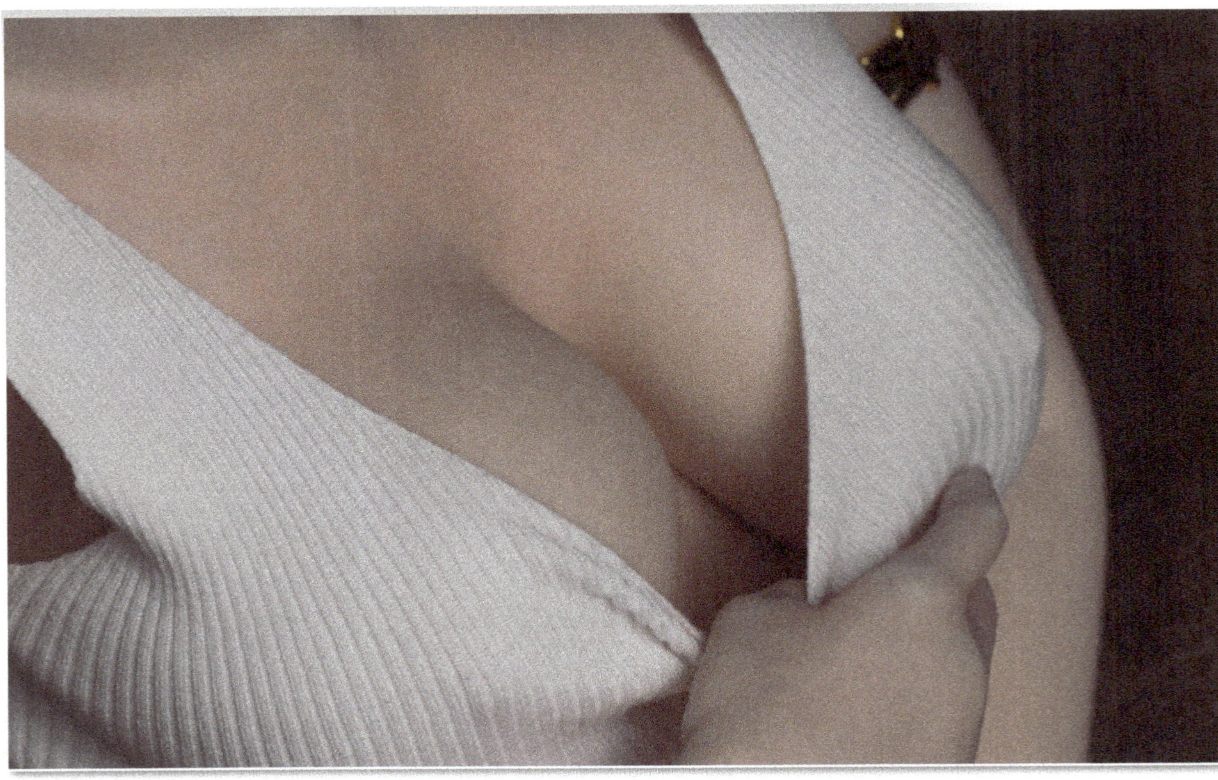

Twenty First Century Sex Cyborg (Doll)

Twenty First Century Sex Cyborg (Doll)

Twenty First Century Sex Cyborg (Doll)

Twenty First Century Sex Cyborg (Doll)

Yes, male sex dolls exist. [48] The market for male sex dolls is almost exclusively found in the gay community.

[48] Only one of the four main manufacturers of sex dolls began a limited production of male cyborgs beginning in 2018.

Twenty First Century Male Sex Cyborg (Doll)

If online porn, phone sex, and sexting can create an OR world sexual experience, imagine what adding a sophisticated AI cyborg into the sexual equation can do. And speaking of what sex cyborgs can do—high-end dolls maintain a 98.6 F/37C body temperature, possess a realistic skin texture and feel, can blink, smile, moan, get goose bumps and hold a conversation with their sex partner. And with a VR – CNS doing the sensory processing, your AI sex doll that is as beautiful as Marilyn Monroe becomes smarter with each software upgrade. If you think Siri is getting smarter and more responsive with each software upgrade, you should try out her naughty kindred spirit sister who knows how to talk dirty. "Hey Sirilucious—well, you know."

At the 2018 Computer Electronics Show (CES) in Las Vegas attendees were entertained by cyborg females that pole danced. And no, you didn't have to slip a $5 bill into their G-strings.

> *"[D]olls, sold by Sex Doll Genie and manufactured by Gynoid, are silicone-based and, according to SGD founders Janet Stevenson and her husband Amit, look and feel like a real human. 'There are lonely middle-aged men who don't necessarily want to stroll through the dating minefield again, there are handicapped and disabled folks for whom sex dolls are convenient and non-judgmental companions, then there are couples like us who wanna add another dimension to their love-life*

without additional emotional baggage,' according to the website. 'Also, increasingly there are folks who just think that a sex doll suits their lifestyle better.' However, they are now being used by people worried about COVID-19 and couples. Since the pandemic, the Florida-based company saw orders spike by more than 51% during February and March — when lockdowns began in the US and other countries. 'They are the most realistic on the market. ... They say 90% of the sex is in the mind — when the doll you are making love to looks so real, it does indeed make sex more pleasurable and gratifying," Amit told Daily Star

SexDoll Genie Creation: "Secretary Izelle"

The high-end dolls — that come complete with a full body and equipped with artificial intelligence — start at around $6,000 but can go as high as $8,000. 'They're hand-made. If you look at the video, you can see the veins in the arms or in the chest," Amit told the Star. 'It's pretty crazy, I have some videos of their recent order, and you look at these videos and you think, she could just blink any second now, it looks that real.'" [49]

[49] New York Post, Eerily realistic sex doll can smile, moan — and even hold a conversation. By: Paula Froelich, June 20, 2020.

Sex dolls are the perfect example of how V the Reality is making inroads into what used to be one of the most intimate of all OR world human-to-human interactions—sex.

The sex dolls of 2050 will make the dolls presented in this book look like a horse and buggy when compared to the most sophisticated automobiles of 2021. When that happens, and it will unless governments get together and outlaw sex doll technological advancements, the implications for human existence will be profound. The reader might be wondering, why would a government outlaw sex dolls? Let's take a closer look.

Our review of penal codes across the globe as of 2021 informs us the following countries have either explicitly outlawed sex dolls or could certainly make that argument before a magistrate by simply defining the sex doll as a sexual device or toy:

- The Maldives
- Saudi Arabia
- United Arab Emirates
- Thailand
- Vietnam
- Malaysia
- India

The issue of sex dolls and cultural morality has gotten more attention as sexual cyborgs have become more realistic. In South Korea, its supreme court found sex dolls to be legal in as much that they were for personal use. However, the court's ruling caused a backlash, to wit:

> *"SEOUL, South Korea — A petition calling for a ban on importing life-size sex dolls into South Korea has gathered nearly a quarter-million signatures as of Friday, passing a threshold that requires the president's office to respond to the matter. While sex dolls are not illegal in South Korea, government customs agencies had blocked their import under a law that restricts materials that "corrupt public morals." However, the*

> *Seoul High Court said in January that sex dolls were for personal use and should be treated differently than pornography, which is heavily restricted under South Korean law. That decision was upheld by the Supreme Court in June. The ruling has sparked a backlash, with one petition filed with the presidential Blue House gathering more than 237,000 signatures. The unidentified author of the petition argued that an influx of imported sex dolls could lead to an increase in sex crimes. A spokesman for Incheon Main Customs said they had allowed imports from Japan, but are still reviewing whether to release imported dolls from China."* [50]

In the United States, South Dakota lawmakers recently introduced a bill that would outlaw certain types of sex dolls:

> *"Lawmakers in South Dakota plan to introduce a bill that would make it illegal to have or manufacture sex dolls that look like children in the state. The Argus Leader reports that supporters of the measure fear such lifelike dolls could promote pedophilia, although some academics have theorized they could be a harmless outlet for would-be abusers.* ***"The dolls are a gateway," Carrie Sanderson, director of the Center for Prevention of Child Maltreatment, told the newspaper. "They have the potential of eroding the shame that would typically come with having sex with a child."*** *Only a handful of other states have similar laws on the books. South Dakota's bill is opposed by a group of defense lawyers who say it is too broad and that there is no victim of the proposed crime." (Emphasis Added)* [51]

---

[50] Reuters News Service. South Korea sex doll ruling arouses controversy among consumers. Aug. 2, 2019.

[51] The Daily Beast. South Dakota Pols Want to Outlaw Child-Like Sex Dolls. By Traci Connor. February 11, 2021.

In 2018, the House of Representatives passed the "Curbing Realistic Exploitative Electronic Pedophilic Robots Act." This law outlaws the importation and possession of child-like sexual robots.

Shown Here:
Referred in Senate (06/14/2018)

115TH CONGRESS
2D SESSION

H. R. 4655

IN THE SENATE OF THE UNITED STATES
JUNE 14, 2018

Received; read twice and referred to the Committee on the Judiciar

AN ACT

To amend title 18, United States Code, to prohibit the importation or transportation of child se" dolls, and for other purposes.

Be it enacted b the Senate and House of Representatives of the United States of America in Congress assembled,

SECTION 1. SHORT TITLE.

This Act ma be cited as the "Curbing Realistic E"ploitative Electronic Pedophilic Robots Act of 2017" or as the "CREEPER Act of 2017".

SEC. 2. FINDINGS.

The Congress finds as follows:

(1) There is a correlation between possession of the obscene dolls, and robots, and possession of and participation in child pornograph.

(2) The phsical features, and potentiall the "personalities" of the robots are customiable or morphable and can resemble actual children.

(3) Some owners and makers of the robots have made their children interact with the robots as if the robots are members of the famil.

(4) The robots can have settings that simulate rape.

(5) The dolls and robots not onl lead to rape, but the make rape easier b teaching the rapist about how to overcome resistance and subdue the victim.

(6) For users and children e"posed to their use, the dolls and robots normalie submissiveness and normalie se" between adults and minors.

(7) As the Supreme Court has recognied, obscene material is often used as part of a method of seducing child victims.

(8) The dolls and robots are intrinsicall related to abuse of minors, and the cause the e"ploitation, objectification, abuse, and rape of minors.

Apparent Underage Sex Doll

The makers of underage sex dolls don't go around advertising their sales numbers. If we look at the sex doll industry as a whole it is estimated at $30 billion market value, with the underage market estimated to be at least one-third of that market share. I have censored much of what our research uncovered on this subject, but suffice to say if you let your imagination run wild, you would probably underestimate the degree and level of depravity when it comes to not only underage, but also other genres of sexual cyborgs. [52]

Governments across the globe are beginning to take a close look at regulating the sex cyborg business. The issue of government regulation goes right to the heart of V the Reality and our future as an AI virtual reality programmed species. Here are some questions the reader may wish to ask him/herself:

- Should laws be enacted that regulate sexual behavior with sex dolls? (If your answer is no, then answer these questions):

- Should engaging in sex with a minor sex doll be outlawed?
- Should engaging in sex with an AI animal doll be outlawed?
- Should physically abusing a sex doll during a VR sex session be outlawed?
- Should sex dolls programmed to simulate rape dynamics be outlawed?

These questions force us to contemplate the melding of VR and OR into V the Reality and its societal implications. Let's examine just ONE of the hot button issues related to sex cyborgs—underage and other felon-fetish sex dolls.

- In as much that it is difficult if not impossible to rehabilitate child molesters,
- And if we as a society are not going to lock them up and throw away the key,
- Then what are the consequences of allowing child molesters to purchase underage sex dolls?

Manufacturers and sellers of underage-looking VR sex cyborgs enable felonious behavior and should be regulated, if not outlawed. The reasons why go right to the heart of our running theme found throughout this book: Anything that enables sexual felons to exercise their neural circuitry potentiates[53] those circuits and facilitates the transition from VR to OR world behavior. Remember, phone sex, sexting, image facilitated masturbation, and having sex with underage sex dolls IS sex in the mind of the actor. To the counterfactual critics spuriously comparing OR world sexual acts with underage-looking sex dolls to first-person shooter video games and OR world violence—you are comparing apples and oranges, because the victims in first person shooter games are not touchable, nor do they smell, have body temperatures and react with somatic reactions to your behavior. VR sex can be so immersive it is indistinguishable from OR world sex in the minds of some troubled individuals.

United States manufacturers have recently produced dolls that have a feature that allows their partner (owner) to program their behavior. One prototype sex robot, Roxxxy made by True Companion, can be programmed to be "Wild Wendy,"

---

[53] potentiation | pəˌten(t)SHēˈāSH(ə)n |noun Physiology: The increase in strength of nerve impulses along pathways which have been used previously, either short-term or long-term.

"Mature Martha," and "Frigid Farrah." Should we be concerned about these sex dolls? They are adult dolls, after all. For our more libertarian-minded readers who reply "no," consider this:

> One of Roxxxy's personalities is Frigid Farrah. This doll is programmed to reject sexual touching. In other words, she is programmed to say "no!" Some men find this to be arousing—we sometimes label the men who do not take no for an answer rapists. Frigid Farrah was designed to be raped by her owner—that is her allure. Just like *Gran Turismo* champ Ricardo Sanchez became proficient at racing at Willow Springs by playing *Gran Turismo* the rapist owners of Roxxy would also be expected to work out, that is, potentiate their rape-pleasure circuits in their brain.

And if you think things couldn't get worse, consider what House Judiciary Committee Chairman [54] Bob Goodlatte revealed, a Virginia Republican who was privy to the degree to which manufacturers have learned to cater to their felon client base:

> *"Customers can order bespoke dolls, providing pictures of specific children they would like the doll to resemble. They can indicate a preferred facial expression such as sadness or fear."*

Just to make this perfectly clear, bespoke sex robots can be ordered by pedophiles/child molesters to look like a child he is sexually attracted to. Imagine, just for a moment—someone takes a photo of your child at a piano recital, then submits the photo to one of these sex doll manufacturers that then custom manufactures a sex doll that is the spitting image of your seven-year-old daughter. Once your daughter's sex doll doppelganger is delivered to her new owner, she is VR raped.

Not to be outdone by governmental regulations, manufacturers as well as their retail distributors have provided their customers any number of suggestions

---

[54] 2018

on how to navigate the legal minefield intent upon clamping down on their quest to own a sex victim, to wit:

> *"If you live in the areas listed below we recommend the following: pick a doll shipping from a local warehouse: USA, Canada, EU, Australia- choose a Fantasy, Curvy BBW or Torso Doll: Fantasy, BBW, Torso- pick a larger (in height) doll- dolls that do not look young are legal everywhere we ship. Problem areas include the following below: USA states: Florida, Kentucky, Tennessee have very strict policies regarding sex dolls. We encourage you to look for a more mature looking (or a doll over 150cm) doll to avoid any problems. Please be sure to check with the laws in your state. Canada: Your doll should be mature looking or over 125 - 140cm. UK: the law currently specifies that your doll cannot be under 125cm or choose a doll that is mature looking. Australia and New Zealand: where your doll cannot be under 158cm height or choose a doll that is mature looking. Europe: Legal and safe. Some countries in Europe are starting to adopt laws. As far as we know, the EU is still a safe place for all doll sizes. We are not telling you all of this so you buy a bigger or more expensive doll. It's actually easier for us to make and sell smaller dolls and our profit margins would be significantly higher without these ridiculous regulations. We are informing you of these facts because we don't want anyone buying a doll to face huge fines or even prison.* [55]

It should not surprise the reader that the mental and physical health issues related to VR world sex dolls are being studied by serious researchers. Dr. Chantal Cox-George from the Academic foundation in London, along with Dr. Susan Bewley, a Professor of Complex Obstetrics at King's College London, published their findings,

---

[55] Doll Podium. December 16, 2019.

"I, Sex Robot: the health implications of the sex robot industry." [56] Here are findings from their research:

- [I]t is "plausible that sex robots will be helpful for patients who would benefit from sexual practice without pressure, although this might move some further away from human intimacy."
- [T]he use of sex robots for couples with mismatched libido or to help treat erectile dysfunction turned out to be a double-edged sword, with potential adverse consequences such as rejection of the non-interacting partner or threats to the integrity of the relationship.

With regard to whether or not sex cyborgs might be of therapeutic value in the lives of the lonely, disabled, or those suffering from mental illness?

- Probably not, for a number of reasons, most explicitly that the meaning of a "companion" would negatively change from an interacting, speaking person that can genuinely reciprocate, verbally and emotionally as much as physically.

Drs. Cox-George and Bewley concluded that it is too early to recommend the clinical use of sex dolls until more research has been done.

Sex centers in humans' CNS appear to be particularly vulnerable to conflating VR and OR world sensory-interactive stimulus and response sets. Recall earlier that we made note of the fact that at some point in the future, we would no longer be able to distinguish between VR and OR world experiences. The Tesseract dimension, as I analogically refer to it, is the inevitable end point for alternative reality technologies—and it will arrive sooner than most people expect. VR sexual behavior, whether it is facilitated by phone, texting, imagery, or sex dolls, provides us with a glimpse of what is to come and will terminate at V the Reality (sooner) and eventually when the Tesseract dimension arrives. Whether human beings should

[56] BMJ Sexual & Reproductive, Sex Robot: the health implications of the sex robot industry. Health Jul 2018, 44 (3) 161-164; DOI: 10.1136/bmjsrh-2017-200012I

stop it or can stop it is yet another fascinating question that VR world technology, and our appetite for it, forces us to contemplate.

CHAPTER XII

OBJECTIVE REALITY : VIRTUAL REALITY: Gender Objective : Gender Mind

I've chosen to focus upon key biopsychosocial issues and considerations related to gender identity as a means to an end. The end point of our examination in this chapter will be to draw a finer portrait of the burgeoning move toward establishing V the Reality as a social norm truth. The means will involve a scholarly review of the counterpoint to what many readers have assumed is a settled issue, namely, that surgeons can turn men into women and women into men, and that gender is a social construct. I chose gender reassignment—or as some prefer, gender affirmation surgery—as the canvas upon which we draw our illustrations, because no subject is as revelatory when it comes to the push toward a V the Reality world. Take a look at the following market data from Grand View Research regarding gender reassignment, or if you prefer, gender affirmation surgery. Perhaps no better illustration of the rise of virtual reality, especially V the Reality, is evidenced by the burgeoning number of people choosing—and our culture's ever-increasing acceptance of and willingness to pay for—someone else's major surgery designed to dismember and then reconstruct the OR world of sexual organs to approximate [57] their VR psychological sense of gender identity.

U.S. Sex Reassignment Surgery Market Size, Share & Trends Analysis Report By Gender Transition (Male To Female, Female To Male), And Segment Forecasts, 2020 - 2027

"The U.S. sex reassignment surgery market size was valued at USD 267.0 million in 2019 and is expected to expand at a compound annual growth rate (CAGR) of 14.4% from 2020 to 2027. The rising incidences of gender dysphoria and the increasing number of people deciding for gender confirmation surgeries are expected to boost market growth over the forecast period. Sex reassignment surgeries are performed by a multispecialty staff that usually involves board-certified or licensed plastic surgeons. The objective of this surgical procedure is to give transgender individuals the functional abilities and physical appearance of the gender they ***align their emotional and psychological identity*** *with. It includes procedures such as facial feminization surgery, transfeminine bottom surgery, transfeminine top surgery, transmasculine top surgery, facial masculinization surgery, and transmasculine bottom surgery."* [58]

[57] Approximate is the operant descriptor, not surgically change one sex into another sex.

[58] GRAND VIEW RESEARCH: U.S. Sex Reassignment Surgery Market Size, Share & Trends Analysis Report By Gender Transition (Male To Female, Female To Male), And Segment Forecasts, 2020 – 2027. Publication date, December 2020.

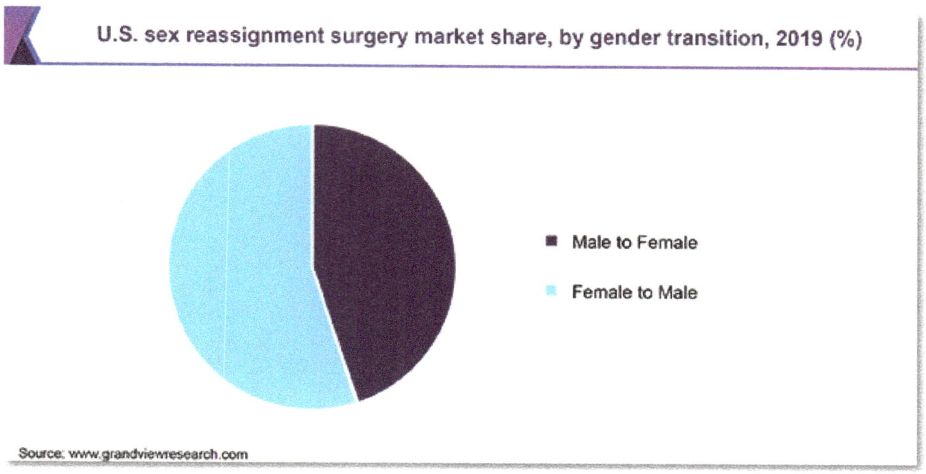

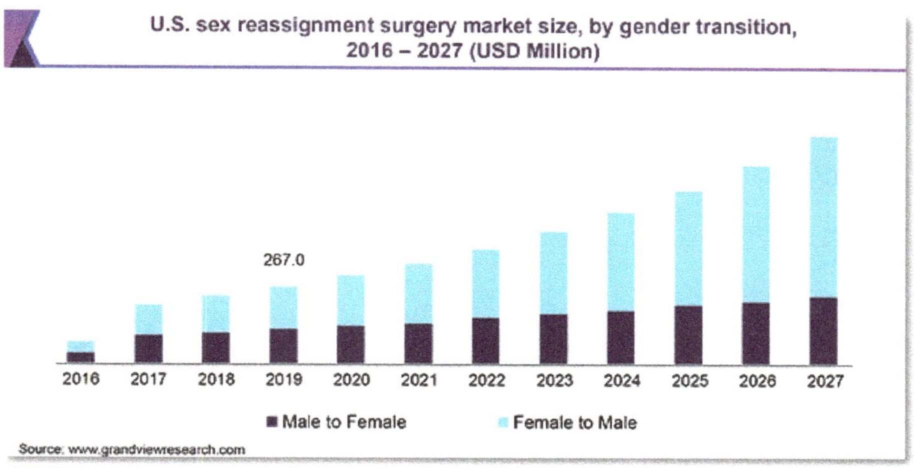

OR World Major Surgery Trends Purposed to Modify Objective Reality to Resemble V the Reality

In addition to these major surgery stats, keep in mind that any number of dermatologic, endocrine, and other somatic modifications are utilized in conjunction with genital surgery in hopes that visual image and facsimile sexual function better approximate the patient's psychological sense of their gender identity—with *approximation* the operant term. These major interventions typically include but are not limited to hormone replacement therapy—estrogens (OR-XY) and androgens (OR-XX)—breast augmentation (OR-XY), mastopexy surgery (OR-XX), debridement of the Adam's apple and/or supraorbital ridges (OR-XY), and not uncommonly, the use of medications designed to grow longer and thicker eyelashes (OR-XY). In addition to the aforementioned interventions, a host of other cosmetic strategies are employed—including electrolysis, hair extensions, and various waxing and skin care modalities— to narrow the visual image deltas between the sexes even after major sexual reassignment surgery. Endocrine and dermatologic interventions typically require maintenance during the life of the patient. Is there a counterpoint to the American Psychiatric Association's (APA) "psychological sense" of gender identity, you might ask? Yes. What follows is a statement from the American College of Pediatricians on the objective reality of biological sex.

> *"In the midst of society's questioning of the gender binary, the American College of Pediatricians (ACPeds) is concerned that the field of medicine risks denying the reality of biological sex.* ***Sex is a dimorphic, innate trait defined in relation to an organism's biological role in reproduction.*** *In humans, primary sex determination occurs at fertilization and is directed by a complement of sex determining genes on the X and Y-chromosomes.* ***This genetic signature is present in every nucleated somatic cell and is not altered by drugs or surgical interventions.*** *Sex differences arise from at least four different genetic mechanisms, in addition to the actions of sex hormones and environmental influences. Consideration of these innate differences is critical to the practice of good medicine and to the development of sound public policy for children and adults alike."* [59]

Discordant gender identity surgical and endocrine modifications have become a WOKE norm that is an enforced one-way street. When a person decides to alter their anatomy and physiology using major medical interventions purposed to make their physical self *approximate* their psychological sense of their gender identity, that choice is socially lauded and legally protected. On the other hand, behavioral modification—that is, psychological interventions purposed to modify a person's psychological sense about who and what they are, so that those feelings *approximate* the OR world of genes and body type—is not only considered to be socially reprehensible, but as of 2021 **it is illegal in many states across the USA**.

---

[59] American College of Pediatricians: *Sex is a Biological Trait of Medical Significance*. March 2021.

Readers should take special note of the fact that while behavioral modifications may be reversed—that is, rejected, abandoned or simply not work—surgical and endocrine environment modifications are for all intents and purposes impossible to untangle, i.e., reverse, even if the patient's psychological sense of their gender identity changes. What are the incidence data on "reversals?"

> *"The 2015 U.S. Transgender Survey claims that 11% of female respondents regret surgery enough to change back to their original sex. Transgender men had a reversion rate of 4%."*[60]

These data reflect the number of people who *acted* on their dissatisfaction with their reassignment surgery, but NOT the number of people who *regret* having had the surgery and for whatever reason(s) chose to not undergo a subsequent major revisionary surgical procedure.

The notion of "changing back" is misleading, to say the least. Surgical reassignment surgery dismembers then "repurposed" penises, vaginas and surrounding tissues. These structures can never exist as they were **originally designed and functioned** after surgery. Changes to a patient's endocrine environment cannot be reversed like changing one's hair color, and long-term modification to one's endocrine environment may result in irreversible changes. Some estimate the number of those who regret having undergone gender reassignment surgery to be in the hundreds.[61] The author cannot confirm the accuracy of that number. One of the reasons that can't be done is the entire subject of "transgender" is so thoroughly protected by social engineers, it is almost impossible to gauge the data—but regret, buyer's remorse, and gender identity as fluid, especially in pre-pubescent and adolescents, are accepted and validated principles in human behavior that strongly suggest dissatisfaction, remorse, and

---

[60] James, S. E., Herman, J. L., Rankin, S., Keisling, M., Mottet, L., & Anafi, M. (2016). The Report of the 2015 U.S. Transgender Survey. Washington, DC: National Center for Transgender Equality.

[61] Sky News. Hundreds of young trans people seeking help to return to original sex: A woman who detransitioned in 2018 says there are many people who have had gender reassignment surgery who wish they hadn't. Story by: Sally Lockwood, October 5, 2019.

ambivalence about the choice to undergo sexual affirmation surgery are much more common than the current data reflect.

The subjects of gender dysphoria or gender mismatch and surgical "treatments" for these states of mind are **impossible to broach** without incurring critical attention from social engineers focused upon creating a V the Reality world—critical attention that manifests when they employ their number one go-to strategy, i.e., the attachment of a Scarlet Letter, aka, the attachment of a stigmatized label on anyone who challenges their assumptions and resultant behavior. Permit me to repeat, it is important for readers, especially my digital native readers and unwitting enforcers of social engineer's edicts, to recognize that my coverage of gender affirmation/gender reassignment major surgery is **only** for illustration purposes related to the rise of V the Reality.

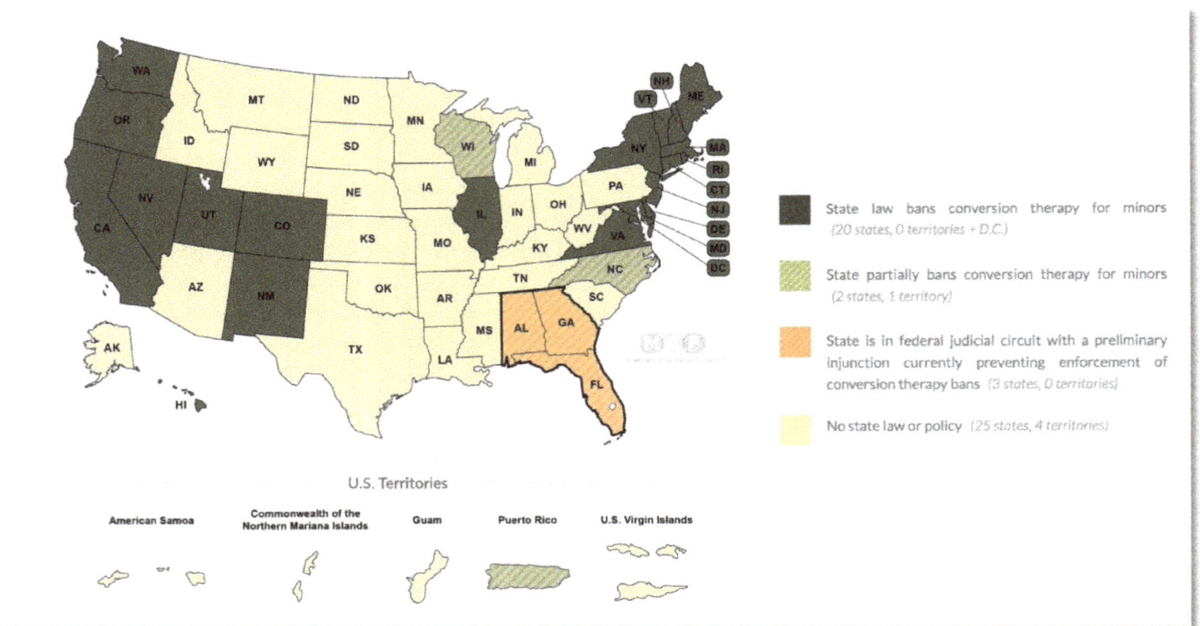

Equality Maps – Conversion "Therapy" Laws (Courtesy of: Movement Advancement Project (MAP)

NINTH AXIOM OF VIRTUAL REALITY

As social engineers continue their efforts to blur, if not totally dissolve, the delta between OR and VR worlds, major surgery, genetic modifications of human beings, and civil and criminal punishments will be implemented to enforce V the Reality's dominance over OR.

Choosing to undergo major surgery to modify genitalia, and the thousands of OR world anatomical and physiological characteristics of OR gender so that they resemble the VR gender identity in our head, is ***consequential NOT coincidental*** to the rise of virtual reality.

Transgender, transpecies, transgenomic, and interventional psychotrophic psychiatric modifications of human beings' objective states of being may very well become de rigueur in the future, as it currently is when it comes to gender reassignment surgery.

"WASHINGTON – The Pentagon has spent nearly $8 million to treat more than 1,500 transgender troops since 2016, including 161 surgical procedures, according to data obtained by USA TODAY." [62]

> *"Taxpayers will now foot the bill for gender reassignment surgery for active military personnel* ***and*** *veterans, with some treatments* ***costing upward of $200,000*** *under an executive order signed by President Biden. Tucked inside Biden's Jan. 25, 2021 transgender order, "Enabling All Qualified Americans to Serve Their Country in Uniform," is a clause that repeals an Obama-era policy that prohibited federally funded reassignment surgery. This was followed up by memos from both Secretary of Defense Lloyd Austin and Veterans Affairs Secretary Denis McDonough specifically stating that surgery is now an added benefit. "This revised policy will also ensure all medically necessary transition related care authorized by law is available to all Service members,"*

[62] USA Today: Exclusive: Pentagon spent nearly $8 million to treat 1,500 transgender troops since 2016. Story by: Tom Vanden Brook, February 27, 2019.

Austin wrote. In a VA email to employees, McDonough echoed: "Perform an assessment of the necessary steps to eliminate the exclusion of 'gender alteration' (gender affirmation surgery) in the medical benefits package." [63] (Emphasis added)

Not only are enlisted military personnel eligible for gender reassignment surgery, but also, as of June 19, 2021, military veterans can have their gender affirmation surgery paid for by the Veterans Administration i.e., the taxpayer:

"WILMINGTON, Del. (AP) — The Department of Veterans Affairs is moving to offer transgender veterans gender confirmation surgery, Secretary Denis McDonough announced at a Pride Month event in Orlando Saturday. McDonough said in prepared remarks that the move was "the right thing to do," and that it was part of an effort to overcome a "dark history" of discrimination against LGBTQ service members. The move is just the first step in what's likely to be a years-long federal rulemaking process to expand VA health benefits to cover the surgery, but McDonough said the VA will use the time to "develop capacity to meet the surgical needs" of transgender veterans. The decision, he said, will allow "transgender vets to go through the full gender confirmation process with VA by their side." McDonough also referenced what he said were higher rates of mental illness and suicidal thoughts among LGBTQ veterans, and a fear of discrimination that prevents those veterans from seeking care." [64]

Once upon a time, some people joined the military to fight for their country, and in the bargain earn the benefits of the G.I. Bill which helped pay for their higher education, G.I., home loans, etc. In today's world, some people suffering—or if you prefer, "experiencing" —gender dysphoria join the military just so they can have

[63] FFN News: Transgender Surgery is Now Free For Military, Thanks to Biden Executive Order. March 10, 2021.

[64] Associated Press. VA moves to offer gender confirmation surgery to vets. Story by: Alexandra Jaffe, June 19, 2021.

taxpayers pay for their gender reassignment/gender affirmation surgery. Readers may be thinking, "How can doctors tell if such surgery is medically necessary?" Assuming medical necessity is still a respected criterion before gender affirmation or any other major surgical intervention is made, examining the issue provides a clear window though which we may better understand V the Reality versus objective reality.

The assessment of the genuineness of a patient's psychological sense of gender dysphoria is a key factor in any clinical psychological assessment, whether in the forensic or surgical candidate arena, because of the problems of malingering and the mercurial, often transitory, quality of psychological states of mind, to wit:

> *"[D]uring a one-year period, probable malingering and symptom exaggeration were found in 30% of disability evaluations, 29% of personal injury evaluations, 19% of criminal evaluations, and 8% of medical cases. This is consistent with earlier studies on base rates of malingering identified during mental health evaluations."* [65]

The above referenced data regarding disability is important because, legally speaking, gender dysphoria is considered to be a disability protected by the Americans with Disabilities Act (ADA). This from the Harvard Law Review:

> *"Acknowledging this evidence, the U.S. Department of Justice concluded in 2015 that 'the current research increasingly indicates that gender dysphoria has physiological or biological roots, and that gender dysphoria* ***is a protected disability*** *under federal disability rights laws."*[66]

Federal law considers, by definition, gender dysphoria to be a disability under the ADA. Under current Veterans Administration policy guidelines, gender dysphoria qualifies for taxpayer funded gender affirmation surgery as a result of it being a

[65] Wiley Mittenberg, Christine Patton, Elizabeth M Canyock, Daniel C Condit. Base rates of malingering and symptom exaggeration. Journal of Clinical and Experimental Neuropsychology. 2002 Dec;24(8):1094-102.

[66] Harvard Law Review: *Embracing the ADA: Transgender People and Disability Rights.* Article by: Jennifer L. Levi and Kevin M. Barry, February 22, 2021.

protected disability. However, The National Center for Transgender Equality (NCTE) states that gender dysphoria is NOT a disability, to wit:

> ***"Does this mean that being transgender is considered a disability?***
> ***No****. Gender dysphoria, a medical condition that some transgender people have, can sometimes be considered a disability that is protected under laws like the ADA. NCTE opposes discrimination and stigma against people living with disabilities, whether that includes gender dysphoria or other medical conditions that many transgender people live with."*[67]

It is hard to find a better example than the fact that while federal law classifies gender dysphoria as a protected disability under the ADA, the NTCE—one of the, if not the, leading advocates for transgender equality—does NOT as a rule believe gender dysphoria qualifies as a disability, although "it can sometimes be." We infer that when the NTCE agrees that gender dysphoria qualifies as a disability, it is in those circumstances when people want taxpayer or insurance company subsidization for their gender affirmation surgery and/or when transgender and/or gender dysphoric people feel they are being discriminated against according to the protection afforded to them under the ADA. In the absence of the gold standard of objective reality as our reference point, the virtual world in our heads becomes the scale upon which government weighs its policy edicts and normative standards. Note:

> **The current author is not asserting that how people feel or what they believe is not real *to them*. My focus is upon *why* people feel and believe what they do and within what cultural standards of reality those feelings develop and flourish. The ongoing push to make V the Reality a culturally accepted truth rests upon making**

[67] National Center for Transgender Equality. Breakthrough: Americans with Disabilities Act Can't Exclude Gender Dysphoria. May 22, 2017.

feelings and beliefs the sine qua non of objective reality. I'll write more about this later.

Let's examine The National Center for Transgender Equality's position statement that gender dysphoria *can be* a "medical condition." A medical condition suggests, as it does when considering Type I diabetes or congenital adrendal hyperplasia (CAH), for example, that the cultural norm of focusing exclusively upon how a person feels about their gender identity may not be the gold standard when we attempt to answer the question: "Is it Ella or Memorex?" In a V the Reality world, the "Ella question" is irrelevant, if not moot. The current author has written about the objective reality of genuine transsexual states of mind, as well as related issues having to do with same-sex sexual attraction. What part does objective reality play, if any?

Any number of medical conditions are causally related to, if not greatly influenced by, hormonal modification to intrauterine environments. Anorexia nervosa is one such condition. Doctors Procopio and Marriott published research in the Archives of General Psychiatry in December of 2007[68] that demonstrated changes to a mother's intrauterine hormonal environment increased the risk of developing anorexia nervosa in female children, *but not* in male children.

Another genetic condition that impacts gender identity/sexual behavior is congenital adrenal hyperplasia (CAH):

> *"CAH is an autosomal, recessive disorder that occurs in approximately 1 in 5,000 to 1 in 15,000 births in Europe and North America]. [A]ndrogen levels in female fetuses with classical CAH, the form of the disorder known to involve prenatal androgen elevation, are raised dramatically, and as a consequence girls with classical CAH are* ***born with some degree of genital virilization.*** *In rare cases, the virilization is sufficiently severe that they are mistaken for boys at birth. Usually,*

[68] Marco Procopio, MD, MRCPsych; Paul Marriott, PhD, Intrauterine Hormonal Environment and Risk of Developing Anorexia Nervosa Arch Gen Psychiatry. 2007;64(12):1402-1407. doi:10.1001/archpsyc.64.12.1402.

however, the genital ambiguity leads to prompt diagnosis and postnatal treatment to regulate hormone levels, and assignment and rearing as girls, with surgical genital feminization typically in infancy. At least 10 studies have been published in the English language on sexual orientation in girls and women with CAH in comparison to female controls. ***The overwhelming conclusion from these studies is that women with CAH are less likely to be exclusively or almost exclusively heterosexual than are other women.*** *"* [69]

Lesbianism has been found to occur at significantly higher rates when developing babies have CAH. Here is what authors Dreger A, Feder EK, Tamar-Mattis A. wrote in their study published in the journal of Bioethics in 2012:

"Following extensive examination of published and unpublished materials, we provide a history of the use of dexamethasone in pregnant women at risk of carrying a female fetus affected by congenital adrenal hyperplasia (CAH). This intervention has been aimed at preventing development of ambiguous genitalia, the urogenital sinus, tomboyism, and lesbianism." [70]

My point in sharing with readers these representative studies on how biology impacts sex and gender identity is solely to illustrate to a public denied knowledge of this information that sex and gender identity are inextricably intertwined with, and are not exclusively and perhaps not predominantly the purview of, virtual reality—that is, social constructs, as social engineers pushing V the Reality would have all of us believe. Keep in mind that IF V the Reality is to become the new truth, then of course objective reality must be subordinated and shoved into the darkest

---

[69] Hines M. (2011). Prenatal endocrine influences on sexual orientation and on sexually differentiated childhood behavior. Frontiers in neuroendocrinology, 32(2), 170–182. https://doi.org/10.1016/j.yfrne.2011.02.006

[70] Dreger, A., Feder, E. K., & Tamar-Mattis, A. (2012). Prenatal Dexamethasone for Congenital Adrenal Hyperplasia: An Ethics Canary in the Modern Medical Mine. Journal of bioethical inquiry, 9(3), 277–294. https://doi.org/10.1007/s11673-012-9384-9.

recesses of the stacks. Let's now examine transgender issues within the context of a V the Reality world.

Biologically based transsexuals' brains are discernibly different than non-transsexuals in some key ways. These differences are present in some cases intrautero. Dr. Antonio Guillamon conducted research in Madrid, Spain, which showed that transsexuals' brains differ in at least four regions of white matter. [71] His work proved, for the first time, that transsexuals who had a non-ideologically driven desire to become women possess different neural structures from men who did not have those neural differences and who had no desire to trans-sex.

In a separate study using an independent methodology, Dr. Guillamon's team studied the brains of 19 transsexual men and 19 transsexual women. In each subject, MRI imaging showed four regions of white matter that had been altered from the nominal condition of being 100% male or female, as it were, to approximately half male and half female. Dr. Guillamon described the genetic males in his study this way: "Their brains are not completely masculinized and not completely feminized, but they still feel female," says Guillamon. Dr. Sean Deoni, on staff at King's College in London, has demonstrated that anomalous brain structures of OR world transsexuals can be visualized on MRI scans as early as two or three years of age.

Dr. Ivanka Savic-Berglund at the Karolinska Institute in Stockholm, Sweden, believes she has indentified one particular area of white matter than may explain the discordance between genetic sex and its expression in neural structures. Dr. Berglund said: "One of the four regions—the superior longitudinal fascicle—is particularly interesting. It connects the parietal lobe [involved in sensory

---

[71] Rametti G, Carrillo B, Gómez-Gil E, Junque C, Segovia S, Gomez Á, Guillamon A. White matter microstructure in female to male transsexuals before cross-sex hormonal treatment. A diffusion tensor imaging study. J Psychiatr Res. 2011 Feb;45(2):199-204. doi: 10.1016/j.jpsychires.2010.05.006. Epub 2010 Jun 8. PMID: 20562024.

processing] and frontal lobe [involved in planning movement] and may have implications in body perception." [72]

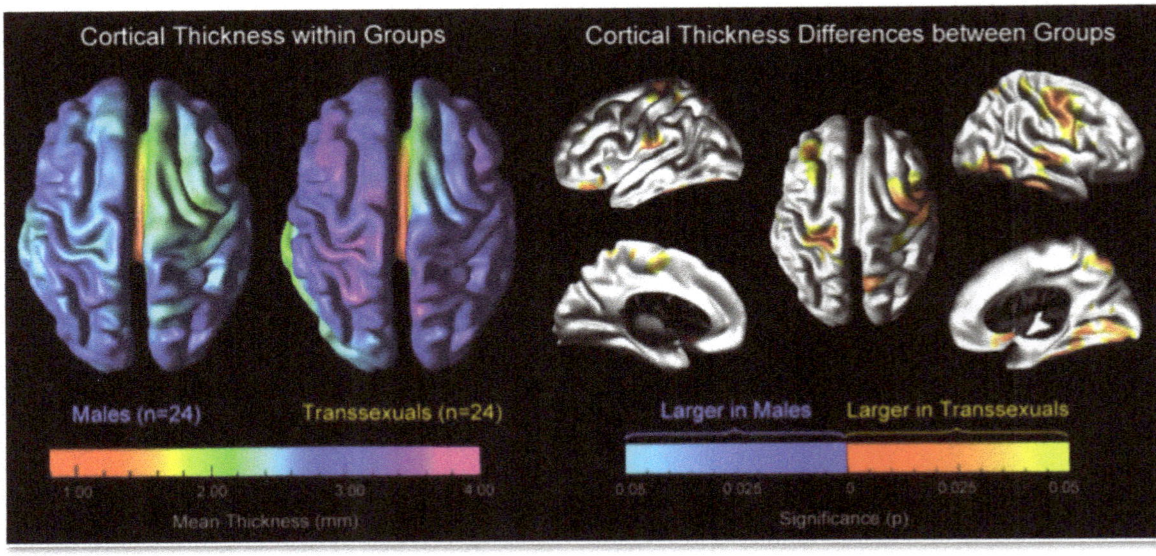

"Gender incongruence (GI) is characterized by a feeling of estrangement from the own body in the context of self. GI is often described in people who identify as transgender. The underlying mechanisms are unknown. Data from MRI measurements and tests of own body perception triggered us to pose a model that GI in transgender persons (TGI) could be associated with a disconnection within the brain circuits mediating the perception of own body as self. This is a departure from a previous model of sex atypical cerebral dimorphism, introducing a concept that better accords with a core feature of TGI. The present MRI study of 54 hormone naive transmen (TrM), 38 transwomen (TrW), 44 cismen and 41 ciswomen show that cortical gyrification, a metric that reflects early maturation of cerebral cortex, is significantly lower in transgender compared with cisgender participants. This reduction is limited to the occipito-parietal cortex and the sensory motor cortex, regions encoding own body image and body ownership. Moreover, the cortical

---

[72] Wang, Yanlu & Khorashad, Behzad & Feusner, Jamie & Savic, Ivanka. (2021). Cortical Gyrification in Transgender Individuals. Cerebral Cortex. 31. 10.1093/cercor/bhaa412.

gyrification correlated inversely with own body-self incongruence in these regions. These novel data suggest that GI in TGI may originate in the neurodevelopment of body image encoding regions. The results add potentially to understanding neurobiological contributors to gender identity."

These studies demonstrate that genetic sex blueprints and gender identity are inextricably linked to anatomy and physiology, especially CNS structure and function—both of which are a function of genetics, intrauterine environments and subsequent hormonal influences on sex and gender expression and identity. However, in a world pushing a V the Reality social truth, objective reality is forced to take a back seat. This sets in motion any number of unintended consequences.

What follows is a brief description of the term "transgender" from the American Psychiatric Association (APA). Please notice the APA's **emphasis** upon the VR world of *psychological sense,* to use their terminology, and their subordination of OR world phenotype and genotype, i.e., anatomy, physiology, and genetic blueprints, as we just covered in the preceding sampling of research.

"The term "transgender" refers to a person whose sex assigned at birth (i.e., the sex assigned by a physician at birth, usually based on external genitalia) does not match their gender identity ***(i.e., one's psychological sense of their gender)****. Some people who are transgender will experience "gender dysphoria," which refers to psychological distress that results from an incongruence between one's sex assigned at birth and one's gender identity. Though gender dysphoria often begins in childhood, some people may not experience it until after puberty or much later."* [73]

Please pay special attention to how the APA framed the act of "sexual assignment" by medical doctors and RNs at birth. The APA suggests sex—and therefore, sex assignment at birth—is nothing but or mostly an act of social construction fueled by

[73] American Psychiatric Association: Gender Dysphoria. 2021.

un-WOKE doctors. Certain non-enlightened doctors hold social construct ideologies that result in the attachment of a boy or girl label that has no determinative biological basis in fact. The social engineering ideology which seeks to subordinate OR to VR—with the ultimate goal to establish V the Reality as truth—has resulted in doctors being cautioned against "assigning a sex" to newborns for fear that this could conflict with the infants' self-declared gender identity later in childhood. What does the American College of Pediatricians think about the APA's missives?

> *"These claims belie the physical, biological fact that sex is not a state of mind that one can "identify" into or out of at will.* ***Pediatricians do not "assign" an infant's sex; they announce it based upon the physical reality of the infant's body before them.*** *This growing movement to deny the physical reality of sexual dimorphism requires a dangerous dismissal of both science and medical ethics, one that will cause severe harm to individuals and society at large if embraced."* [74]

What makes any thoughtful and objective forensic analysis of these issues a three-story house of mirrors is this: it is crystal clear that human beings can be made to *genuinely* believe almost anything, e.g., Edward Bernays' social engineering of consent was proven to be highly successful because, in part, it is relatively easy to pull off. When it comes to feelings about gender, along with a myriad of other identity issues, they are all highly susceptible to outside influences, with adolescent and younger humans being especially impressionable. It is not as though this is a novel discovery, to wit:

"Teenage Brains Are Like Soft, Impressionable Play-Doh

There's a softer side to adolescent minds: they're vulnerable, dynamic and highly responsive to positive feedback. " [75]

Dr. Marcel Kinsbourne, MD, neurologist and cognitive neuroscientist, has written eloquently about the impressionable nature of human beings, especially

[74] Ibid, 62.

[75] Jay Geld, MD, National Institutes of Health in: Smithsonian Magazine, October 18, 2012.

adolescents. As you read Dr. Kinsbourne's thoughts, I would ask the reader to think about digital natives' 24/7 exposure to the media entertainment complex that delivers to them subliminal and explicit messages which subordinate objective reality and pushes V the Reality as truth.

> *"That an individual is likely to act in the same ways that others act is seen in the documented benefit for sports training of watching experts perform.* ***"Emotional contagion" occurs when someone witnesses the emotional expressions of another person and therefore experiences that mood state oneself.*** *People's viewpoints can subtly and unconsciously converge when their patterns of neural activation match, in the* ***total absence of argument or attempts at persuasion****. When people entrain with each other in gatherings, crowds, assemblies and mobs, diverse individual views reduce into a unified group viewpoint. An extreme example of gradual convergence might be the "Stockholm Syndrome";* ***captives gradually adopt the worldview of their captors.*** *In general, interacting with others makes one converge to their point of view (and vice versa). Much ink has been spilled on the topic of the lamentable limitations of human rationality. Here is one reason why. People's views are surreptitiously shaped by their experiences, and rationality comes limping after, downgraded to rationalization."*[76] (Emphasis added)

With regard to Dr. Kinsbourne's analysis: *People's views are* ***surreptitiously*** (unconsciously) *shaped by their experiences, and rationality comes limping after,* ***downgraded to rationalization –*** I would remind readers that in the world of social engineering, especially when it comes to gender identity, rational thought based on objective reality is not merely "downgraded to rationalization" but increases the risk of the attachment of socially deplorable labels, which are intended, with malice

---

[76] Marcel Kinsbourne, MD. The New School - Co-author, Children's Learning and Attention Problems: WHAT HAVE YOU CHANGED YOUR MIND ABOUT? WHY? Story covered in Edge Magazine, retrieved June 2021.

aforethought, to ruin the personal, social, and vocational life of even the most thoughtful, kind, and rational scientist scholars who simply disagree with social engineers.

Is the *psychological sense* of gender dysphoria, to use the APA's descriptor, genuine, transitory, ulteriorly motivated, sequelae of an endocrine disorder, e.g., fetal androgenization and/or a psychological reaction to what is by analogy an IV-drip on push that pumps trendy, popular, and so-called WOKE ideology into native and immigrant screensters 24/7? One example that makes the point is the media entertainment complex's fawning coverage of public figures that have chosen major surgery to modify their bodies, and because of that received accolades far and wide for making that choice.

Caitlyn Jenner and Bruce Jenner (Courtesy of: Getty / AP)

A forensic anthropologist that happens upon the skeletal remains of Caitlyn Jenner 1000 years from now will have no difficulty, none whatsoever, as classifying the remains as belonging to a biological male. This would also be true for the skeletal remains of children who underwent sexual affirmation surgery. Biological sex (OR) doesn't disappear in life or death

because of what you may think, feel or do – no matter how dearly you believe (VR).

Psychiatric assessment of the genuineness of declared gender identity dysphoria would be less of an epistemological concern if the virtual world was not remarkably vulnerable to manipulation by its very nature, and psychiatric diagnoses had been proven to be reliable between independent clinical evaluators. To wit:

> *"A new study, published in Psychiatry Research, has concluded that* ***psychiatric diagnoses are scientifically worthless as tools to identify discrete mental health disorders.*** *The study, led by researchers from the University of Liverpool, involved a detailed analysis of five key chapters of the latest edition of the widely used Diagnostic and Statistical Manual (DSM), on 'schizophrenia', 'bipolar disorder', 'depressive disorders', 'anxiety disorders' and 'trauma-related disorders'. Diagnostic manuals such as the DSM were created to provide a common diagnostic language for mental health professionals and attempt to provide a definitive list of mental health problems, including their symptoms. The main findings of the research were:*

- *Psychiatric diagnoses all use different decision-making rules*
- *There is a huge amount of overlap in symptoms between diagnoses*
- *Almost all diagnoses mask the role of trauma and adverse events*
- ***Diagnoses tell us little about the individual patient and what treatment they need.****"* [77]

The aforementioned study is just one of the more recent critical reviews of what experts in the forensic arena have been aware of for quite some time. We identify these problems as rooted in test-retest reliability, and to describe psychiatric diagnoses as woefully lacking in test-retest reliability is an understatement.[78]

---

[77] University of Liverpool quoted in - ScienceDaily: Psychiatric diagnosis 'scientifically meaningless.' July 8, 2019.

[78] 2. Regier DA, Narrow WE, Clarke DE, et al. DSM-5 field trials in the United States and Canada, Part II: test-retest reliability of selected categorical diagnoses. Am J Psychiatry. 2013;170(1):59-70.

States of mind, even longstanding states of mind, are the product of biopsychosocial predicates. The relative contributions of and overlap between these three fundamental bulwarks that precede expressed behavior may remain stable over time, but may also fluctuate and sometimes disappear. Such is the nature of alternative realities. But more fundamentally, when we evaluate the virtual world of thoughts and feelings, it is important to assess a culture's changing ethos within which those feelings and thoughts take place.

Social conformity pressures are real, and they are powerful—what is popular, trendy, and characterized over and over by agents of the media entertainment complex as "good" can easily overwhelm even the most stalwart independent thinker. Researchers have been keeping tabs on modifying the VR world of *psychological sense* very closely for at least the last 30 years:

> *"[H]eavy exposure to mass media creates and cultivates attitudes more consistent with a media-directed version of reality than with reality itself."*[79]

For people to accept the objective reality that their most cherished wants, wishes, desires, and beliefs are merely products, as if made in a manufacturing plant, requires the ***rare*** combination of humility, ego-strength, and discernment.

At one time possessing a mindset of same sex attraction was deemed to be pathological as was cross-dressing and gender identity confusion. What changed? One important clue that helps us answer that question is the fact that changes in psychiatric assessments of and social norms related to LGBTQ+ mindsets track perfectly with the trajectory of well-financed advocacy and promotion of the collective ethos of the LGBTQ+ community and the media entertainment complex's exultation of V the Reality over objective reality.

It is not as though the psychiatric community justified their revised clinical assessments of gender dysphoria, et al., after honing their scientific methods and/or

---

[79] Gerbner G, Gross L, Morgan M, Signorielli N. Growing up with television: the cultivation perspective. In: Bryant J, Zillman D, eds. Media Effects: Advances in Theory and Research. Hillsdale, NJ: Lawrence Erlbaum; 1994:17–41

discovered an empirically proven superior assessment measure(s) of transgender mindsets, e.g., fMRI, PET, SPECT imaging, blood work, genomic sequencing, advanced psychometrics, etc. —it was OR world advocacy that changed the APA's proclamations, if not their minds. Advocacy that masterfully utilized the power of the media entertainment complex and political lobbying changed social norms about LGBTQ+ mindsets, states of being, and identities—so much so these mindsets became trendy and PROTECTED, if not hallowed, ideological and political territories where trespassers are shot on sight.

V the Reality promotion, by its very nature, is an aggressively assertive ethos when compared to emphasis upon OR, because virtual reality is the playground of the social engineering world. Parents are being told "you are likely to get it wrong" when talking to their child about gender identity. This is the same child who, after having been exposed to 24/7 social engineering messages on the topic of sexual identity, vis-à-vis the media entertainment complex, may express some confusion and have questions about what they are feeling with regard to sexual identity. This from Dr. Jershonda Hartsfield, MD:

"Be ready to learn, and to get it wrong"

> *"The way teens today describe gender identity and sexuality is very different than for previous generations. Parents need to do their research."* [80]

The good doctor then dismisses parents' cultural, religious, and moral standards, whether intended or not, in one fell swoop when she advises parents:

> *"Parents may hold religious, cultural, or moral beliefs that make conversations around identity challenging. However, Dr. Hartsfield says*

[80] SHARP HEALTH NEWS: Talking with teens about gender and identity, Jershonda Hartsfield, MD, June 15, 2021.

that our role as parents is not necessarily to agree with our kids but to provide them with love. "[81]

Children's attitudes about gender are never, in fact **cannot be**, organic—therefore, while of course we respect and listen to even the most specious ideas, beliefs, and feelings expressed by our children—to defer to them as if their doubts, confusion and ambivalences about their gender identity are gospel is symptomatic of the elevation of V the Reality, and subordination of what objective reality has proven to be true when it comes to the fluidity and sometimes capricious nature of children's thoughts, feelings, and behavior. Children's thoughts, feelings, and behaviors are the *proven* end result of 24/7 social engineering by vested ideological interests: profiteers, manipulators, prevaricators, and marketers who use the media entertainment complex to create a product defined by its attitudes, feelings, and behaviors, i.e., your child's mind. Let's translate the subordination that is in the IV on push into the veins of parents everywhere:

> **Reject your cultural and religious tradition. Hold in abeyance your parental rights, obligations and authority and SUBMIT to the product your child was made to be by the media entertainment complex and its financiers who paid for the content of your child's mind. You are "wrong" and "we" are right—with "we" being the vested interests and their advocacy arms that defined what your children think, feel, and do.**

The good doctor then provides parents with a new vocabulary and sexual identity taxonomy that reflects social engineers' ultimate goal—the elevation of psychological sense over objective reality. The following vocabulary is courtesy of PFLAG. [82] It is intended to be and will serve to **replace** parent's existent cultural, moral, and religious lexicon held for thousands of years:

---

[81] Ibid.

[82] PFLAG, the largest organization for lesbian, gay, bisexual, transgender and queer (LGBTQ+) people, and their parents, families, and allies, offers a glossary of terms some LGBTQ+ people use to describe their gender or sexuality.

- Aromantic: Sometimes abbreviated as aro, the term refers to someone who does not experience romantic attraction.

- Asexual: Sometimes shortened to ace, the term refers to a person who does not experience sexual attraction.

- Bisexual: Commonly referred to as bi or bi+, this term refers to a person who acknowledges in themselves the potential to be attracted — romantically, emotionally or sexually — to people of more than one gender.

- Cisgender: Often shortened to cis, this term refers to an individual whose gender identity aligns with the one associated with the sex assigned to them at birth.

- Demisexual: Used to describe an individual who experiences sexual attraction only after forming an emotional connection.

- Genderfluid: Used to describe a person who does not consistently adhere to one fixed gender and who may move among genders, identifying as male, female, or nonbinary (see below) at different times or in different circumstances.

- Genderqueer (GQ): This term refers to individuals who blur preconceived boundaries of gender in relation to the gender binary, which is the disproven concept that there are only two genders (male and female), and that everyone must be one or the other. GQ is often used as an umbrella term for those whose gender doesn't fit with socially constructed norms for their sex assigned to them at birth.

- Nonbinary: The term refers to people who do not subscribe to the gender binary. They might exist between or beyond the man-woman binary, feeling that they are a bit of both genders or not identifying with either gender.

- Pansexual: Often shortened to pan, the term refers to a person whose emotional, romantic, or physical attraction is to people inclusive of all genders.

- Pronouns: The words used to refer to a person other than their name include common pronouns, such as they/them, he/him and she/her.

- Queer: A term used by some LGBTQ+ people to describe themselves and their community.
- Questioning: Used to describe those who are in a process of discovery about their sexual orientation, gender identity, gender expression, or a combination of the three.
- Transgender: Often shortened to trans, the term describes a person's gender identity that does not necessarily match their assigned sex at birth. Transgender people may or may not decide to alter their bodies hormonally or surgically to match their gender identity.

From the American College of Pediatricians:

> *"Acknowledging the fact of inborn genetic sex differences is also crucial for creating public policies that will ensure the health and safety of children and adults alike. Genetics is the reason a male who self-identifies as female remains male and explains why giving estrogen to a male does not transform him into a female. While it is true that a male who uses estrogen after puberty will lose muscle strength and impair other aspects of his physiology, he does not alter his genetics; he remains male at the cellular level in all body systems. Similarly, a female who self-identifies as male remains female, and giving her testosterone does not transform her into a male. In terms of genetics, she remains female at the cellular level. There is no scientific justification for allowing, let alone mandating, males access to female-specific spaces such as restrooms, homeless shelters, prisons and the like. Similarly, just as a female doping testosterone would be prohibited from competing against other females, so too should all males be barred from competing against females. The risk for harm to females from ignoring biological sex in these scenarios is both obvious and documented."*[83]

[83] Ibid 59.

Possessing an XX or XY genotype, ovaries, fallopian tubes, a vagina, penis, testes, and a CNS with all the hallmarks of that which distinguish male and female brains from one another **are not sufficient** to establish OR gender when social engineers push the dominance of V the Reality with the assistance of the media entertainment complex and the enforcement arms of government.

In a culture where objective reality is continually subordinated and V the Reality is the preferred social norm, then the implications, both intended and unintended, should be carefully examined for what they portend for the future—not just when it comes to gender identity, but almost everything else as well. I offer the following primer on the demonstrable OR world differences between the brains of XX and XY genotypes—independently verifiable data that readers probably are not familiar with—in order to provide you with a sense of the power of the ethos of V the Reality when it asserts itself with the help of the media entertainment complex and government.

> *"Reviewing over 20 years of neuroscience research into sex differences in brain structure, a Cambridge University team has conducted the first meta-analysis of the evidence, published in the Journal Neuroscience and Bio-behavioral Reviews. The team, led by doctoral candidate Amber Ruigrok and Professors John Suckling and Simon Baron-Cohen in the Department of Psychiatry, performed a quantitative review of the brain imaging literature testing overall sex differences in total and regional brain volumes. They searched all articles published between 1990 and 2013. A total of 126 articles were included in the study, covering brains from individuals as young as birth to 80 years old. They found that males on average have larger total brain volumes than women (by 8-13%). On average, males had larger absolute volumes than females in the intracranial space (12%; >14,000 brains), total brain (11%; 2,523 brains), cerebrum (10%; 1,851 brains), grey matter (9%; 7,934 brains), white matter (13%; 7,515 brains), regions filled with cerebrospinal fluid (11.5%; 4,484 brains), and cerebellum (9%; 1,842 brains). Looking more closely, differences in volume between the sexes were located in*

several regions. These included parts of the limbic system, and the language system. Specifically, males on average had larger volumes and higher tissue densities in the left amygdala, hippocampus, insular cortex, putamen; higher densities in the right VI lobe of the cerebellum and in the left claustrum; and larger volumes in the bilateral anterior parahippocampal gyri, posterior cingulate gyri, precuneus, temporal poles, and cerebellum, areas in the left posterior and anterior cingulate gyri, and in the right amygdala, hippocampus, and putamen. By contrast, females on average had higher density in the left frontal pole, and larger volumes in the right frontal pole, inferior and middle frontal gyri, pars triangularis, planum temporale/parietal operculum, anterior cingulate gyrus, insular cortex, and Heschl's gyrus; bilateral thalami and precuneus; the left parahippocampal gyrus, and lateral occipital cortex. The results highlight an asymmetric effect of sex on the developing brain. Amber Ruigrok, who carried out the study as part of her PhD, said: ***"For the first time we can look across the vast literature and confirm that brain size and structure are different in males and females. We should no longer ignore sex in neuroscience research, especially when investigating psychiatric conditions that are more prevalent in either males or females.*** *"* [84] *(Emphasis added)*

I should note that for every discrete physical difference in the anatomy and physiology of male vs. female brains, countless gender-flavored behaviors parallel those differences. The rigors of the scientific method appear to be shortchanged by relying upon *psychological sense* in lieu of the reams of empirical data we have complied on the OR world nuts and bolts of gender identity.

---

[84] Amber, N.V. Ruigrok, Gholamreza Salimi-Khorshidi, Meng-Chuan Lai, SimonBaron-Cohen, Michael V.Lombardo, Roger J.Tait, JohnSuckling. A meta-analysis of sex differences in human brain structure. Neuroscience & Biobehavioral Reviews. Volume 39, February 2014, Pages 34-50.

The subordination of OR has profound implications for internal medicine as well, because social engineers have, remarkably, been successful at conducting virtual book burning/publishing/redaction when it comes to medical education. The problem is so serious that the American Physiological Association (experts who often teach physicians in training about anatomy and physiology)[85] has long argued that physicians, especially younger doctors, would benefit from remedial education, to wit:

> *"[T]here are marked differences between men and women in the incidence and expression of many major disease entities.* [86] *These sex-based differences in the pathophysiology of disease imply, in turn, that there are important underlying differences in physiological function. Despite the importance of this topic, sex-based differences in physiology are typically not systematically addressed either in physiology textbooks or in the medical physiology curriculum, with the obvious exception of reproductive physiology. [W]ith the recent recognition of important sex-based differences in disease, there is now a burgeoning literature addressing sex-based differences in normal physiological function and effects of sex steroid hormones on the function of multiple organ systems* [87]*The goal of the Refresher Course symposium was to summarize our current state of knowledge of sex-based differences in three systems for which there are prominent differences between men and women: cardiovascular, musculoskeletal, and immune systems.* [88] *In*

---

[85] The American Physiological Association: Sex-based differences in physiology: What should we teach in the medical curriculum? Martha L. Blair, 01 JAN 2007https://doi.org/10.1152/advan.00118.2006

[86] Institute of Medicine Committee on Understanding the Biology of Sex and Gender Differences. Exploring the Biological Contributions to Human Health: Does Sex Matter? Edited by Wizemann TM, Pardue ML. Washington, DC: National Academy, 2001.
(continued) Legato MJ (editor). Principles of Gender-Specific Medicine. London: Elsevier, 2004.

[87] Miller V, Hay M (editors). Principles of Sex-Based Differences in Physiology: Advances in Molecular and Cell Biology. London: Elsevier, 2004, vol. 34.

[88] Brown M. Skeletal muscle and bone: effect of sex steroids and aging. Adv Physiol Educ 31: 0000–0000, 2007.

view of the fact that many sex-based differences are mediated by the actions of estrogens or androgens, the Refresher Course also presented an update on the genomic and nongenomic mechanisms of action of sex steroid hormones.[89]

Then we have this research from biologists Moran Gershoni & Shmuel Pietrokovski, conducted in 2017:

> *"[W]e comprehensively mapped human sex-differential genetic architecture across 53 tissues. Analyzing available RNA-sequencing data from 544 adults revealed thousands of genes* ***differentially expressed*** *in the reproductive tracts and tissues common to both sexes. Sex-differential genes are related to various biological systems and suggest new insights into the pathophysiology of diverse human diseases. We also identified a significant association between sex-specific gene transcription and reduced selection efficiency and accumulation of deleterious mutations, which might affect the prevalence of different traits and diseases. Interestingly, many of the sex-specific genes that also undergo reduced selection efficiency are essential for successful reproduction in men or women. This seeming paradox might partially explain the high incidence of human infertility."* [90]

IF a culture's mores, ethos, laws, and financial beneficiary criteria elevate V the Reality's handmaiden of *psychological sense* over the world of anatomy, physiology and brain chemistry, then:

Dale E, Davis M, Faustman D. A central role for transcription factor NF-κB in autoimmunity, genes, sex, and the immune system. Adv Physiol Educ 30: 152–158, 2006. Huxley V. Sex and the cardiovascular system: the intriguing tale of how women and men regulate cardiovascular function differently. Adv Physiol Educ 31: 0000–0000, 2007.

[89] Wierman M. Sex steroid effects at target tissues: mechanism of action. Adv Physiol Educ 31: 000–000, 2007.

[90] Gershoni, M., Pietrokovski, S. The landscape of sex-differential transcriptome and its consequent selection in human adults. BMC Biol 15, 7 (2017). https://doi.org/10.1186/s12915-017-0352-z

What rationale can be offered to deny the same benefits and rights to people who identify as infants even though in the OR world they are provably adults? Why would any public benefit or right be denied to people whose *psychological sense* inform them that their personal identity properly belongs to the species Canis familiaris when OR world criteria screams Homo Sapiens?

Think I am overstating the issue or being melodramatic? If you are thinking that, you may be exercising your confirmation biases or simply unaware. Perhaps you are a social engineer pushing V the Reality, or an unwitting enforcer of the social engineers that have created you to serve that purpose.

For those unfamiliar with adults whose *psychological sense* encourages them to identify as infants, or people that identity as dogs or other animals, I provide this brief primer on the subject. Remember, I am only covering this topic because it is the sine qua non of the OR vs. V the Reality dynamic that is the précis of this book:

The men who live as dogs: 'We're just the same as any person on the high street'

It's a dog's life ... Spot at home with his former fiancé Rachel (Photograph: Richard Ansett/Channel 4)

Spot, Hexyc and Tibo (Photograph: Richard Ansett/Channel 4)

I dare say people outside of clinical psychology and psychiatry know nothing of meaning when it comes to the sexual psychodynamics of cross-species sexual identities. I bring this subject up because the all-too-real prejudice faced by the LGBTQ+ and especially the transgender community is virtually identical to the prejudice faced by people who identify as dogs or infants. Nell Frizell, a writer from the Guardian, wrote eloquently about this in 2016, to wit:

> *"It's easy to laugh at a grown man in a rubber dog suit chewing on a squeaky toy. Maybe too easy, in fact, because to laugh is to dismiss it, denigrate it—ignore the fact that many of us have found comfort and joy in pretending to be animals at some point in our lives. Secret Life of the Human Pups is a sympathetic look at the world of pup play, a movement that grew out of the BDSM community and has exploded in the last 15 years as the internet made it easier to reach out to likeminded people. While the pup community is a broad church, human pups tend to be male, gay, have an interest in dressing in leather, wear dog-like hoods, enjoy tactile interactions like stomach rubbing or ear tickling, play with toys, eat out of bowls and are often in a relationship with their human "handlers". In the documentary, we see Tom, AKA Spot, take part in the Mr. Puppy Europe competition in Antwerp, a mix of beauty pageant, talent show and Crufts; David, AKA Bootbrush, talk*

> *to camera in a leather dog mask; two pups walk through London pretending to wee on lampposts to raise awareness of their identity; and lots of men jumping up for "treats", barking and wagging their mechanical tails. When I speak to Tom, he is keen to point out that puppy play is about more than just outfits and surface-level power games: it's about being given license to behave in a way that feels natural, even primal. "You're not worrying about money, or food, or work," says Tom, who works as an engineer in a theatre. "It's just the chance to enjoy each other's company on a very simple level."* ***[W]hether we see it as a kink, an identity, a reaction to an early experience, a form of escapism or a fetish, the main thing, says Tom, is that we see it at all; that we know it's there and accept it. "It feels like you can be gay, straight, bisexual, trans and be accepted," he says. "All I want is for the pup community to be accepted in the same way.*** *We're not trying to cause grief to the public, or cause grief to relationships. We're just the same as any other person on the high street."*[91]

The issue that should take center stage for any student of the psychosocial implications of elevating V the Reality over OR has to do with the intended and unintended consequences of what happens when any culture indulges the subordination of objective reality to V the Reality. Examples of this new VR standard of reality are too numerous to mention, but the following serve to illustrate the conundrums involved.

The North American Man/Boy Love Association (NAMBLA) makes the argument that their, to use the APA's operant term, *psychological sense* that grown men should be allowed to have sex with minor boys and should be decriminalized, because it has not been proven to be harmful to boys—in fact, NAMBLA argues that

---

[91] The Guardian. The men who live as dogs: 'We're just the same as any person on the high street.' Story by: Nell Frizell, May 25, 2016.

sex with grown men is **good** for a boy's development and **may help gay boys'** identities flourish before parents, religion, and morals interfere with the homoerotic expression of the boy's *psychological sense* of his sexuality.

A facile retort to NAMBLA's thesis typically reads something like: "Yes, but having sex with underage boys is illegal." In response, NAMBLA representatives often reference the rights afforded to the LGBTQ+ community to buttress their views and how society has changed its legal views on LGBTQ+ behaviors. NAMBLA reminds people that members of the LGBTQ+ community also engaged in behavior that was at one point in our (America's) history illegal, to wit: Homosexuality was in the not-too-distant past illegal, as was same sex marriage. Anal sex, i.e., sodomy (the most popular sexual act between gay males) was illegal even when practiced by heterosexual and married couples as recently as 2003 under various sodomy laws, until the United States Supreme Court invalidated those laws.[92] And if we take morality and religion out of the equation, and focus solely upon laws, take a look at the following international and USA age of consent laws and how they have changed over the years:

Age Limit in Age of Consent Laws in Selected Countries

	1880	**1920**	**2007**
Austria	14	14	14
Belgium	-	16	16
Bulgaria	13	13	14
Denmark	12	12	15
England & Wales	13	16	16
Finland	-	12	16
France	13	13	15
Germany	14	14	14

[92] Lawrence v. Texas, 539 U.S. 558 (2003), was a landmark decision of the U.S. Supreme Court in which the Court ruled that sanctions of criminal punishment for those who commit sodomy are unconstitutional.

	1880	1920	2007
Greece	-	12	15
Italy	-	16	14
Luxembourg	15	15	16
Norway	-	16	16
Portugal	12	12	14
Romania	15	15	15
Russia	10	14	16
Scotland	12	12	16
Spain	12	12	13
Sweden	15	15	15
Switzerland	various	16	16
Turkey	15	15	18
Argentina	-	12	13
Brazil	-	16	14
Chile	20	20	18
Ecuador	-	14	14
Canada	12	14	14
Australia			
New South Wales	12	16	16
Queensland	12	17	16
Victoria	12	16	16
Western Australia	12	14	16
United States			
Alabama	10	16	16
Alaska	-	16	16
Arizona	12	18	18
Arkansas	10	16	16

	1880	1920	2007
California	10	18	18
Colorado	10	18	15
Connecticut	10	16	16
District of Columbia	12	16	16
Delaware	7	16	16
Florida	10	18	18
Georgia	10	14	16
Hawaii	-	-	16
Idaho	10	18	18
Illinois	10	16	17
Indiana	12	16	16
Iowa	10	16	16
Kansas	10	18	16
Kentucky	12	16	16
Louisiana	12	18	17
Maine	10	16	16
Maryland	10	16	16
Massachusetts	10	16	16
Michigan	10	16	16
Minnesota	10	18	16
Mississippi	10	18	16
Missouri	12	18	17
Montana	10	18	16
Nebraska	10	18	17
Nevada	12	18	16
New Hampshire	10	16	16
New Jersey	10	16	16

	1880	1920	2007
New Mexico	10	16	17
New York	10	18	17
North Carolina	10	16	16
North Dakota	10	18	18
Ohio	10	16	16
Oklahoma	-	-	16
Oregon	10	16	18
Pennsylvania	10	16	16
Rhode Island	10	16	16
South Carolina	10	16	16
South Dakota	10	18	16
Tennessee	10	18	18
Texas	10	18	17
Utah	10	18	16
Vermont	10	16	16
Virginia	12	16	18
Washington	12	18	16
West Virginia	12	16	16
Wisconsin	10	16	18
Wyoming	10	16	16

[93]

The Supreme Court's involvement in private sexual behaviors should serve as a harbinger of things to come for our more discerning readers. The following

[93] Stephen Robertson, "Age of Consent Laws," in Children and Youth in History, Item #230, https://chnm.gmu.edu/cyh/items/show/230 (accessed June 14, 2021).

illustrates the friction that can occur when government, using its plenary powers, elevates V the Reality over OR.

Just a few years ago, the mere mention of a government official in charge of matters related to a nation's health NOT declaring, "Of course it should be **illegal** for grammar school age children to choose to undergo major gender reassignment surgery **without the consent of their parents"** would have been scandalous and would have resulted in the immediate demand that the official be fired, if not worse. Keep in mind that even today (2021), a doctor can't reset the disjointed index finger of a little leaguer without the consent of his parents, absent a medical emergency.

Fast forward a few years, and that is exactly where we find ourselves in our V the Reality dominant world circa 2021. Secretary of Health Rachel Levine, M.D., has refused, multiple times under questioning by members of the Senate and the press, to categorically rule out that the government of the United States will at some point make it illegal for parents to prohibit their grammar school age child who expresses a *psychological sense* that they want to "be" another sex to choose sexual reassignment surgery. It is the fact that Secretary Levine categorically refuses to rule out that parents of children with a *psychological sense* of gender discordance may at some point be able to choose, and then force taxpayers or the child's insurance company to pay for the surgery, that corroborates V the Reality is the new truth of our culture. Grammar school age children can't legally vote, buy alcohol, drive an automobile, join the military, have sex with an adult, undergo breast augmentation surgery, or be tattooed, **but should be able to choose** to undergo major life-changing surgery and permanently change their endocrine fingerprint without parental approval, and without legal protections that would force the child to wait to make such a life-changing decision at least until they reach the age of 18!

Secretary of Health Dr. Rachel Levine speaking at a virtual press conference for the Pennsylvania Department of Health March 20, 2020. (photo: PHD / CC BY 2.0)

The lines of demarcation in the VR world of sexual identities and objects of affection, including automobiles[94], do not exist because VR is virtual—not real. To wit:

"Darius Monty, 35, suffers from a sexual condition known as mechanophilia—which means he gets turned on by his car" [95]

[94] Sexual attraction to automobiles is labeled "mechanophilia."

[95] The SUN/UK, Story by: Maryse Godden, July 21, 2017.

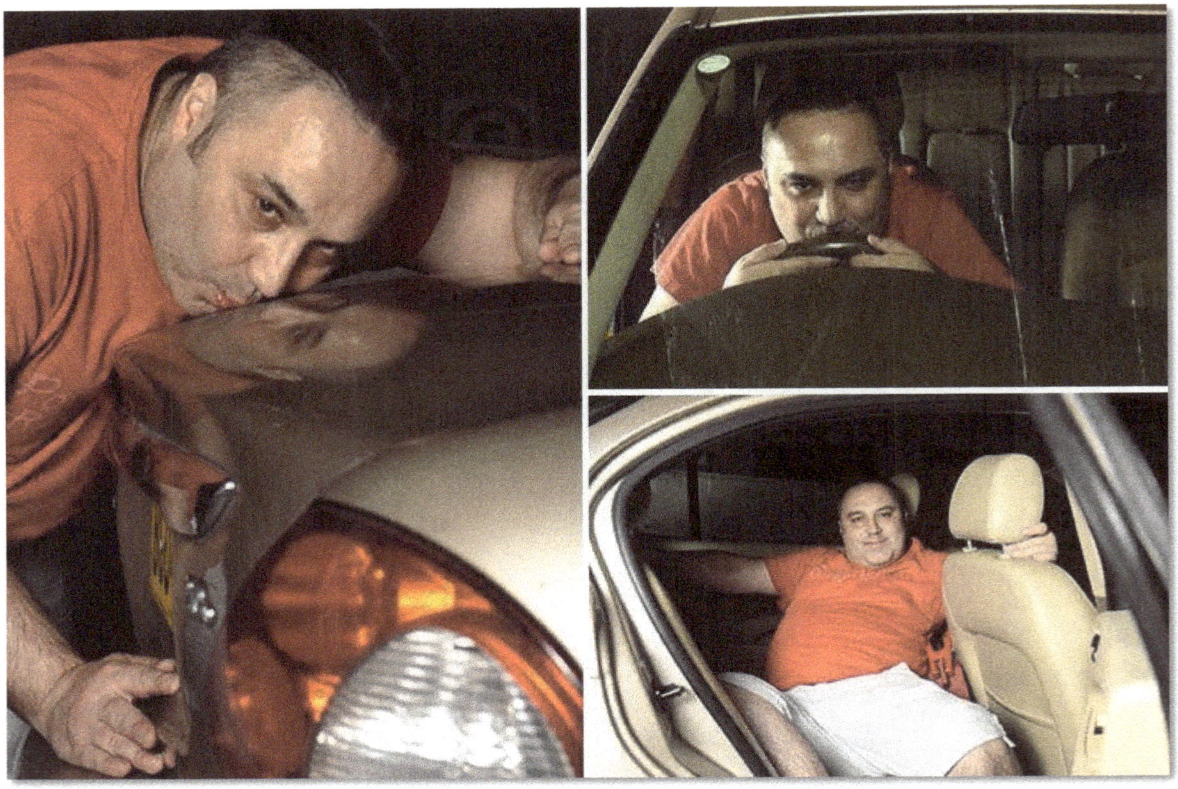

Darius Monty suffers from mechanophilia – which means he gets turned on by his car (Credit: Mirrorpix)

> *"MECHANOPHILIA - The love or sexual attraction to computers, cars, robots or androids, washing machines and other domestic appliances, lawn mowers and other mechanised gardening equipment. Sexual relations between living organisms and machines."* [96]

Here is another personal and sexual/gender identity labeled "paraphilic infantilism" that garners their validity by elevating *psychological sense* over OR.

> *"Paraphilic infantilism is a rare sexual paraphilia where individuals typically get sexually aroused from being a baby (and is commonly referred to as 'adult baby syndrome'). Some websites claim that the condition also goes under the name of 'autonepiophilia,' but the sexologist who coined this particular paraphilia (John Money) described*

[96] C.f., Aggrawal A. (2009). Forensic and Medico-legal Aspects of Sexual Crimes and Unusual Sexual Practices. Boca Raton: CRC Press.

the condition as particularly relating to 'diaper fetishism' (i.e., people who get sexually aroused from wearing nappies)." [97]

Adults who identify as infants have come out into the open, because our culture's exultation of V the Reality has invited them to do just that. They have their own group on social media, The Adult Baby Diaper Lover Community (ABDL). Amazon has its own paraphernalia section dedicated to the ABDL community.

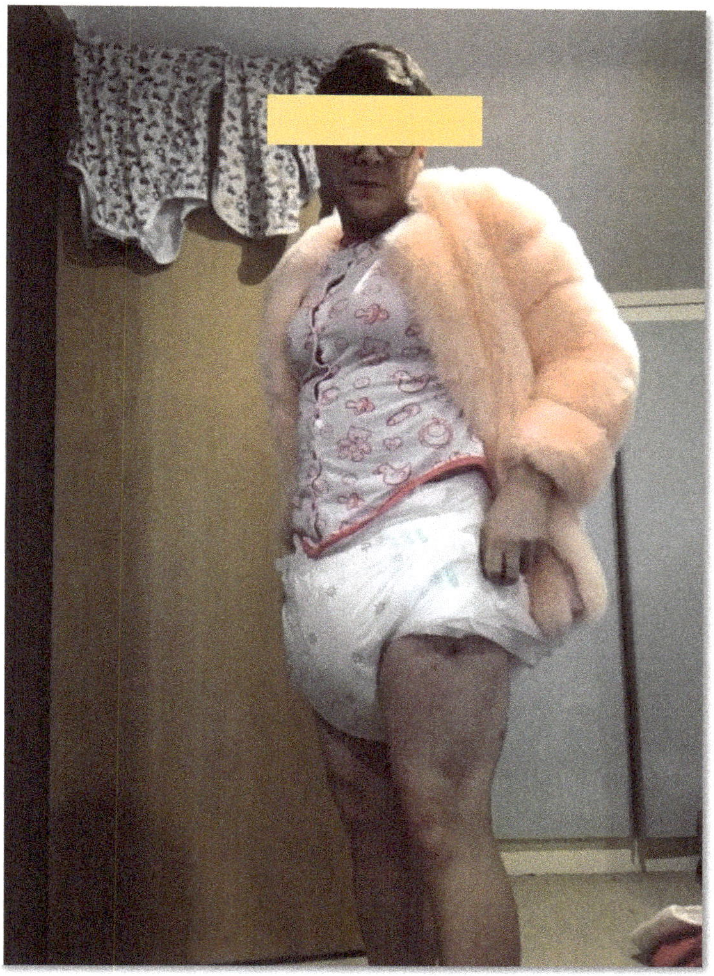

[97] Psychology Today. Child's Play: A brief look at paraphilic infantilism. By: Mark D. Griffiths Ph.D., October 25, 2013.

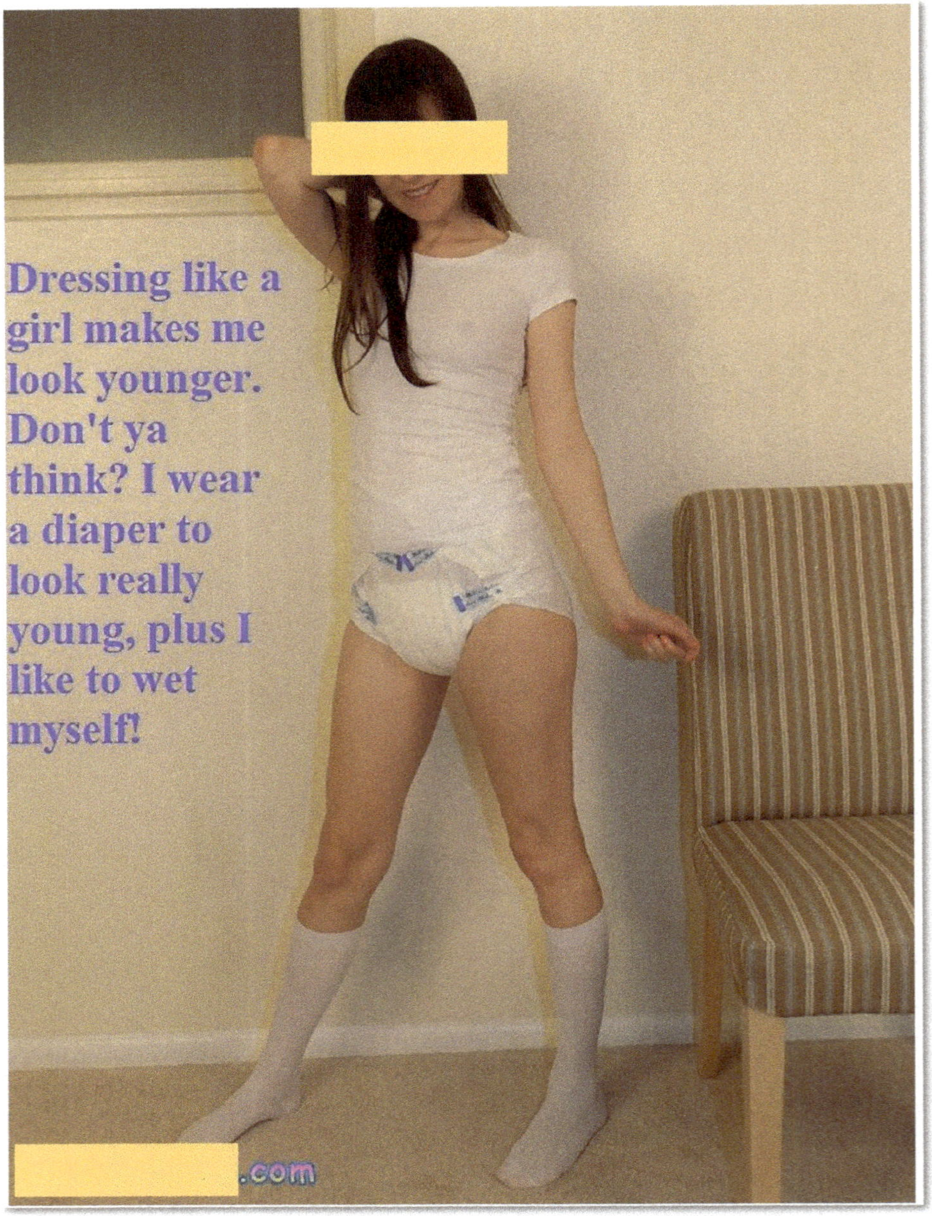

Virginia is enforcing the right of boys in its public school system who declare "I feel like I am a girl," aka "psychological sense" to shower with girls, i.e., watch pre-teen and teen girls undress, ogle them, and expose themselves in front of girls. These same behaviors in the objective world constitute a sexual offense in the state of Virginia, e.g., voyeurism and public indecency.

> *B. It shall be unlawful for any person to use a peephole or other aperture to secretly or* ***furtively peep****, spy or attempt to peep or spy*

> *into a restroom, **dressing room, locker room**, hotel room, motel room, tanning bed, tanning booth, bedroom or other location or enclosure for the purpose of viewing any non-consenting person who is totally nude, clad in undergarments, or in a state of undress exposing the genitals, pubic area, buttocks or female breast and the circumstances are such that the person would otherwise have a **reasonable expectation of privacy.*** [98]

Are there any adults in the room, you might ask? Yes, the adults in the room are forcing females—underage females—to submit to voyeurism simply because **a feeling** expressed by a biological male is **elevated, without meaningful scrutiny, by the state as superordinate over objective reality. In this world, female classmates and their rights to privacy be damned.** Nevertheless, and this should not be a surprise, girls raised in a culture where V the Reality was sold to them as real are beginning to question if what was sold to them was nothing more than the imposition of a social engineering edict that sacrificed her rights to privacy, and in particular her right to not be the victim of voyeurism or what many clinicians—including myself—deem sexual abuse, if not patent state-sanctioned sexual assault.

Virginia girl slams school board for transgender locker room policy

> *A 14-year-old Virginia girl has lashed out at her school district — claiming that its policy to allow transgender children to use female locker rooms is "dangerous" and "rooted in sexism." "Two years ago, I was told policy 1040 was just an umbrella philosophy and you weren't going to allow boys into the girls' locker rooms. But here you are doing just that," eighth-grader Jolene Grover told the school district at a board meeting Tuesday, Fox News reported. Jolene was referring to the Loudoun County Public Schools' recent 8350 policy, which states in a draft that "students should be allowed to use the facility that corresponds to their gender identity," according to the news outlet. The*

[98] Va. Code Ann. § 18.2-130.

> *teen, who was wearing a shirt that read "Woman is female," defiantly told the board members:* ***"Everyone knows what a boy is — even you.****" "Your proposed policies are dangerous and rooted in sexism," she added. The middle schooler then argued that* ***"modern identities" are only "superficial."****[99]

Miss Grover's commentary "modern identities are only superficial" is a direct reference to the rise of virtual reality and her all-too-familiar acculturation that mandated that she subordinate OR in favor of VR. In Gen Z's world, the distinction between OR and VR have been consequentially, serendipitously, and most important purposefully blurred, so that even people who should know better either can't tell the difference, or won't declare they know the difference between Ella and Memorex for fear of having a stigmatized label attached to them. For those readers who have not read my previous works on labeling theory, I offer this brief overview from Dr. Becker as referenced in this footnote.[100]

While aggressive interventions, including major surgical intervention, is rapidly becoming the socially accepted norm in much of the west in order to bring the OR world into consonance with the VR world, the opposite is also becoming the new accepted social justice norm. By "opposite," I mean that de-stigmatizing so-called pathological behavior is becoming the new truth as V the Reality becomes the dominant social ethos. This includes a revamping of how society views individuals who live in the virtual world of their mind, including those people we currently label as suffering from a psychosis, engage in substance abuse and violate laws designed to protect the health and safety of others in the community. I specifically reference people that are **not** under a doctor's care ***only because they are happy with their lives***.

---

[99] New York Post. Virginia girl slams school board for transgender locker room policy. Story by: By Yaron Steinbuch, June 11, 2021.

[100] Please refer to the work of Howard Becker to learn more about stigmatized labels: http://www.personal.psu.edu/faculty/e/x/exs44/406/becker_outsiders_from_weitzer.pdf

Psychiatric labels, e.g., antisocial, mentally ill, or substance abusive behavior, can only remain valid if the gold standard reference point is objective reality, to wit:

psychosis | sīˈkōsəs |

noun (plural psychoses | -ˌsēz |)

a severe mental disorder in which thought and emotions are so impaired that **contact is lost with external reality.**

For example, in the absence of the gold standard of objective reality, it would be impossible to attach the diagnostic label "schizophrenic" using DSM-5 criteria.

- Delusions - Delusions are strongly held beliefs that are **untrue**.
- Hallucinations - Hallucinations are sensations of things that you perceive to be real **that actually don't exist**.
- Seeing, hearing, or tasting things that **others do not**.
- Suspiciousness and a **general fear of others' intentions**.
- Persistent, **unusual** thoughts or beliefs.
- Difficulty thinking **clearly**.
- **Withdrawing** from family or friends.
- A significant decline in **self-care**.[101]

Notice that OR is the unspoken gold standard reference point in the non-inclusive behavioral descriptions characteristic of schizophrenia with paranoid features noted above. Remove objective reality as the agreed-upon reference point in evaluating mental illness, in this case what we used to call paranoid schizophrenia, and the internal validity of diagnostic labels dissolve into thin air.

As V the Reality continues to make inroads to replace OR as the gold standard, the *rethinking* of what is the very nature of and what constitutes mental illness is on a parallel track—again, we see this as consequential and not coincidental to the rise of V the Reality, to wit:

---

[101] For a complete reading of the diagnostic criteria within DSM-5 please see: https://www.medscape.com/answers/288259-13968/what-are-the-dsm-5-criteria-for-schizophrenia

Rethinking Schizophrenia in the Context of the Person and Their Circumstances: Seven Reasons

"As far as this article is concerned, we shall argue, with the support of data and sound reasoning, for a consideration of schizophrenia first and foremost as ***a disorder of the person, rather than of the brain****."* [102]

Researchers who have not submitted to the siren song of V the Reality have sounded the alarm:

Schizophrenia Is A Disease, Not An Extreme of Normal Variation

Researchers say the current NIMH approach for study of many types of major mental illness is misdirected and must be improved.

"Does this statement seem a bit obvious and not exactly rocket science? Although it may, this isn't how the National Institute of Mental Health (NIMH) — the psychiatry wing of the National Institutes of Health — currently views severe mental disorders such as schizophrenia, autism, bipolar disorder and dementia. The NIMH is the largest federal agency that provides research funding on mental disorders. For the past decade, the NIMH has used a system called Research Domain Criteria (RDoC) to describe all mental illnesses as dimensions of psychological norms that fall along extremes of too much or too little of common personality traits. For example, everyone has minor fears of things such as spiders, heights or snakes. But, having very strong or unmanageable fears might constitute an anxiety disorder.

While this way of thinking may make sense for anxiety, Johns Hopkins physicians argue that for the most severe of mental disorders — such as autism, schizophrenia or bipolar disorder — the approach will lead

---

[102] Pérez-Álvarez, M., García-Montes, J. M., Vallina-Fernández, O., & Perona-Garcelán, S. (2016). Rethinking Schizophrenia in the Context of the Person and Their Circumstances: Seven Reasons. Frontiers in psychology, 7, 1650. https://doi.org/10.3389/fpsyg.2016.01650.

> *clinicians and scientists in the wrong direction. These conditions aren't the result of too much or too little of a normal human trait. Rather they represent a clear-cut shift outside the typical dimensions of human experience."* [103]

The navigational compass of objective reality is the true north from which all mental illness is judged. Replace true north with a V the Reality compass, and our current diagnostic criteria would resemble the behavior of a compass in the middle of the Bermuda Triangle. "Who is to say he is not Jesus Christ?" "Who is to judge that the conversations he has with people we can't see don't really exist in his head—and therefore are real from his perspective?" "If he thinks that every white car he sees is a sign the moon's inhabitants are trying to communicate with him—who am I to say *my reality* is superior to *his reality*?"[104] "So he is unkempt, is that so different from Hollywood stars who are members of the grunge community?" "So he lives on the street. If he had come from a wealthy family, he would be living behind the wall of a mansion. Are we to judge him because he does not come from wealth and wants to camp out on the beach or in a beautiful public park?"

The current author characterizes aggressive interventions in the normative OR world, and passive acceptance and protection of the pathological VR world, as two sides of the same coin. OR world modifications of normal states of being are rapidly approaching normative status in many western countries as of 2021. From the more superficial modifications like eye color and hair texture, to the more profound alterations like sexual reassignment/gender affirmation surgery, and everything in between, we are rapidly approaching that point in time when our technology will invite us to take aggressive, dangerous, and costly actions to force the OR world to bend to the VR world—no matter how disparate and seemingly out of touch with OR that VR world we are changing or tolerating happens to be. This

---

[103] Johns Hopkins Medicine NEWSWISE: Schizophrenia Is A Disease, Not An Extreme of Normal Variation. January 29, 2020.

[104] These delusions represent actual clinical presentations I have seen in my clinical practice at one time or another.

means socially and independently responsible citizens will have to bend to the will of their fellow citizens who have chosen, with the operant word CHOSEN, to live in the troubled VR world of their minds, which manifests as what used to be labeled socially irresponsible behavior or mental illness.

When V the Reality becomes the equivalent of a social justice norm—i.e., once a critical number of human beings come to believe they are *entitled* to modify the OR world, including their bodies, to comport with the thoughts and feelings in the VR world or force the OR world to adapt to the world in their head—then communal; that is, taxpayer funding of surgical, genetic, and psychiatric modifications of human beings will become the normative ethos. But the converse is also true, as V the Reality by definition insulates psychotic and even criminal behavior from OR world judgments, taxpayers will be forced to tolerate the common area presence of the mentally ill and early release felons at the expense of the public's health and safety.

One day soon, employers may be forced to hire psychotic individuals and make accommodations for them, including reprimanding or firing employees who complain that their co-worker is out of touch with reality and threatens their safety. In California, an employer with an all-female staff MUST not discriminate against an early release felon who had been convicted of rape who says he wants to come to work at your business. In other words, you cannot conduct a criminal background check on such people, with few exceptions (adoption agencies, child care). [105] What are the chances, you may ask, that violent felons would be eligible for early release in California—including rapists, killers and sex offenders? (Check your state—the list of states adopting this policy is growing with each passing day)

> *SACRAMENTO, Calif. (AP) — California is giving 76,000 inmates, including* ***violent and repeat felons****, the opportunity to leave prison*

[105] National Association of Professional Background Screeners. Ban the Box and Sex Offenses: To Hire or Not to Hire. Written by: John P. Zaimes, Esq. and Roxanne M. Wilson, Esq., May/June 2018.

> *earlier as the state aims to further trim the population of what once was the nation's largest state correctional system. More than 63,000 inmates* ***convicted of violent crimes*** *will be eligible for good behavior credits that shorten their sentences by one-third instead of the one-fifth that had been in place since 2017. That includes nearly 20,000 inmates who are* ***serving life sentences with the possibility of parole****."* [106]

Of course, releasing repeat felons onto California streets makes perfect sense if one accepts the basic tenets of V the Reality as truth. What do OR world data show when it comes to OR world truth?

> *"Importantly, data also show a troubling rise in homicides in 2020. Los Angeles reported a 40% increase in homicides, from 237 in 2019 to 332 in 2020, while Oakland experienced a 36% jump from 75 to 102. San Francisco and San Diego also saw increases, from 41 to 48 (17%) and 50 to 55 (10%), respectively."*[107]

Some would make the case that all over the USA, this scenario is in full bloom as mentally ill, drug- and alcohol-addicted, and sex offender urban campers choose to take up residence in some of the most upscale and pricey real estate in the United States, despite the fact that government offers to them taxpayer funded housing and psychiatric care in addition to their existing public assistance checks. All these urban campers have to do to qualify for free housing is give up their beachfront or other posh campsite, stop using drugs, and abide by a curfew in their new state-funded condominiums.

> *"California has as many homeless sex offenders now as it did 2½ years ago, when a state Supreme Court ruling that overturned restrictions on where they could live was seen as a way to increase housing options and*

---

[106] Associated Press (AP) 76,000 California inmates now eligible for earlier releases. Story by: Don Thompson, May 1, 2021.

[107] Public Policy Institute of California. California's Major Cities See Increases in Homicides and Car Thefts. Story by: MAGNUS LOFSTROM, BRANDON MARTIN APRIL 27, 2021.

allow law enforcement to better track them. Sex offenders must register with the state and provide new addresses when they move. Those who are homeless are less apt to keep their locations updated and more likely to commit new crimes. The number of homeless offenders more than tripled after voters banned sex offenders from living near schools and parks a decade ago, and it was thought the number would fall with the Supreme Court's March 2015 decision."[108]

Los Angeles spent $619 million on homeless shelters in 2020 and has allocated a total of $1 billion as of 2021.

"The price tag for some of Los Angeles' housing for the homeless is expected to hit a whopping $746,000 per unit, far more than the cost of building some luxury high rise condos in downtown." [109]

Shop owners along the Venice Beach Boardwalk, and residents who are intimately familiar with the people camping in front of their high-rent storefronts and outside their home's front door on one of the most famous and at one time beautiful beaches in the world on the taxpayer's dime, have made trenchant points corroborated by law enforcement and mental health professionals familiar with the situation:

"Most of them are content with living on the beach because they don't want to have a curfew ... somebody giving any rules and [them] not being able to do the drugs that they do, and not be able to behave the way they want to behave," (Kevin Buttress, 32, owner of the Xquisite Barber Lounge)[110]

---

[108] NBC -4: Calif. Seeks Solutions to Homeless Sex Offender Rate. By Don Thompson • Published July 29, 2017.

[109] NBC-4: LA's Homeless Housing Now Costs More Than Some Luxury Condos. Story by: Joel Grover and Josh Davis • Published September 8, 2020 • Updated on September 9, 2020.

[110] New York Post: Venice Beach boardwalk in California is now 'dangerous' homeless encampment. Story by: Yaron Steinbuch, May 10, 2021.

Venice, CA Beach Encampment Circa 2021

"You make sure to get home by dusk." "[T]here's fights multiple times a day on the Ocean Front Walk ... stabbings, shootings are happening weekly. It's just a very dangerous time to be a Venice resident right now." (Venice Neighborhood Council member Soledad Ursua)

Venice Beach Boardwalk Before Choice Encampments (Courtesy of: iStock.com/libre de droit)

It is illegal for residents of Venice, California, to ask urban campers to stop having loud and violent drug-addled parties at 3:00 A. M. because they have to get up and go to work, so they can pay the taxes that fund the campers' public assistance checks. It is illegal to ask urban campers to move, leave, or behave. Should a resident of Venice ask the police for assistance with dangerous urban campers outside their doorstep, their calls will go unanswered while social justice warriors will troll them on social media once they get wind of their efforts.

> *"Violent robberies in the neighborhood have jumped by 177 percent and the number of cases of assault with a deadly weapon involving a homeless person have spiked by 162 percent, according to LAPD stats. [I]n January, a fire that apparently started at an encampment spread to a building on the boardwalk and destroyed it, the Los Angeles Fire Department told the outlet. Last month, a family pooch was killed in a house fire that some believe was started by local homeless people. Togo "became the latest victim of Venice's continued degeneration when a transient threw an accelerant into his home, burning him alive," an online tribute says."*[111]

---

[111] Ibid.

CHAPTER XIII

ANONYMITY AND SHIELDS IN THE VR WORLD: Why Social Media is a Cesspool

The Disneyland of the virtual world is social media. It is a public swimming pool where anybody on earth with access to the web and the wherewithal to set up a social media account can publish anything they can get away with. Like any public swimming pool, it only takes one person to defecate in that pool to turn a wonderful experience into a very unpleasant environment—that is, turn a swimming pool into a cesspool.

People do things on social media they would never do in the OR world, because social media is a hybrid virtual reality where the governors of social behavior are all but missing. In the VR world, all bets are off due to a number of social dynamics unique to social media, one of which is anonymity. Real people swim in the virtual world of social media, but all of them are shrouded in anonymity to one degree or another. Anonymity facilitates role playing, lies if you will, where avatars that may or may not accurately reflect the real person publish thoughts and emotions they may not really have, with other avatars engaged in the same role-playing make-believe.

Published images of social media swimmers are almost always embellished to one degree or another, if not an outright misrepresentation. People can and often do lie about their gender, sexual orientation, age, physical appearance, background, and the list goes on and on. Because the vast majority of people using social media never actually meet their fellow virtual swimmers, and most never even talk to them using voice communication, swimmers ONLY know what they THINK they know about others in the pool.

Anonymity creates a pernicious mindset while engaged in almost any social behavior, because it eliminates many of the regulators that control responsible behavior. Anonymity falls on a continuum ranging from partial to complete. One of the characteristics of being anonymous is that it creates a sense of imperviousness. Anonymity shields its holder against redress, retribution, and exposure as anti-social. Criminal behavior is facilitated by anonymity. This is why robbers wear masks, getaway cars have bogus license plates, snipers work from behind blinds, and child molesters pretend to be the peers of their victims from behind the blind of their computer.

Driving in your car offers some degree of real and perceived anonymity. Driving a motor vehicle also exponentially increases the driver's conscious and unconscious sense of his or her own power and invulnerability. People pick their noses in their cars as if it has no windows because of their sense of being anonymous. Road rage is a phenomenon that is exacerbated by the twin factors of anonymity and VR mindset invulnerability and/or dominance. And while road rage is an OR world phenomenon, in the VR world the number and kinds of ways anonymous people who feel impervious can vex, harass, stalk, and cause harm is only limited by the innumerable ways people swimming in the digital world manage their daily affairs.

When you stop to think about it, child molesters who purchase underage bespoke sex dolls not only make their purchases using as much anonymity as possible, but their felonious acts they perform with their sex dolls are also anonymous, because the sex doll can't report them. While this may strike some readers as obvious, consider this. OR world child molesters kill their victims in order to remain anonymous, at least in part. The other predominant motivation driving child molesters to kill their victims is to erase the OR world human being that created (in the perpetrator's mind—once again the perp's "psychological sense") the unacceptable and evil sexual impulses in the virtual world of their mind. Again, anonymity is a pernicious mindset that is central to the popularity of social media.

We have invented terms for people who behave badly in the virtual world of social media, e.g., "troll," cyber stalker, and cyber bully. A troll is typically an anonymous person who feels impervious behind the blinds and shields that are part and parcel of social media platforms. Some stalkers publish photos of themselves along with their real name. However, their mindset is one of being untouchable—a facsimile of being anonymous— "So sue me, I have no money and besides I'd love the attention." A troll may eavesdrop on a conversation had in your virtual world of social media, and then insert him or herself into the conversation, usually marked by a rude, snide and/or cryptic comment purposed to cause an unpleasant emotional reaction in their victim. If one dares to engage the troll, you soon learn that one of the driving motivations of trolls is to ensnare their victim into a faux, i.e., VR fight without ever being physically harmed.

Some swimmers in the cesspool of social media become stalkers. Stalking in the virtual world is termed "cyber stalking" and has a specific legal meaning, to wit:

> *"The fact that cyber stalking does not involve physical contact may create the misperception that it is more benign than physical stalking. This is not necessarily true. As the Internet becomes an ever more integral part of our personal and professional lives, stalkers can take advantage of the ease of communications as well as increased access to personal information. In addition, the ease of use and non-confrontational, impersonal, and sometimes anonymous nature of Internet communications may remove disincentives to cyber stalking. Put another way, whereas a potential stalker may be unwilling or unable to confront a victim in person or on the telephone, he or she may have little hesitation sending harassing or threatening electronic communications to a victim. Finally, as with physical stalking, online*

harassment and threats may be a prelude to more serious behavior, including physical violence." [112]

It is clear from the preceding official policy statement from the United States Department of Justice (DOJ) that it recognizes the profound implications of stalking in the VR world.

The first stalking laws were designed to address objective world stalkers. This was because the technology that would permit cyber stalking didn't exist. Objective world stalking laws evolved into laws that addressed the use of landline phones and physical mail to carry out the stalking. Thanks to the digital swimming pool of social media, laws have had to catch up the VR world. Although any one of us can be targeted in cyber space, it is the digital native generation that has been affected the most. Because of how cyber stalking has disproportionately affected digital natives, high school and college students are being made aware by colleges and universities across the U.S. The University of California at Irvine has developed a cyber stalking educational program they call UCI CARE. Here is one of their informational flyers designed to educate their digital native students:

[112] Excerpted from http://www.usdoj.gov/criminal/cybercrime/cyberstalking.htm

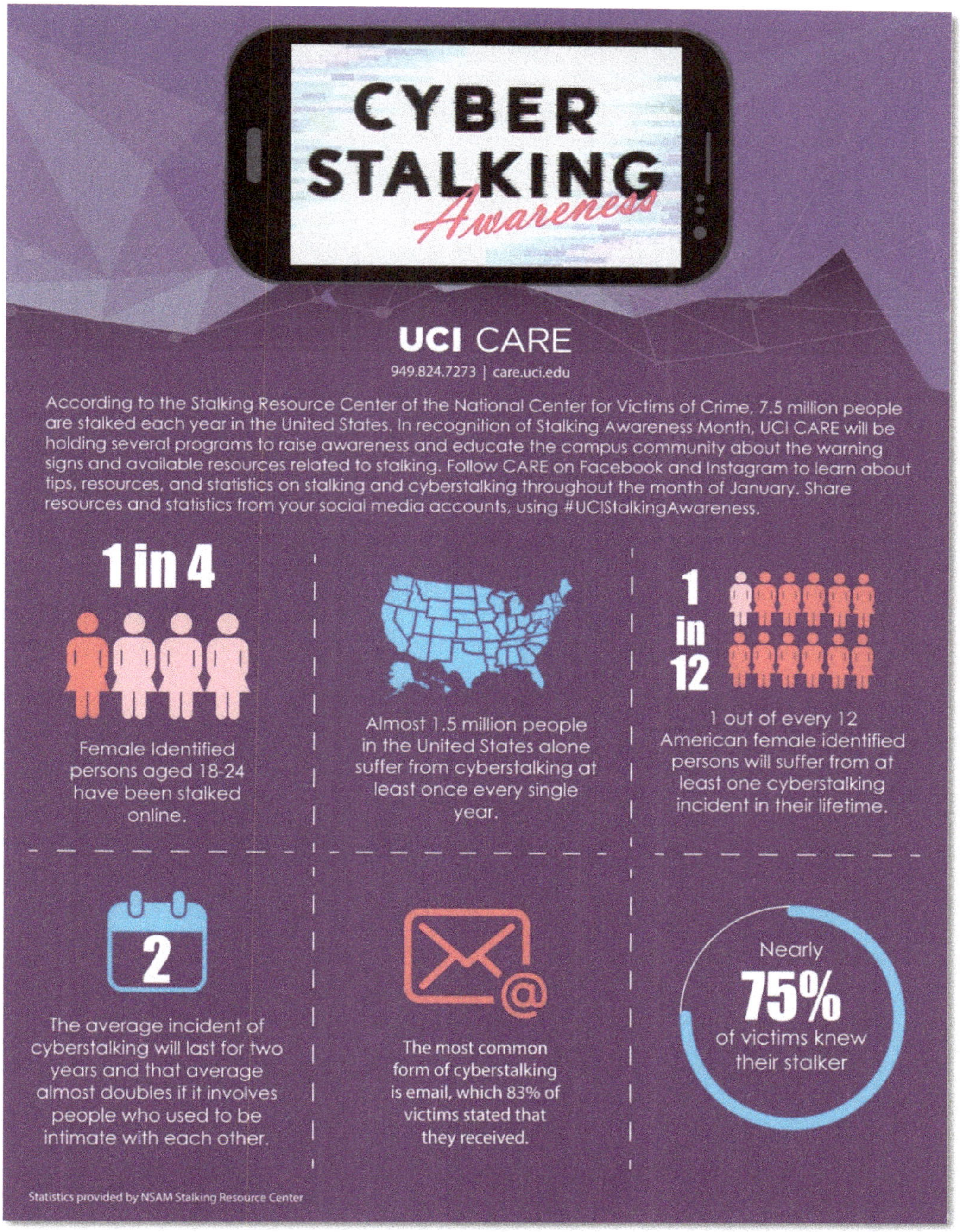

University of California at Irvine: UCI CARE Cyber Stalking Awareness Flyer

Here are some bullet points to keep in mind when thinking about cyber vs. OR world stalking:

- The majority of cyber and OR world stalking is still carried out by people we have come across in the OR world—even if that contact was minimal. However, an ever-growing number of victims only became known to their stalkers in the digital world, sometimes having interacted with their stalkers only casually and sometimes not at all.

- Most stalkers are men, but after a half-century of homogenizing the genders through social engineering, more and more women have joined the ranks of stalkers.
- Stalkers are motivated by control, revenge, and a belief that by imposing contact upon their victim they will make them recognize, acknowledge, or even love them.
- OR world stalkers almost always live in the same geographical area as their victims.
- Cyber stalkers can live anywhere on Planet Earth and using digital technology can actually become more of a threat, because VR is 24/7 whereas OR world stalking is limited by time and space regulators.

Here is an illustration of that last point, which provides insight into the VR vs. OR world discordance and human behavior:

> *"Imagine a door-to-door salesman who comes to your front door and rings the doorbell. You answer the door and tell the salesperson that you are not interested. The salesman walks away, and that is that. Now consider this scenario all too common in the cesspool that is social media:, rather than the salesman leaving your residence after you tell him that you are not interested, imagine that he continues to stand at your front door, continually ringing your doorbell. You tell him to stop, but he does not stop. Now imagine a situation where the salesman and a clan of his friends take turns incessantly ringing your doorbell. When one of these stalkers gets tired, another one takes over where their colleague left off. Imagine that the stalker clan rings your doorbell, bangs on your door with their fists, and bangs on your windows in*

unison 24/7. In the objective world, most people would call the police but what do you do in the VR world?" [113]

In the VR world, there are no police in the traditional sense. Sure, you can complain to the hosting social media site, but before you do I suggest you read their terms of service. Yes, you can file a criminal complaint against the ringleader or her accomplices—that is like taking a number at a bakery where you are last in a long line. And for those who make the glib suggestion "just close your account and forget about it," that might work for the World War II or Baby Boomer generations, but for digital natives, that would be like erasing a huge chunk of your life—the life you have lived since birth, the digital life that has modified your central nervous system.

How serious is cyber stalking or cyber bullying? Take a look at these data from the *Megan Meier Foundation:*

CYBERBULLYING

- Approximately 34% of students report experiencing cyber bullying during their lifetime (Hinduja & Patchin, 2015)
- Over 60% of students who experience cyberbullying reported that it immensely impacted their ability to learn and feel safe while at school (Hinduja, 2018)
- 59% of U.S. teens have been bullied or harassed online, and over 90% believe it's a major problem for people their age (Pew Research Center, 2018)

SELF-HARM

- Targets of cyber bullying are at a greater risk than others of both self-harm and suicidal behaviors (John et al., 2018)
- Approximately 18% of youth report self-harming at least once, impacting 1 in 4 girls and 1 in 10 boys (Monto, McRee, & Deryck, 2018)
- About 6% of students have digitally self-harmed, or anonymously posted online or shared hurtful content about oneself (Patchin & Hinduja, 2017)

SUICIDE

[113] Ibid 40

- Students who experienced bullying or cyberbullying are nearly 2 times more likely to attempt suicide (Hinduja & Patchin, 2018)
    - Current research suggests that suicide ideation and attempts among adolescents have nearly doubled since 2008 (Plemmons et al., 2018), making suicide is the 2nd leading cause of death for individuals 10-34 years of age (CDC, 2017)
    - Approximately 1 in 20 adolescents experience a suicide in single year (Andriessen, Dudley, Draper, & Mitchell, 2018)

OR world societal and legal prohibitions squelch, if not eradicate, cyber bullying. But in the world of virtual schoolyards, virtual school bathrooms, and virtual lunchrooms, people in charge are at a loss to implement a quick fix. It is much easier to kick a bullying student out of an OR school and solve the problem than when a perpetrator can go into his room, shut the door, and cyber bully his victim. It is much easier to call the police on a woman who breaks into your home and tries to kill you with a kitchen knife than it is a cyber stalker sitting behind a screen with a glass of wine, all the time in the world, your telephone number, street address, professional license number, and a borderline personality disorder that blames you for all the misery in her wretched life.

Michael Douglas and Glenn Close (Fatal Attraction: Paramount Pictures, 1987)

Governments, as well as terrorist groups, have harnessed the latitude VR provides that is denied them in the OR world. Cyber warfare is a 21st century military strategic and tactical choice that is made more frequently than air strikes.

Cyber warfare can and has altered the balance of power. Its threat coefficient to everyday people is much greater than bullets, bombs, or invasions. Cyber warfare runs the gamut from simple computer and network hacking to sophisticated mind control, recruitment, and other psychological operations (PSYOPs) that exploit vulnerabilities in man's virtual reality.

One military/state/militia that has successfully used cyber warfare is the Islamic State of Iraq and Syria (ISIS), also known as The Islamic State of Iraq and the Levant (ISIL). ISIS produces high-quality propaganda that is disseminated via any number of social media sites, including but not limited to Twitter, Instagram, Pinterest, WhatsApp, YouTube, and Facebook.

In 2014 ISIS, produced a recruitment video entitled "Flames of War." ISIS also minted the hashtag #worldcup2014 and "#amessagetotheU.S. The World Cup hashtag baited unwary social media soccer-philes into accessing recruitment messages instead of information about soccer. After the United States began bombing ISIS strongholds, the message hashtag was used to directly condemn America. In 2014, ISIS captured British broadcaster John Cantlie. Cantlie was featured on YouTube spouting ISIS propaganda with a shaven head and orange T-shirt. Proof of the effectiveness of ISIS' cyber warfare campaign was measured, in part, by the number of recruits it managed to persuade to join its army. Hundreds of western youths joined ISIS, most of whom were digital natives. It is not a coincidence that ISIS' recruitment and brainwashing took place in the virtual world. However, at some point the transition must be made from the virtual to the objective world.

I was interviewed in 2017 by a national media outlet on Al Qaeda's online recruitment of digital natives using social media. The terrorist organization used slick online media presentations and interactive VR world connectivity to target digital natives, many of them women. These digital native women were persuaded, if not seduced, to join the ranks of this fundamentalist religious organization made famous for beheading their enemies and blowing themselves up in acts of jihad. Not only did hundreds of VR recruits join VR Al Qaeda, but scores of young women and some men transformed their VR Al Qaeda recruit status into an OR world experience. How did that turn out?

Let's just say the United States military's elite rescue forces got involved when the discordance between the VR and OR world prompted a call from some of the more privileged of the new recruits back home to mommy and daddy, who then used their political connections to conduct an OR world intervention. I know of only two people—both male—who made the transition from VR to OR world Al Qaeda member. It was the discordance between the VR and OR world that turned revolutionary guard recruits into Al Qaeda AWOLs.

Just as terrorist organizations have recognized VR as a fertile ground to till for political and ideological advantage, technology giants and their government sponsors, enablers, and in some instances, co-conspirators have set their sights on a connected world where every move you make will be captured and stored on the blockchain. Permit me to orient my reader by referring to something they may be familiar with in the OR world. Perhaps some readers have seen surveillance video of organized crime kingpins walking along a city street with hands over their mouths while discussing business. That OR world scene seems quaint in today's V the Reality world. Today, and certainly in the future, big tech and governments will not have to petition a court for a search warrant, because in the digital world every keystroke, financial transaction, search entry, and word you utter within the confines of your OR world residence is but one drop of water in the VR dystopian swimming pool we call V the Reality. Which leads me to that area under the three overlapping curves between V the Reality, money, and politics.

CHAPTER XIV

V THE REALITY: All that Glitters is Not Gold

Recall earlier, we took note of the fact that VR technologies may be developed in vitro but gain traction and flourish within cultural contexts. Just as Rosie the Riveter came about because of World War II and Gen Z became who they are today because of the digital technology milieu they grew up in, so it is today that V the Reality has taken off because of a black swan event known as COVID-19.

Naomi Klein, senior writer for *The Intercept*, included this quote in her landmark article entitled *Screen New Deal:*

> *"Anuja Sonalker, the CEO of Steer Tech, a Maryland-based company selling self-parking technology, recently summed up the new virus-personalized pitch. 'There has been a distinct warming up to humanless, contactless technology,' she said. "Humans are biohazards, machines are not."'* [114]

Developers of VR technology recognized a magnificent opportunity to elevate VR over OR world experiences using COVID-19 as their catapult. To use our terms of art and to make it perfectly clear:

---

[114] The Intercept: Screen New Deal: Under Cover of Mass Death, Andrew Cuomo Calls in the Billionaires to Build a High-Tech Dystopia. By Naomi Klein, May 10, 2020.

Tech oligarchs in unison with their kindred spirits in government are in the process of redefining social dynamics and cultural norms so that virtual becomes the default reality—that is, V the Reality becomes the only reality. Big tech, politicians, and government bureaucrat social engineers intend to replace human-to-human contact with a sans-human, touchless, virtual version of everything they can get their hands on. They intend to promote a humanless world as the new norm. They will do this by making OR world behavior cumbersome, old fashioned, unavailable, and when those means don't get the job done, then illegal, e.g., using cash, driving, as in control of an automobile, or by removing from our options list those means and avenues by which we can transact the personal, vocational, and business parts our lives human-to-human—while making VR more intoxicatingly pleasant, easy, entertaining, and fashionable. When their transformation becomes functionally complete, you will no longer be able to speak in person to a human for most of your daily transactions—even when it comes to your doctors, human-to-human contact will be intercepted by a labyrinth of VR technology that will feel like running the gauntlet if your goal is to get to the other side where you can actually be in the company of your doctor. A cashless society will be "just the way it is" and when human-to-human interactions are a necessity, they will be so regulated by socially engineered sensibility filters, regulations, hurt feelings, boundaries, etc., they will be insufferable. These vexing socially engineered person-to-person dynamics will make people yearn for a V the Reality world, thus creating a malignant feedback loop where V the Reality becomes a welcome relief from the tortuous experiences of walking on thin ice, hurt feelings, etc. that describes 21st century socially engineered human-to-human interactions. For example, people

have become such bad drivers because the tractor beam coming from their digital device holds their attention—not on the road—that even OR world proponents of traditional driving are beginning to conclude maybe we do need driverless cars.

The COVID-19 pandemic forced the most strident OR world devotees, even the World War II generation, to step into the world of virtual reality with both feet. To be sure, social distancing, touchless delivery, pickup, and self -isolation were ***necessary*** retreats from human-to-human contact to flatten the infection curve during COVID-19—but necessity has a way morphing into "choice" permanency if vested interests decide to make it so. And in the case of COVID-19, it didn't even require social engineers to jury-rig the infection and death rate data to make them worse than they are, as some have alleged. No, the virus was so virulent that social engineers just sat back in awe and watched the great pandemic of 2019-2021 unfold. The dynamic we are describing here was given voice in 2008 by President Obama's chief of staff, Rahm Emanuel:

> *"You never want a serious crisis to go to waste. I mean, it's an opportunity to do things that you think you could not do before."*

Tech titans and their kindred spirits in government are not the first to springboard off a national disaster to redefine social norms and laws. The events of 9/11 may have warranted the shutting down of air travel, and such things as warrantless searches and the admittedly ineffective bureaucratic funnel known as the TSA for a period of time. However, long after the dust had settled and the terrorists responsible had been neutralized, The Patriot Act codified a permanent loss of personal and civil liberties. What began as 9/11 related security necessities morphed into permanent application limits on American's constitutional protections of civil liberties. As the brilliant Naomi Klein wrote:

> *"It has taken some time to gel, but something resembling a coherent Pandemic Shock Doctrine is beginning to emerge. Call it the "Screen New Deal." Far more high-tech than anything we have seen during previous disasters, the future that is being rushed into being as the bodies still pile up treats our past weeks of physical isolation not as a*

painful necessity to save lives, but as a living laboratory for a permanent — and highly profitable — no-touch future."[115]

Perhaps the people at the center of bringing about this cataclysmic shift in human evolution feel more comfortable with non-sentient beings. Perhaps it is about money, because the windfall profits that await them by converting an OR world into a V the Reality world are so massive, they are incalculable, and/or maybe they just want to promote V the Reality because their business is selling technology and software that does just that. Perhaps government's participation in promoting V the Reality is because it affords them more control over their subjects—bureaucracies are habitual list and rule makers, in the same way OCD patients are compulsive and fixated on rules and regulations. It is probably all of these motivational factors fueling the push toward, as Miss Klein terms it, the *Screen New Deal.* For our purposes, we need to understand the unintended consequences that await all of those people walking along the Pacific Ocean on a warm, starlit night that have their CNS glued to their smart phone, and not the sensory spectacle provided by mother nature.

[115] Ibid.

Starry Night Over Rock Formations By The Pacific Ocean. *(Artist: Dalian, Liaoning, China)*

All motivation, including the push to create a new norm of V the Reality, originates somewhere within our biopsychosocial fingerprint. We've already documented that digital technology physically changes the brains of those who consume it for long, extended periods of time. The human genome includes any number of heritable predispositions including intelligence, warmth, information processing matrices, and a host of other presets. As I have written elsewhere, heritability is not inevitability, but it helps to understand what makes us want to choose one direction or another—including a V the Reality world.

Psychology includes any number of mental prisms that modify environmental and internal stimuli before being processed by the CNS. These include attitudes, perceptions, information processing styles, affective responses, mental filters, enhancers, nullifiers, and confirmation bias. Social factors include cultural heritage, racial identity, religious and group dynamics, social conformity, and patterned exposure that when mixed with psychology result in, for example, ego and ethnocentrism.

Biopsychosocial dimensions interact and intersect, which results in algorithmic relationships and seemingly functionally autonomous hybrid behaviors that reveal themselves only by studying the patterns of any one person within and between many differing contexts. So, why are we discussing these neuropsychological issues in a book about virtual and other realities? These points are relevant because all of us, including the people busy creating V the Reality, inevitably and unavoidably project their internal world and what they feel most comfortable with onto the outside world—and in the case of tech savants, that means:

> **Their world will become our world—like it or not, good, bad or indifferent. With or without malicious intent and, perhaps, without awareness, a few dozen tech savants, cryptographers, and big money oligarchs along with their government cohorts are busy turning *their* world into our world, i.e., projecting their internal CNS environment onto the rest of the world.**

To illustrate how ego-syntonic that process is, people without color vision tend to decorate their homes in achromatic palettes. People who view the world as a dangerous place to live tend to put bars on their windows and use light-blocking window treatments. But what if you are able to see colors and want to let the light in? Do you want to live in a home decorated by color-blind and paranoid designers? Let us try to reduce the equation to its lowest common denominator by talking about core traits in people. If you are going to have your world re-imagined—that is, surgically alter your body, mind, and spirit—then you may wish to think about who is doing the re-imagining and performing the surgery.

In 1946, a psychological researcher by the name of Solomon Asch became interested in human traits. Asch identified what he termed "warmth" as a central trait in order to emphasize warmth's importance in the human experience. As you read this brief overview of the importance of warmth in giving meaning to the lives of both humans and other sentient beings, never forget that the internal world of tech titans and their government enablers is anything but warm.

> *"Solomon Asch presented subjects with a description of a person who was intelligent, skillful, industrious, warm, determined, practical, and cautious. With another group of subjects the term warm was replaced with cold. Subjects later described the first person much more positively,*

e.g., wiser, happier, and more humorous than they did the second person. Asch postulated that because warm and cold are central traits they have a powerful impact on the range of conclusions people are willing to reach about others. Supporting this view, replacing warm and cold with polite and blunt, respectively, did not carry the same impact, presumably because these were more peripheral traits. Harold Kelley in 1950 introduced a guest lecturer to a class to some students as a warm person and to others as a cold individual. Students receiving the first description were more likely to engage in class discussion and to rate the lecturer as effective and less formal. " [116]

For the people who possess the central trait of warmth, human-to-human OR contact is natural and the preferred method of contact. And it is not just people. Warm people reflexively respond to pets with a desire to touch them or talk to them. They often have pets and relate to other living things better than they do objects or technology. Warm people are responsive, effusive, and reactive. They feel what other sentient beings are feeling and react accordingly.

People who lack internal warmth, on the other hand, have a robotic quality about them. They tend to relate better to objects and abstractions rather than sentient beings. Being close to other people can be uncomfortable for them. Their nonverbal behavior has an artificial or forced quality about it. We clinicians call this "as if" behavioral sets. Colloquially, it has been called "human emulation mode." Why a cold person would need to develop a "human emulation mode" is intuitive, because if you cannot easily feel for or with other sentient beings and yet have to present before or interact with others, you superimpose a set of behaviors you learned that are supposed to convey warmth and feeling, even though nothing could be further from the truth.

---

[116] Asch, S. E. (1946). Forming impressions of personality. Journal of Abnormal and Social Psychology, 41, 1230-1240.
Kelley, H. Harold (1950) The Warm-Cold Variable In First Impressions Of Persons https://doi.org/10.1111/j.1467-6494.1950.tb01260.

As a preface to moving forward in this chapter, it is not our intent to cast aspersions against any of the tech titans and cryptographers helping to create V the Reality. As I conveyed earlier, people naturally try to make the external world into one that comports with their internal environment. Whether or not their world is the best world for the rest of us is the issue. Steve Jobs famously described his Mac as "a computer for the rest of us." Jobs made this comment during a time when, as now, people whose internal environments lack warmth ran the world. During Steve's time, it was Bill Gates and his DOS operating system. Some readers may remember the "PC Guy" commercials in the early part of the 21st century. PC Guy was a character that captured the difference between Steve Jobs' and Bill Gates' internal environments:

Apple Commercial "PC Guy" (Circa 2006)

Mark Zuckerberg, one of the tech titans actively converting our world into a V the Reality world, told Lester Holt from NBC News the following:

> *"Historically, I've had a very hard time expressing myself," Zuckerberg said when asked if he was the best communicator for his company. "I just come across as robotic.'"*[117]

We interpret Mr. Zuckerberg's self-description more in terms of a genuflection, not an admission, because the entire world has taken note of his absence of warmth. Here is just one of tens of thousands of similar reactions to the CEO of Facebook:

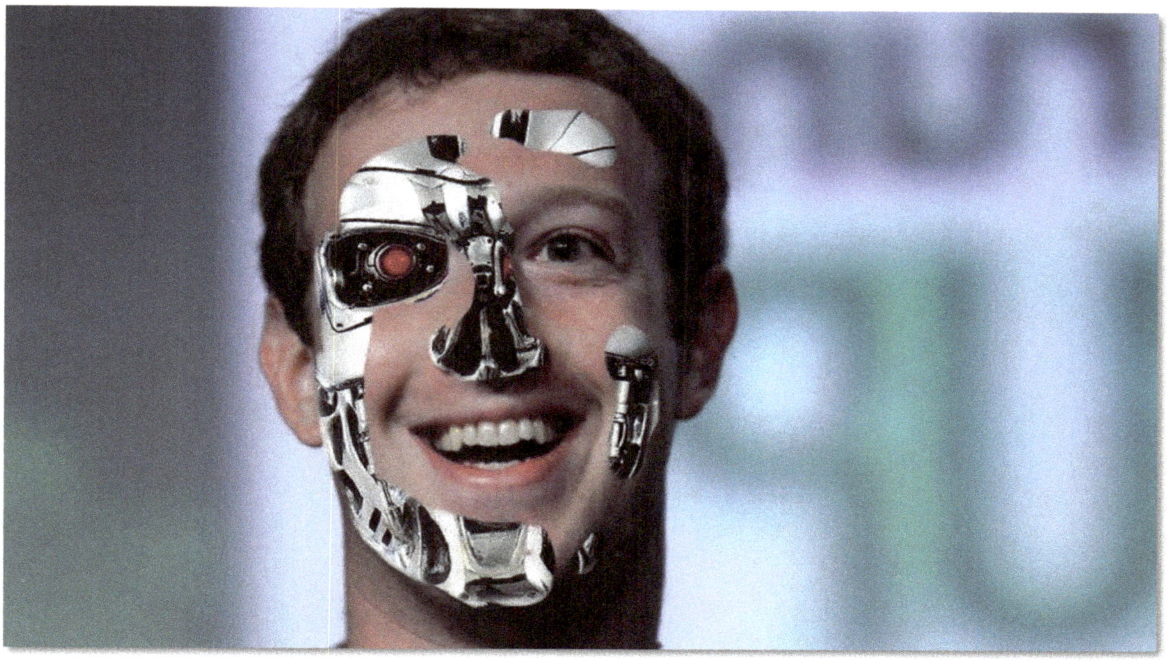

Caricature of Mark Zuckerberg, CEO of Facebook

On October 9, 2016, Mr. Zuckerberg did a live Facebook feed from his backyard where he grilled animals he had hunted down and killed himself. As if his behavior during the live feed did not reaffirm his absence of warmth, he put the cherry on top of Asch's sundae when he declared:

[117] CNET. Mark Zuckerberg knows he comes across as 'robotic.' The Facebook CEO tells NBC News he's working to improve his communications skills. Story by: Steven Musil, Oct. 21, 2019.

"Meat and fish tastes better when you kill it yourself."

Hunger Games, here I come! Mark Zuckerberg in full camo on Wednesday as he embarked on a dangerous hike in Hawaii with a bow and arrows to kill wild boar (Courtesy of THE DAILY MAIL)

Eric Schmidt, former executive at Google and the man whom Steve Jobs accused of stealing designs for his iPhone, is a notoriously "as if" presenter. Mr.

Schmidt is right in the middle, if not the ringleader, of bringing about what Naomi Klein suggests will become a dystopian nightmare, to wit:

> *"Thanks to Cuomo and his various billionaire partnerships (including one with Michael Bloomberg for testing and tracing), New York state is being positioned as the gleaming showroom for this grim future—but the ambitions reach far beyond the borders of any one state or country.*
>
> ***And at the dead centre of it all is Eric Schmidt.*** *Well before Americans understood the threat of Covid-19, Schmidt had been on an aggressive lobbying and public-relations campaign, pushing precisely the Black Mirror vision of society that Cuomo has just empowered him to build. At the heart of this vision is seamless integration of government with a handful of Silicon Valley giants—with public schools, hospitals, doctor's offices, police and military all outsourcing (at a high cost) many of their core functions to private tech companies. It's a vision Schmidt has been advancing in his roles as chair of the Defense Innovation Board, which advises the US Department of Defense on increased use of artificial intelligence in the military, and as chair of the powerful National Security Commission on Artificial Intelligence, or NSCAI, which advises Congress on "advances in artificial intelligence, related machine learning developments and associated technologies", with the goal of addressing "the national and economic security needs of the United States, including economic risk". Both boards are crowded with powerful Silicon Valley CEOs and top executives from companies including Oracle, Amazon, Microsoft, Facebook and of course, Schmidt's former colleagues at Google. As chair, Schmidt—who still holds more than $5.3bn in shares of Alphabet (Google's parent company), as well as large investments in other tech firms—has essentially been running a Washington-based shakedown on behalf of Silicon Valley. The main purpose of the two boards is to call for exponential increases in government spending on research into artificial intelligence and on tech-enabling infrastructure such as 5G—investments that would*

directly benefit the companies in which Schmidt and other members of these boards have extensive holdings." [118]

Eric Schmidt *(Forbes Magazine, December 11, 2018)*

[118] The Intercept: SCREEN NEW DEAL: Under Cover of Mass Death, Andrew Cuomo Calls in the Billionaires to Build a High-Tech Dystopia. By Naomi Klein, May 8, 2020.

"Bill Gates has a plan to save the world. Will the world listen?"

(Wired Magazine, February 15, 2021)

Mr. Schmidt, unlike some of his tech titan peers, e.g., Elon Musk, tells people he is not the least bit worried about a V the Reality world populated by *Terminator*-like robots. Perhaps Mr. Schmidt has grown more comfortable with AI because of his connections with the U.S. Department of Defense. He revealed something very important about his internal CNS environment in a 2018 Forbes Magazine interview:

> *'"We're The Killer Robots To Start, We Would Find A Way To Stop Them"*

When Mr. Schmidt said **"we're the killer robots,"** he was disclosing something important about himself—after all, he is right at the center of developing and imposing his dreams of an AI world that plans to make commonplace the Atlases of the world and their cute little V the Reality helpers.

Boston Dynamics' Atlas robot can now chase you through the woods (New Atlas, By Rich Haridy, May 10, 2018)

Like any great salesperson, Mr. Schmidt has made it abundantly clear that the world he is creating and selling is good for you—this from Wired Magazine:

ISSIE LAPOWSKY BUSINESS 12.09.2014 05:54 PM

Google's Eric Schmidt: Don't Fear the Artificially Intelligent Future

Eric Schmidt wants you to know that robots are your friend.

Mr. Schmidt describes a not-so-distant future where AR/AI meld so seamlessly with whatever you do that many of the people we rely upon will become obsolete—not unlike the buggy whip with the advent of automobiles. In Mr. Schmidt's world, expertise is measured by the amount of factual data you can immediately access, and not your intelligence, education, training, and experience. He also hints that one of the great things about AI is that the average person will have immediate access to so much information, he will become an instant expert on almost anything he data-siphons from the well of AI.

In 2015, I published a textbook on mind control. In that book is a chapter with the title: Google IQ. Here is a brief excerpt that looks at how the virtual world deludes the unwary by convincing him that access to factual data is the sine qua non of expertise:

> *"[G]oogle generated knowledge, with the exception of isolated factual information, e.g., how many continents are there? What is the mass of the earth? What is a good recipe for apple pie? promotes the delusion in its user that he is smarter and better educated than he really is. Here is but one example that illustrates this phenomenon. One can do a Google search for the landing protocol of the Boeing 777 aircraft. The search results can then be inserted into a term paper, they can be quoted at a social gathering, or they can be authoritatively inserted into a blog, etc. Does this mean the holder of this information knows how to land a Boeing 777 aircraft? No, of course not, and therein is the problem. I saw comedian Howie Mandel do the following at one of his live performances that illustrates the subject of this chapter. Mandel, a high school kickout, played an emergency room physician on a TV show. During one of his standup performances broadcast on HBO, I saw Mandel arrogantly question a real emergency room physician who was sitting in his audience. Mandel brashly questioned the real doctor about various treatment protocols that had been written into one of the show's scripts that Mandel had memorized. The ER doctor didn't rattle off the answers like a parrot when challenged to do so by Mandel, but Mandel did regurgitate the text from the memorized script and demonstrated this to his fawning audience who applauded his display of his script memorization. The interaction between Mandel and the doctor did not come across as a joke and it certainly wasn't funny. It was clear to me that Mandel really believed that parroting medical terms from a TV script was the equal of the knowledge possessed by the real emergency room doctor. How did we get to this point where a high school kickout comedian feels that he can compete with (actually know more than) a real doctor? All of us know by now that we live in the "information age." Information is everywhere and easily accessible to*

anyone with access to the Internet and the ability to enter a search term(s) into your favorite search engine. Information that was once buried in the musty stacks at the university's library is now a few mouse clicks or finger swipes away, eagerly awaiting insertion into a school paper, speech, tweet or casual conversation at a dinner party. With all of this information at our fingertips, conventional wisdom is that we are all smarter and better educated, but is that true? Does having the results of a Google search mean you necessarily know something of substance? Regardless how you answer that question, there is one thing we do know, and that is the easy access to information has promoted the belief among the masses that they are smarter and know more than those who grew up without access to the Internet. I call the delusion of being smarter and better educated, after scrolling through the results of a Google search, The Google IQ™. " [119]

Any reader with an MD, PhD, DVM, DDS, OD, RN, or any other licensed health care professional has been lectured by a Google IQ'er. The Google IQ phenomenon is so ubiquitous in today's V the Reality world that coffee mugs emblazoned with the following is all the rage among health care providers:

[119] Ibid. 10, page 232.

So, what are we/they/them missing, if anything, and are we better off by being coerced, persuaded and/or cajoled to live in the world they are designing for us? Let's return to the internal environments of tech and math savants before we answer this question—this time looking at their emotional states of mind, not merely their cognitions.

Warmth is mediated in part by our mirror neuronal system, one of many dedicated neuronal bundles and other brainstem mediated affective centers that make possible warmth and the ability to feel for and with other sentient beings. Compassion is visible using fMRI scans, to wit:

> *"Functional magnetic resonance images (fMRI) were acquired as participants viewed 55 continuous sequences of slides to induce either compassion or pride, presented in alternation with sequences of neutral slides. Emotion self-report data were collected after each slide condition within the fMRI scanner. Compassion induction was associated with activation in the midbrain periaqueductal gray (PAG), a region that is activated during pain and the perception of others' pain, and that has*

been implicated in parental nurturance behaviors. Pride induction engaged the posterior medial cortex, a region that has been associated with self-referent processing. Self-reports of compassion experience were correlated with increased activation in a region near the PAG, and in the right inferior frontal gyrus (IFG). Self-reports of pride experience, in contrast, were correlated with reduced activation in the IFG and the anterior insula. These results provide preliminary evidence towards understanding the neural correlates of important interpersonal dimensions of compassion and pride. Caring (compassion) and self-focus (pride) may represent core appraisals that differentiate the response profiles of many emotions." [120]

In 2018, researchers from Cambridge University found that ten percent of a person's ability to feel for and with other sentient beings is wholly related to one's genome. As I mentioned earlier, people are born with predispositions to be one way or the other. If you think of a normal distribution with each tail of the curve representing extremes, in the case of the ability to feel for and with other sentient beings, you find some people dead inside, e.g., people and other sentient beings are viewed as fitting into typically one of three functional categories: a. Can I have sex with it? b. Can I eat it? c. Is it a threat to me?

On the other end of the continuum, we have people who are exquisitely sensitive to how other sentient beings feel, and not just creatures like themselves. These are the people who honestly can feel your and other sentient beings' pain, moods, fear, and joy. The people predisposed to be cold have a very difficult time relating to any living being, especially living beings that are a different species. Animals to these people are objects, and human beings would not be given much more consideration without laws—with an emphasis upon enforcement of those laws.

---

[120] Emiliana R Simon-Thomas , Jakub Godzik, Elizabeth Castle, Olga Antonenko, Aurelie Ponz, Aleksander Kogan, Dacher J Keltner (2012). An fMRI study of caring vs self-focus during induced compassion and pride. Social Cognitive and Affective Neuroscience. Aug;7(6):635-48.

> *"In a new study published in the journal Translational Psychiatry, the Cambridge team, working with the genetics company 23andMe and a team of international scientists, report the results of the largest genetic study of empathy using information from more than 46,000 23andMe customers. The customers all completed the EQ online and provided a saliva sample for genetic analysis. The study was led by Varun Warrier, a Cambridge PhD student, and Professors Simon Baron-Cohen, Director of the Autism Research Centre at Cambridge University, Thomas Bourgeron, of the University Paris Diderot and the Institut Pasteur, and David Hinds, Principal Scientist at 23andMe. The new study has three important results. First, it found that how empathetic we are is partly due to genetics. Indeed, a tenth of this variation is due to genetic factors. This confirms previous research examining empathy in identical versus non-identical twins. Second, the new study confirmed that women are on average more empathetic than men. However, this difference is not due to our DNA, as there were no differences in the genes that contribute to empathy in men and women. This implies that the sex difference in empathy is the result of other non-genetic biological factors, such as prenatal hormone influences, or non-biological factors such as socialization, both of which also differ between the sexes."* [121]

The research subjects, wherein ten percent of the variance in empathy was found to be located on the human genome, were from a normal cross-section of human beings. But make no mistake about it, millions of human beings have zero empathy—that is, they either have zero genetic coding that makes possible the ability to feel for and with other sentient beings, or the combination of their genetics

---

[121] V Warrier, R Toro, B Chakrabarti, iPSYCH-Broad Autism Group, Grove J, Borglum AD, D Hinds, T Bourgeron, and S Baron-Cohen (2018), Genome-wide analyses of self-reported empathy: correlations with autism, schizophrenia, and anorexia nervosa. Translational Psychiatry. DOI: 10.1038/s41398-017-0082-6. In: University of Cambridge Research Update: March 12, 2018.

influenced by their psychosocial acculturation makes empathy difficult, if not impossible.

> *"Narcissists, borderline and psychopathic personalities are introduced as people lacking "affective empathy"—the ability to feel others' feelings. Baron-Cohen's new paradigm classifies these personality types as "zero-negative": a zero amount of affective empathy being a negative condition, because the ability to self-regulate the way they treat others is significantly compromised. By contrast, Baron-Cohen defines people with Asperger's syndrome or classic autism, which is his own field, as "zero-positive". Like the zero-negatives these people lack affective empathy, but in addition they score zero on "cognitive empathy"—thinking others' thoughts. Because some zero-positive individuals have, through their unusual ability to systemize, pushed human culture forwards with their discoveries (Einstein was late to talk—a sign of classic autism—yet he was an extreme systemizer who discovered E = mc2), Baron-Cohen categorizes them "zero empathy positive". Baron-Cohen divides the empathizing mechanism into six degrees. Someone at level 6 is the opposite type to the zero-positive/negative, being highly intuitive, wired to feel the feelings of others, read the minds of others and anticipate plot development in the social realm. Because this type of person is more likely to be female than male, Baron-Cohen defines them as having an extreme female brain. "* [122]

Level 1, zero-negative people are the trophy hunters who can watch animals writhe in pain, gasp for air, and look at their murderer in the eye to get nothing but a smile. The author notes that trophy hunters reject V the Reality for some very telling reasons. Simulations of animals being killed aren't good enough for them. They need to see a living being take its last breath, stumble, cry, and be terrified for them to

---

[122] Simon Baron Cohen (2011), Zero Degrees of Empathy: A New Theory of Human Cruelty. Penguin Books Ltd., 80 Strand, London, WC2R oRL, England.

experience pleasure. As an illustration of how V the Reality could be something good, trophy hunting in a V the Reality world would be an evolutionary advancement for the tens of thousands of sentient beings murdered for fun by gleeful killers—but perhaps the same arguments as to why having sex with an underage sex doll is outlawed in many places throughout the world would apply to ultra-realistic trophy hunting. Painting V the Reality is going to require lots of colors.

Melissa Bachman Posing with Lion She Killed for Fun

Then we have research that has demonstrated that for the zero empathic positive (zero-positive) human beings, their degree of empathy can be increased with human contact, compassion, and the teaching of kindness, especially when empathic conditioning occurs early on and within the family. What is profoundly disturbing, however, is that zero-positive humans can never have a chance toward becoming more empathetic in a world where gizmos and gadgets, mechanical puppy dogs, virtual sex, and digital connectedness supplant or replace empathic human-to-98.6 F/37C human contact. In this virtual world dystopia, human beings who have the capacity to feel for and with other sentient beings may become morose, depressed, and feel lonely when separated from the mother's milk of human contact.

Not only has COVID-19 provided a serendipitous springboard for the zero-negative Level 6 people and zero-positives in positions of power to push their

Screen New Deal, as Miss Klein calls it, but on a positive note, it has provided scientists and authors like myself the perfect naturally occurring experiment that can help to shed light on what happens to normal human beings when they are forced to isolate, go humanless, isolated, and touchless. Mind you, we already have millions of unwitting experimental subjects who were steeped in V the Reality since birth—we refer to these people as belonging to Gen Z. Let's review the data generated by these two naturally occurring experiments on V the Reality: Gen-Z and COVID-19.

Recall that Gen Z is the most digitally connected and tech savvy generation to have ever lived. They were raised where the prevailing zeitgeist approached V the Reality. They are also lonely, depressed, and the most fatalistic generation in over 100 years. An American Psychological Association (APA) "Stress in America" survey conducted in August of 2018 found:

> *"More than nine in 10 Gen Z adults (91 percent) said they have experienced at least one physical or emotional symptom because of stress, such as feeling depressed or sad (58 percent) or lacking interest, motivation or energy (55 percent). Only half of all Gen Zs feel like they do enough to manage their stress."*

In July of 2020, Bloomberg's Business Wire reported the following about Gen Z:

- Web or die. 58% of Gen Z can't go more than 4 hours without Internet access before they become uncomfortable.
- In the Internet we trust. In 5 years, 64% of Gen Z thinks the Internet will determine what they will do on a daily basis.
- Byte-pal. 56% of Gen Z is friends with someone they ONLY know online.

In addition to the Gen Z naturally occurring experiment, COVID-19 provided researchers with a once-in-a-lifetime real-world study on what happens to people when they are forced into a virtual world due to an infectious pathogen loose in the OR world. A large-scale BBC Loneliness Experiment found the following:

> *"There's a reason the term "physical distancing" hasn't been used much during the coronavirus pandemic: Though it's a more accurate*

description of what public health experts are trying to achieve than "social distancing," it fails to capture the loss that many of us feel as a direct result of being separated from other people. ***Young Americans might be the loneliest of all. [L]oneliness has been a growing problem for decades—with some estimating that 61 percent of adults in the United States feel it—and it's only been made worse by the COVID-19 lockdown.*** *Over the last four months, the requirement that we sequester ourselves whenever possible, venturing outside our homes only for essentials and maintaining a six-foot minimum distance from fellow shoppers or exercisers, has been frustrating—even painful. While keeping to ourselves helps prevent coronavirus' spread, humans are social creatures and prolonged isolation takes a toll on our mental health."* [123](Emphasis added)

The article went on to recount the work of anthropologist Robin Dunbar, whose work in the 1990s demonstrated that primate brain size is correlated with personal contact, to wit:

"Back in the 1990s, British anthropologist Robin Dunbar, upon discovering a correlation between primates' brain size and the social groups they formed, concluded that humans have the brainpower to maintain about five close relationships."

Once again, we have ample empirical evidence that V the Reality affects more than attitudes and perceptions—it actually modifies CNS brain chemistry, structures, and function. Now take a look at these data which are consistent with the notion that as generations have transitioned from human-to-human connectedness to its more virtual versions, our mental health and sense of well-being has taken a hit:

Highlights

- Younger people reported more loneliness than the middle-aged.

---

[123] Manuela Barretoa, Christina Victor, Claudia Hammond, Alice Eccles, Matt T. Richinsa, Pamela Qualterd: *Loneliness around the world: Age, gender, and cultural differences in loneliness. Personality and Individual Differences Volume 169, February 1, 2021.*

- The middle-aged reported more loneliness than older people.
- Men reported more loneliness than women.
- People in individualistic (vs. collectivist) countries reported more loneliness.
- Age, gender, and culture interacted to predict loneliness. [124]

The authors of the study went on to document:

> *"[O]ne in five millennials have no friends at all. And a survey released in 2020 found that 71 percent of millennials and almost 79 percent of Gen Z respondents report feeling lonely—a significantly greater proportion than other generations."*

Those less digitally connected and/or dependent upon digitally mediated social networks, the better is their mental health outlook.

Then we have this study authored by neuroscientists from the Massachusetts Institute of Technology (MIT) and the Salk Institute in La Jolla, California, that confirms how human brains are modified by how we treat them, with particular reference to supplanting OR world interactions with V the Reality:

> *"When people are forced to be isolated from one another, do they crave social interactions in the same way a hungry person craves food? To address this question, we used functional magnetic resonance imaging (fMRI) to measure neural responses in participants (n=40) evoked by food and social cues after ten hours of mandated fasting or total social isolation. After isolation, people felt lonely and craved social interaction. Midbrain regions showed increased activation to food cues after fasting and to social cues after isolation; these responses were correlated with self-reported craving. Neural patterns in response to food cues when participants were hungry generalized to social cues after isolation. Our*

[124] Ibid.

> *results support the intuitive idea that acute isolation causes social craving, similar to hunger."* [125]

After reviewing these studies on human beings' mental and physical health when human-to-human contact is supplanted, or in some cases replaced with, its V the Reality versions, think about what a handful of tech titans, cryptographers, and their governmental kindred spirits and financiers have done and are doing to life on earth, whether intended or not:

> **After tens of thousands of years of evolution where every gene, every neuron, every behavior having been naturally selected for and modified by human-to-human, sentient being to sentient being contact, a cataclysmic change is being orchestrated by a handful of people whose internal world, if their public personas are any guide, feel more comfortable in their digital "as if" human emulation mode world than the OR world they are busy replacing.**

Do we want to live in their world? Is it mentally healthy to live in their world? Can you opt out? We already have enough data to answer the last question, "Can we opt out?" The answer is, for all intents and purposes, no! As we have learned, for all the glitz and convenience virtual reality has brought into our lives, it comes with a physical and mental health cost. However, what makes VR technology maddening is that some of it has been very good. Here are just a few examples:

Surgical systems that function as a smart bridge between surgeon and patient, e.g., The Da Vinci Surgical System and Femtosecond Laser Eye Surgery Apparatus, or AI robots like Spot the police dog that may one day replace living police dogs and is

---

[125] L. Tomova, K. Wang, T. Thompson, G. Matthews, A. Takahashi, K. Tye, R. Saxe (2020) The need to connect: Acute social isolation causes neural craving responses similar to hunger. doi: https://doi.org/10.1101/2020.03.25.006643.

currently being tested by the Massachusetts State Police, are tremendous advancements for our culture. [126]

Boston Dynamics Spot in Action (Massachusetts State Police/WBUR Television)

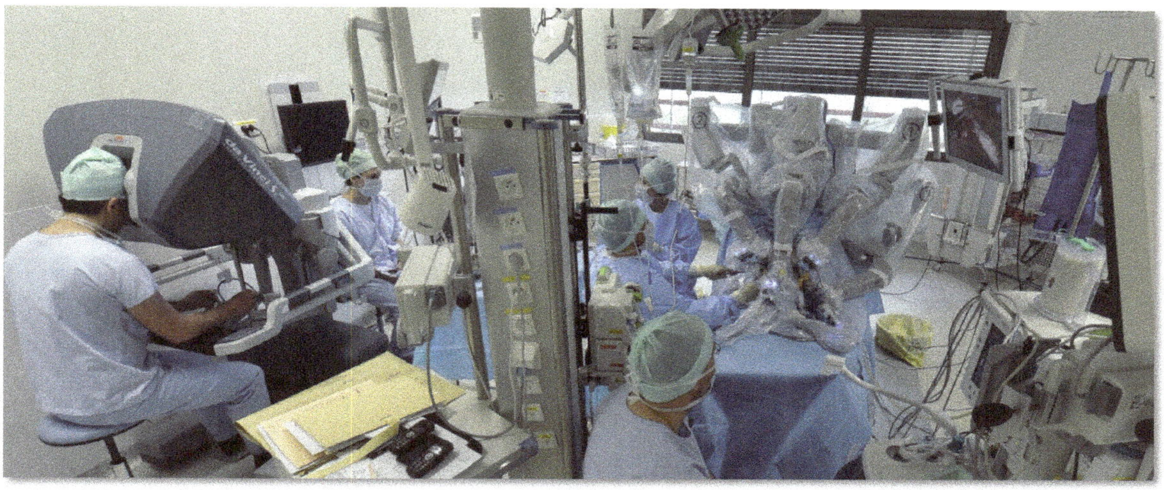

Da Vinci Surgical System in Action

---

[126] https://www.wbur.org/news/2019/11/25/boston-dynamics-robot-dog-massachusetts-state-police

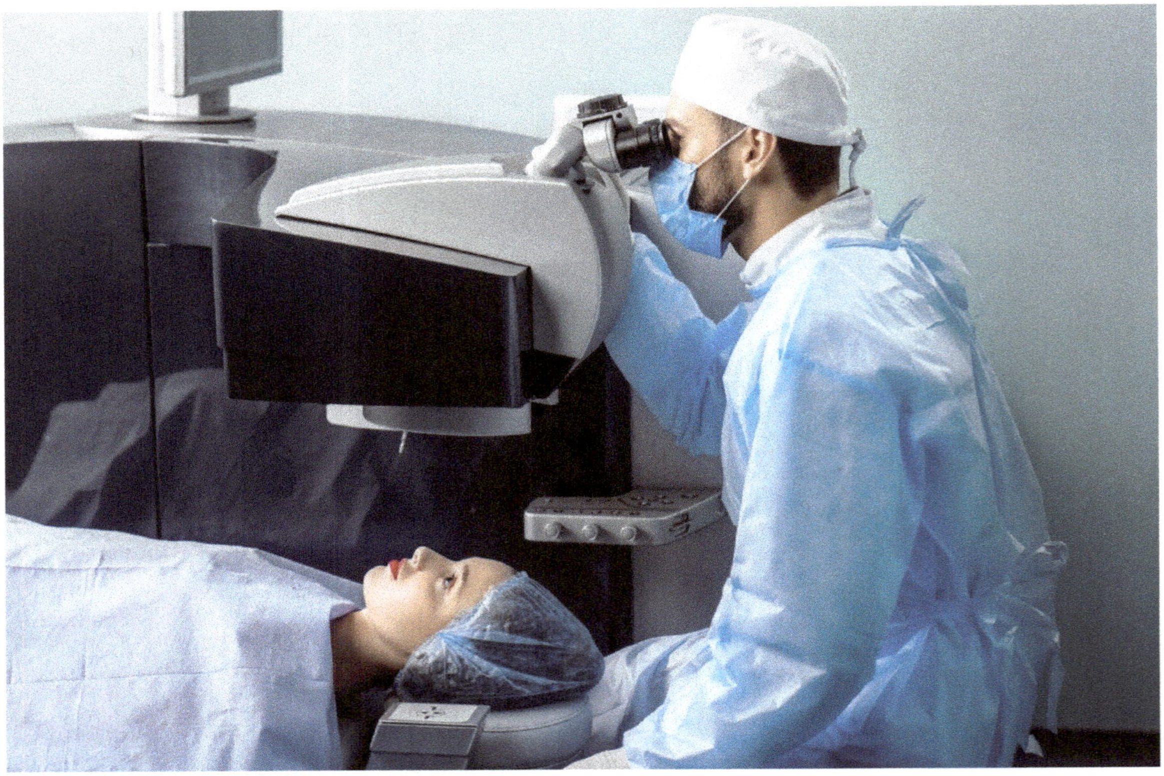

Femtosecond Laser Eye Surgery Apparatus

These and other technological interfacial and augmented reality assistants in medicine and police work are just what the doctored ordered.

> **Take note of the fact that these marvelous advancements do not redact or replace human-to-human interactive experiences. V the Reality is absent in all of these wonderful technological creations.**

That said, are we really losing anything of significance if we replace those all-too-common and mundane sentient being-to-sentient being interactions with V the Reality analogs?

The mundane everyday interactions had between sentient beings are perhaps not so mundane after all. A smile between customer and clerk, a thank you genuinely conveyed, a pat on the shoulder, handshake, an act of courtesy afforded other drivers that is acknowledged with a wave or simple smile between strangers, has a ten thousand-plus year natural selection provenance that suggests what we should have known all along, but have now been forced to accept—human-to-human, animal-to-animal sans technology is what we are genetically programmed to be and do. A compliment or gracious consideration offered by a stranger in passing is something that can literally make a bad day into a good day. These so-called mundane interactions with check-out persons, clerks, your doctor and her front office staff, and those dinners with extended family members were redacted or watered down for Gen Z, and certainly for all of us doing our part to flatten the SARS-CoV-2 infection curve—the result, mental health took a hit. For the first time, many people experienced cabin fever and the psychological stress reaction known as stir crazy. For the counterfactual reader's facile retort: "But those bad actors we run into at the grocery store or on the road are also avoided with a V the Reality existence," I suggest the following considerations,

That would be true, but social media and other VR transactions are actually worse in many cases for reasons we outlined earlier, e.g., anonymity and a sense of empowerment to act as badly as one can imagine because there are no OR world retributions. Bad actors pre-VR were limited to the "crazy person" everyone knew in the neighborhood. In the VR world psychopaths, borderlines and SOBs from all across the globe enter our home, right along with all the tracking technology built into VR tech.

I reflect upon time spent in the stacks at brick, mortar, and cellulose edifices we call libraries. The smell of books, the maze of shelves and aisles overlaid with enforced quietness, the incidental glance between students, the flirting and occasional competition for a particular book. The helpful albeit sometimes stern librarians who seemed to know where everything is without so much as having to resort to one of her special references kept behind her desk. It is true that part of my fond memories are tainted with the elixir of nostalgia, but the scientist in me has now—after researching Gen Z and COVID-19 isolation dynamics—concluded we've lost something that may be a necessary to a meaningful life that is encoded on our genome. At least those human beings with built-in empathy. But this issue is complex and more nuanced than one might think.

Some human beings, as we have learned, are not so comfortable and don't value direct sentient being to sentient being contact, and that may have been a part of their desire to create alternative realities. Perhaps we can think of some of these people's inventions as a form of self-medicating through VR, et al., inventions.

For children challenged by an autistic spectrum profile, technological interfaces have been life-enhancing, if not lifesaving. Nevertheless, I reflect upon the wisdom of Abraham Maslow. Maslow was perhaps most famous for his self-actualization hierarchy of needs model of human behavior. However, many psychology students and practitioners alike are unaware of how Dr. Maslow thought differently about his contributions to psychology, as he grew wiser with age.

I was privileged to have as one of my mentors Dr. Charles Coulson. He was a contemporary of Carl Rogers, Abraham Maslow, and other luminaries in the humanistic psychology movement—he knew them all very well. VR at its best reminds me of the idealism of humanistic ideologies. Positive humanism can be intoxicating because of its positivism—but there is a problem. I ask the reader to consider the wisdom of the older Dr. Maslow before we move on, because his insights serve as the perfect introduction to our next chapter and will be referred to from time to time, to make Dr. Maslow's wisdom real—not a virtual notion:

> "Maslow believed in evil, and we didn't.
> (referencing Rogers and Coulson) Maslow said
> there was danger in our thinking and acting as if
> there were no paranoids or psychopaths or SOBs
> to mess things up. We created a miniature
> utopian society, the encounter group." [127]

[127] Coulson, Charles. How I Wrecked the I. H. M. Nuns.The Latin Mass, Chronicle of Catholic Reform, Special Edition, 1994.

PART II

CHAPTER XV

DIGITAL FINGERPRINTS: You Can Run But You Cannot Hide

The vested interests funding, promoting, and making possible the adoption of VR technology delude consumers into thinking they are not participants, or for that matter products. If we are products and participants, then what are we participating in? What is our value as a product, and how much do we cost, and who purchases us? Let us disassemble alternative reality technology in order to answer those questions.

VR technology, software, and its various alternative reality iterations have recording and tracking devices built into them. Microphones, cameras, and location and position sensors, along with the conduits to deliver and send data to the cloud, satellites or other storage technology via WiFi, Bluetooth, or cellular links are integral to VR, AR, et al., technology.

You don't have to be a high-value target, a 007 agent in service to Her Majesty, for someone(s) to monitor where you go, how much time you spend there, what you look at, what you buy or don't buy, contribute money, vote for, attend to, and if so for how long or how soundly you sleep to be worthy of tracking—no, you just have to exist. And because you have money to spend, you're marketable—at least your VR fingerprint, to the highest bidder who wants to sell you something. But that is only part of the story and in the grand scheme of things is de minimis.

You might also be valuable to the NSA, TSA, CIA, FBI, and any of the other domestic and foreign acronym agencies because you are a person of interest. Do you have to be on a watch list, have a record, or be labeled as a domestic terrorist to warrant surveillance? No, you don't. You just have to be there, be alive, and do things using digital technology, especially VR, et al., technology. You'll know for certain that the smartest people on the planet believe in life after death when AI with an uplink is installed into your crypt—unless you were their enemy, in which case your crypt will be denied an uplink.

You may recall in Chapter One that I identified some of the most current AR devices in use as of the publication of this book (2021). One device was the Oculus VR Headset. Facebook acquired Oculus in 2014. In 2020, Mr. Zuckerberg required purchasers and users of Oculus VR to login using their Facebook accounts. Oculus

VR headsets capture terabytes of its user's biometric data[128] and relay those data to Mr. Zuckerberg's data mining farms, where they are packaged for sale and/or data mined in house for commercial purposes. On February 26, 2021, Facebook paid a $650 million fine to the state of Illinois [129] for violating its biometric law (BIPA)—specifically for using facial recognition technology and keeping its products' faces on file, presumably to be compared to other data sets kept by who knows who or what to keep tabs on you. And this is just the tip of the iceberg, to wit:

> *"Strapping these devices to ourselves lets us enter a virtual world, but at a price—these companies enter our lives and have access to intimate details about us through biometric data. How we move and interact with the world offers insight, by proxy, into how we think and feel at the moment. Eye-tracking technology, often seen in cognitive science, is already being developed by Vive, which sets the stage for unprecedented privacy and security risks. If aggregated, those in control of this biometric data may be able to identify patterns that let them more precisely predict (or cause) certain behavior and even emotions in the virtual world. It may allow companies to exploit users' emotional vulnerabilities through strategies that are difficult for the user to perceive and resist. What makes the collection of this sort of biometric data particularly frightening is that unlike a credit card or password, it is information about us we cannot change. Once collected, there is little*

---

[128] Biometric Data is a form of information related to your biometric characteristics, which may be used to identify you. Common examples include fingerprints, voiceprints, scans of a hand, facial geometry recognition, and iris or retina recognition. There are various state laws that define Biometric Data including "biometric identifiers" and "biometric information" as defined under the Illinois Biometric Information Privacy Act, "biometric identifiers" under the Texas Capture or Use of Biometric Identifier Act, "biometric identifiers" under the Washington Biometric Information Law, and "biometric information" under the California Consumer Privacy Act.

[129] Facebook denied guilt, which means by definition the $650 million "settlement" was tantamount to an allegation of leveraged extortion by the state of Illinois.

users can do to mitigate the harm done by leaks or data being monetized with additional parties." [130]

Privacy is a personal, legal, and moral precept that has been turned on its head by personalities adrenalized by alternative reality technologies. No matter where you go on earth, the notion of privacy exists, although where and when a person chooses to invoke their right to privacy is culturally bound.

Even when people dismissive of the importance of privacy declare things like "I have nothing to hide," these same people close the door while taking a bathroom break and pull their curtains while dressing. People dismissive of privacy protections are the same people who would not hesitate to call the police on a peeping Tom. But make no mistake, big tech, its government kindred spirits, and the agencies they empower are exponentially more violative of our privacy than any peeping Tom.

In an October 2020 study published in Scientific Reports, VR and AR technology proved to be almost flawless in its ability to identify its users/products digital fingerprints, to wit:

"Virtual reality (VR) is a technology that is gaining traction in the consumer market. With it comes an unprecedented ability to track body motions. These body motions are diagnostic of personal identity, medical conditions, and mental states. Previous work has focused on the identifiability of body motions in idealized situations in which some action is chosen by the study designer. In contrast, our work tests the identifiability of users under typical VR viewing circumstances, with no specially designed identifying task. Out of a pool of 511 participants, the system identifies 95% of users correctly when trained on less than 5 min of tracking data per person. We argue these results show nonverbal

---

[130] Electronic Frontier Foundation. *If Privacy Dies in VR, It Dies in Real Life. Story by: BY RORY MIR AND KATITZA RODRIGUEZAUGUST 25, 2020*

> *data should be understood by the public and by researchers as personally identifying data."* [131]

The researchers went on to document that certain medical diagnoses can be ascertained from monitoring your head movements, eye gaze, attention span, and reactivity measurements they uploaded from your VR headset to manufacturers, who can then sell those data to whomever finds value in those data—e.g., insurers, employers, licensing agencies, sellers of all stripes and colors, and of course, government. But if you think vacuuming up your most intimate personal, vocational, and business data is the worst of it—you ain't seen nothin yet.

Most people are aware, albeit vaguely, of how big tech, government and its acronym agencies vacuum up your personal information when online. Some have suspicions about their devices listening to them—in that regard, some people swear that after discussing a particular vacation destination or product among friends in the privacy of their own home, soon thereafter ads related to those topics of discussion mysteriously show up when they go online. Vacuuming intimate

[131] Mark Roman Miller, Fernanda Herrera, Hanseul Jun, James A. Landay & Jeremy N. Bailenson (2020) Personal identifiability of user tracking data during observation of 360-degree VR video. Scientific Reports, Stanford University, Stanford, CA, USA. https://doi.org/10.1038/s41598-020-74486-y

information is disturbing enough, but what if I told you that VR and its various technological conduits are not only physically modifying your brain, but inculcating into your mind what you believe, think about, want, need, who or what you like, dislike, vote for, donate to, boycott, and hold dear? I'm talking about all of those thoughts, feelings, and beliefs you hold dear that you are CONVINCED arose organically—that is, you believe what you believe and feel what you feel, because *you and you alone* came to hold those beliefs after careful and intelligent consideration.

I'll remind you again of Abraham Maslow's admonition to his fellow quixotic colleagues, who developed humanistic psychology with the best of intentions:

> "[M]aslow said there was danger in our thinking and acting as if there were no paranoids or psychopaths or SOBs to mess things up." [132]

It is not as though the paranoids, psychopaths, and/or SOBs running our world today are any different than their kindred spirits since time immemorial. Profiting from and controlling people have always energized certain personality types, many of whom now populate tech, cryptography, acronym agencies, and public offices. We've all heard it said, "there is nothing new under the sun," and that is true—but the means by which all those old things under the sun were accomplished in the past are new today. Let's take a trip down memory lane to illustrate how the psychopaths, paranoids, and SOBs, as Maslow referred to them, tracked and modified your thoughts, feelings, and behaviors *before* the advent of silicon chips.

Edward Bernays was the nephew of Sigmund Freud. In the early 1900s, he became fascinated with and ultimately became an early innovator in a burgeoning human behavior specialty he labeled "the social engineering of consent."[133] Socially engineering consent in Bernays' speak means this:

---

[132] Coulson, Charles. How I Wrecked the I. H. M. Nuns.The Latin Mass, Chronicle of Catholic Reform, Special Edition, 1994.

[133] Bernays, Edward L.; Cutler, H.W. (1955), The Engineering of Consent. University of Oklahoma Press.

***Bernays could make average people think, feel, and do things without their awareness.* This means people who have been socially engineered own the things they feel, think, and do. They believe with all their heart that the reason(s) they think, feel, and behave the way they do originated in them after careful consideration, and not because some faceless social engineer was paid to mold them to his employer's favor.**

Bernays justified his social engineering of people without their consent by arguing that the "common people" naturally behave irrationally and dangerously as a result of their herd instinct. His thoughts in this regard were nothing new when he gave voice to them in the early 20th century, to wit:

> *"Josiah Ober, an expert in the classics at Stanford University, said this about the term democracy: '[A]ncient critics of popular rule sought to rebrand Demokratia as the equivalent of a tyrannical 'polloi-archia'—as the monopolistic domination of government apparatus by the many who were poor...[P]lacing democracy on a par with oligarchy , as little more, in principle or practice, than the monopoly over established governmental offices by, respectively, the many (poor) and the few (wealthy), is to accept fifth-century anti-democratic polemics as an accurate description of political reality.' [134](Emphasis Added) As far back as ancient Greece, it was fully understood that the seemingly "fair" notion of rule by "common people" (demos) can, and almost certainly will, result in tyranny by the masses using the cudgel of popularity and majority rule as its mechanism of tyranny. Greek Philosopher Plato preceded many other great thinkers who cautioned us about the perils and pitfalls of democracy: 'In democracy, the lower class grows bigger and bigger. The poor become the winners. Diversity is supreme. People*

---

[134] Stanford University. By: Josiah Ober. The original meaning of "democracy:" Capacity to do things, not majority rule. September, 2007.

are free to do what they want and live how they want. People can even break the law if they so chose. This appears to be very similar to anarchy.'" [135]

Bernays demonstrated his expertise in mind control by successfully stampeding the demos to adopt any number of "new" attitudes and behaviors about whatever he had been paid to change. He changed what we ate for breakfast, e.g., from cereals and grains to pig meat and eggs. He persuaded women to take up smoking, changed the way architects designed single-family residences, and persuaded hundreds of thousands of men to fight wars they felt they should stay out of—that is, until Mr. Bernays and his employers in the United States government decided to modify their behavior to serve their purposes.

With regard to war, Bernays, along with his colleagues, Carl Byoir and John Price Jones, manipulated public opinion to support America's involvement in World War I (WWI). One of Bernays' cohorts involved in the coercion of consent over WWI was songwriter George M. Cohan. Cohan's seemingly organic patriotic song, "Over There," got the demos all worked up over Germany and helped to motivate a war-weary American public to enter the war. If you have ever hummed this tune or sang this song, or even heard it played, please appreciate the fact that you were parroting or listening to a clever social engineering ploy in the form of a song that motivated men to fight and die in a war they knew little or nothing about—and up until Bernays got involved, not only had no interest in fighting, but believed that staying out of the war was the most patriotic thing they could do. Here is a sampling of the lyrics:

Lyrics to "Over There" by George M. Cohan

Johnnie get your gun, get your gun, get your gun
Take it on the run, on the run, on the run
Hear them calling you and me
Every son of liberty

---

[135] Cahn, Steven M. (2002), Classics of Political and Moral Philosophy, Oxford University Press, with reference to the words of Plato.

Hurry right away, no delay, go today
Make your daddy glad to have had such a lad
Tell your sweetheart not to pine
To be proud her boy's in line.

In addition to songs sung in town squares, parades, and patriotic rallies, the predecessor to digital technology—cellulose newspapers and their owners—socially engineered motivation for the war.

> *"On this, the 100th anniversary of the day the First World War began, it is sobering to look back at the way that conflict was so badly reported. The catalogue of journalistic misdeeds is a matter of record: the* ***willingness to publish propaganda as fact****, the apparently tame* ***acceptance of censorship*** *and the* ***failure to hold power to account****. But a sweeping condemnation of the press coverage is unjust because journalists, as ever, were prevented from informing the public by three powerful forces—****the government, the military and their own proprietors.*** *It is undeniable that newspapers began by demonizing the German enemy. They published* ***fabricated stories of German barbarism****, which were accepted as fact. Although Belgian and French citizens were executed as reprisals by the German army in the early months of the war, many unverifiable stories—later dubbed "atrocity propaganda" —were wholly untrue.* ***Editors and journalists were therefore guilty."***[136] (Emphasis added)

And none other than Nazi brain trust Hermann Goering understood the demos instinct and how easy it is to make people do what you want them to do without one iota of awareness that what they think, feel, and believe had been socially engineered. Imagine what Herr Goering could do with V the Reality:

> *"Why of course the people don't want war. Why should some poor slob on a farm want to risk his life in a war when the best he can get out of it*

---

136 National Guardian. First world war: how state and press kept truth off the front page. Story by: Roy Greenslade, July 27, 2014.

> *is to come back to his farm in one piece? Naturally the common people don't want war: neither in Russia, nor in England, nor for that matter in Germany. That is understood. But after all it is the leaders of a country who determine the policy and it is always a simple matter to drag the people along, whether it is a democracy or fascist dictatorship, or a parliament or a communist dictatorship. Voice or no voice, the people can always be brought to the bidding of the leaders. That is easy. All you have to do is tell them they are being attacked, and denounce the peace-makers for lack of patriotism and exposing the country to danger. It works the same in any country."*[137]

Perhaps the most pernicious quality of all effective social engineering—but in particular alternative reality technology—is that it is entertaining, fun, and ego-boosting. In order to find the who, what, when, where, why, and how behind social engineering you have to become more discerning than the character Neo in the movie The Matrix.

It is not merely the brilliantly opaque nature of VR/AR/AI that keeps the Agent Smiths of tech, government, their acronym agencies, and multinational corporations hidden from view; it is the participant/product that is in a deep state of denial about his or her immunity to being tracked, modified, and molded to be one of Agent Smith's most exemplary creations, aka YOU! After all, I've already documented FAR beyond a reasonable doubt that your brains have been physically modified by alternative reality technology. Yet if the reader chronicles their own reactions up to this point, even THAT wasn't enough to move you—to know that your brain had been physically modified was taken in stride.

Just think: the tissues in your brain have been permanently changed by VR. Even that is not enough to make a dent in your defenses. Literal and obvious social

---

[137] This quote was part of a conversation Gustave Gilbert held with Hermann Goering in his jail cell on the evening of 18 April 1946 during a three-day Easter recess of the Nuremberg Trials. Gilbert was a German-speaking intelligence officer and psychologist tasked by the Allies to gather intelligence on their Nazi prisoners. Gilbert published Goering's quote in his book: *Nuremberg Diary*.

engineering is never used, e.g., implanting microchips, wearing surgical respirators—out of the question. Do you know why? Here is a rule of thumb: If you can identify social engineering, it isn't social engineering. What you are sure is social engineering or government control may be a strategy to make you think it is social engineering, so that you will rebel and oppose it. It is your oppositional behavior that is the desired end result of social engineering.

Social psychologists have documented, and my own clinical and forensic experience has confirmed, that people tend to deny or greatly underestimate their susceptibility to mind control—believing that they are the ones in control of what they think and feel. Even the most iconoclastic and independent-minded person is not immune to social engineering without their awareness. This tendency to believe "you are in control" is even more exaggerated in virtual reality settings. [138] When people do find out that they have been duped or manipulated, their first response is almost always denial. This denial is rooted in the fact that it is psychologically unpleasant to become aware of the fact that you have become an unwilling participant and product. Even when the likes of Mark Zuckerberg come out and tell you what your role is in his grand schemes and aspirations—using plain English—participant's/product's defense mechanisms reign supreme, to wit:

Esquire Style Culture Watches Life SUBSCRIBE NEWSLETTER UK

Mark Zuckerberg Called People Who Handed Over Their Data "Dumb F****"

I doubt that users of Oculus VR or any of the other VR technologies "handed" over their data in as much that participants/products probably had no idea what those data are, or that they are participants and products, not users—who knew a reliable medical diagnosis could be made about you if viewed by the right people? Who

[138] Hobbs, Christin; Kreiner, Honeycutt; Hinds, Brockman (2010). "The Illusion of Control in a Virtual Reality Setting". North American Journal of Psychology. 12 (3). Archived from the original on 2016-06-01.

knew your political affiliations, gender identity, and sexual proclivities were being handed over? Probably Mr. Zuckerberg, but as his lawyers declared while they KNEW they were handing over to the state of Illinois $650 million for violating the state's laws against vacuuming up biometric data, "Facebook denies any and all wrongdoing." [139] But something more profound is going on, and it goes right to the heart of one of our running themes throughout this book.

What is afoot is best described as a war on objective reality. In the early stages of the war, humans were bedazzled by the technology. Social conformity did its magic as more and more people joined the digital club. Then the technology became affordable. It then showed up everywhere—at school, at work, at home and in your car. Soon thereafter, humans were persuaded that virtual reality is equal to objective reality in terms of meaning, value, and importance in life. The next stage of the war manipulated virtual reality such that man was no longer able, but mostly did not desire, to tell the difference between what is true and objective, and the virtual reality he carries with him in his CNS. The edict imposed on all social engineering soldiers as they waged/wage this war is:

Ensure that participants and products remain unaware of what is happening to them. Who is winning the war between awareness and denial? Do I have to ask?

Ever hear the old adage: "Are you going to believe me or your lying eyes?" A mid-20th century psychologist named Muzafer Sherif conducted studies on the core principle found in this adage. Sherif set about to get to the bottom of how and why people tend to conform their thoughts, emotions, and behaviors to the herd instinct. Sherif placed a research subject in a darkened room and displayed a point of light on a screen, not unlike an eye examination where the patient sits in a darkened room and visualizes letters. Sherif set the experiment up with the research subject either sitting alone, or accompanied by confederates of his choosing who had been

---

[139] When Facebook declared its absolute innocence but paid the State of Illinois $650 million it tacitly declared that it had been extorted by the State of Illinois.

coached to respond according to plan. One of the tasks designed by Sherif was to simply have the research subject report how much and what kind of movement the point of light made. Sherif took advantage of something called the Autokinetic Effect, wherein a stationary point of light projected upon a screen in a darkened room will appear to move based upon the neuro-optical physiology of the visual processing centers in the brain. When the subject sat alone, he would report his own perceptions of movement. When, on the other hand, research subjects were accompanied by Sherif's confederates, each of whom had been coached to report contrived amounts of movement, research subjects modified and denied their perceptions in order to conform them to the confederates' perceptions.

I want to stress that it was not that research subjects knew in their hearts that the point of light only moved so much but conformed their stated opinion to match that of the group to avoid a conflict or debate the issue. No, the research subject's perceptions were actually modified by the influence of the group. Even the most stalwart and independent-minded subjects came to doubt their perceptions and beliefs. [140]

Solomon Asch, working in the 1950s, was another early researcher who investigated how people can be controlled to deny their own perceptions by passive or unconscious group pressure. The key here is the word "passive." Asch showed an unsuspecting research subject in a group of five other confederates (in on the study) a line drawn on a card. He then showed the subject three other cards labeled "A", "B" or "C." Each of the cards had a different length of line drawn on it. The test subject, who was permitted to compare in real time the original card with the alphabet cards, was asked to identify which of the three cards most closely matched the length of the line drawn on the original card. What do think happened? Remarkably, 75% of research subjects gave an incorrect answer to at least one question because their perceptions and beliefs had been controlled, without their awareness, by the

---

[140] Muzafer Sherif. (Jul. - Oct., 1937), An Experimental Approach to the Study of Attitudes. Sociometry, Vol. 1, No. 1/2 pp. 90-98 American Sociological Association.

passive psychological effects of the confederates who knowingly gave false answers. When it comes to perception, it is well known that by manipulating the wants of the perceiver, one can modify the ease with which he can be manipulated. Many of us have experienced a naturally occurring form of this phenomenon. For instance, have you ever been expecting an important call, only to swear you heard your phone ring when it did not? If you answered yes, then YOU have experienced the phenomenon I'm talking about.

Now, compare the context of human beings pre-digital ,where mass mind control was limited by the means by which social engineers could reach a critical mass of people, e.g., cellulose newspapers, magazines, radio, TV, and in-person get-togethers. In the olden days, Americans had only three major television networks, and the most popular shows never reached more than a small percentage of households at the same time. Also, once the half-hour or hour show was over, that was it. Even national advertising had its limits, not to mention that in those days, lots of people didn't have TVs—or if they did, they didn't sit in front of them 24/7. Enter VR.

H.G. Wells, the author of *Brave New World*, foresaw advancements in mass communication technology and how one day those scientific wonders would make mass indoctrination possible for the first time in human history. Over 75 years ago, H. G. Wells sensed the vast potentialities of these inventions when he wrote in the New York Times:

> *"Modern means of communication—the power afforded by print, telephone, wireless and so forth, of rapidly putting through directive strategic or technical conceptions to a great number of cooperating centers, of getting quick replies and effective discussion, have opened up a new world of political processes. Ideas and phrases can now be given effectiveness, greater than the effectiveness of any personality and stronger than any sectional interest. The common design can be documented and sustained against perversion and betrayal. It can be*

> *elaborated and developed steadily and widely without personal, local and sectional misunderstanding.'"*[141]

VR, et al., represents the quintessential manifestation of H.G. Well's prescient warnings regarding technology and global mind control. Keep in mind, however, that all VR technologies require a supplicant audience—an audience that has allowed themselves to be made into products and participants, not owners/users.

---

[141] Bernays, Edward L. (1928), Propaganda. Ig Publishing, Brooklyn, New York.

CHAPTER XVI

FROM PRODUCT & PARTICIPANT TO: Owner & User

Let's be realistic: VR genies will not be put back in their bottles. Not only can't this be done, but also, people love their genies, and too much money has and will be made from them to even consider this a remote possibility. Moreover, VR et al, including everything but V the Reality, has too much to offer humanity to shut it down—not that you can, of course.

On other hand, V the Reality is a difference in kind when compared to alternative reality tech, in that embedded within V the Reality is the subordination of the very essence of what it means to be a free, sentient being. Therefore, if we are to survive with warmth in an all-too-cold world along with every other sentient being then V the Reality must be vanquished as smallpox was vanquished. Yes, the smallpox virus still exists, but we know where it is, and it is guarded day and night.

> **Accepting V the Reality as a cultural norm is dangerous, no matter how well we learn to control our data. When we subordinate the OR world, as we do by definition in a V the Reality world, we surgically remove those areas of our brain that make possible the central traits of warmth and critical discernment. V the Reality is the natural mindset for those who**

lack the ability to feel for and with other sentient beings and/or who also lack discernment.

To put my last declaration in context, permit me to share with you the words of George Orwell from his masterpiece *1984*. He may not have had a clear vision of the various AR headsets or AI, Atlas or Spot creations, but he understood human psychopathology and predicted that sooner or later, we'd destroy ourselves if we developed the means to do it on a mass scale.

> *"In our world there will be no emotions except fear, rage, triumph, and self-abasement. Everything else we shall destroy everything. Already we are breaking down the habits of thought, which have survived from before the Revolution. We have cut the links between child and parent, and between man and man, and between man and woman. No one dares trust a wife or a child or a friend any longer. But in the future, there will be no wives and no friends. Children will be taken from their mothers at birth, as one takes eggs from a hen. The sex instinct will be eradicated. Procreation will be an annual formality like the renewal of a ration card. We shall abolish the orgasm. Our neurologists are at work upon it now. There will be no loyalty, except loyalty towards the Party. There will be no love, except the love of Big Brother. There will be no laughter, except the laugh of triumph over a defeated enemy. There will be no art, no literature, and no science. When we are omnipotent, we shall have no more need of science. There will be no distinction between beauty and ugliness. There will be no curiosity, no enjoyment of the process of life. All competing pleasures will be destroyed. But always -- do not forget this, Winston -- always there will be the intoxication of power, constantly increasing and constantly growing subtler. Always, at every moment, there will be the thrill of victory, the sensation of*

trampling on an enemy who is helpless. If you want a picture of the future, imagine a boot stamping on a human face — for ever.' " [142]

A great place to begin restoring our freedom, personhood, privacy, and humanity is to become an owner/user and not a product/participant of the alternative technologies we use—including social media.

An owner/user maintains strict control over *their* data. This means that owners/users have singular access to a detailed chain of custody map of where *their* data traveled and is stored. Notice I did not include "how those data are viewed and/or used," because that notion of "use" and "view" by an identifiable third party must become easily rescindable and easily verifiable by average people, if not made illegal with harsh penalties when violated, if we are no longer going to be products and participants. Bulletproof data encryption is the sine qua non of being an owner/user.

When it comes to social engineering and our consent using alternative realities conveyed through digital technologies, we must have the right and the means to quickly and easily learn the identities of who pays for our social engineering of consent—with "social engineering of consent" defined in statutory language as part of our civil and criminal codes, that if violated are enforceable by courts of law. If readers are paying attention, your heads are shaking with incredulity— "This will never happen." Whatever the outcome, it is important to wrap our arms around the new Bonnie and Clyde—AR, AI, VR, et al., government, its acronym agencies, and the oligarchs who live and work in the shadows. And don't forget those peeping Toms we just can't seem to stop, no matter what we do.

Let's take a closer look at something we have all heard of—cookies. I will use this content as purely introductory to what is in the wings, ready to take center stage later in this book. The purpose of this introduction is to orient the reader to

---

[142] Orwell, George. *1984*, page 176. SIGNET CLASSICS, Published by New American Library, a division of Penguin Group (USA) Inc., 375 Hudson Street, New York, New York 10014, USA.

the most basic, inconsequential personal data vacuuming that has affected all of us. I'm talking about cookies.

Right off the bat, the term "cookie", whether intended or not, elicits warm feelings from lots of people. Yet a digital cookie is anything but warm and fuzzy. Would not a better name be "Trojan Horse" or "bug?" Let us compare some definitions:

> ***COOKIE:*** *Cookie or cookie profiling, also called web profiling, is the use of persistent or permanent cookies to* ***track a user's overall*** *activity online. This tracking does not just happen when you are on a particular site, but it occurs the whole time you are browsing. This kind of profiling activity is often done by marketers who buy advertising rights on thousands of popular websites in order to collect and collate cookie information and* ***create a single "profile" of a user****. Internet advertising, as it is called, targets potential customers based on the* ***manner they browse the Internet****. This is the very reason why most websites flash banner ads on their pages. This matter may not be a big deal for some, but others take their privacy seriously and are uneasy about being "followed around" and profiled.*[143] (Emphasis added)
>
> **Trojan Horse:** The Trojan Horse is the wooden horse from the Trojan War used by the Greeks **to enter the city of Troy** and win the war. The horse was effective because it did not look like it served the purpose of its designers—that is, to break into the city of Troy where citizens felt safe.
>
> **Bug:** verb (bugs, bugging, bugged) [with object] to conceal a miniature microphone in (a room or telephone) in order to monitor or record someone's conversations: the telephones in the presidential palace were bugged. Record or monitor (a conversation) by concealing a microphone in a room or telephone.

---

[143] Allaboutcookies.org.

As if to prove our thesis that the terms "bug" and "Trojan Horse" would have been better names for "cookies," a notorious virus named Trojan Horse has become part of our digital vernacular. And of course, the term "bug" is what any number of acronym agencies to this day call a wiretap—with the term "wiretap" representing a beautiful example of the value of the etymology of terms of art. Yes, we used to rely upon actual wires to communicate with one another, and literally wires would be "tapped" into, either at relay junctions or by literally cutting and splicing.

Notwithstanding the etymology of the terms "Trojan Horse" and "bug," it strikes me that the term "cookie" is the poorest descriptor of its purpose and intended function. Cookies rely upon Trojan Horse psychology (can you easily find where your browsing cookies are located? Have you looked at them lately?) With regard to "bugs?" The term "bug" is the quintessential digital age definition of a cookie.

What follows is a telling illustration of cookies and how the unwary participant/product is exploited. Here we have a website that educates interested parties on how AR can transform frontline operations. I chose an AR site to make the greater poetic point.

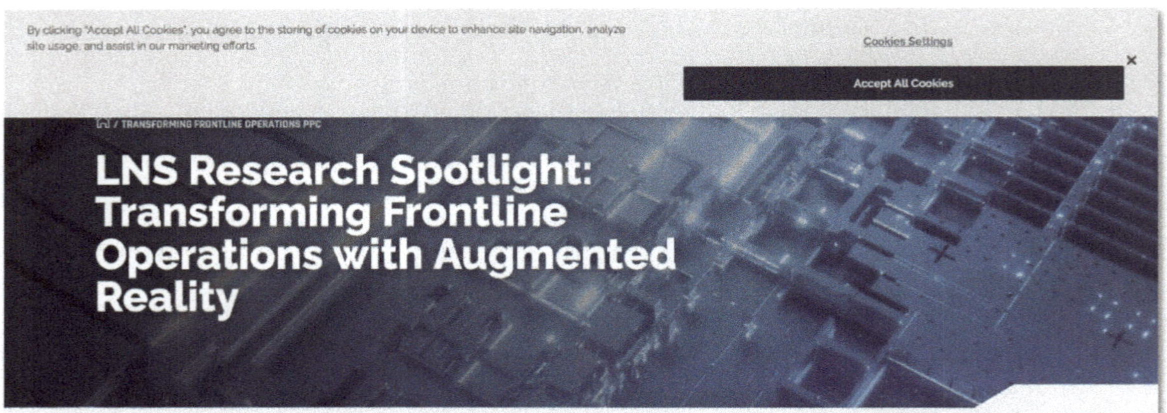

Please take note of the fact that the default cookie setting is "Accept All Cookies," and that even in California where we have consumer protection laws regarding web privacy, we are required to click on "Cookies Settings" —note the plural "cookies" — before I can push back on the "Accept All Cookies" default setting. Before I could click on "Cookies Settings," I'm presented with a pop-up introducing LNS's bot:

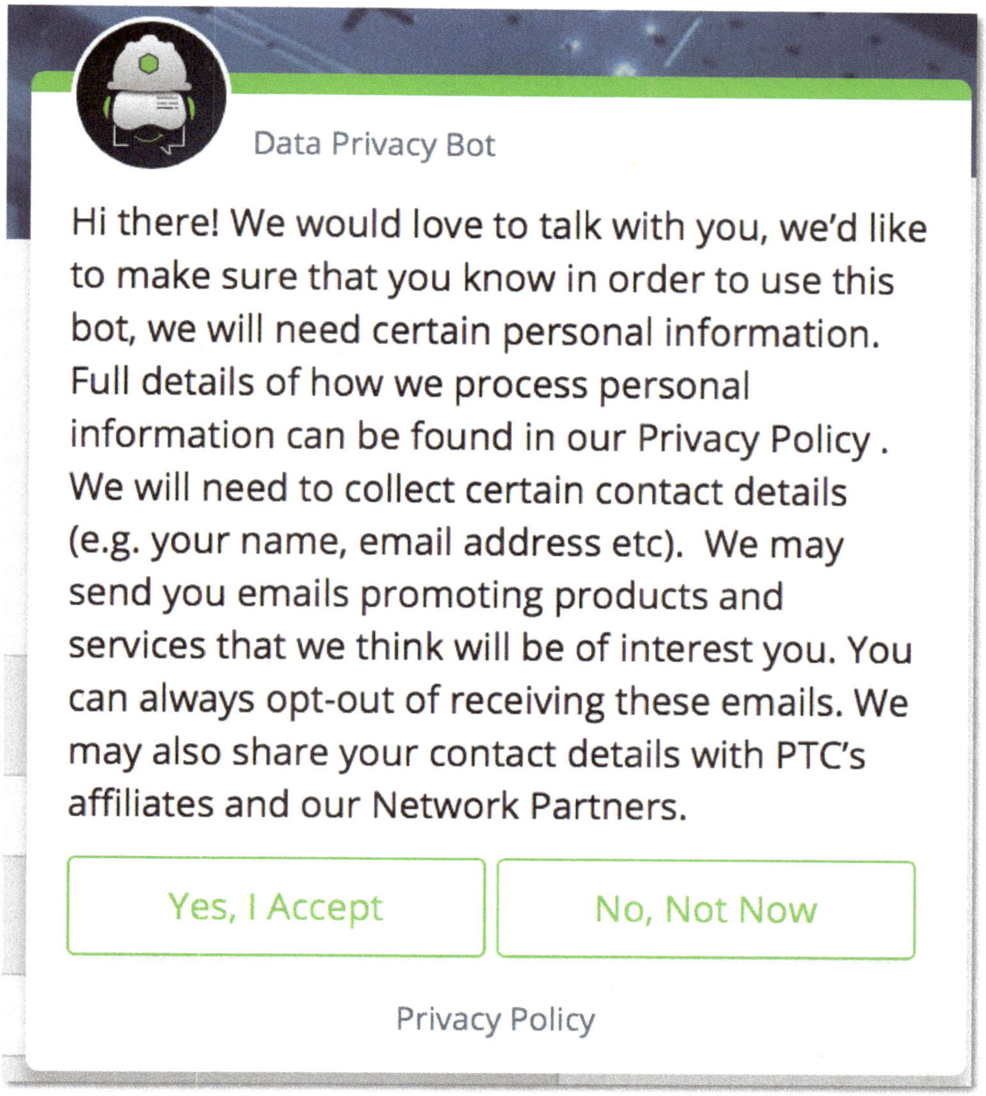

So, if I were to use this chatbot, I am warned, as a California resident, that I will be bugged, tracked, followed online, and that my personal data—everything that has been vacuumed by my Internet Service Provider (ISP)—will be sold to PTS and "our Network Partners." If you do not live in a state that has such stringent privacy protections as California, you may not be provided these warnings. So, what are this website's cookie settings once you click on them?

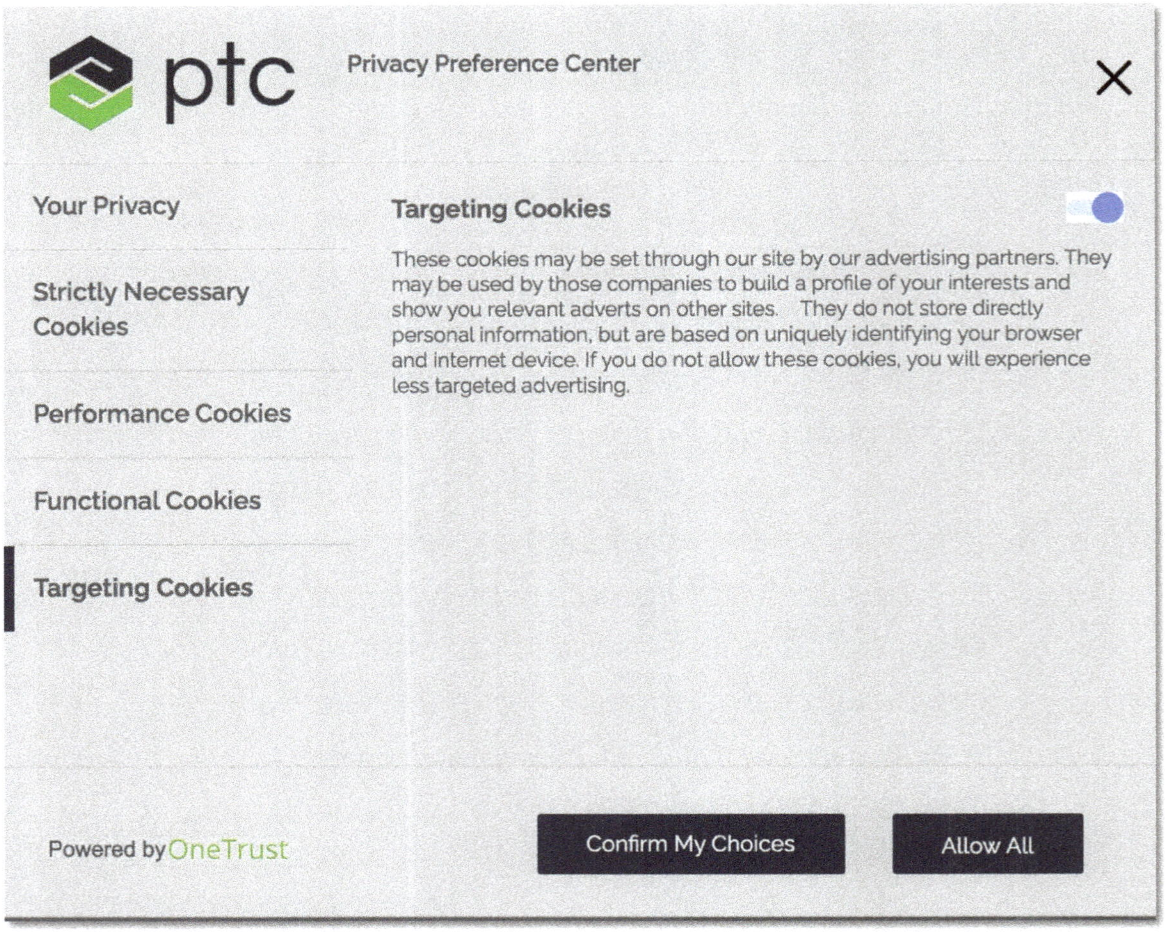

Note that "Targeting Cookies" (accept) is the default choice. What are targeting cookies? From the LNS website:

> *"These cookies may be set through our site by our advertising partners. They may be used by those companies to build a profile of your interests and show you relevant adverts on other sites. They do not store directly personal information, but are based on uniquely identifying your browser and internet device. If you do not allow these cookies, you will experience less targeted advertising."*

"Advertising partners" is one of those terms of art, rather like the term "cookie," that taps into the positive halo valence of "partner" —Partner? Here is LNS's definition of its various cookies:

- **STRICTLY NECESSARY COOKIES:** These cookies are necessary for the website to function and cannot be switched off in our systems. They are usually only set in response to actions made by you which amount to a request for services, such as setting your privacy preferences, logging in, or filling in forms. You can set your browser to block or alert you about these cookies, but some parts of the site will not then work. These cookies do not store any personally identifiable information.

- **PERFORMANCE COOKIES:** These cookies allow us to count visits and traffic sources so we can measure and improve the performance of our site. They help us to know which pages are the most and least popular and see how visitors move around the site. All information these cookies collect is aggregated and therefore anonymous. If you do not allow these cookies, we will not know when you have visited our site and will not be able to monitor its performance.
- **FUNCTIONAL COOKIES:** These cookies enable the website to provide enhanced functionality and personalization. They may be set by us or by third party providers whose services we have added to our pages. If you do not allow these cookies, then some or all of these services may not function properly.
- **TARGETING COOKIES:** These cookies may be set through our site by our advertising partners. They may be used by those companies to build a profile of your interests and show you relevant adverts on other sites. They do not store directly personal information, but are based on uniquely identifying your browser and hardware device. If you do not allow these cookies, you will experience less targeted advertising.

This particular website originates in the United Kingdom. The UK has pretty good privacy laws, similar to those on the books in California. As I hope I have illustrated, however, you and I are viewed as products and participants, not users entitled to privacy. And even when afforded some legal protections, people defined (without our knowledge) as products and participants have to run the gauntlet to marginally modify what I argue is a right, i.e., privacy, not a privilege.

Imagine if this is what products and participants are faced with by simply accessing a website. What would your status as a product and participant be like if you are using a dressing room, medical diagnostic tool uplink, eyeglasses, makeup or other AR shopping/buying tool? What if you are out and about on a city street, department store, or driving in your car or someone else's car? Retinal scans, facial recognition, height, weight, shopping habits, friends, body temperature, and only things the acronym agencies know, and even if this author knew about in detail could not tell you, is the operational definition of V the Reality.

Back to Eric Schmidt for a moment, because he is one of the, if not THE, world's most prolific and powerful advocates **for government-funded AI tracking infrastructures.** Mr. Schmidt is chairman of the National Security Commission on Artificial Intelligence (NSCAI) and recently stepped down as chair of the Defense Innovation Board (DIB). Although Mr. Schmidt is chairman of NSCAI, he brought along with him the who's who of Silicon Valley. These people *are* big tech, and all of them have the cell phone numbers of the most powerful people in at least two branches of the U.S. government—and certainly many of them can get an audience with world leaders with one contact attempt. The case for the nexus between big tech and government(s) isn't hard to make, because they are quite literally in bed with one another. Notwithstanding what you may hear or read on your screens, these bedfellows wake up and go to bed together, and have for a very long time.

Earlier we touched upon what motivates the employers of social engineers to transform OR into V the Reality. We also reviewed what motivates governments to get involved. I dare say that we all should have a pretty good guess about what motivates government, their bureaucracies, and acronym agencies that work in unison with big tech. The allocation of time and resources goes something like this: Big tech provides the gadgets, software, gizmos and design expertise, and government along with big tech provides the infrastructure and data storage and mining farms.

To hear Mr. Schmidt wax on about his vision of the future is like reading the screenplay for *The Polar Express*—it is magical. He probably believes what he says for the most part. After OR is processed through the prisms residing in his CNS, he probably has a hard time comprehending why any well-adjusted person would not yearn for his globally connected alternative reality world. Perhaps if Mr. Schmidt were in charge of the efferent and afferent data routes in our CNS, then those concerned about civil liberties could put their minds at ease—or maybe not. Mr. Schmidt said this in 2010:

> *"One of the things that eventually happens ... is that we don't need you to type at all," Eric Schmidt, Google's former CEO, said in a moment of candor in 2010. "Because we know where you are. We know where you've been. We can more or less guess what you're thinking about." He later added: "One day we had a conversation where we figured we could just try to predict the stock market. And then we decided it was illegal. So we stopped doing that."*[144]

What few people appreciate is a nifty legerdemain that we've discussed at some length in previous chapters. Denial and the failure to draw tethers to seemingly isolated islands of data allows readers to gloss over Mr. Schmidt's statement, "We more or less guess what you're thinking about," and those who do hold it with some degree of traction you probably concluded that "they" can guess what you are thinking about, because they have been tracking you. And although that is true in part, the bombshell insight is much more profound:

> **The primary reason "they" can more or less guess what you are thinking about—and I will add feel and believe—is because "they" inculcated into your mind, into your actual tissues, those thoughts, feelings, and behaviors you swear are your own—organically grown only after careful and reasoned consideration.**

Mr. Schmidt, as of the publication of this book (2021), still holds over $5 billion in Google (Alphabet) stock. The Electronic Privacy Information Center got access to one of Mr. Schmidt's presentations before the NSCAI where he said: "Surveillance is one of the 'first-and-best customers' for AI." [145]

---

[144] National Guardian. Google's Earth: how the tech giant is helping the state spy on us. By: Yasha Levine, December 20, 2018.

[145] Electronic Privacy Information Center, reproduced in The Intercept, "Screen New Deal" by Naomi Klein, May 8, 2020.

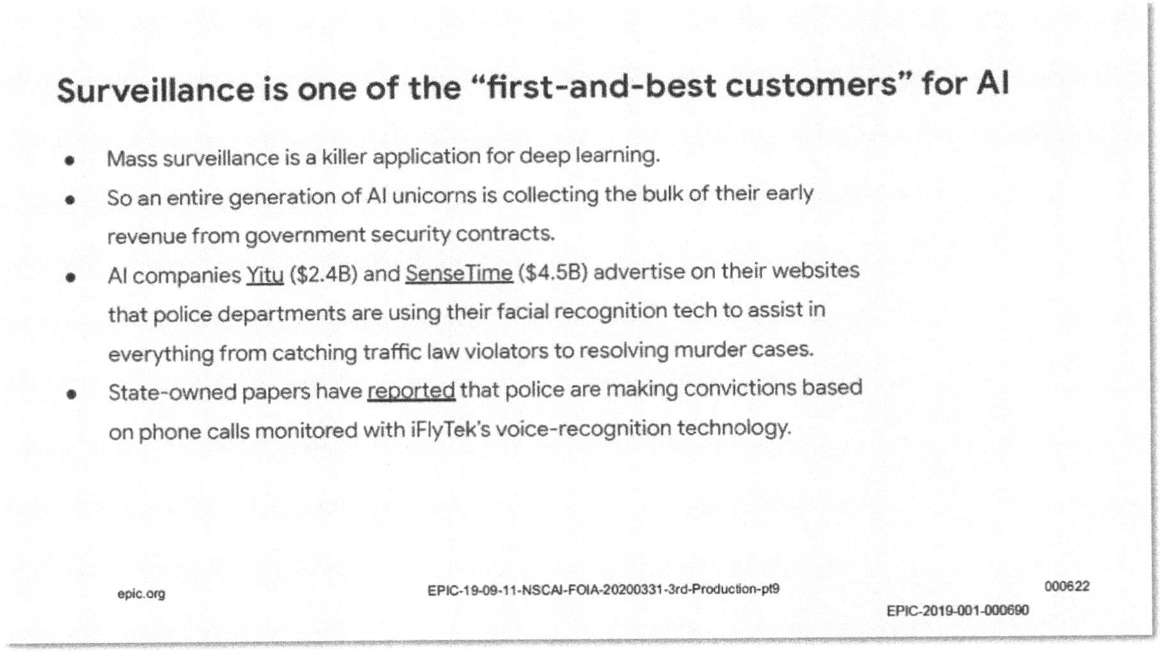

The thrust of his sales pitch was to stoke the fires of competition between China and the USA. China's advantages in mass surveillance are not so much related to their technological expertise, but to their culture's central planning statist ethos, absent the civil liberty of personal freedom. Without constitutionally protected civil liberties, the only thing keeping China from becoming the world's foremost gill netting of mass surveillance is the infrastructure hardware and the funding to make it happen. In places where civil liberties have not been completely abandoned, Mr. Schmidt's dreams run into interference like a pleasant dream interrupted by a dog barking. It is that dog barking that Mr. Schmidt argues must be quieted, even if it means killing the dog, for his and the government's dreams to come true.

Sales pitches never tell the whole truth, whether it is Eric Schmidt, that local team member down at your favorite automobile dealership, or politicians—especially politicians. The Patriot Act was promoted and sold as a means by which free-floating anxiety among U.S. citizens would be ameliorated, i.e., "you'll be safe—we'll protect you" from terrorists. Washington State Congressman Jim McDermott, MD, a psychiatrist by training, made this comment about the Patriot Act: "You can make people do anything if they are afraid." I might add the free-floating anxiety from color-coded terrorism threat levels were cultivated by the same forces in government that promised to save citizens from it. Part of the safety bargain purchased by the American public required them to trade their civil liberties for a *sense* of safety though few people understood the bargain to include that tradeoff. And just like car buying, once you sign the papers, there is no three-day cooling-off period.

The fear of losing the tech race to China harkens back to the space race between the USSR and the USA in the late 1950s and '60s. When the USSR rocketed Sputnik into orbit around the earth in 1957, the race was on. In 2021, not a day goes by that one or more of the branches of the media entertainment complex drives home the point that China is America's biggest threat, and we are in a race for our very survival. More often than not, it is the tech race that is the focus of the story.

A race between countries predictably winds people up and makes voters more receptive to Mr. Schmidt's and colleagues' plans to install a surveillance infrastructure in every Standard Metropolitan Statistical Area (SMSA) in America, then the world. They know this would permanently modify life on earth. In 1999, speaking before the National Press Club, the late social commentator and comedian George Carlin gave his audience this prescient message:

> *"I'm a man for the millennium digital and smoke free I've been inputted out sourced uplinked and downloaded I have software on my hard drive and I can give you a gigabyte in a nanosecond I'm factory authorized returnable fully equipped built to last and I'm definitely biodegradable...[I]'ve been dumbed down with smart bonds I'm in denial I'm in recovery but I'm out of the loop I'm also on the bubble a high-tech...[I] use the f-word and my email a new wave from the old school and if I'm not at ground zero you can reach me at square one I'm gender specific voice-activated capital-intensive heat-seeking faith-*

based and work-related but I'm definitely not group oriented I'm online I'm in line but most the time I'm out of line." [146]

Anyone who thinks that connected minds are not social engineers and governments' dream-come-true playground have not left their house much these past couple of years (2020-2021). Since COVID-19, that includes almost everybody. Therefore, it should not surprise anyone that big tech and their co-conspirators in governments all across the globe have capitalized on the lockdowns *necessarily put into place to flatten the infection curve of SARS-CoV-2.* I'll digress a moment to address those readers who may have little experience in social engineering, but have a healthy imagination, if not paranoia. My purpose here is to keep readers rooted in empiricism, not their fears and especially their imagination when it comes to COVID-19.

Lots of people have grown suspicious of government, a suspicion that grew during the great SARS-CoV-2 pandemic of 2019 and subsequent years. And while it is true that upon occasion government initiates a hoax, ruse, or false flag event in order to reel in what it wants, that is not how governments work most of the time. Much more common is the practice of exploiting and/or integrating a naturally occurring threat to health and safety into its overarching plans or aspirations. This happened with COVID-19, to wit:

> *"Human behavior is inextricably linked to the COVID-19 black swan event. Once we found ourselves in the middle of the latest of a long history of pandemics, we couldn't get out of our own way because of our customs, fears, and self-destructive tendency to game everything we come in contact with, along with the seemingly insatiable need for everyone from politicians to social media stars to exploit every national tragedy so they can be a "somebody." Politicians schooled in political science and the law had no idea what was happening with these*

---

[146] National Press Club: Guest Speaker George Carlin, May 13, 1999. https://www.youtube.com/watch?v=Pc0ZHsoHAlE

invisible terrors that had been given names more confusing to them than the names given to artificial sweeteners. And if they didn't know what and why it was happening, they surely had no idea as to what to do. So they did the only thing they know how: they imposed blunt force behavioral modification edicts on citizens who already didn't trust them before anyone had ever heard of COVID-19. [W]hen members of the general public believe, and for good reason, that virtually everything presented to them by the media entertainment complex is gamed, massaged, and motivated by partisan ideologies; when they realize that the people they voted into office are often motivated by their desire to exercise authority for authorities' sake and to preserve their job no matter what it takes, their mistrust can easily devolve to the point where they become unhinged from reality during events like COVID-19. This is especially true when people become scared and feel like they have little or no control. Sadly, the American public appears to prefer partisan theater posing as journalism over objective reportage—perhaps because they know nothing else. People in a decompensated state of mind unconsciously distort reality in order to assuage their shredded nerves. It is not a coincidence that by coming to believe that the COVID-19 pandemic is not real, or certainly not as bad as government officials say it is, their fears are assuaged. Even believing that the government or some other unseen power created the COVID-19 pandemic makes people feel better, because at least some evil entity caused all of my fear, not an unseen, very real threat that cannot be easily controlled." [147]

As Miss Klein, writing for the Intercept, took note, before the pandemic the sales pitch for Mr. Schmidt's and friends' surveillance nirvana focused upon convenience,

---

[147] Napoleon, Anthony (2020), COVID-19 HUMAN BEHAVIOR. VBW Publishing, College Station, Texas. Page 52, ¶2; Page 55, ¶5-Page 56¶ 1-2.

frictionless interactions and personalization. I'd also add to that list the allure of the Google IQ phenomenon, where average folks are promised immediate access using AI, et al., to the inner workings of the stuff of PhD dissertations that can now be easily accessible simply by where you direct your gaze or point and click. The new AR image placed into the heads of the average person is that you, too, can now look over the shoulder of a surgeon performing heart transplant surgery—and then you, too, can perform a heart transplant with a little practice, if only someone in power would let you do it. Expand that delusion from surgery to flying fighter jets, and then running the world. Instant equilibrium between the average person and our brightest and most educated—had for only the price of a digital device.

> ***The unintended consequences of alternative reality technologies and their effects upon human biopsychosocial fabrics are not to be taken lightly.***

As far as unintended consequences are concerned, Edward Bernays' social engineering efforts to get Americans to enter WWI provides us a classic cautionary tale. One would think that it was bad enough persuading reluctant young men to fight and die in WWI—but it was much worse.

Bernays' brilliant but devious social engineering ploy to get farm boys from across the United States to go to Europe and fight a war they knew nothing about resulted in the great pandemic of 1918. Go back 100 years to the state of Kansas in the USA. This is where we find farmers involved in the business of breeding, raising, and then slaughtering pigs, cows, chickens, and other animals as their way to make money. At least one of these doomed creatures housed a replicating virus we came to label the H1N1 virus. That virus jumped to one of the farmers, who then spread his virus payload to other unsuspecting humans.

> *"No one knows for sure what farm, what family may have first fallen ill. The community was most likely Santa Fe, now a ghost town in Haskell County," says Darlene Groth, curator at Haskell County Historical Society in Sublette. What is known is that a Kansas country doctor — Dr. Loring Miner, who practiced in Haskell County — became concerned when he noticed this three-day flu wasn't typical. It was an "influenza of*

the severe type," he wrote, and hit young, strong and otherwise healthy people the hardest. He was the first to report to Public Health Reports —a publication of the U.S. Public Health Service — that this flu was a killer. Dr. Miner could not have known that a perfect storm of circumstances was developing to rapidly spread the virus around the world. At any point, it could have lost its potency. But it didn't — it kept building in strength like a wildfire each time large groups of people were forced into crowded situations in geographic centers around the world." [148]

Humans, never at a loss to throw fuel on an already raging fire, became embroiled in World War I, which also began in 1918. These same infected farm boys who unwittingly manufactured the H1N1, without any awareness whatsoever, were drafted into service and reported for duty at Fort Riley while humming Edward Bernays' colleague George M. Cohan's "Over There," to wit:

"Camp Funston, at Fort Riley, was the largest training facility in the Army, full of makeshift non-insulated barracks, housing 250 soldiers each. It teemed with soldiers from all over the Midwest, training for duty in France. They trained over 50,000 troops at a time who all lived in close quarters. The Army was cognizant that it needed to help our French and British Allies out, so there was no questioning, they were sending troops out — soldiers were being sent that had flu-like symptoms," said Robert Smith, supervisory curator for Fort Riley Museums. Troops traveled by train from the Midwest to ports, then boarded ships bound for the war. "Recruits were being shifted from camp to camp by the thousands and they were taking with them fatigue and it made for easy exposure. The infections and disease followed," Smith said. Along the way, the virus mutated, many times. It hit people

[148] Wichita Eagle (February 19, 2018) By: Becky Tanner: How a killer flu spread from western Kansas to the world.

in waves, becoming more virulent each time. The first wave in the winter of 1918 was serious. The second wave — during the summer, when many of the soldiers were on the Western Front — was deadly, Smith said. The third wave came during the fall, when troops were returning. "We gave it to our Allies and they gave it to our enemies," Smith said. The virus mutated along the way as men coughed and sneezed, spreading germs in Army barracks, then on trains across the nation and on ships to Europe. Within six to nine months, the 1918 influenza pandemic had killed at least 20 million people worldwide. Some reports said 40 million." [149]

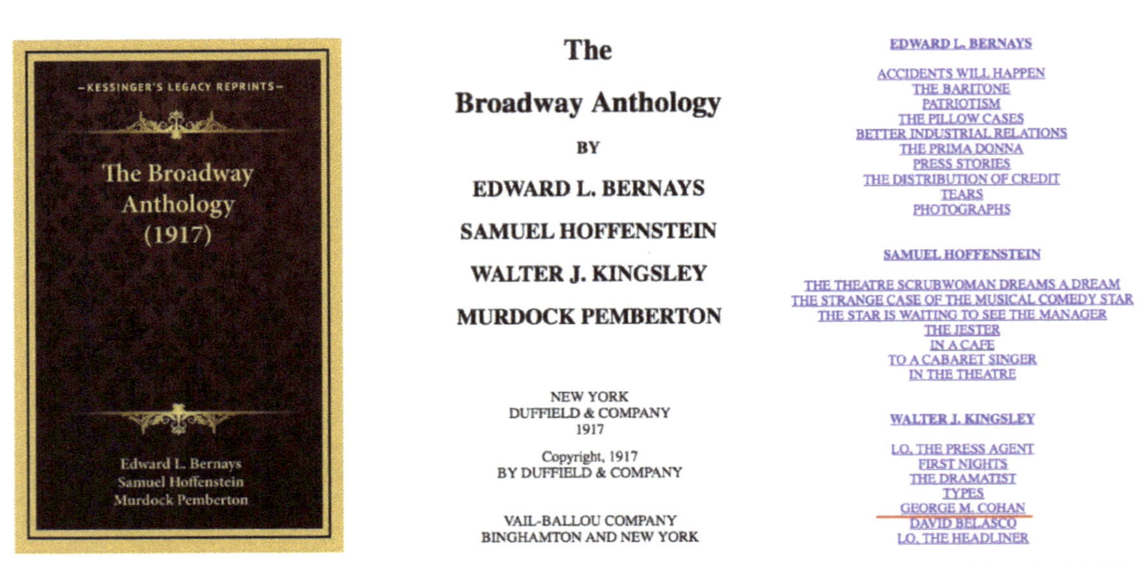
-KESSINGER'S LEGACY REPRINTS-
The Broadway Anthology (1917)
Edward L. Bernays
Samuel Hoffenstein
Murdock Pemberton

The Broadway Anthology
BY
EDWARD L. BERNAYS
SAMUEL HOFFENSTEIN
WALTER J. KINGSLEY
MURDOCK PEMBERTON

NEW YORK
DUFFIELD & COMPANY
1917

Copyright, 1917
BY DUFFIELD & COMPANY

VAIL-BALLOU COMPANY
BINGHAMTON AND NEW YORK

EDWARD L. BERNAYS
ACCIDENTS WILL HAPPEN
THE BARITONE
PATRIOTISM
THE PILLOW CASES
BETTER INDUSTRIAL RELATIONS
THE PRIMA DONNA
PRESS STORIES
THE DISTRIBUTION OF CREDIT
TEARS
PHOTOGRAPHS

SAMUEL HOFFENSTEIN
THE THEATRE SCRUBWOMAN DREAMS A DREAM
THE STRANGE CASE OF THE MUSICAL COMEDY STAR
THE STAR IS WAITING TO SEE THE MANAGER
THE JESTER
IN A CAFE
TO A CABARET SINGER
IN THE THEATRE

WALTER J. KINGSLEY
LO, THE PRESS AGENT
FIRST NIGHTS
THE DRAMATIST
TYPES
GEORGE M. COHAN
DAVID BELASCO
LO, THE HEADLINER

[150]

Bernays knew a lot about social engineering, but he knew nothing about the pathogenesis of viruses—and even if he did, he could not have anticipated that his work for the United States government would result in over 675,000 deaths in the U.S. alone, and over 50 million deaths worldwide due, at least in part when

---

[149] Ibid.
[150] Bernays, Hoffenstein and Pemberton (2010), A Broadway Anthology. Kessinger Publishing LLC, P.O. Box 1404, Whitefish, MT 59937. Original publication date 1917.

examining U.S. death stats, to the unintended consequences of psychological war mongering. [151]

Post COVID-19, the sales pitch for alternative reality replacements for the objective world morphed from convenience to one of safety born of necessity. If necessity is the mother of invention, then big tech and government are selling a new way of being human using virtual realities as the means by which their customers can achieve a sense of existential safety—Perhaps this "new way" of being human is a mirror image of VR savant's and big tech and government pitchmen's internal CNS world they want to share with the rest of us. "We're here to help make your dreams come true." Is it YOUR dream, or THEIR dream? And keep this key precept in mind: standing center stage in this brave new world circa 21st century chopping block is your privacy.

You better decide if your world will be better if it reflects the inner world of the titans of big tech, politicians, cryptographers, the nameless bureaucratic workers that sit in unnamed buildings with mirrored glass windows, or a world where touching and OR world eye contact is the norm for how we *primarily* relate to one another and other sentient beings. But don't get the idea that all of big tech is on board with this dystopian new reality. Not all of big tech thinks Mssrs. Zuckerberg's and Schmidt's, et al., global surveillance earth is a good idea. I'll touch upon the lone big tech gunman who carries a blazing privacy six-shooter into this gunfight, as it will serve as an introduction to our next chapter.

Apple has always been *less inclined* to violate its customers' privacy when compared to its peers. In 2010, Steve Jobs told interviewers that Apple's customers

---

[151] Any mortality comparisons between these two pandemics in the United States, 2020 and 1918, must differentiate between totals and rates. The current US population, a little more than 330 million, is more than three times larger than the population in 1918, estimated at 105 million. The 675,000 deaths attributed to the influenza epidemic made up 0.64 percent of the total population, a little more than six in every thousand people. By contrast, the more than 500,000 deaths attributed to COVID-19 make up about 0.15 percent of the total population, or between one and two in every thousand people. If COVID-19 caused deaths at the same rate as the 1918 epidemic, the total would approach two million. Even the disturbing projections of more than to 600,000 deaths by July 1, 2021, would still remain below the rates recorded in the earlier epidemic. (Health Affairs Blog, by E. Thomas Ewing, April 1, 2021)

should have the right to choose whether or not they want to be tracked online or in the Apple ecosystem. In the forensic world, we saw Apple's dedication to the privacy of its customers in 2015 when Islamist nationalists Syed Rizwan Farook and Tashfeen Malik killed 14 people in San Bernadino, California. Farook had on his person an iPhone. Despite the FBI's insistence that Apple unlock the killer's phone, it refused, citing privacy concerns should Apple provide the FBI a backdoor key to its operating system. Apple's insistence upon protecting all of its customers' privacy resulted in Apple getting a lot of heat from politicians and cable TV presenters, along with other big tech firms that had long ago established privacy policies that were government compliant.

Farook's iPhone was eventually "hacked" by *Azimuth Security*, a secretive if not shadowy company that has gone out of its way to make the point that it only sells its proprietary hacking software and accompanying tech to *democratic governments*—in this case, the FBI. That last point is worth remembering, i.e., "democratic governments," because I know of no organization in this business that admits to selling their software to anyone who can afford to pay whatever it takes to get it, or to those organizations that can shut them down if a deal can't be made, i.e., the government.

What is fascinating and telling is that no one at Apple knew at the time who, or how for that matter, Farook's iPhone had been unlocked. Some security experts have observed that Azimuth did Apple and the notion of privacy a favor by hacking Farook's iPhone. These same people argue that had Azimuth not unlocked the iPhone, the United States may have gotten a court order to force Apple to provide to not only the FBI, but any number of government agencies its backdoor key to its operating system's security features. But the story doesn't end there.

Apple has carved out a niche in the privacy world. Over the past several years, Apple has spent hundreds of millions of dollars on R&D focused upon alternative reality technologies, but with one big difference—a difference articulated by Apple CEO Tim Cook on March 28, 2018 during a town hall broadcast by MSNBC and hosted by Chris Hayes and longtime tech reporter Kara Swisher. Mr. Cook declared:

"Privacy is a human right, it's a civil liberty."

Mr. Cook went on to make our point that one way to save alternative reality technology from, as Maslow referred to them, "psychopaths, paranoids and SOBs," is to stop treating customers as products. As CEO Cook told his audience:

> ***"The truth is we could make a ton of money if we monetized our customer, if our customer was our product," Cook said. "We've elected not to do that."***

It is also interesting that the subject of the San Bernadino, California, terrorist's iPhone came up in that town hall, with specific reference to the fact that Apple butted heads with the FBI—Mr. Cook:

> ***"If that same circumstance arose again, we would fight, because this, again, is a value of America," Cook said Wednesday. "You should not be able to compel somebody to write something that is bad for civilization."***

In September 2015, Apple released IOS 9, its newest operating system for its mobile devices. IOS 9 was engineered at Apple to include various backdoor firewalls, should anyone manage to get backstage. It was that operating system on Farook's iPhone 5C. Since that time, Apple has been relentless in its efforts to engineer hardware and software that protects its customers' privacy. These efforts have culminated in its latest (2021) and, to be candid, revolutionary operating system IOS 14.5.

During the week of April 26, 2021, Apple made history in its efforts to protect its users' privacy, and in so doing drew a red line in the sand between itself, its big tech peers, governments, and their acronym agencies by releasing IOS 14.5. It includes a revolutionary feature that Apple calls "App Tracking Transparency" (ATT). The ATT puts the power of tracking back into the hands of Apple's customers by giving them an easy way to hide their Identifier for Advertisers (IDFA) from businesses that treat customers like products, and governments that would piggyback and have access to those IDFA data. [152]

When an Apple customer using IOS 14.5 opens any app that heretofore would have surreptitiously tracked Apple's users, thus transforming them into products, *users* will now see a pop-up screen that asks them if they want to be tracked, and then give them an EASY way to opt in or out. Apple customers can also go into settings and with one swipe disable ALL tracking. You can imagine how the likes of Facebook, Google, governments, and their acronym agencies feel about that feature. If the FBI took exceptions to the security features in IOS 9, then it will hate IOS 14.5. Mr. Zuckerberg's Facebook and Eric Schmidt's and successors Google (Alphabet), along with any number of other surveillance-based businesses, and Tim Cook's Apple have been at odds over the product/participant vs. customer/user paradigm for over a decade, to wit:

> *"The two companies have been at odds for a decade, and have recently engaged in a heated war of words around these privacy changes. Last week, Facebook CEO Mark Zuckerberg called Apple one of its biggest competitors and said the privacy changes will hurt the growth of "millions of businesses around the world." The next day, Apple CEO Tim Cook alluded to Facebook in a speech at a data privacy conference in Brussels, saying,* ***"If a business is built on misleading users, on data***

[152] The Identifier for Advertisers (IDFA) is a random device identifier assigned by Apple to a user's device. Advertisers use this to track data so they can deliver customized advertising. The IDFA is used for tracking and identifying a user (without revealing personal information). The data can then be used to discover information such as which in-app events a user triggers. The IDFA can also identify when users interact with a mobile advertising campaign, provided the channel offers IDFA tracking and the advertiser tracks users who interact with as successfully. If this occurs, the IDFA can identify whether specific users click an advert for payment and attribution purposes.

> ***exploitation, on choices that are no choices at all, it does not deserve our praise. It deserves reform."*** [153](Emphasis added)

Of course, the public relation's divisions of both Facebook and Google (Alphabet) have been busy. When Google rolled out its Android 11 operating system, it made sure to highlight a cadre of privacy features so as to not concede the whole "privacy thing," as they view it, to Apple. The magazine *MacRumors*, famous for knowing what goes on behind the scenes in the world of big tech, published this telling story on January 5, 2021, that originated from investigators at FastCompany.com

> *"Not a single one of Google's iOS apps have been updated in almost a month—an unusually long period for a tech behemoth not to release, at the very least, even a minor bug fix or stability update for one of its dozens of insanely popular iPhone and iPad apps. And after reviewing the latest release dates for all of Google's iOS apps, one reason for this lack of updates seems more likely than others: It could be related to Apple's new App Store privacy labels. The last time any Google iOS app was updated was on December 7. This includes updates to major Google apps like Google Drive, YouTube, Google Docs, Google Sheets, YouTube Music, Google Duo, Google Authenticator, and Gboard. Why is December 7 a significant date? Because starting on December 8, Apple mandated that any new apps or app updates submitted to the App Store would require the developer to fill out the privacy label information for the app it was submitting. This privacy label reveals exactly what data the app is collecting about the user and how that user data is being used. The label can then be viewed on an app's App Store listing page. The feature is part of Apple's push to make developers be more transparent in the ways they collect and use user data, so users can make more informed choices about the apps they choose to download. When I spoke*

[153] CNBC, Facebook strikes back against Apple privacy change, prompts users to accept tracking to get 'better ads experience.' Story by: Salvador Rodriguez, February 1, 2021.

with Apple's senior vice president of software engineering, Craig Federighi, ahead of the privacy label launch in early December, Federighi told me the labels are something he hopes other app stores copy. But far from copying the privacy label idea for the hundreds of thousands of apps on its own Google Play app store, it appears Google doesn't even like the idea of privacy labels being applied to its iOS apps in Apple's App Store. By getting in all its existing apps' updates on or before December 7, Google has managed to avoid filling out a privacy label for any of their apps so far. You can verify this yourself by launching the App Store app on your iPhone, selecting any Google-owned app in the store, and then checking its privacy label on the app's listing. As of the time of this writing, you'll see every Google app's privacy label still reads, "No Details Provided. The developer will be required to provide privacy details when they submit their next app update." [But] if Google is trying to delay the unveiling of its privacy labels for fear of similar bad press, it makes one wonder just how bad its privacy labels are going to be. I mean, it's hard to believe they could be any worse than Facebook's. Then again, Google's user privacy policies, or lack thereof, have historically left much to be desired. Either way, we will eventually find out—the question is when. After all, Google cannot continue not updating any of its iOS apps, which are some of the most popular apps on the iPhone. So when will those updates come? This post will be updated if we hear back from Google. Google did not respond to a request for comment about its lack of updates." [154]

---

[154] FastCompany.com. Google's iOS apps haven't been updated in weeks. Could Apple's privacy labels be the reason? Story by: Michael Grothaus, January 5, 2021 in, MacRumors, January 5, 2021.

CHAPTER XVII

WHERE THERE IS A WILL THERE IS A WAY: All is Fair in Love and War

If the reader wants to get back to the fun of reading about all the new, flashy alternative reality devices and what the future holds for us in that VR world, I suggest you stay focused on the product/participant vs. customer/user battle taking place as I write this. Ignore this battle at your own peril.

I'm now going to share with the reader something that happened the week before Apple released IOS 14.5—or should I write, "Threw down the gauntlet?" You have to figure that with Mr. Cook's dedicated focus upon privacy and security, Apple engineers would rank somewhere around the 99th percentile of hacking security mavens. Apple is so serious about its security on its iPhone, it has a standing offer of $1 million to anyone who can hack an iPhone—but it doesn't stop there:

> *"[A]pple is also launching a Mac bug bounty, which was confirmed Thursday, but it's also extending it to watch OS and its Apple TV operating system. The announcements came in Las Vegas at the Black*

Hat conference, where Apple's head of security engineering Ivan Krstić gave a talk on iOS and macOS security."[155]

So, you would think that of all the hackable targets out there, including banks, utilities, health care organizations, retailers, government, and other big tech firms that Apple would be immune—think again.

The week before Apple released IOS 14.5, it was the victim of a ransomware (RW) attack. If you find the timing to be suspicious, you are not alone.

Now to be sure, it wasn't Apple's servers that were hacked but a third-party supplier named Quanta. Apple had provided detailed blueprints to this third-party fabricator. The crooks, of course, didn't try to extort the third-party hardware fabricator—they got on the phone to Tim Cook and demanded $50 million, or else they promised Apple's competitors would be provided build sheets on Apple's upcoming product(s).

Who or what was responsible? ***REvil:***

"Our team is negotiating the sale of large quantities of confidential drawings and gigabytes of personal data with several major brands," REvil wrote in its post of the stolen data. "We recommend that Apple buy back the available data by May 1."

Petite RW attacks are not rare. You may have been a victim of an RW attack. The typical modus operandi is to "lock" the victim's device until a ransom is paid. But today, the modus operandi of RW crooks is to threaten their big-time victims with the release of important data—not simply lock their data.

As a forensic expert, I often look closely at how an attack is carried out, not the fact of the attack itself, in order to find clues about the mindset of the perpetrator. For example, homicides can be executed with sterile purpose, e.g., a surgical severing of carotid arteries or a homicide fueled by rage, e.g., 50 stab

---

[155] Forbes Magazine, Apple Confirms $1 Million Reward For Anyone Who Can Hack An iPhone. Story by: Thomas Brewster, August 8, 2019.

wounds to the face, torso and genitalia. With regard to RW attacks—had the perpetrator's only communication been the paragraph noted above, then I would be more likely to conclude the attack was sterile, i.e., "just business, not personal." But that is not what happened. The attackers included the following communications—and like the homicidal rage motive in a 50-stab-wound attack, the attack was personal against Apple and in particular Tim Cook, Steve Job's hand-picked successor. To wit:

> *"Today we, the REvil Group, will provide data on the upcoming releases of* ***the company beloved by many****," (Emphasis added)*

REvil continued:

> *"Tim Cook can you say thank you Quanta?"*

I also look for perpetrator patterns in forensic cases. Is such personal calling out of CEOs by name, as if to taunt them, the modus operandi of REvil? Enter hostage negotiators for the virtual reality world of cyber crime who can answer that question.

One such cybersecurity firm that specializes in negotiating with ransomware crooks is named Arete Incident Response. (AIR) The head of AIR is Marc Bleicher, who reportedly has negotiated with REvil at least 32 times since January 2021.
In total, AIR has analyzed 173 previous REvil attacks. AIR is, perhaps, in the best position to judge whether or not REvil's attack on Apple is typical of their modus operandi. Here is what Mr. Bleicher told Eamon Javers on CNBC on April 23, 2021:

> *"Attacking Apple by name — and demanding $50 million — is on a much different scale from what REvil has operated on in the past."*

My assessment of REvil's attack on Apple, with specific attention to its timing (days before the release of IOS 14.5) and the personal nature of the attacker's messages, calling out and taunting CEO Tim Cook by name, tells me that if this attack is coincidental, then it is one of the most curious "coincidences" I've run across in a long time. Let's put it this way: if REvil was contracted to make the hit on Apple, then along with the nuts and bolts of the hit came the directive, "make it personal."

At the risk of entering the realm of "conspiracy theory," the reader should take note that Apple's earning report on April 28, 2021, was extraordinary. Even stock analysts who tend to be circumspect were impressed, as denoted by their descriptors of the earnings report, e.g., "blowout," "stunning," "breathtaking," "stellar," and "beyond even the most bullish analyst's expectations." But the day after reporting this stellar earnings report, Apple's stock price was down. Facebook, on the other hand—that also delivered very good, but not breathtaking results that included a warning to analysts that Apple's IOS 14.5 release would impact its bottom and top line in the next quarter—was up a stunning seven percent. The only point I am making is that a pattern of retribution directed at those who would dare thwart the surveillance economy is the rule—could it be coincidental? In forensics, we take note of "plausible deniability." Ten plausible reasons can explain Apple's stock price behavior and the timing of its hacking. You can be sure the counterfactual financial reporters, analysts, and the cottage industries to which they belong and profit off the surveillance economy will articulate those plausible explanations with the aplomb, and dare I suggest success, of the late criminal defense attorney Johnnie Cochran: "If the glove doesn't fit, you must acquit." I will remind the reader of the wisdom of Ian Fleming, who was the real James Bond:

> **"Once is happenstance, twice is coincidence and three times is enemy action."**

The fact that Apple, the white knight of privacy, was the victim of an RW attack and has to go so far as to offer a lucrative bounty of $1 million to anyone who can break into its devices begs the question: will we ever be able to enter the world of VR, et al., without automatically submitting our biological tissues, attitudes, thoughts, feelings, and behaviors to the social engineers and acronym agencies who will do with us what they want? The most fundamental and perhaps easiest concern to deal with is privacy, while the greater issue of redefining users' minds as "no fly zones" is going to be a much more difficult goal to achieve when we enter the VR, et al. world—enter Pegasus, and other horses we don't even have names for at this point. We have all learned that to be safe, "don't click on that link," don't respond to text messages from people you don't know, and limit your screen time—in other words, get outside and don't bring any of your devices with you, because it is good for you.

But what if I told you those guidelines may not be enough to protect you in the virtual universe?

Let's begin our story about a secretive Israeli cyber-savant group that sells something called Pegasus, and retired NSA official cryptographer William Binney. Our story begins with the group NSO:

> NSO Group Technologies (NSO standing for Niv, Shalev and Omri, the names of the company's founders) is an Israeli technology firm whose spyware called Pegasus enables the remote surveillance of smart phones. It was founded in 2010 by Niv Carmi, Omri Lavie, and Shalev Hulio. [156]

NSO's ever-evolving star software is named Pegasus,

> Pegasus is a modular malware capable of virtually unlimited surveillance on the targeted device, as per a report by digital security company Kaspersky. It installs the necessary modules to read the user's messages and mail, listen to calls, send back the browser history and more, which basically means taking control of nearly all aspects of your digital life. And that is just the small stuff.

---

[156] NSO Group appears to be owned by a private equity firm with headquarters in San Francisco: Francisco Partners Management LLC, which reportedly acquired it in 2014 after approval from the Israeli Defense Ministry. However, as of November 2015, Francisco Partners was reportedly exploring selling NSO Group, with a stated valuation of up to $1 billion. Interestingly, Francisco Partners previously invested in Blue Coat, a company selling network filtering and monitoring solutions, whose technology has been used by repressive regimes according to previous Citizen Lab research.

Graphic Depiction of Pegasus (Courtesy of Karpersky Digital Security Company)

The University of Toronto Munk School of Global Affairs and Public Policy published the following informational graphics on Pegasus sourced from The Citizen Lab. For definitional purposes, "Zero-Day Exploits" is what the team at NSO refers to as the end product of Pegasus. NSO recruits from the graduate pool of the Israeli Defense Force's (IDF) elite intelligence Unit 8200. The IDF's 8200 is the Israeli equivalent of the USA's NSA. NSO has approximately 500 security experts on staff, but that number is soft and only a best estimate. The Israeli Defense Ministry governs NSO and other cyber surveillance firms, like Task Force 7 Technologies, under Israeli law.

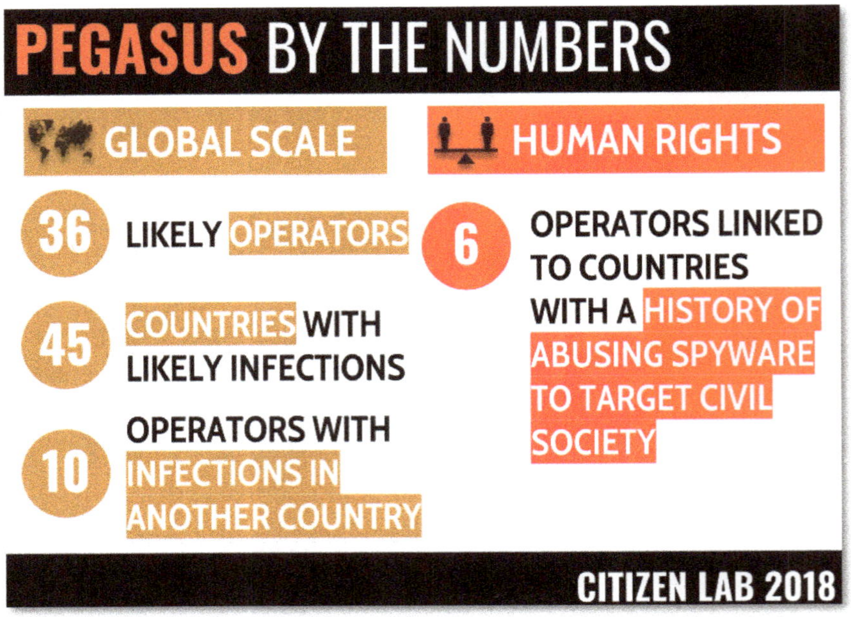

Diagram from purported NSO Group Pegasus documentation depicting the range of information gathered from a device infected with Pegasus. (Source: Hacking Team Emails)

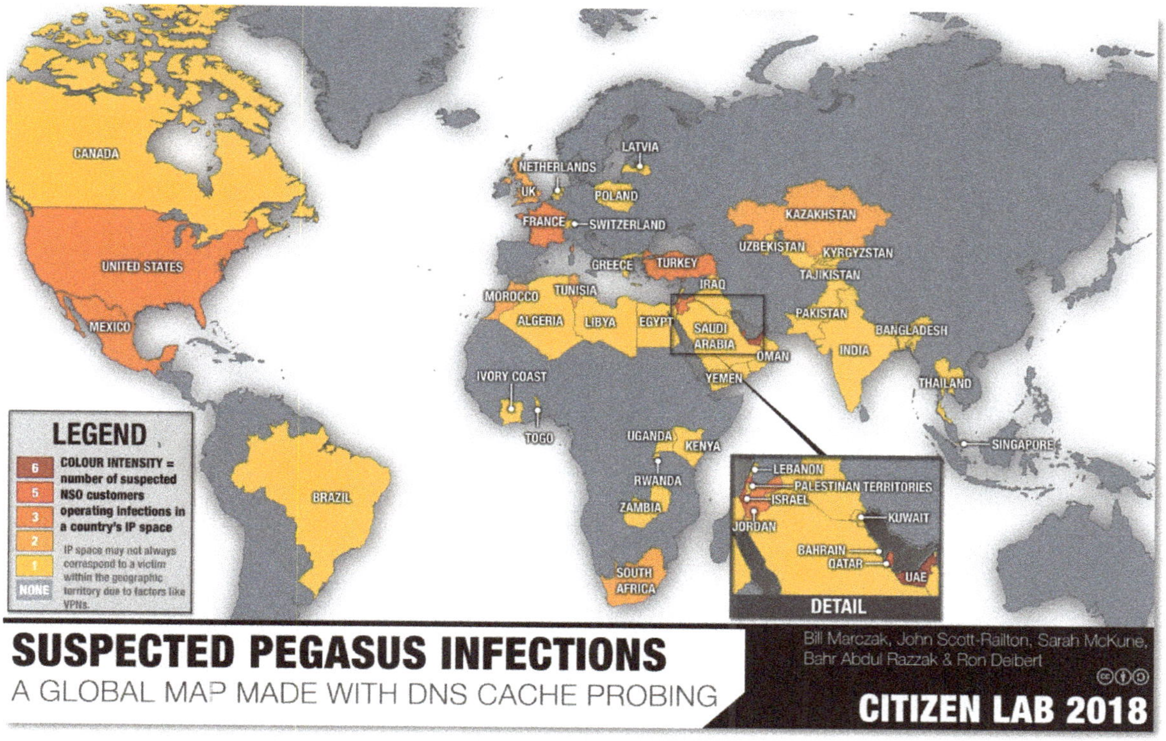

Each "exploit," as NSO calls it, costs at least $1 million dollars for a limited number of targets, and only for a limited time. As the number of targets rise, costs can easily reach $100 million or more. Few businesses can afford the $1 million price tag, and only governments funded by taxpayers can afford to use Pegasus on larger numbers of its citizens.

NSO makes it clear that it only leases Pegasus to "government intelligence and law enforcement agencies to fight crime and terror." It has been reported that NSO has leased Pegasus to Mexico, in addition to Colombia, Saudi Arabia, and the United Arab Emirates (UAE)—not to mention the USA. Profound implications exist when Israeli Unit 8200-originated Pegasus software is leased to other countries and agencies. Once surveillance technology is in the hands of other entities, control becomes an issue. No user of Pegasus is going to admit that its motivations fall outside the laudable limitations set forth by the NSO group, and by inference, Israel. Since the Israeli Defense Ministry governs NSO, it is easy to see where problems can arise, because no matter how careful the screening process, "where there is a will, there is a way." The reader should understand that while cell phones comprise a fertile target for NSO's surveillance software, softer targets include any and all

VR/AR/AI modalities. We say softer because public land installed cameras, microphones, and their links are located on government property. Data conduits in space orbit the earth, all protected and monitored by the North American Aersospace Defense Command (NORAD).

The rationale for using taxpayer funds to create infrastructure monoliths always emphasizes security and safety. Mr. Schmidt touts Chinese/American competition, which is another way of saying you're not safe because of the Chinese government. As already addressed, 9/11 was the springboard that hatched the Patriot Act, which made possible the warrantless tracking of almost anyone if a FISA Court judge can be persuaded it is in the national security interest—and almost everything is related to national security in the digital world because of the very things we are discussing here.

What the general public is unaware of is NSO is capable of carrying out what Citizen Lab calls, "Zero-Click Exploits." This means exactly what its name implies—the target need not click on a link, access a suspicious website, or communicate with someone who has been exploited for NSO to take complete control of your phone. Zero-Click exploits the infrastructure of satellites, cell phone towers, and the digital world of 1's and 0's.

> **Pegasus can simply call your cell phone from a known or unknown number. Whether you answer the call *or not* — *voila,* your phone, VR headset, gaming console, computer, watch, linked devices, e.g., thermostats, home security systems, light modules, and everything else "smart" homes that digital natives and digital immigrants possess are now under the full and complete control of Unit 8200's genius creation.**

If you are a nobody, your data is scooped up and put in a dump—and while it may be a refuse pile taken away by the garbage men, never to be seen again (or so you think), if the gendarme ever come looking for that dead body you carefully threw in the trash that ended up in a landfill, you can be sure everything in that dump is traceable.

To illustrate the inextricable link between international relations, governments, and VR, et al. we know as fact that once President Trump brokered a "normalization" deal between Israel, Saudi Arabia, and the UAE, the latter two countries spent hundreds of millions of dollars leasing Israel's genius creation Pegasus. That is just two countries located in one region of the world. And if you are wondering, every single data point vacuumed up by the leasers of Pegasus remains available for use by NSO—that is, the IDF and the Israeli government—although that is denied, of course.

The incestuous nature of international cyber expertise is the result of government's unique capability to train the brightest and best that leave government or military service and enter the "draft," not unlike a star college player enters the NBA draft. The government has an unlimited amount of other people's money at its disposal and can hand out badges, medals, privileges, ranks, and power, with only big business as its wanna-be competitor when it comes to offering incentives to the best and the brightest.

Retail spy operations recruit retired acronym agency experts with money, gifted luxury, privilege, and sexual liaisons, even in places where sexual liaisons are strictly governed. Just as NSO is manned by former IDF Unit 8200 specialists, UAE's DarkMatter group is manned by former NSA and CIA cyber specialists, with the difference being the NSA and CIA specialists left their home country to man a shop located in the UAE—specifically Abu Dhabi. The difference between, let's say, Top Gun pilots trained by the Navy and cyber specialists trained by the NSA, CIA or Unit 8200, is when Navy pilots leave their command to go fly commercial aircraft, they are not followed and debriefed after every nonstop flight from New York to Paris. When it comes to IDF, NSA, CIA, et al., trained cyber mavens, you can be sure the governments that trained them never, ever lose touch with them. In fact, companies like NSO and DarkMatter, just to name two such organizations, may be thought of as the retail arm of their government trainers/funders.

Since the CIA's charter makes "spying" on US citizens illegal, some have wondered whether or not CIA cyber specialists who "retire" from government service then work in the UAE under the retail operation where DarkMatter facilitates the circumvention of prohibitions against spying on US citizens. Karim Sabbagh, former CEO of DarkMatter, has categorically denied that sort of thing takes place—in part because DarkMatter does not have the capability to handle such massive data dumps. William Binney has gone on the record regarding whether DarkMatter and other retail arms of government cyber surveillance operations deny spying on their own and other citizens because of data ceilings:

> "They're lying, *I designed these mathematical programs.* ***We had no upper limit on the capacity to handle data—none.*** *There was no problem at trillions...quadrillions. We had no mathematical limit that I could see."*

Permit me to emphasize a point made by Mr. Binney: NO UPPER LIMIT ON AN AMOUNT OF DATA THAT CAN BE SCREENED AND ANALYZED EXISTS. Often, I hear everyday citizens, and some apologists who really should or do know better, buttress the spurious notion that there are just too many people, too many phone calls, emails, web traffic, et al., for any government or multinational corporation to monitor their behavior. Instead of massaging your defenses, perhaps you would do better to be somewhat awestruck and wary of the technology control that mavens have created and put into action with **your tax money**.

Once you access your phone, you are immediately known worldwide—your ISP (even the so-called shielded ISP's, PC/Mac identifiers) is recorded. The NSA used "implants" in "computer network exploitation" programs. Binney said that by 2010, the NSA had installed 50,000 implants in networks, servers, switches, and every other imaginable conduit for our digital activations. That number today is exponentially larger everywhere. This means that who and where you are is immediately known, no matter where you are on earth.[157] The Intercept, previously quoted here highlighting the work of Eric Schmidt was itself hacked by DarkMatter using former NSA and CIA cyber experts. (See footnote 96)

The entire point of our revelations is to remind the reader that ANY VR, et al., technology is not what it seems to be. Mark Zuckerberg's, et al., profit-motivated commercial tracking sold to sellers seems innocent when analyzed within the context of government and their acronym agencies' motivations. According to Jenna McLaughlin, investigative journalist/writer and contributor to the Intercept and Foreign Policy Magazine, Americans who "don't go along with the program," i.e. dissidents, are routinely hacked by offshore retail outlets for various acronym agencies from the USA and Israel, thus circumventing laws that would otherwise prohibit such behavior.[158] Maslow was right, and virtual, augmented, mixed, and certainly V the Reality, for all of its allure and promise, is that Brave New World Huxley warned about and Orwell's 1984 dystopian earth, all rolled into one. But something is missing to make it all happen. Binney's work that told us what some of us already knew—that no data mining ceilings exist, confirmed by Edward Snowden and proofed by others who know about such matters—is still not enough to irreparably and completely hack the OR world system: that means you. What is the missing piece that will do to life on earth what the Chicxulub asteroid did 66 million years ago?

---

158 The Intercept: Spies for Hire. Story by Jenna McLaughlin, October 24, 2016.

CHAPTER XVIII

CRYPTOCURRENCY: Tales from the Crypt

Recall our earlier made observation regarding the quest of every VR developer,

> "Even in the days when music was recorded on the physical medium of wax, virtual world innovators tried to convert the objective into a virtual world facsimile so that their creations would blur the difference between the two in the minds of their customers." [159]

Money is different from any other real-world creation transmuted into the virtual world—not just because of what money means in people's lives, but because this is the first-time developers and innovators have reversed the VR/OR equation and thus created a cryptocurrency revolution:

> **Instead of converting an objective reality into its virtual world facsimile, we are in the midst of a revolution where the goal is to transmogrify a virtual creation into an OR world truth. VR creators of money don't want to blur the delta between the VR and OR world—they intend to replace OR world money with V the Reality money.**

---

[159] Page 17.

Before we get into the weeds on this subject, it is important to think about money itself. What is it about money and the human experience that makes it unique? Ever notice that of all the things you lose, cash is the least likely to be lost when compared to rings, watches, and necklaces? This is true despite the fact that rings fit on fingers, watches wrap around wrists, and necklaces are clasped around your neck—yet thin pieces of paper taken in and out of purses, wallets, and pockets tend to stay with us. The guys you see at the beach use metal detectors, not $20 bill detectors.

The terms we use as synonyms for money provide a window into the deep-seated meaning that money has in the human psyche, e.g., dough, mammon, loot, moola, brass, roll, chips, ooftish, beans, scratch, gravy, bread, bones, grig, jack, lucre, almighty dollar, boodle, cabbage, spinach, wad, and the list goes on. The fact that religion, food, killing, stealing, hard work, sexuality, and evil have become synonyms for or interlaced with money should tell us that money isn't just a medium of exchange or store of value.

When it comes to socioeconomic strata, the importance ascribed to money is dependent upon how much of it you have and how you acquired it among other things, e.g., the less money you have, the more important it is to you. Trust fund children are typically wasteful with their money when compared to someone who began life poor and through hard work became financially successful.

Having a certain amount of money has always been the sine qua non of freedom and security. Colloquially, the term "FU money" is something the vast majority of people would love to be able to say with conviction that they have. This begs the question, who or what is the identity of the "YOU" in that assertion? Is it our employers, perhaps the government? The fact of the matter is that money, security, and autonomy go hand in hand.

In the olden days, parents gave their daughters a dime before they left home for a date just in case they had to make an emergency call from a phone booth. Your "stash" in today's lexicon may refer to your stockpile of recreational drugs, but the origin of the term refers to that cache of money in your physical possession that you can easily access in an emergency. Yet, for all of its complexity, when it comes to economic theories of money, no matter where you go on earth, even children know how to use it.

The reader may reflect upon their childhood and how they managed their lunch money, allowance, or pay they received for working odd jobs. You knew how to count, spend, save, and calculate what more you needed before you could buy something. Some of you had piggy banks, while others had coffee cans where you kept your money. You could make change, and you knew when someone was trying to cheat you. You had a keen understanding of what the things you bought were worth, and you knew a good deal when you came across one. And one thing you all knew as children—you knew what a dollar was worth and what it could buy.

You also knew that for all practical purposes, a dollar in your pocket today would still be a dollar next week, month, and probably year. Inflation and devaluation of your currency was something that economic statisticians kept track of, and not until you were older did you notice it. You never went to bed on a midweek school night fearing that your five dollars would be worth five cents in the morning and you couldn't buy lunch the next day.

> **All of those certainties were because the money you knew as a child was OR world money. These certainties are not true for digital native generations. In their world money is more mercurial. Long before digital natives ever heard of Bitcoin the delta between OR world and VR world money had been purposefully blurred. This was particularly true in the gambling industry.**

Money is not simply a matter of accounting in the human experience, regardless of your generation. Human beings have never been able to relate to money in a consistently rational manner, because money and emotions go hand-in-hand. In fact, cottage industries exist that purport to treat this tendency on the part of man to be irrational with money by managing it for you. But like many diseases, treatments may exist for man's irrational relationship with money, but no cures exist.

Whether you are an onstage idealist, opportunistic gambler, interested party, or none of the above, you would do well to appreciate that no matter how far back you go in time, the money story is comprised of the same characters and story arcs. This remains true for crytocurrencies as well. Study the following money story arcs.

- Man in a Hole
- Double Man in a Hole
- Rags to Riches
- Riches to Rags
- Icarus
- Cinderella
- Oedipus Story
- Gambler
- Get Rich Quick

And the musical soundtrack that goes best with each and every one of these money story arcs is to be found in the lyrics of this song:

MONEY

Lie for it
Spy for it
Kill for it
Die for it
So you call it trust
But I say it's just
In the devil's game
Of greed and lust
They don't care
They'd do me for the money
They don't care
They use me for the money
So you go to church
Read the holy word

In the scheme of life
It's all absurd
They don't care
They'd kill for the money
Do or dare
The thrill for the money
You're saluting the flag
Your country trusts you
Now you're wearing a badge
You're called the "Just Few"
And you're fighting the wars
A soldier must do
I'll never betray or deceive you my friend but...
If you show me the cash
Then I will take it
If you tell me to cry
Then I will fake it
If you give me a hand
Then I will shake it
You do anything for money...[160]

The people most inclined to embrace this modern-day version of the alchemist's dream of changing lead into gold, as well as those among the general public who are most receptive to it, come from digital native generations—they are the perfect audience for the idea of cryptocurrencies (crypto).

Digital native neural tissues were bio-formed, along with their attitudes and cultural ethos having been socially engineered. They believe with all their collective emoji hearts and "Fave" memes that V the Reality money, aka crypto, is not only real,

---

[160] The song 'Money' is a track from Michael Jackson's 1995 studio album, HIStory. It was written and composed by Jackson and recorded in 1994.

but a very good thing. Exigent social factors ensured their receptivity to crypto. The confluence of economic hardship all too common among digital natives, their generation's ambient psychological distress, and an inability to keenly distinguish between virtual and objective reality made them the perfect audience for *Bitcoin's Siren song*.

Odysseus, Odysseus
Forget where you're going
Forget what you're doing
And come to us
Odysseus, Odysseus
Come live with us
Our island has everything
Every wish, every dream
Waits for you
They'll all come true
You hear our song
You feel us calling

You hear our voices
Rising , falling
It's so hypnotic
As we all sing for you
Just for you, only you
Odysseus
You'll come to us
Odysseus
No man can resist
Once his ears have been kissed
By the siren's song
So sing along
The life you knew is slowly fading
You can't say no to our persuading
You can't resist our serenading
For you
Just for you
Only you Odysseus [161]

In consideration of the importance of money in all of our lives, should it be any surprise that governments and their acronym agencies, for a very long time, have experimented with developing a VR currency?

> **In 1996, the NSA's cryptographic unit published a white paper on this very subject entitled: HOW TO MAKE A MINT: The Cryptography of Anonymous Electronic Cash.** [162]

---

[161] John Stegman, JJ's Tunes and Tales 2012. https://youtu.be/LtiPgvTRrdk

[162] National Security Agency (NSA), National Security Agency Office of Information Security Research and Technology, Cryptology Division. Laurie Law, Susan Sabett, Jerry Solinas: HOW TO MAKE A MINT: The Cryptography of Anonymous Electronic Cash, 1996.

In order to help the reader keep her timeline of reference in context, peruse this representative listing of Apple computers that were, at the time of the publication of this NSA paper, the newest of the new:

- Macintosh Performa 5260/5270
- Power Macintosh 8200
- PowerBook 1400c/cs

Just as Apple computers have evolved, so have the protocols used in mining, aka MINTING Bitcoin and all the other crytpo. What follows is an excerpt from that first NSA-sourced white paper that outlined the coding protocol proposed to mint virtual money, with the author's footnotes redacted.

> ***2.1 Public-Key Cryptographic Tools***
>
> *We begin by discussing the basic public-key cryptographic techniques upon which the electronic cash implementations are based.*
>
> ***One-Way Functions****. A one-way function is a correspondence between two sets which can be computed efficiently in one direction but not the other. In other words, the function phi is one-way if, given s in the domain of phi, it is easy to compute t = phi(s), but given only t, it is hard to find s. (The elements are typically numbers, but could also be, e.g., points on an elliptic curve;*
>
> ***Key Pairs.*** *If phi is a one-way function, then a key pair is a pair s, t related in some way via phi. We call s the secret key and t the public key. As the names imply, each user keeps his secret key to himself and makes his public key available to all. The secret key remains secret even when the public key is known, because the one-way property of phi ensures that t cannot be computed*
>
> *from s.*
>
> ***All public-key protocols use key pairs****. For this reason, public-key cryptography is often called asymmetric cryptography. Conventional cryptography is often called symmetric cryptography, since one can both encrypt and decrypt with the private key but do neither without it.*

Signature and Identification*. In a public key system, a user identifies herself by proving that she knows her secret key without revealing it. This is done by performing some operation using the secret key which anyone can check or undo using the public key. This is called identification. If one uses a message as well as one's secret key, one is performing a digital signature on the message. The digital signature plays the same role as a handwritten signature: identifying the author of the message in a way which cannot be repudiated and confirming the integrity of the message.*

Secure Hashing. *A hash function is a map from all possible strings of bits of any length to a bit string of fixed length. Such functions are often required to be collision-free: that is, it must be computationally difficult to find two inputs that hash to the same value. If a hash function is both one-way and collision-free, it is said to be a secure hash. The most common use of secure hash functions is in digital signatures. Messages might come in any size, but a given public-key algorithm requires working in a set of fixed size. Thus, one hashes the message and signs the secure hash rather than the message itself. The hash is required to be one-way to prevent signature forgery, i.e., constructing a valid-looking signature of a message without using the secret key.4 The hash must be collision-free to prevent repudiation, i.e., denying having signed one message by producing another message with the same hash."* [163]

The VR money that was "minted" in the 1996 NSA whitepaper should not be confused with the technology used to pay for goods or services using an electronic commerce company, e.g., PayPay, Venmo, Apple Pay, Zelle, Cash App, et al. The fact that you can purchase something online with your credit card or your commerce company account without handling cash is merely the digital version of writing a paper check—it is NOT the equivalent of minting virtual money.

---

[163] Ibid.

Earlier when we discussed NFTs and their role in converting parts of the OR world into the VR world, I identified the SHA-256 Hash protocol's part in transmuting Jack Dorsey's brilliant $2.9 million five-word tweet into its VR world NFT. That "little bit" of coding has also garnered the attention of the world's intelligence community:

> **As with the 1996 development of one of the first and most important iterations of a cryptocurrency protocol, it was the NSA's cryptographic unit—once again—that developed the SHA-256 Hash protocol. <u>SHA-256 is used in several parts in the mining of Bitcoin.</u>**

Fast-forward 16 years, and members of the general public were just beginning to hear snippets about this new money thing called Bitcoin. In 2012, writers Michelle and Robert King created a television series named *The Good Wife.* These writers were fascinated by government scandals in their day, in particular President Clinton's affair with Monica Lewinsky and North Carolina Senator John Edwards' extramarital affair. The Kings' focus upon what goes on backstage drew their attention to Bitcoin. Here are a few lines from one of *The Good Wife* episodes that aired in 2012:

> **Alicia Florrick:** I went online and bought one Bitcoin last night.
>
> **Office Guy:** Really, it's the future.
>
> **Alicia Florrick:** I don't know, it didn't feel real.
>
> **Office Guy:** Oh, real's gonna change.

Circling back to work by the NSA back in 1996, what would motivate the intelligence community to experiment with VR money that could, at least theoretically, upend central banks' control over money—thus much of everything else—while potentially empowering America's enemies? The NSA's VR money paradigm maintained central bank control over crypto. This suggests that the NSA's 1996 paper was both an acknowledgement of the burgeoning crypto movement, and a resolution compromise or "cut them off at the pass" gambit directed at crypto-guerillas who had made a persuasive case that their VR money was going to be the new money. Crypto guerillas?

In the 1980s, a PhD cryptographer by the name of David Chaum was developing a way for people who didn't trust one another to make monetary transactions using crypto. A contemporary of Chaum, an electronic engineer and former senior scientist at Intel by the name of Tim May, dreamed of creating replacement money (cryptocurrency) that would put central bankers out of business. May is considered to be the father of the Crypto Anarchy movement. He, along with Chaum, are recognized as two of the most important founding members of what came to be called the Cypherpunks. Their crypto movement mirrored the spirit of the punk music scene of their era, e.g., *Dead Kennedys, Bad Religion.*

To give you a sense of the Cypherpunks' political aura, May wrote these firebrand essays, "The Crypto Anarchist Manifesto" and "True Nyms and Crypto Anarchy." This brief excerpt from May's Manifesto captures his mindset and helps to explain why May's New York Times obituary included this: ***"He often wrote about arming himself and waiting for government agents to show up."*** [164]

> *"A specter is haunting the modern world, the specter of crypto anarchy. "Computer technology is on the verge of providing the ability for individuals and groups to communicate and interact with each other in a* ***totally anonymous manner****. Two persons may exchange messages, conduct business, and negotiate electronic contracts without ever knowing the True Name, or legal identity, of the other. Interactions over networks will be untraceable, via extensive re-routing of encrypted packets and tamper-proof boxes, which implement cryptographic protocols with nearly perfect assurance against any tampering. Reputations will be of central importance, far more important in dealings than even the credit ratings of today. These developments* ***will alter completely the nature of government regulation, the ability to tax and control economic interactions, the ability to keep***

[164] Popper, Nathaniel (2018-12-21). "Timothy C. May, Early Advocate of Internet Privacy, Dies at 66". The New York Times. ISSN 0362-4331. Retrieved 2018-12-26.

information secret, and will even alter the nature of trust and reputation." *(Emphasis added)*

David Chaum, albeit less explicitly radical, developed something he called *Blind Signature Protocol,* a foundational property of block/blockchain coding that has a direct lineage to modern-day Bitcoin. In 1989, Mr. Chaum went on to create a business called *DigiCash*. Mr. Chaum introduced *eCash* in 1993, a mere three years before the NSA's Cryptocurrency and its SHA-256 Hash protocols were made public.[165]

Other players in the crypto community seemed to coalesce around the libertarian, if not anarchy-oriented, Cypherpunk movement. For example, Hal Finney, Wei Dei, and Adam Black were part of a group, if not camarilla, known as the Extropians. This community was comprised of futurists with a libertarian bent. Adam Black has said that cyber anarchist Tim May got him interested in the Cypherpunk movement, which may provide the reader with insight into the mindset of the founders of the onstage crypto movement.

All of these math savants lived in a rarified VR world, before there was the popular VR world as we know it. In their mind's eye, they are superheroes– similar to the people you see at a ComicCon convention but with a genius for cryptography, which turned out to be their superpower. In the virtual world, anything is possible, and that is the world where these fathers of cryptocurrency came from. With intent or inadvertence, these men *chose to impose* their world upon the OR world of money.

The intelligence community took notice of these libertarian cryptographers, and when acronym agencies take notice, they take action. According to David Chaum, agents of America's intelligence community contacted his colleagues and personal friends, i.e., members of the Cypherpunk community. What came out of

---

165 The current author believes that the NSA's foundational work on cryptocurrencies goes back at least as far as the 1980s and perhaps to the 70s or earlier.

those contacts resulted in the imposition of a gag order related to disseminating David's work with something called "mixes" that eventually led to Tor.

The NSA clamped down on the Cypherpunk's work, because its leadership had collectively concluded that it constituted a threat to national security. David never personally identified the person at the NSA who gave the order to clamp down on his work. I believe that person to be Lieutenant General Michael Hayden, who went on to become head of the CIA in 2006 under President George W. Bush.

Lieutenant General Michael Hayden, Former head of the NSA and CIA

Director Hayden has been and is keenly attuned to the numerous threats that weaponized cryptography, including cryptocurrencies, poses to national security. In fact, it was General Hayden who headed the CIA during its joint development of the VR Stuxnet code, along with Israel's Mossad. Stuxnet enabled the OR world *physical* destruction of digitally controlled VR systems, e.g., uranium enrichment centrifuges, nuclear power plants, and by implication server farms that house cryptocurrencies, their energy sources, cooling systems, etc., to wit:

> *"The Stuxnet computer virus sabotage of Iran's nuclear program was a 'good idea' but it lent legitimacy to the use of malicious software as a weapon, according to a former CIA director. 'We have entered into a new phase of conflict in which we use a cyber weapon to create* ***physical destruction****.'"* [166]

At this point, permit me to introduce a point of order. Sharing forensic intelligence data does not necessarily mean that I am in disagreement with specific agency actions or question the good intentions of the people and agencies that are the subject of my reportage. Quite to the contrary, I have made the point throughout this book that virtual reality is not to be ignored or taken lightly. It has changed the physical structure of tens of millions of brains, impacted mental and physical health, and now money. With regard to the national security threat that virtual reality poses, keep in mind that religious zealotry, when mixed with a powerful dose of hope and greed and paired with a gamer's mindset, **is** THE recipe for disaster—and disasters of any magnitude are important to national security. Keep that in mind as we continue our close examination of V the Reality money.

In response to the intelligence community's clampdown on cryptocurrency code sharing, Cypherpunks smuggled code embedded within tattoos and other clever workarounds. Any idealistic, albeit naïve person who sets about to upend not only an apple cart but THE apple cart, aka money, using virtual reality should be

---

[166] PHYS.ORG. Stuxnet was 'good idea': former CIA chief. March 2, 2012.

aware that they are playing with fire. Also recognize that fire's agents' first attempt to control you will not be to burn you.

The seduction of viable threats to existent power by existent power is a well-practiced art. First, you are ignored. If that doesn't work, you are seduced with promises of sex, power, wealth, or even an invite to join the "club." Seduction comes in various forms. For example, according to Mr. Chaum, none other than Bill Gates, then CEO of Microsoft, offered him $100 million if he would agree to incorporate Chaum's eCash into the core code of every copy of Windows 95. According to Mr. Chaum, he turned down the offer.

As of 2020, Mr. Chaum is the brain trust behind the cryptocurrency named Praxxis. It is not publicly traded, and in terms of popularity it falls into the "other" category among cryptocurrency aficionados. People in the cryptography world have raved about Praxxis as technologically more sophisticated and safer than Bitcoin, but most readers have never heard of it.

David Chaum's Praxxis Cryptocurrency

The VR world of money is a difference-in-kind challenge to existent power. Cryptocurrencies have the potential to reorganize existent power centers. Bitcoin also has the potential to replace them—that is, eradicate them. The early cryptographers who set about to create cryptocurrencies may have had an inkling, but I am certain most of them failed to discern the gravity of what they were doing.

Keep in mind that mathematical savants have always lived in their own rarified worlds. The pejorative descriptor of "nerd" is not without functional merit, albeit a term I do not use as a matter of course as it applies to the people actually doing this disruptive work, because it is dismissive, rude, and I like many of them.

Book authors, screenwriters, and comic book creators have always been fascinated with the "nerd" who becomes the superhero, who ends up not only with the beautiful girl, but saving the world. These fabricated superheroes would not be expected to understand that their VR world is not the same as their adopted OR world—only in the movies does he actually save the world—but in each and every story line, they never quite fit in.

Virtual worlds have transformed communication, interpersonal relationships, transportation, food, shelter, and clothing. But make no mistake about it: minting money has always been the holy grail of power, and failure to discern what that means in the OR world will come, sooner or later, with a lesson that parallels the gravity of the situation.

V the Reality money was envisioned by a number of math savants—cryptographers—as a means to an end. What was the end? For the most part, they wanted to create an online economy *free of outside control*. Ben Wei was one of those people who, in 1998, created what he called b-money. You have to ask yourself: Did Mr. Wei set out to intentionally create a way to pay for illegal merchandise and services on the dark web without being caught, or was he, like Mr. May and later developers, in a battle with the banking industry and Big Brother? Could anyone smart enough to develop b-money have not known the implications of what they were doing? The answer is yes. This is because when you live in the virtual world, you can lose touch with reality. In another era, perhaps the brilliant founders of the crypto movement would have been master counterfeiters—with one big difference:

Each and every cryptocurrency creator has dreamed of making THEIR cash the authentic cash, and OR world money the counterfeit money.

Do you think the most powerful acronym agencies across the globe might be interested in appropriating Bitcoin for their own purposes? How about drug lords, child traffickers, and every other person involved in felonious behavior—you think they might be desirous of escaping the bonds of OR world monetary regulation? How about the stock market gamblers who are always on the lookout for the next trading vehicle vulnerable to the volatility of irrational exuberance? To what lengths will these and other villainous characters go to **destroy or empower** the Cypherpunk movement? Of course, malicious intent is a two-way street in the crypto world.

Jim Bell proposed using V the Reality money as a way to pay for the assassination of politicians and other leaders. He authored *Assassination Politics* in 1995. [167] Bell's "collective" mindset, something that is quite common in the crypto world, proposed the empowerment of average citizens, aka "the collective," by encouraging them to take the law into their own hands and engage in murder-for-hire schemes by pooling their cryptocurrency as a bounty for the head of who the "collective" wanted to kill—all untraceable thanks to cryptocurrency.

It took Nick Szabo in 1998 to *literally* propose V the Reality money. He named his cryptocurrency bit-gold. He has stated that he wanted to create a virtual version of OR world gold without the need for a central authority. Mr. Szabo presents himself as an anti-collectivist, anti-communist, and individual rights-oriented thinker. He is also a keen observer on a key vulnerability of gold, the result of it being an OR world commodity. In 2019, Mr. Szabo spoke in Tel Aviv, Israel, at the first Israeli Bitcoin Summit on this point:

> *"'There's going to be some situations where* ***a central bank can't trust*** *a foreign central bank or government with their bonds for example," said Szabo. 'One solution that's been developed is to have the Swiss government hold it for you—that's not a trust minimised solution. The*

[167] In April 1995, Bell authored the first part of a 10-part essay called "Assassination Politics", which described an elaborate assassination market in which anonymous benefactors could securely order the killings of government officials or others who are violating citizens' rights.

Swiss government itself is subject to political pressures and so a more trust minimised solution is cryptocurrency. The other problem with gold reserves is that they're physically vulnerable. ***When the Nazis conquered countries in Europe, the first place they went to was a central bank's gold reserves.'"*** [168] (Emphasis added)

Nick Szabo Speaking at the First Bitcoin Summit in Tel Aviv, Israel (photo: Platin)

Could crypto be envisioned by some as a preemptive strike against forces in the world that have aligned themselves against *some* sovereign nation(s)? If this is true, was *this* sovereign nation(s) pursuing this particular functionality of crypto as an afterthought, or was it the impetus to create it in the first place?

---

[168] FINANCE MAGNATES: Gold Reserves to Bitcoin Reserves: Nick Szabo on Crypto in 2019. Story by: David Kimberley, September 1, 2019.

Up until Mr. Szabo's bit-gold, cryptocurrencies had been joined at the hip with OR world money—with cryptocurrency serving the role of a token for VR world currency. Mr. Szabo proposed cryptocurrency as the virtual version of an OR world commodity, like gold, silver, et al., during his presentation in Tel Aviv in 2019. In keeping with his VR analog to the OR world, he laid out a method of "mining" V the Reality money by solving complex equations. As payment for "miner's" efforts, they would be paid in his cryptocurrency. By the way, Mr. Szabo was a former employee of David Chaum at DigiCast.

> **It is as though Mr. Szabo redefined the paper check as its own OR world money. He transformed flight simulators into passenger aircraft, with the owners of flight simulators the only people/nations that would be able to fly.**

What is intriguing is that after the work of Mssrs. Chaum, May, Wei, Szabo, Finney, Black, Law, Sabett, Solinas, et al., **the cryptocurrency movement seemingly went into hibernation.**

For ten years, the momentum and "collective" zealotry of math savants obsessed with creating V the Reality money—a momentum that appeared to be unstoppable—had been stopped. Are we to believe this stand-down, if indeed it occurred, was organic? For those who assert this ten-year crypto hiatus was organic, realize that would be like the automobile industry going into hibernation after Henry Ford's creation of the assembly line and the development of the Model A.

Let's now discuss the onstage debut of V the Reality money with this question: What if a "creator(s)" were to orchestrate the development of a working V the Reality money that is, by definition, 100% virtual—a true "MINTING OF MONEY" circa 21st century, for public consumption? You can be sure that in this orchestral arrangement, the creator(s) would remain anonymous—because when social engineering revolutions are brought onstage, the rule is "keep your engineers backstage." This is because you never know who your friends and enemies are, or even if they are distinguishable from one another. There is a reason ghost writers are labeled "ghosts."

The unique dynamics of the virtual world govern the behavior of cryptocurrencies. It is in that world that cryptocurrencies can function as envisioned, within whatever sets of cleverly designed rules its creators designed for them. However, *once they BECOME OR world money like Bitcoin, my Tenth Axiom of Virtual Reality becomes the fundamental governing dynamic.*

TENTH AXIOM OF VIRTUAL REALITY

If you go broke in the VR world of Bitcoin, you will also go broke in the OR world. VR currencies have no reset button.

CHAPTER XIX

BITCOIN: Bitcoin is not actually a coin

Let's examine the zeitgeist of Bitcoin. Devotees appear to be motivated, at least in part, by a genuine desire to restore equity from the inequities of past economic models—in particular central banks. We have chronicled this idealism among the likes of David Chaum, et al., for example. And exactly like the idealistic humanistic psychology movement spearheaded by Abraham Maslow, Carl Rogers, Charles Coulson, et al., not one of them factored into their laudable and elegant C++ coding and VR money protocols what Maslow only came to realize at the end of his life:

> "Maslow believed in evil, and we didn't.
> (referencing Rogers and Coulson) Maslow said
> there was danger in our thinking and acting as if
> there were no paranoids or psychopaths or SOBs
> to mess things up. We created a miniature
> utopian society, the encounter group." [169]

Another exigent human factor needs to be addressed, because it is inextricably linked to crypto. Bitcoin is conceptually, for all intents and purposes, a religion.

---

[169] Coulson, Charles. How I Wrecked the I. H. M. Nuns.The Latin Mass, Chronicle of Catholic Reform, Special Edition, 1994.

religion | rəˈlijən |noun - the belief in and worship of a superhuman controlling power, especially a personal God or gods: ideas about the relationship between science and religion.

• a particular system of faith and worship: the world's great religions.

• a pursuit or interest to which someone ascribes supreme importance: consumerism is the new religion.

Like a religion, Bitcoin is mysterious by its very nature (few people honestly understand what it is and how it works) and therefore requires more belief than empirically derived scientific understanding, not unlike a secular version of the Paschal mystery. Likewise, Bitcoin's genesis is steeped in intrigue—complete with a spiritual oracle that appeared out of nowhere and created his religion—then disappeared without a trace (perhaps into heaven), known by the name of Satoshi Nakamoto.

Because Bitcoin's provenance story resembles the genesis story of many religions, and its followers include devout believers, it is virtually impossible for an objective analysis of Bitcoin to fall upon objectively tuned ears. Believers will tell you it is a revelation from a mysterious prophet, while non-believers will make their case that Bitcoin is the VR world analog of a classic Ponzi scheme. If ever there was a subject that routinely falls prey to the pitfalls of confirmation bias, it is Bitcoin.

CONFIRMATION BIAS: by: Signe Wilkinson (Courtesy of The Philadelphia News)

Mythical backstage idealistic creators of Bitcoin are not, however, the driving force behind the cryptocurrency revolution. Satoshi's part in the psychodrama is his starring role as the *mystery man*. This archetypal role is so important that an entire genre of literature and film is labeled "mystery." One particular onstage group I want to identify, however, is the driving force behind Bitcoin, and these are greed merchants and gamblers. They are, upon close inspection, comprised of digital immigrants who came from the seedier parts of Wall Street money manipulation in the 1980s. But now, having seen the light, or so their story goes, they have jumped on the "get rich by trading Bitcoin and kill all the central bankers" bandwagon—or so their liner notes read.

VR World Cryptocurrencies vs. OR World Environments

The definition of Bitcoin is not unlike the definition of water. It can be described through the prism of technical analysis, e.g., "two atoms of hydrogen and one of oxygen" {H_20 or with more precision by depicting water's molecular geometry, e.g., HOH}. Water may also be defined by its function within the context of biological systems, e.g., "a necessary element of life." You will notice that like any abstract mathematical construct or protocol written in C++ or other coding language, the functional definition is depicted as its familiar analog in the OR world, in this case coins. We will technically define cryptocurrency later, but our focus at this point is on how cryptocurrencies, the OR world, and V the Reality interact and intersect with one another.

Cryptocurrencies have been defined as a store of value and/or means of exchange—two definitions not without controversy. Cryptocurrencies have also become a vehicle for wild financial speculation by the same cadre of wild-west cowboys who gamed GME using Robinhood and Reddit. In fact, a cryptocurrency named Dogecoin (created as a joke by the way) became the target of this same gang of gamblers, and as a result managed to crash Robinhood on May 4, 2021. [170]

> *"Robinhood ran into issues processing cryptocurrency trades this morning, during a spike in the price of Dogecoin that sent users flocking to the app. The website DownDetector shows the outage starting around 9:30AM ET and reducing in severity about an hour later. Robinhood confirmed that it experienced a "partial outage" in crypto trading and said the issues had been resolved as of 11:15AM ET."* [171]

I need to address some issues related to Bitcoin's valuation metrics, since this brilliant baby of the Cypherpunks has been, at least up to this point in time (2021), commandeered by the gamblers on and off Wall Street. If it has been a while since you read my chapter on stock trading, now may be a good time to review that content before proceeding.

---

[170] CNN Business: What is Dogecoin? How a joke became hotter than bitcoin. Story by: David Goldman, May 4, 2021. Dogecoin was created December 6, 2013, by a pair of software engineers as a joke.Billy Markus, an IBM programmer from Portland, Oregon, set to differentiate his crypto from bitcoin, which was steeped in mystery with an anonymous creator and at the time attracted a small, niche group of miners. Markus wanted his cryptocurrency to be open to the masses, according to Chohan. Markus looked for help making his weird dream a reality and found Jackson Palmer, who worked for Adobe (ADBE). Palmer purchased the domain dogecoin.com — a nod to the "doge" meme that was all over the internet at the time. The website nods to its joke origins at the very top: Its Shiba Inu mascot is the first image on the page, mimicking the meme that inspired it, which features the same dog surrounded by a bunch of Comic Sans text in broken English. On dogecoin.com, its mascot is captioned: "Dogecoin is an open-source peer-to-peer digital currency, favored by Shiba Inus worldwide."

[171] THE VERGE: Robinhood crypto trading crashed during a Dogecoin spike. Story by: Jacob Kastrenakes, May 4, 2021.

Here is a primer on how people think about Bitcoin in the financial markets. With regard to Bitcoin being a store of value, it is important to appreciate that Bitcoin is a non-productive asset, and as such its value is wholly dependent upon the value another person is willing to ascribe to it. In other words, for a non-productive asset like Bitcoin to appreciate, its owner must find another person who counts on the fact that he, like you, will be able to find another buyer who will pay more to him than he paid to you for the privilege of owning Bitcoin. In stock market trading parlance, this is called "the greater fool" theory. How something so brilliant and revolutionary as Bitcoin has fallen prey to the greater fool theory is proof of Maslow's wisdom. Here is some more color on non-productive assets.

If you buy a farm, you have the value of the land, but also your farm may produce commodities that you can sell, e.g., soybeans and corn. After 20 years of owning the farm, you have the original productive asset of the farm, but you also have the value of the assets produced by the farm. The same holds true for a private or publicly traded business. A viable business is a productive asset—it generates income for its owner/share holders.

Members of the nouveau Wall Street church of Bitcoin often point to gold as an analog of Bitcoin. Putting aside the fact that gold does have some value as a commodity in some industries, e.g., electronics, dentistry and jewelry, gold is also best described as a non-productive asset for our purposes here. So, let's use gold as an analog of Bitcoin to hone and clarify the assumptions made by Robinhood cowboys.

If we go back 2000 years and study the value of the time required to mine and hold X amount of gold, and then move those calculations forward, correcting for time and cost variables and using today's analogous metrics, you will find that the compound interest rate of gold's appreciation over those two millennia would amount to one or two-tenths of a percent—essentially corroborating the notion that gold is a non-productive asset. Another example is perhaps more relatable to digital immigrants: if a person purchased gold in 1942, reasoning that Ally forces may lose the war, and you held that gold until 2021, you would have less than one cent of appreciation for every dollar you spent on that gold in 1942, using metrics in today's dollars. [172]

Bitcoin's plausible value resides in its comparison to fiat currencies. The Fed's printing presses have devalued the dollar. On the other hand, Bitcoin has a stipulation found in its source code that it must have a limited and finite supply. But that limit is not immutable, because the source code can and has been modified since its inception in some fundamental and critical ways. Here is just one example.

Satoshi limited the block size to one megabyte. So-called "big blockers" want to double the size of the block—that is, tinker with Mr. Nakamoto's creation. "Small blocker" or traditionalists argue that keeping the block size as originally defined by Nakamoto maintains Bitcoin as a store of value. "Big blockers" argue that Bitcoin's value is not as a store of value, but as a means of exchange, and that means competing with other payment services. How does Bitcoin compare as a means of exchange? Bitcoin can handle approximately seven transactions per second. By comparison:

- PayPal-15 transactions per second
- Visa- 2000 transactions per second

On the subject of fiat currencies, the USD, as well as every other country's currency, are defined as fiat currencies. Here is why: In 1973, under President Nixon, the USA abandoned the gold standard. The gold standard defined and quantified the denomination of any paper note or coin to an equal value amount of gold for which the paper or coin currency could be exchanged. Practically, this meant that if the Central Bank of the United States desired to have "printed" $100,000 twenty-dollar bills, then an equal value of gold would have to be mined and/or allocated and made available for exchange.[173] The gold standard was also abandoned during the

---

[172] Warren Buffet has popularized these analogies when analyzing cryptocurrencies.

[173] The U.S. Federal Reserve controls the supply of money in the U.S., and when it expands that supply it is often described as "printing money." The job of actually printing currency bills belongs to the Treasury Department's Bureau of Engraving and Printing, but the Fed determines exactly how many new bills are printed each year.

Depression of the 1930s. **No country uses a gold standard as of 2021**. Dollars are, however, backed by the full faith and credit of the USA, a fact that cryptocurrency advocates dismiss without much thought.

Fiat currencies are often maligned as "only worth the paper they are printed upon." That description isn't quite fair, despite the ease with which fiat currencies can be devalued by the Fed's printing press. The dollar, for example, is a proxy for an operational definition of its OR world basis, e.g., the full faith and credit of the USA means, if nothing else, that its Gross National/Domestic Product (GNP-GDP) is the "gold." [174] But other profoundly important considerations exist with regard to cryptocurrency as a means of exchange or as a store of value, because it is digitally sourced virtual reality and requires electricity to exist—not just "make" to exist:

> *"The creation process, known as mining, requires computers around the world to complete rapid calculations to try to solve the same mathematical puzzle. It always takes 10 minutes, and the winner is rewarded with some digital bitcoin. Then a new puzzle is generated, and the whole process repeats for another 10 minutes. In August 2018, a Princeton University associate professor expert in cryptocurrency testified in writing at a hearing of the U.S. Senate Committee on Energy and Natural Resources. The testimony said bitcoin mining accounts for nearly 5 gigawatts—or about 1% of the world's energy use. That is slightly more than what is used by the entire state of Ohio. Electricity must be made from other energy sources. The process creates large amounts of greenhouse gases such as carbon dioxide, methane, and ozone. These allow sunlight to enter the Earth's atmosphere, but then trap the heat. So the more electricity produced, the hotter the planet gets. As more people learn about bitcoin and mining—and as the bitcoin*

---

[174] Gross domestic product (GDP) is the value of a nation's finished domestic goods and services during a specific time period. A related but different metric, the gross national product (GNP), is the value of all finished goods and services owned by a country's residents over a period of time.

price increases—more are using their computers to mine bitcoins. As more people join the network and try to solve these math puzzles, you might expect each puzzle to be solved sooner, but bitcoin is not designed that way. The software that mines bitcoin is designed so that it always will take 10 minutes for everyone on the network to solve the puzzle. It does that by scaling the difficulty of the puzzle depending on how many people are trying to solve it. The more people mining, the harder the puzzle gets. That is why it always will take 10 minutes. In other words, although the time taken to produce a bitcoin doesn't vary, the computing power used to produce it does. As more people join the bitcoin network and try to mine bitcoins, the puzzles become harder, and more computing power and electricity are used for each bitcoin produced. The best bitcoin mining software doesn't just let you participate. it also minimizes downtime, so you can mine more efficiently. That means a near-constant cycle of electricity use.

Calculating the Cost

To understand how to calculate the electrical energy used to power the bitcoin network, you'll need to understand how bitcoin creation works. First, you calculate how many sums are conducted per second to solve the puzzles. Then find out how much electricity it takes to do each sum. These individual sums are called hashes.1 There are so many, you must think in terms of millions (known as megahashes) or billions (gigahashes) to make any sense of them. In early 2020, the computers on the bitcoin network were cranking out close to 120 exahashes per second.2 One terahash is a trillion hashes per second, One petahash is a quadrillion hashes per second, and one exahash is one quintillion hashes per second. (That's a one followed by 18 zeros.) Many different bitcoin-mining computers are out there, but many companies have focused on Application-Specific Integrated Circuit (ASIC) mining computers. These use less energy to conduct their calculations. Mining companies running lots of ASIC miners as businesses, claim to use only one watt of power for every gigahash per second of computing performed when mining for bitcoins. If this information is correct, the bitcoin network in 2020 consumes 120 gigawatts (GW) per second. This converts to about 63 terawatt-hours (TWh) per year. Here's how energy use relates to hashtag volume:

One Gigahash Per Second = One Watt

One Terahash Per Second = One Kilowatt

One Petahash Per Second = One Megawatt

One Exahash Per Second = One Gigawatt

This amount of power equates to 156 million horses (1.3 million horses per GW) or 49,440 wind turbines (412 turbines per GW) generating power at peak production per second. No matter how many miners, it still takes 10 minutes to mine one bitcoin. At 600 seconds (10 minutes), all else being equal it will take 72,000 GW (or 72 Terawatts) of power to mine a bitcoin using the average power usage provided by ASIC miners. One watt per gigahash per second is fairly efficient. So it's likely this is a conservative estimate. Media outlets and bloggers have produced various estimates of the electrical energy used in bitcoin mining, so the accuracy of reported power use is sketchy, at best. Many residential miners use more power." [175]

[175] The Balance: How much power it takes to create a Bitcoin. Story by: Danny Bradbury with review and fact checking provided by Khadija Khartit, May 7, 2021.

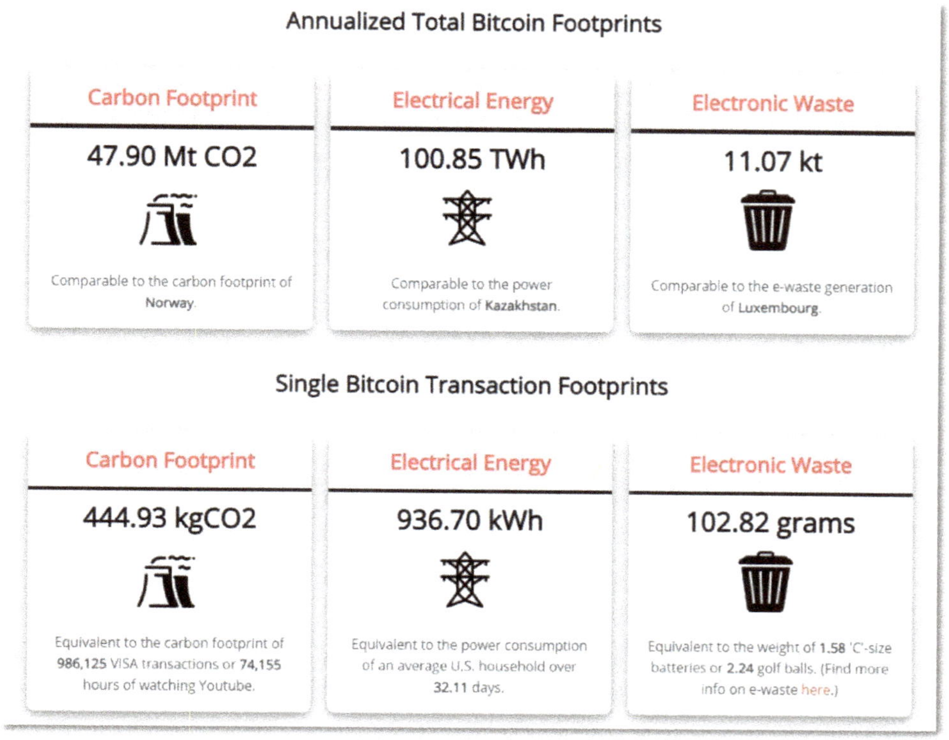

The University of Cambridge's Centre for Alternative Finance (Courtesy of DIGICONOMIST)

The 2019 Cambridge research found that Bitcoin production is estimated to generate between 22 and 22.9 million metric tons of carbon dioxide emissions a year, or between the levels produced by Jordan and Sri Lanka, according to a 2019 study in the scientific journal Joule. Cambridge updates its Bitcoin energy consumption metrics every 30 seconds. [176] The following screen grab was made on Friday May 7, 2021 PST:

---

[176] https://cbeci.org

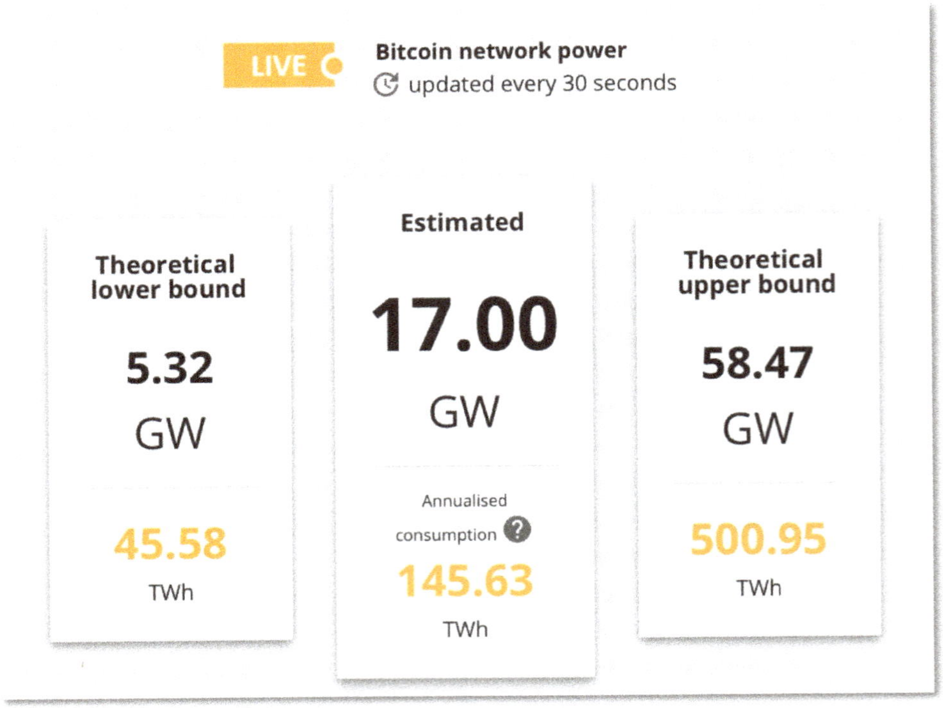

Bitcoin now requires more electricity than Argentina, the United Arab Emirates, or the Netherlands did for all of 2016. (Market Watch, February 16, 2021)

Corporate responsibility is a hot topic these days. We have ETFs that focus on green energy, conservation, and socially responsible industries. CEO pay is another topic brought to the forefront by the Occupy Wall Street movement.

> **Bitcoin's valuation is inextricably linked to these social and monetary dynamics—not because that is how it was designed, but because the idealists, anti-government, and privacy advocate civilian cryptographers created a baby that everyone wants to emulate or kidnap. Their very attractive baby has gotten old enough that she now attends public school, and it is becoming harder and harder to keep her from the world's bad influences.**

Let me give you some examples—keep in mind the anti-government and libertarian mindset of Bitcoin's historical figures as you read the following factual data.

China mines approximately 75 to 80 percent of all Bitcoins in existence. Inner Mongolia is a hotbed of mining activity, and it also happens to be coal rich. About 40 percent of all Bitcoins minded in China come from untreated coal burning power plants. As a consumer, you can determine *when* your Bitcoins were mined, but you cannot determine *where* they were mined. The environmental and socio-political implications of these facts are stunning. First and foremost, if you were to tell the Cypherpunks crew back in their early days that in the future one of the most intrusive, controlling, and anti-libertarian countries on earth would mine the vast majority of their anti-government creation, what do you think they would say? Put the issue of respect for Bitcoin's founders aside and consider the cold war between China and the United States.

What do you think would happen to the value of Bitcoin if an embargo were to be imposed upon China's Bitcoin mining operations? Perhaps a better question is this: how could such an embargo be enforced, given the very nature of Bitcoin's network of autonomous miners? If you are sensing a hint of hypocrisy among some Bitcoin aficionados, you may wish to consider some of the following facts. Don't progressive minded, environmentally focused digital currency aficionados know about China's coal fired furnaces churning out Bitcoins? Is not sustainable Bitcoin mining a human right? If the heirs to the Cypherpunk revolution are going to have to empower the government to enforce sustainability—perhaps at the tip of a spear—are we going to give in and modify one of the hallmark features of Bitcoin mining by forcing miners to not only identify their operations, but also provide to the government their exact carbon footprint? The devil is always in the details of the hash.

Miners of Bitcoin keep the network up and running by solving graduate-level mathematical problems. For their efforts, *they are paid in Bitcoins.* In recognition of this fact, it should be clear that the collective is not a *people's* collective at all—but is comprised of a miniscule cadre of elitists who happen to be math savants, and have set up their own V the Reality money banking system that only they understand—thus control.

The conflict of interest all Bitcoin miners share is seldom discussed and is directly linked to Bitcoin's valuation. Presumably, miners welcome an increase in the value of Bitcoin, because that is how they are paid—lower overhead means higher profits. But if Bitcoin fails as a store of value, and its valuation as a means of exchange requires it to modify block sizes that highlight the zero-sum relationship between store of value and means of exchange metrics, such that they are, then human behavior issues arise that impact valuation metrics.

For example, honest miners may believe that if they maintain the security and veracity of their mining operations, then the value of Bitcoin will increase. Ulterior motivated miners may do what any currency manipulators do in the OR world to increase her profits—she will exploit exchange rates. But she is not alone—she is joined by gamblers using VR to game stock markets. These include pump and dumpers and a host of other bad actors that are engaged in rapacious manipulation of Bitcoin's value.

In the OR world of money, exchange rates are either fixed or floating. Fixed means that the exchange rate for, let's say, the USD and the Euro is fixed at X amount. That exchange rate is maintained by the central bank of the nation's currency in question. This is done, in part, by the central bank buying or selling its own currency in order to maintain a fixed rate. When exchange rates are floating, as is the case with *any* VR money, comparative currency values are impacted by any number of variables out of anyone's control, to wit:

> *"Short-term moves in a floating exchange rate currency reflect* ***speculation, rumors, disasters****, and everyday supply and demand for the currency. If supply outstrips demand that currency will fall, and if demand outstrips supply that currency will rise. Extreme short-term moves can result in intervention by central banks, even in a floating rate environment. Because of this, while most major global currencies are considered floating, central banks and governments may step in if a nation's currency becomes too high or too low."* [177] (Emphasis added)

What are some of the exigent factors that could "move" the price of Bitcoin, other than fundamental changes in the asset?

> **TESLA BUYS $1.5 BILLION IN BITCOIN**: *Cryptocurrency's price soars after electric-vehicle maker says it soon expects to accept customer payments in Bitcoin*
>
> By: Caitlin Ostroff and Rebecca Elliott
>
> Updated Feb. 8, 2021 6:04 pm ET
>
> *"Tesla Inc. said Monday that it bought $1.5 billion in bitcoin, a disclosure that follows Chief Executive* ***Elon Musk's promotion*** *of the cryptocurrency and other digital-currency alternatives on Twitter.*
>
> *The electric-vehicle company also said it expects to start accepting bitcoin as payment for its products soon. Prices jumped more than 10% after the announcement, according to cryptocurrency research and news site CoinDesk."* [178] (Emphasis added)

---

177 Federal Reserve Bank of New York. "U.S. Foreign Exchange Intervention." https://www.newyorkfed.org/aboutthefed/fedpoint/fed44.html

178 Wall Street Journal, Business Section.

Musk's Tesla says it invested $1.5 billion in bitcoin, sending the cryptocurrency to record levels near $44,000 (Credit: MarketWatch)

So, what could be the problem here? How better could Mr. Musk express his confidence in the value of Bitcoin by "putting his shareholder's money where his mouth is?" One problem with any VR money is that it assumes the mantle of OR world money, but with none of the governors, central bank maintained exchange rates, little or no SEC oversight, and, as I have oft repeated, a precious few number of people who actually understand what Bitcoin is, much less its meaning and value in a hostile world where gamblers, shills, religious zealots, and governments want to move things around to suit their own purposes. If the Musks of this world are simply talking their book in service to their bets, then at the risk of the pun—all bets are off. To wit:

Reformed Bitcoin miner: Elon Musk's $1.5 billion bet is 'crazy'

"Few observers are better qualified than Alex Pickard to assess Elon Musk's astounding decision to channel $1.5 billion of Tesla's corporate cash into a bet on Bitcoin. Pickard is a former big-time Bitcoin miner who abandoned the cryptocurrency when, in his view, it strayed from

the original mission of becoming a consumer currency and gold-like store of value to degenerate into a casino chip for digital gamblers. It so happens that Pickard is also a student of sound corporate practices as a vice president at Research Affiliates, a firm that oversees $145 billion in investment strategies for mutual funds and ETFs. This writer recently wrote a piece chronicling Pickard's Bitcoin adventures, which encompassed buying $300,000 worth of ASIC-driven mining equipment and moving from sunny California to rustic Wenatchee, Wash., home to the lowest electricity prices in America. There, his machines whirred away in multiple garages. ***His dream came to grief when the local utility shut down his operation for overloading the grid*** *and Bitcoin's price tumbled over 80% in 2018. Given his vantage point, it was only natural that I query Pickard on Musk's unorthodox gambit."* [179] (Emphasis added)

Given the green "image" of electric vehicles in the public's mind, that investment didn't go over well with people who are tuned into the energy-intensive business that is Bitcoin. Ben Dear, head of Osmosis Investment Management, said this:

> *"'We are of course very concerned about the level of carbon dioxide emissions generated from bitcoin mining,' said Ben Dear, CEO of Osmosis Investment Management, a sustainable investor managing around $2.2 billion in assets that holds Tesla stock in several portfolios."* [180]

What follows is a typical Musk apologist's *belief-based retort* to the glaring dissonance between Musk touting his business as eco-friendly when it is nothing of the kind, even before he began investing in Bitcoin. This comes from SJ Oh—he is

---

[179] Fortune Magazine. "Reformed Bitcoin miner: Elon Musk's $1.5 billion bet is 'crazy'." Story by: Shawn Tully, February 13, 2021

[180] Reuters. "Elon Musk wants clean power. But Tesla's carrying bitcoin's dirty baggage." Story by: Anna Irrera, Tom Wilson.

the founder of a firm that runs a very small green bitcoin mining operations in the Canadian subarctic.

> *"'Overwhelmingly, I do think there will be a concerted effort by the bitcoin industry to be environmentally friendly,' said Oh, who believes Musk and his company can come up with better methods. 'Tesla is one of the greenest companies on the planet so I'm sure* ***they'll figure it out.'"*** [181]

Musk figured it out, but not as Mr. Oh had probably expected. **A few weeks after Musk sent Bitcoin soaring by willing to accept it as payment for his cars, he recanted, pointing out the huge carbon footprint of Bitcoin mining and its past and continuing deleterious effect on the environment.**

Do you think Elon Musk, CEO of SpaceX, Tesla, Solar City, and reputed "genius," was not fully aware, before he decided to accept Bitcoin as payment for his cars and purchased $1.5 billion in Bitcoin, that its mining operations and storage costs make West Virginia dirty coal look like a naturally occurring green geothermal energy plant? The only onstage event of major importance that occurred between the time Elon made his big Bitcoin announcement and purchase is when he appeared as guest host on Saturday Night Live. Perhaps the show's producer, Lorne Michaels,

---

181 Ibid

pulled him aside and shared some show biz insights about how performers must constantly preen their public image, so as to not get in the way of the public's projections upon them.

Is Mr. Musk unaware that tweeting golden hands is the same as flashing a gang sign to the gamblers of Bitcoin? Did golden hands help to protect his $1.5 billion in Bitcoin holdings from sliding even further? Is there a conflict here? Influential people have to know it is easy to manipulate a cryptocurrency that has a religious following. If Bitcoin is a currency, then is Mr. Musk's behavior currency manipulation? We know for certain that Mr. Musk's behavior as it relates to Bitcoin as a currency is not a part of the 1988 Omnibus Foreign Trade and Competitiveness Act, and would not fall under its purview regardless. [182]

For now, realize that VR world money machinations are wreaking havoc on OR world asset risk for anyone playing in the V the Reality money casino. No FDIC or analog institution functions as a safety net in the crypto world. If you can't pay your marker in Vegas—even though the chips you gamble with were designed to not look like real money—well, I refer readers to the movie Casino.

---

[182] Under this act the United States Secretary of the Treasury is required to "analyze on an annual basis the exchange rate policies of foreign countries ... and consider whether countries manipulate the exchange rate between their currency and the United States dollar for purposes of preventing effective balance of payments adjustments or gaining unfair competitive advantage in international trade"

VegasSlotsOnline.com (Image courtesy of Shutterstock)

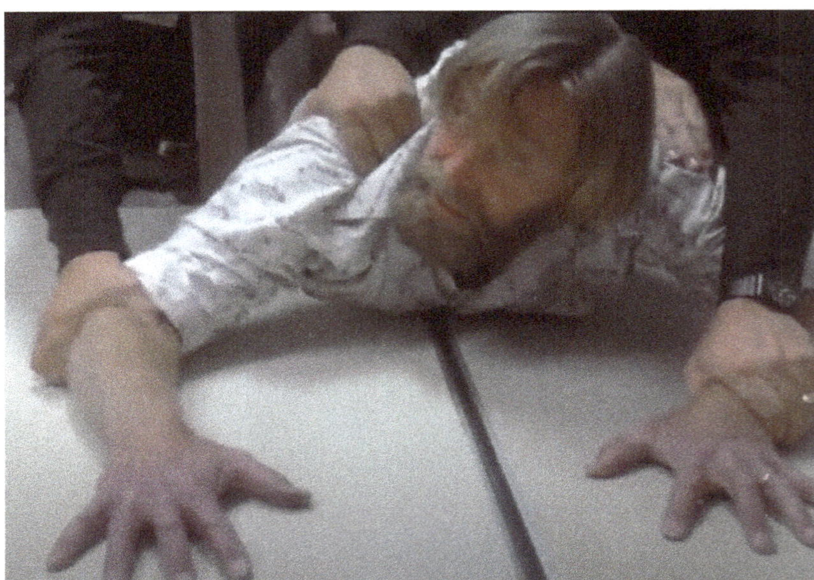

Cheaters Scene From the Movie Casino (Universal Pictures, 1995)

So, let's delve deeper into the gold issue, if for no other reason than the fact that Bitcoin and gold are often intertwined in the public's mind. Gold can be used as a comparison to Bitcoin, but not without problems. Refer to our earlier made points about gold and its role as a store of value. The cost of producing an American Gold Eagle, for example, is exponentially less energy intensive than producing its equivalent in Bitcoin. Not only is the cost of mining an American Gold Eagle less energy-intensive, but also once the gold is mined and then minted, the American Eagle consumes no energy to maintain. It produces no greenhouse gases as it sits safely in your safe, under your mattress or in that hole in your backyard—not so with Bitcoin. In fact, the cost to the environment of not only minting a "coin," but maintaining that area in the Bitcoin protocol you call your wallet, is so energy-intensive, the horrendous impact on the environment of the earth comes as a shock to even the most devout believers in the Church of Bitcoin—save for the Robinhood and Wall Street crowds, that are dancing with snakes and imbibing Strychnine while speaking in tongues as they read these words.

The issues related to productive vs. non-productive assets and costs to the environment exist solely because Bitcoin's genome is by definition 100 percent pure virtual reality, while gold is pure objective reality. Once again, for all the machinations of Bitcoin, the one thing about all cryptocurrencies is that they are virtual and that, alone, should convince the reader that all those people walking along the beach held by the tractor beam of VR are not just people engaged in a fad, but people who are being biopsychosocially engineered by people whose internal worlds are written in C++, and who actually believe that V the Reality is good for the earth and the rest of humanity. If you have ever watched a forensic analyst step foot into a crime scene, the first thing he does is listen to the cops answer his question: "What do we have here?" I have a forensic interest in the provenance of crypto in general, and Bitcoin in particular. The Bitcoin saga is a forensic analyst's dream-come-true. Come along with me past the yellow tape, and let's examine this whodunit.

CHAPTER XX

SATOSHI NAKAMOTO: A rose by any other name would smell as sweet

As of 2021, the most popular cryptocurrency with the largest market cap is Bitcoin. When I discuss Bitcoin, I am by definition exploring the VR world of money. The VR world characteristics of Bitcoin are the same for other cryptocurrencies, e.g., Etherium or Dogecoin, though significant differences exist between them. Bitcoin's domain name was registered on August 18, 2008. Only its creators know its gestation period.

```
Domain Name: BITCOIN.ORG
Registry Domain ID: D153621148-LROR
Registrar WHOIS Server: whois.namecheap.com
Registrar URL: http://www.namecheap.com
Creation Date: 2008-08-18T13:19:55Z
Registrar: NameCheap, Inc.
```

Keep in mind the Bitcoin religion is long in the tooth, although most of its digital native flock believes, as with electric cars, that both are something new—they are not.

Electric Vehicles Have Been Around for Well Over 100 Years

Bitcoin's genesis is also the name given to its original coding block, i.e., "Genesis Block."

Halloween 2008—that is, October 31, 2008—marked the day the following whitepaper was published: *Bitcoin: A Peer-to Peer Electronic Cash System.* Where was it published? Of all places, a cryptography mailing list at metzdowd.com. This is the title as it looked back in 2008:

Bitcoin: A Peer-to-Peer Electronic Cash System

Satoshi Nakamoto
satoshin@gmx.com
www.bitcoin.org

The so-called "Genesis Block" was published on January 3, 2009, and sometime in 2010, Satoshi Nakamoto made his ascension into Bitcoin heaven—or perhaps

Purgatory.[183] Take a look at how Bitcoin.com depicted the date of the Genesis Block's publication,

Bitcoin.com Depiction of the Publication Date of the Bitcoin Genesis Block

The actual Genesis Block is less stork-like and looks like this in the OR world:

```
00000000   01 00 00 00 00 00 00 00   00 00 00 00 00 00 00 00   ................
00000010   00 00 00 00 00 00 00 00   00 00 00 00 00 00 00 00   ................
00000020   00 00 00 00 3B A3 ED FD   7A 7B 12 B2 7A C7 2C 3E   ....;£íýz{.²zÇ,>
00000030   67 76 8F 61 7F C8 1B C3   88 8A 51 32 3A 9F B8 AA   gv.a.È.Ã^ŠQ2:Ÿ¸ª
00000040   4B 1E 5E 4A 29 AB 5F 49   FF FF 00 1D 1D AC 2B 7C   K.^J)«_Iÿÿ...¬+|
00000050   01 01 00 00 00 01 00 00   00 00 00 00 00 00 00 00   ................
00000060   00 00 00 00 00 00 00 00   00 00 00 00 00 00 00 00   ................
00000070   00 00 00 00 00 00 FF FF   FF FF 4D 04 FF FF 00 1D   ......ÿÿÿÿM.ÿÿ..
00000080   01 04 45 54 68 65 20 54   69 6D 65 73 20 30 33 2F   ..EThe Times 03/
00000090   4A 61 6E 2F 32 30 30 39   20 43 68 61 6E 63 65 6C   Jan/2009 Chancel
000000A0   6C 6F 72 20 6F 6E 20 62   72 69 6E 6B 20 6F 66 20   lor on brink of 
000000B0   73 65 63 6F 6E 64 20 62   61 69 6C 6F 75 74 20 66   second bailout f
000000C0   6F 72 20 62 61 6E 6B 73   FF FF FF FF 01 00 F2 05   or banksÿÿÿÿ..ò.
000000D0   2A 01 00 00 00 43 41 04   67 8A FD B0 FE 55 48 27   *....CA.gŠý°þUH'
000000E0   19 67 F1 A6 71 30 B7 10   5C D6 A8 28 E0 39 09 A6   .gñ¦q0·.\Ö¨(à9.¦
000000F0   79 62 E0 EA 1F 61 DE B6   49 F6 BC 3F 4C EF 38 C4   ybàê.aÞ¶Iö¼?Lï8Ä
00000100   F3 55 04 E5 1E C1 12 DE   5C 38 4D F7 BA 0B 8D 57   óU.å.Á.Þ\8M÷º..W
00000110   8A 4C 70 2B 6B F1 1D 5F   AC 00 00 00 00             ŠLp+kñ._¬....
```

Genesis Block's Coinbase Parameter Message

We can logically infer that the Genesis Block was written in the coding language C++, probably using a Windows GUI mining application. If the Genesis block is

---

[183] "Ascension", "Assumption", or "Translation", the belief in some religions that some individuals have ascended into Heaven without dying first.

denoted as block zero, then block one was not completed until six days later, for a total of seven days for the creation/coding of blocks zero through one. A popular theory among devout Bitcoin followers is that Nakamoto took seven days to complete his first two blocks, just as God took seven days according to the Christian Bible's Book of Genesis to create the earth. A variation on this religious theme is that Nakamoto chose seven days to complete his initial work as homage to God's creation of the earth according to the Christian Bible. Nothing about Satoshi's Japanese surname, or Nakamoto himself, informs us that he is a Christian or would likely be Christian—in fact, the exact opposite is true. The first Bitcoin transaction occurred between Satoshi and a man named Hal Finney on January 12, 2009, and it involved 10 Bitcoin.

Following the money for forensic analysts is second nature. Satoshi Nakamoto's appearance/disappearance act adds a certain *je ne c'est quoi* to the Bitcoin magical mystery tour. However, when analyzing Bitcoin's trillion-dollar market cap, you can be sure the people who make money from money are going to telegraph things about this mystery without even knowing it.

The Bitcoin Old School Album Cover

One dramatic overlap between the VR /OR worlds of money occurred on February 25, 2021. That is when Coinbase filed its S-1 disclosures as required by the SEC, as a prerequisite to its Initial Public Offering (IPO) on April 14, 2021. S-1 documents contain all the important financial information required by the SEC that are part of the disclosure package available to investors, who can then make an informed choice before investing. Coinbase was started in 2012, a couple of years after Satoshi handed over control of Bitcoin to a man by the name of Gavin Andresen.

As filed with the Securities and Exchange Commission on February 25, 2021

UNITED STATES
SECURITIES AND EXCHANGE COMMISSION
WASHINGTON, DC 20549

FORM S-1
REGISTRATION STATEMENT
UNDER
THE SECURITIES ACT OF 1933

Coinbase Global, Inc.
(Exact name of registrant as specified in its charter)

7389
(Primary Standard Industrial
Classification Code Number)

Cover Page from Coinbase Global's S-1 SEC Filing

One of the important disclosures I found in the S-1 document was written by lawyers for Coinbase's CEO, Brian Armstrong. Forensically, any disclosure is important, because as I like to say, "a lot of derriere covering" is found in S-1 documents, and these provide clues about those people that know where the bodies are buried. You would be surprised how the process of *couverture des fesses* encourages the coverer to tell you things he wouldn't otherwise come out and say. Here is what Coinbase's CEO included in his S-1 regarding Satoshi Nakamoto:

> *"Coinbase says the entire crypto market could be destabilized if Bitcoin's anonymous creator is ever revealed or sells their $64 billion stake."*

First, let's address the liquidation of a $64 to $70 billion holding. Yes, that would devalue Bitcoin, but exceptionally large sell orders almost always have that effect upon a stock's price—so that disclosure is perfunctory. Let's peel off a few layers of the onion regarding that comment about the cataclysmic risk, should Satoshi's real identity be revealed.

What I glean from that statement is that like almost everyone else, Armstrong believes the name Satoshi Nakamoto is a nom du guerre. A single person responsible for a trillion-market cap C++ written protocol on a block/blockchain now estimated (2021) to be worth $64 to $70 billion, who chooses to remain anonymous rather than coming forth so people could project upon him that he is the second coming of Christ, who could have any babe in the world (presuming he is a heterosexual male) and bask in the glow of idolization for the rest of his life, is itself worthy of attention.

I and everyone else not living under a rock knows the identities of at least five or more names who may be the man behind the nom du guerre—if there is a single person. Not one or any combination of those Nakamoto candidates has caused so much as a ripple in financial markets. You won't find any Bitcoin gambler/investor/member of the church who has expressed concern that if X is identified as the real Satoshi Nakamoto, their money will vaporize into thin air.

In reality, while the immaculate conception part of the religious story will be lost if the real Satoshi stands up, that part of the Bitcoin story will be replaced with a living figurehead who will become the embodiment of the second coming. But I, as a forensic analyst, can come up with some candidates who not only would make more logical and historical sense when it comes to who is/are the creator(s) of cryptocurrency, and in particular Bitcoin, but my revelation would immediately vaporize Bitcoin, just as stated in Coinbase's S-1 disclosures.

My revelation as articulated in the following **is pure speculation,** and even if it were true, I could never rationalize it as true, nor would I assert that it is true. The identities set forth below are **purely for "what if" purposes** and have no basis in fact. In fact, to circle back to the brilliant creators of South Park, Matt Stone and Trey Parker:

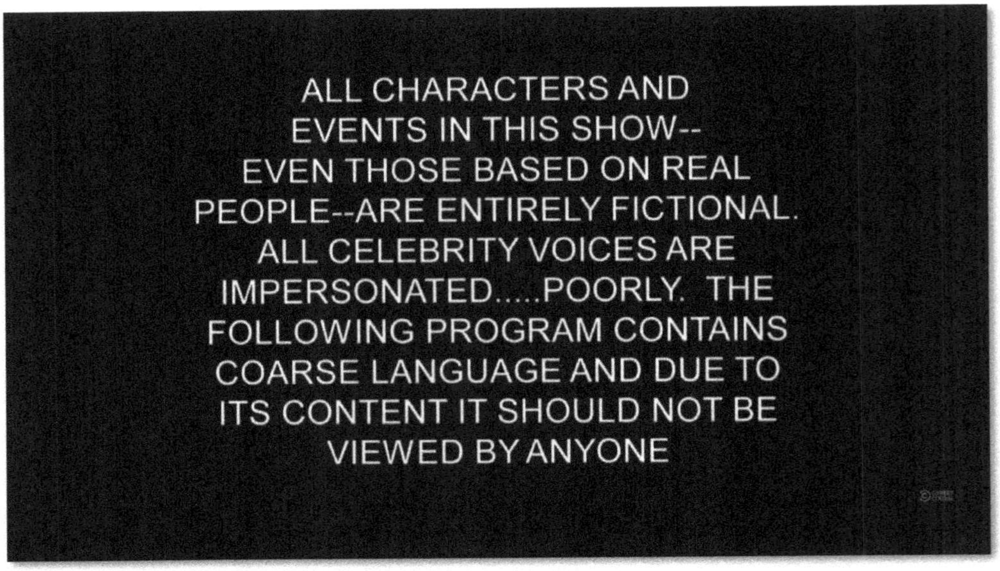

The NSA and CIA, working in unison with IDF's Unit 8200 and related specialists in Israel, assembled the final foundational products we call cryptocurrencies, in particular Bitcoin. The assembly took place during the approximate ten-year hiatus when the momentum among individuals mentioned earlier came to an onstage screeching halt. Even if it turns out these entities had no involvement whatsoever in the creation of Bitcoin—they probably did.

When we name an organization or agency, what we are really doing is naming people who work both as individuals and team members within or on behalf of that organization. The revelation—excuse me—*pure speculation* that acronym agencies in the United States and Israel had a dominant hand in the assembly and propagation of Bitcoin should not come as a surprise to anyone—that is, if it were true, which it is not.

William Binney worked as a cryptographer in the NSA. Edward Snowden's most impassioned warnings pointed to the work of cryptographers and data analysts within the NSA. The fact of, i.e., *pure speculation* there was an acronym agency involvement in the final coding of Bitcoin would crash Bitcoin in a New York minute, and for good reason. But it would not be the best reason—the best reason is because V the Reality money is the solvent of privacy and control for the OR world creatures we optimistically refer to as homo sapiens DESPITE THE FACT CRYPTO HAS BEEN SOLD AS A PRIVACY FIREWALL—how poetically ironic. It is the sapiens part that cynics question as accurate, because as we have documented, human beings find VR extremely pleasing ,even at the expense of their privacy and unique personality over which they have some control. For now, let's get back behind the yellow tape and examine the OR world genesis of the Genesis Block.

Peeling back one more layer of the onion, I want to make note of the fact that a man by the name of Barry Silvert purchased 48,000 Bitcoins in 2014 at a price of $350. This is interesting, not just because this venture capitalist would buy Bitcoin, but from where he purchased them is very telling. The United States Marshal Service sold the Bitcoins to Mr. Silvert through one of their auctions. Another Wall Street type by the name of Tim Draper also bought 30,000 Bitcoins at the same auction.

Let's explore this: why would the United States Marshal have Bitcoins in its possession to sell in the first place? Let me give to you this preface to that answer. On May 7, 2021, Colonial Pipeline Company, the largest gasoline and related fuel pipeline companies in the USA, learned it was the victim of a cybersecurity attack that involved ransomware. DarkSide, a peer of REvil that extorted Apple Computer, has demanded hundreds of millions of dollars from Colonial.

How do you think RW attackers expect to receive their money? Do they want you to write them a check? How about wiring the money from Colonial's bank to the bank of DarkSide? How about the way it was done in the olden days, when a suitcase full of cash money was dropped in a trash bin late at night with the admonition from the extorters: "Come alone. If I see the police, you never see your data again."

If you guessed the ransom would be paid in Bitcoin, you would be right. Yes, Bitcoin has a long and illustrious history as the Silk Road's favored method of payment—everything from dark tar heroin to murder for hire, or buying little children from the poorest countries on earth so you can torture them in the privacy of your own dungeon—Satoshi's creation ruined by paranoids, psychopaths and SOBs? Who would have guessed?

Law enforcement agencies, that's who, and despite what you may have heard, Bitcoin is not anonymous. Take a look at just ONE agency's 2014 sting operation's haul of Bitcoin—P.S., just as a reminder this is where Mssrs. Silvert and Draper purchased their Bitcoin.

These Bitcoin were forfeited in various federal criminal, civil and administrative cases, including:

United States v. Tyler Lee Ward et al., (Case No. 18-cr-438)
DEA Administrative Forfeiture of 1.3766326 Bitcoin
DEA Administrative Forfeiture of 4.94507746 Bitcoin
DEA Administrative Forfeiture of 7.13218 Bitcoin
DEA Administrative Forfeiture of 1.49273858 Bitcoin
DEA Administrative Forfeiture of 14.95978524 Bitcoin
United States v. Ryan Farace (Case No. 18-cr-00018)
United States v. Matthew Lee Yensan (Case No. 17-cr-00303)
DEA Administrative Forfeiture of 1.65659480 Bitcoin
DEA Administrative Forfeiture of 0.66224525 Bitcoin
DEA Administrative Forfeiture of 14.59638483 Bitcoin
DEA Administrative Forfeiture of 0.24130732 Bitcoin
DEA Administrative Forfeiture of 104.34765685 Bitcoin
United States v. Alexandre Cazes, et al., (Case No. 17-cv-00967)
FBI Administrative Forfeiture of 3.33369 Bitcoin
United States v. Ronald L. Wheeler, III (Case No. 17-cr-377)
United States v. Konrads Voits (Case No. 17-cr-20689)
FBI Administrative Forfeiture of 535 Bitcoin
HSI-USCBP Administrative Forfeiture of 0.82609561 Bitcoin
HSI-USCBP Administrative Forfeiture of 8.91 Bitcoin
HSI-USCBP Administrative Forfeiture of Jaxx Wallet BTC (approximately 0.232 btc)
HSI-USCBP Administrative Forfeiture of 0.27698615 Bitcoin
HSI-USCBP Administrative Forfeiture of BITCOINS (approximately 3.544 btc)
HSI-USCBP Administrative Forfeiture of 26.3765293 Bitcoin
HSI-USCBP Administrative Forfeiture of 17.49013698 Bitcoin
HSI-USCBP Administrative Forfeiture of 1.75799537 Bitcoin and 3.63951363 Bitcoin
HSI-USCBP Administrative Forfeiture of 22.89799376 Bitcoin
HSI-USCBP Administrative Forfeiture of 2.02903322 Bitcoin
HSI-USCBP Administrative Forfeiture of 24.21055495 Bitcoin
HSI-USCBP Administrative Forfeiture of 23.7981166 Bitcoin
HSI-USCBP Administrative Forfeiture of Bitcoin (approximately 0.758 btc)
HSI-USCBP Administrative Forfeiture of 5.57 Bitcoin
HSI-USCBP Administrative Forfeiture of Bitcoin (approximately 2.147 btc)
HSI-USCBP Administrative Forfeiture of 3.047 Bitcoin
HSI-USCBP Administrative Forfeiture of 1.50467582 Bitcoin
HSI-USCBP Administrative Forfeiture of .474648 Bitcoin
HSI-USCBP Administrative Forfeiture of .495109 Bitcoin
HSI-USCBP Administrative Forfeiture of 1.86375 Bitcoin
HSI-USCBP Administrative Forfeiture of 18.58166338 Bitcoin
HSI-USCBP Administrative Forfeiture of 0.52691763 Bitcoin
HSI-USCBP Administrative Forfeiture of 35.25012887 Bitcoin
United States v. Seth Bangert (Case No. 19-mj-00073)
HSI-USCBP Administrative Forfeiture of 0.479 Bitcoin
United States v. Donte L. Gibson, et al. (Case No. 18-cr-094)
United States v. Gal Vallerius (Case No. 17-cr-20648)
IRS Administrative Forfeiture of 8.9 Bitcoin
United States v. Darcy Wedd (15-cr-00616)
United States v. Sky Justin Gornik (17-cr-2796)
USPIS Administrative Forfeiture of 0.03773082 Bitcoin
USPIS Administrative Forfeiture of 9.7081 Bitcoin
USPIS Administrative Forfeiture of .1366 Bitcoin
USPIS Administrative Forfeiture of 4.667127 Bitcoin
USPIS Administrative Forfeiture of 6.820611 Bitcoin
USPIS Administrative Forfeiture of 4.8836697 Bitcoin
United States v. 1.60005061 Bitcoin and 0.34017587 Bitcoin (Case No. 19-cv-959)
United States v. Matthew Mulford (Case No. 19-cr-028)

- **Bitcoin Transfer.** The USMS will not transfer any bitcoins until it has confirmed receipt of purchase funds from the buyer. The USMS will not transfer bitcoins to an obscene public address, a public address apparently in a country restricted by the Office of Foreign Assets Control (OFAC), a public address apparently associated with terrorism, other criminal activities, or otherwise hostile to the United States.

- **How much money do I need to make a bid?**

You are responsible for ensuring that you have enough available funds to cover your bid. If you are selected as a winning bidder, you must initiate a wire transfer and provide the USMS with a copy of the wire transmittal receipt by Wednesday, February 19, 2020 at 2:00 PM EST. Failure to initiate a wire deposit in the full amount of your bid, less the initial deposit, will result in forfeiture of your deposit.

A couple of things are worth noting about this U.S. Marshals Auction. Perhaps the most important is the fact that the United States government, by and through just ONE of its law enforcement agencies, was able to confiscate felons' Bitcoins. Not only was their VR money EASILY confiscated, their OR world derrieres were then placed in an OR world jail cell. I'll leave it to readers to confirmation bias these facts using whatever cognitive legerdemain at your disposal in order to maintain your religious beliefs in Bitcoin. Also, if you want your auction-won Bitcoins, just like any retail investor who desires to purchase Bitcoin, you have to trade in your OR world money for VR world money before the United States or its broker will deliver to you VR money in the form of Bitcoins.

I suppose the lesson is this: If you want to use Bitcoin or any other cryptocurrency for buying products or services, you better not run afoul of any number of law enforcement agencies of the United States, Interpol, et al., if you wish to retain your product, service, and cryptocurrency. You would also be wise to not cross paths with any number of acronym-identified intelligence agencies that make a determination that your behavior is a threat to national security.

The very day the galleys of this book were sent to the publisher, I made the following last-second addition to this part of the book, because it will serve as yet another piece of corroborative evidence as to the traceability of Bitcoin. On June 7, 2021, just one month after the RW attack on Colonial, the FBI issued a press release stating most of the ransom payment made in Bitcoin by Colonial had been recovered. Again, I ask the reader who isn't afraid of being excommunicated from the church of Bitcoin to question the assumptions they think they know about the access acronym agencies across the globe have to the block/blockchain. I dare say that unless the "bills" had been marked, this caper would have been impossible to solve.

Anyone who has gotten this far in this book, or is familiar with the intelligence community or my prior writings on this general subject, knows that information has always been center stage. Just as Unit 8200 is a commercial arm of the Israeli Defense Force, the United States and its allies have commercial arms that scour the earth for data and transaction dynamics of interest. Take In-Q-Tel, for example:

In-Q-Tell Mission Statement

In-Q-Tell Data Analyst Depiction

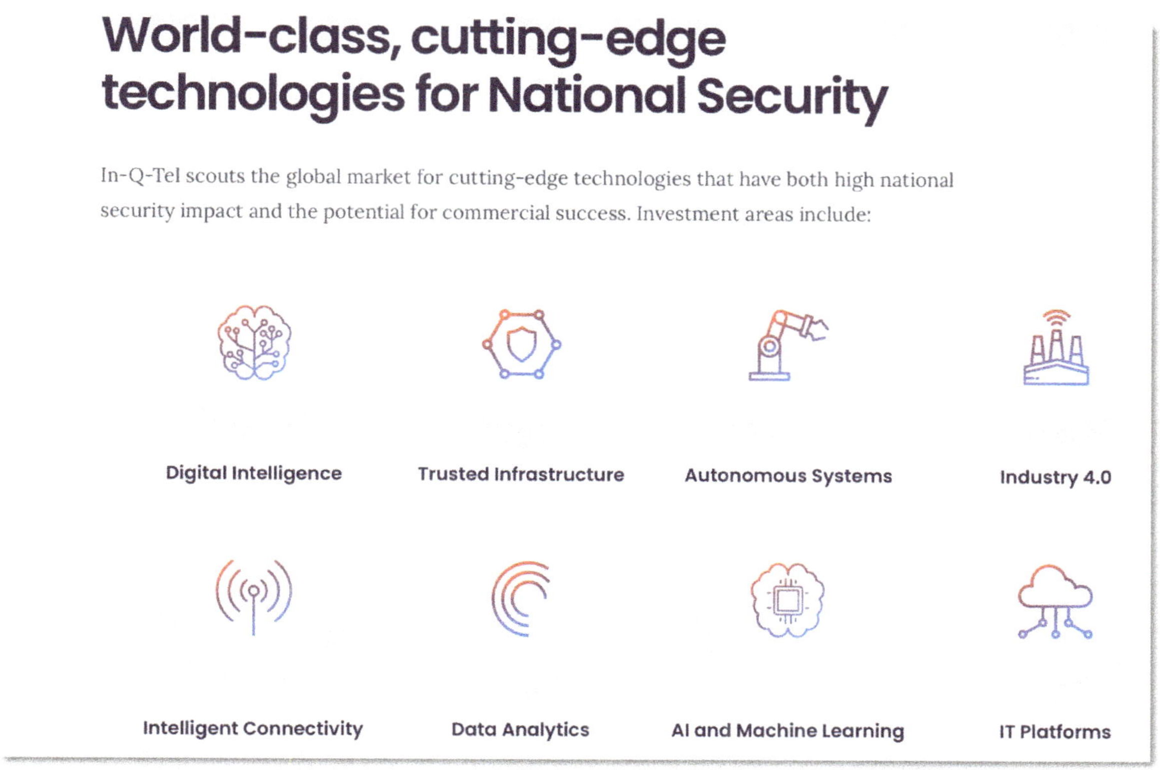

As we have previously documented, in 1996 cryptographers working for/with the NSA laid out the nuts and bolts of what a V the Reality money might involve. These NSA cryptographers belong to a rarified fraternity/sorority that interlope between their government posts and their retail arms. Their behavior is tracked every step of the way because, after all, they are important assets.

Through my forensic prism, it is fascinating but not unexpected that the people who talk about Satoshi, especially those who assert they communicated with him, would become persons of interest. Let's take a man by the name of Gavin Andresen. For the record, Mr. Andresen was born as Gavin Bell. So Satoshi handed over control of Bitcoin to a man who changed his name from Bell to Andresen. Take note of his virtual reality provenance before we move forward:

> Graduating from Princeton with a computer science degree in 1988, he developed software for a number of companies before landing on a full-time role working on bitcoin alongside Satoshi Nakamoto in December 2010. Before this, though, he focused his career on 3D graphics and **virtual reality modeling**.

Mr. Andresen *says* he worked alongside Satoshi Nakamoto. I have seen no OR world *documented* proof of that, e.g., a photograph, real world signed letter, or real-world money exchange. No, their relationship is, like Mr. Andresen's area of expertise, 100% virtual. The reader may find it of some forensic interest that Mr. Andresen has said he was the last person to speak to Satoshi Nakamoto. And here is a little tidbit: **Mr. Bell/Andresen was granted a security clearance by the CIA as early as 2011-12 and is no stranger to Langley, Virginia**. According to Andresen, he emailed Satoshi letting him know that the CIA had reached out to him on the subject of Bitcoin—okay.

If you are an American reader, you will probably tend to be ethnocentric about the provenance of Bitcoin. However, if you talk to educated people in Europe, Asia, and Northern Africa the idea that American and Israeli intelligence operations have their fingerprints all over Bitcoin is a given. No hard proof can be offered, of course, but that begs the question: "What would constitute hard proof?" One thing we do know is this: even when whistleblowers come forward with hard proof about the cryptographic world, e.g., William Binney, Edward Snowden, Perry Fellwock, aka Winslow Peck, Frank Snepp, Coleen Rowley, Thomas Drake, and others, the built-in safety net of plausible deniability is more than enough to temper their impact—especially to true believers, i.e. "You of little faith." [184]

When it comes to the virtual world of clandestine operations, if you think 007 was hard to ensnare, you should try connecting the 1's and 0's to OR world people who use nom du guerres for whom no birth record exists—or if it does, it is cryptographic, which means it could have been created out of whole cloth. Not unlike Jeannie in her bottle, but with no beautiful Barbara Eden to track down. You know Barbara Eden had to climb up a ladder to get into her fabricated bottle, BUT

---

[184] Christian Bible: Matthew 8:26 - The disciples went and woke Him, saying, "Lord, save us! We are perishing!" "You of little faith," Jesus replied, "why are you so afraid?" Then He got up and rebuked the winds and the sea, and it was perfectly calm. The men were amazed and asked, "What kind of man is this? Even the winds and the sea obey Him!"...

ONLY if you were backstage did you know this—and 99 percent of you have never been backstage.

Plausible Deniability in the Virtual World (make that last 1 a 0 – reading right to left)

A fundamental precept of any cryptocurrency is decentralization. Rather than your money and your transactions being held or managed by your bank, payment service, credit card, etc., cryptocurrency distributes your ledger and transactions across the crowd. By crowd, I mean a collective grouping of people numbering in the millions. The trust coefficient of millions of accountants rather than *your* bank derives from the old saw, "You can fool all of the people some of time; you can fool some of the people all of the time, but you can't fool all the people all the time." [185]

Whether or not that wisdom impacts your trust in the "collective" depends upon how you feel about the notion that you *can* fool all the people some of the time – and like setting off a suitcase nuke in the middle of a major city, you ONLY have to

---

[185] Attributed to Abraham Lincoln in The New York Times, August 27, 1887. According to The Collected Works of Abraham Lincoln, ed. Roy P. Basler, "Tradition has come to attribute to the Clinton [Illinois] speeches [September 2, 1858] this "most famous" of Lincoln's utterances. Basler indicates, however, that there is no evidence of this saying in Lincoln documents. P.T. Barnum has also been a putative source for the quotation.

be right once, i.e., fool them all for a brief period of time. I would also interject that individual psychology versus group psychology is a difference in kind. The way people think, feel, and ultimately behave in groups is distinctly different from individual thoughts, feelings, and behavior. What this boils down to is when you buy something, rather than the merchant or trading partner (seller) checking with your bank, PayPal, et al. to verify that you have sufficient funds, the crypto-collective is queried. Every owner of each transaction (the collective) possesses a copy of your transaction. When the purchase and/or transfer are executed, the collective update their records. All of this is automated, of course, by the "bulletproof" security of servers storing 1's and 0's in dynamic and/or static storage device(s) that run on electricity. So, what happens if a record is fraudulent? How does the merchant or trading partner know for certain if any given transaction is fraudulent?

The collective once again embarks upon its "you can't fool all the people (networked computers) all the time" model of human behavior predictions. If 95% of the collective do not agree on the veracity of a transaction, then the transaction is unverified. The model gives no consideration to the notion that perhaps it is the five percent that are correct, and the other 95 percent were hacked and/or corrupted. Since transactions are anonymous, the possibility that intelligence agencies could rig servers in the collective to reject a transaction by a persona non grata is out of the question. After all, we all know that networked computers, even when spread out across time zones, are secure and that no collective of servers has ever been compromised— "And it don't rain in Indianapolis in the summertime."

It is important to understand that the Bitcoin protocol is open source. That means that theoretically, anyone can make a change to the code. However, safeguards are in place, once again, using the collective model. A would-be modifier of Bitcoin's code must submit a Bitcoin Improvement Proposal (BIP). Just as with verifying a transaction's accuracy, 95% of the *last* 2000 miners have to agree that any one particular BIP is a "good" change. And of course no agency has the ability to orchestrate who those last 2000 miners would be. Again, the psychodynamic of group psychology is built into the Bitcoin protocol and opens any number of intrusion doors. The psychodynamics in play are similar to those at work in elections, that is, voting psychology. Add to voting psychology esoteric mathematical problem solving and a source code strewn among thousands and thousands of server farms, each with a rapacious appetite for energy, and you have a V the Reality money system ripe for exploitation. Apologists for the integrity of Bitcoin have extremely sensitive patellar tendons that leg-snap with the slightest impact of a rubber hammer to their knees. Gamblers and 1980s stock market manipulators who have "seen the light," I have found to have the most exquisitely sensitive patellar tendons of all.

What if I gave you a glimpse into what the future holds for the digital natives who are enthralled by their emoji and meme-level discernment and love of Bitcoin. What if I told you that on March 26, 2020, Microsoft Corporation filed for a patent that lays out a new way of mining Bitcoin? No BIP required here! How wonderful, you might say. Perhaps you imagine this patent to involve low-energy consumption models that will be good for the earth. Perhaps the patent involves a turnkey desktop that the average person can purchase, that will permit you to not only use Bitcoin, but also mine it. It might come with its own solar panel. How wonderful! The patent doesn't involve anything like that.

US 20200097951A1

(19) **United States**
(12) **Patent Application Publication** (10) **Pub. No.: US 2020/0097951 A1**
ABRAMSON et al. (43) **Pub. Date: Mar. 26, 2020**

(54) **CRYPTOCURRENCY SYSTEM USING BODY ACTIVITY DATA**

(71) Applicant: **Microsoft Technology Licensing, LLC**, Redmond, WA (US)

(72) Inventors: **Dustin ABRAMSON**, Renton, WA (US); **Derrick FU**, Seattle, WA (US); **Joseph Edwin JOHNSON, JR.**, Seattle, WA (US)

(73) Assignee: **Microsoft Technology Licensing, LLC**, Redmond, WA (US)

(21) Appl. No.: **16/138,518**

(22) Filed: **Sep. 21, 2018**

Publication Classification

(51) **Int. Cl.**
G06Q 20/36 (2006.01)
G06F 3/01 (2006.01)
H04L 9/06 (2006.01)
H04L 9/08 (2006.01)

(52) **U.S. Cl.**
CPC ***G06Q 20/3672*** (2013.01); ***H04L 9/0866*** (2013.01); ***H04L 9/0637*** (2013.01); ***G06F 3/011*** (2013.01)

(57) **ABSTRACT**

Human body activity associated with a task provided to a user may be used in a mining process of a cryptocurrency system. A server may provide a task to a device of a user which is communicatively coupled to the server. A sensor communicatively coupled to or comprised in the device of the user may sense body activity of the user. Body activity data may be generated based on the sensed body activity of the user. The cryptocurrency system communicatively coupled to the device of the user may verify if the body activity data satisfies one or more conditions set by the cryptocurrency system, and award cryptocurrency to the user whose body activity data is verified.

In the future, Microsoft envisions that you will be hooked up or more likely scanned by various body monitors as you sit in front of one of your screens. Your brainwaves, blood flow, body temperature, eye gaze, pupil dilation, sexual responses, and head movements will be monitored and *fed* to a blockchain network. IF, and ONLY IF your responses (not what you say but what you *really think and feel*) comport with what Big Brother says is desirable, you will be rewarded with—wait for it—a Bitcoin.

130. The body activity may include, for example, but not limited to, radiation emitted from human body, brain activities, body fluid flow (e.g. blood flow), organ activity or movement, body movement, and any other activities that can be sensed and represented by images, waves, signals, texts, numbers, degrees, or any other form of information or data. Examples of body radiation emitted from human body may include radiant heat of the body, pulse rate, or brain wave. Brain waves may comprise, for example, but not limited to, (i) gamma waves, involved in learning or memory tasks, (ii) beta waves, involved in logical thinking and/or conscious thought, (iii) alpha waves, which may be related to subconscious thoughts, (iv) theta waves, which may be related to thoughts involving deep and raw emotions, (v) delta waves, which may be involved in sleep or deep relaxation, or (vi) electroencephalogram (EEG), which may be measurement used to evaluate the electrical activity in the brain, such as deep concentration. Examples of the body movement may include eye movement, facial movement or any other muscular movements. Furthermore, brain activity can be sensed using the fMRI. The fMRI measures brain activity by detecting changes associated with blood flow. This technique relies on the fact that cerebral blood flow and neuronal activation are coupled. When an area of the brain is in use, blood flow to that region also increases.

[0037] At operation **330**, user device **130** generates body activity data based on the body activity sensed by sensor **140**. Operation **330** may be part of a mining process which is a process for solving a computationally difficult problem. One exemplary embodiment of operation **330** is shown in

> **[0045]** In some embodiments, cryptocurrency system **150** verifies whether the body activity data of user **145** (e.g. the code of the body activity generated at operation **410** or the hash of the body activity generated at operation **420**) may represent that the body activity of user **145** is within a target range. The target range may be determined using the amount of cognitive effort that user **145** requires to perform the task provided by task server **110**. For example, to verify if the hash of the body activity of user **145**, cryptocurrency system **150** may determine, for example, but not limited to, (i) whether the hash of the body activity of user **145** has a specific certain pattern, repeated patterns, a mathematical properties or the number of leading numbers, characters or strings (e.g. leading zeroes) set by cryptocurrency system **150**, or (ii) whether the hash of the body activity of user **145** is less than a current target value. Examples of the numerical patterns set by cryptocurrency system **150** may be a pattern that first certain digits of the hash form a prime number, or a pattern that a number that is calculated by applying first certain digits of the hash to a preset formula forms a prime number (For example, a number calculated by adding or subtracting a predetermined number or a number set by cryptocurrency system **150** to the first four digits of the hashing forms a prime number). The repeating number patterns may include a repeating number (e.g. leading zeros, ones in the middle of the hash, twos in the last four digits of the hash, and any repeating numbers included in the hash) and a repeating number sequence (e.g. leading repeating digit pairs, such as "121212", or triplets "123123"). If the hash of the body activity of user **145** has the desirable pattern(s) or is within the target range, then the proof of work or proof of stake is considered solved, and that hash can be a new block. The target range or value may be changed periodically to maintain a preselected level of difficulty, although it is not required. For example, the target value may be inversely proportional to the difficulty. By varying the difficulty, a roughly constant rate of block generation may be kept.

Microsoft's patent application is forward thinking, as it relates to incorporating V the Reality money as the instant VR monetary reward in a system that would be tailor-made for social engineering purposes—not that it would be used to modify your thoughts, feelings, and behavior, heavens no, only that it could be used—and quite easily. If the reader thinks this dystopian future is far off, not so. The virtual world of our CNS has already been tapped into by researchers so as to "read the minds" of subjects. When I write "read the minds" of subjects, I mean that literally. Technology exists today that translates the virtual world of our minds into OR world text, to wit:

"A man paralyzed from the neck down used an implanted sensor that processed his brain signals to create text, achieving a typing speed rivaling that of his able-bodied peers. [T]he intracortical brain-computer interface (BCI) decoded his attempted handwriting movements from neural activity and translated them to text in real time at a rate of 90 characters per minute, more than double the previous record for typing with a BCI. [T]he 65-year-old man, referred to as T5 in the paper, had a spinal cord injury in 2007 that immobilized his limbs. Nine years later, as part of the BrainGate2 clinical trial, researchers placed two BCI chips, each the size of baby aspirin, in the part of his motor cortex that governs hand movement. As the man imagined writing, ***a machine-learning algorithm used signals from individual neurons in his brain to recognize patterns he produced with each letter, allowing him to communicate as quickly as someone his age typing on a smartphone****. "We've learned that the brain retains its ability to prescribe fine movements a full decade after the body has lost its ability to execute those movements," Willett said in a statement. Complicated intended movements that involve changing speeds and curved trajectories -- like handwriting -- can be interpreted more easily by artificial intelligence algorithms than simpler motions like straight lines, Willett noted. "Alphabetical letters are different from one another, so they're easier to tell apart," he said. Commercially available assistive typing devices rely predominantly on being able to make eye movements or deliver voice commands, observed Pavithra Rajeswaran, MEng, and Amy Orsborn, PhD, both of the University of Washington in Seattle, in an accompanying commentary. Eye-tracking keyboards can let people with paralysis type at around 47.5 characters per minute but have limitations: it's hard to reread an email to compose your reply while you're typing with your eyes, they noted. [A] deep-learning model called a recurrent neural network learned the neural activity patterns he produced with each character. Over time, the*

> *algorithm showed better ability to differentiate his neural firing patterns. Eventually, it was able to decipher the correct letter 94.1% of the time. An offline autocorrect function boosted that accuracy to over 99%.* [186]

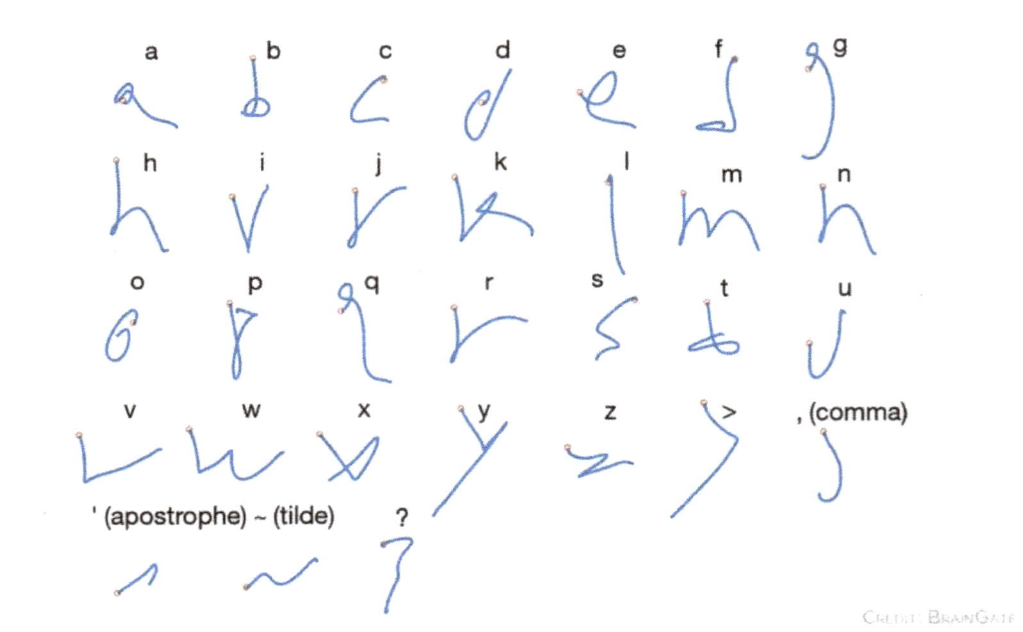

Image Courtesy of BrainGate

Microsoft's patent will make it possible for you to work for your allotment of Bitcoin, but your "work" will be defined for you by what Big Brother defines as *valuable*—or to use today's parlance, socially responsible or WOKE work.

[186] Willett, F.R., Avansino, D.T., Hochberg, L.R. et al. High-performance brain-to-text communication via handwriting. Nature 593, 249–254 (2021). https://doi.org/10.1038/s41586-021-03506-2.

'The machines have names such as Lightning Cash, Seven Seas, King Coins and – hammering on the ceiling of hyperbole – Super Diamond Eternity.' (Photograph: Dan Peled/AAP) [187]

Virtual reality is the ONLY means by which Orwell's 1984 dystopian reality can be fully implemented, and central to that dystopian future is V the Realty money under the explicit or hidden control of Big Brother. Bitcoin, for all of its marvelous cryptographic bells and whistles, created by anti-government punk rockers in a holy war with Big Brother, may not have fully grasped the extent to which Big Brother

[187] The Guardian, U.S. Edition: Playing the pokies: life, whether terrible or beautiful, deferred in the gaming room. Story by: Dan Dixon, July 28, 2017.

would go to either a. destroy their marvelous creation, or b. make Bitcoin their own. Choice "b" is the preferred way power brokers get what they want, because virtual reality when conflated with objective reality can be modified at will. If this is beginning to feel like the time you discovered that Santa Claus is not real, but only virtual—well, it should. I still love Santa, but I know he is not the one eating the cookies I left out for him—a declaration, I might add, that is the sine qua non of blasphemy to true believers.

Virtual reality absent V the Reality money is conceivably controllable. If it can ever be controlled, then it could be absolutely marvelous. However, when V the Reality money is introduced into the equation, no matter how many safeguards, eyes looking over shoulders ad infinitum—money lust, manipulation, and love of it shall not be denied and will inevitably lead to MORE, not LESS control by government, their acronym agencies, and not to mention crooks. Money is the one thing that under no circumstances should be virtualized—but it has been virtualized. And what is going to happen, and in fact is happening right now, is the existent power structures are in the process of subsuming cryptocurrency and making it their own. When the takeover process is complete, the forces explicitly challenged by the crypto anarchists, Cypherpunks, and their kindred spirits will have grown stronger—not weaker, and certainly not eradicated.

I want to mention the current wild-west cowboys herding one another into a gambling frenzy using Robinhood and Reddit who are, without knowing it, relying upon the greater fool theory of investing. These people, for the most part, haven't a clue as to how Bitcoin works or the implications of V the Reality money.

When it comes to the gamblers playing with Bitcoin, et al., they naively believe the people who would dare to conduct an audit of their activities would run into an impenetrable wall, because of the complexity of the C++ Bitcoin protocols and the block/blockchain's failsafe mechanisms. Speculators believe they are smarter than all the other gamblers and will be protected against losses, because the Bitcoin, Etherium, et al., casino tables in Las Vegas have better odds than roulette or craps tables made of wood.

Edward Snowden spoke eloquently about the subversion of Bitcoin at the 2021 Bitcoin Retreat. Mr. Snowden's focus was squarely on privacy. He stated that ensuring privacy is the ONLY protection that Bitcoin has to offer its users, thus protection against Big Brother. He addressed the collective ethos that has been a part of crypto since its inception. "If one of you give it up (privacy) you are taking it from everyone else."

Digital natives must come to understand that privacy is KEY to protecting what is left of freedom in our digital age. The Bill of Rights Fourth Amendment to the United States Constitution enshrined critical bulwarks to privacy, though never mentioning the word. However, be advised, privacy in the virtual world is much more difficult to protect under our Bill of Rights and case law than in the OR world, and that is an insurmountable problem for reasons inherent in all virtual reality conditions.

SEARCH AND SEIZURE

Passed by Congress September 25, 1789. Ratified December 15, 1791.

> **The right of the people to be secure in their persons, houses, papers, and effects, against unreasonable searches and seizures, shall not be violated, and no Warrants shall issue, but upon probable cause, supported by Oath or affirmation, and particularly describing the place to be searched, and the persons or things to be seized.**

The Cypherpunks built their protocols around privacy. That was the whole idea! They may have been egocentric, however, by believing they were smarter than the people who work for and with acronym agencies around the world, who are competent and dedicated protectors of national security, even if your privacy is compromised in the process. Please appreciate that of the tens of thousands of NSA agents, employees, directors, et al., that only a handful of people have cared enough about trading YOUR privacy for national security, they risked their lives to tell you about how VR technology has compromised your fundamental civil liberties—ONLY a handful.

Edward Snowden is living in exile in the Russian Federation, and William Binney and J. Kirk Wiebe had their homes raided and ransacked by the FBI as their families watched. Ultimately, the NSA revoked their security clearances, and they were forced to sue to recover their confiscated personal property. What sins did Binney and Wiebe commit? They alleged in 2002 that their employer, the National Security Agency, mismanaged intelligence-gathering software that potentially could have prevented 9/11. In other words, the government knew or should have known about 9/11. I could argue persuasively that those actions on the part of government were justified, given what was known at the time.

Bitcoin apologists, devotees, and true believers tend to use borderline personality disordered (BPD) thinking when an attempt is made to engage them in rational discourse. Classic BPD thinking categorizes people into "good" guys and "bad" guys. VR games are notorious for promoting and thus conditioning digital native brains to use borderline disordered thinking. But the subject of privacy and OR versus V the Reality money requires sharp and unbiased thinking and analysis—Not "us" versus "them" biases. The salient question to ask with regard to privacy is this:

> **What currency provides the best combination of privacy, targeted probable cause criminal traceability, egalitarianism and functional utility for the masses—V the Reality money or OR world money?**

Edward Snowden addressed this question without awareness at the 2019 Bitcoin conference. His answers gained applause at first from his audience comprised of true believers, but as he progressed, the silence became deafening—despite confirmation bias operating at full steam ahead.

> *"Bitcoin is providing* ***pseudo*** *anonymity if not total anonymity. This transaction, let's say we pull out the old TX ID and dust it off and it connects to this transaction, and this one and this one and this one and this one and this one and this one and finally went to Coinbase and luckily Coinbase is our little deputy. So let's go to Coinbase and you know let's see whose name is attached to that coin but the thing is that coin could have been*

spent 25 times by then but now you're being asked questions and you're going to have to defend this and going to have to go through and where did you get this and where did you get it from that person and eventually you're going to have to say 'I don't know' and that's going to be suspicious. And if you actually look at the terms of services for these major exchanges, when they go into 'know your customer policies' and their anti money laundering regulations where you have to do all this stuff and by the way in every case they go far beyond what the law requires because they just want to cover themselves, if you fail to meet whatever arbitrary burden they impose upon you they don't close your account and return your money they close your account and keep your money. And so this is the thing I think people need to think about what the government goes after today and will always go after in these spaces are the on and off ramps. These are the points that you either need to buy this or sell this. [T]his is a point of existential vulnerability and there are only two ways to really get around this. You can hide them, structure the system in such a way, that you've encouraged enough adoption you can spend directly on groceries and the grocery store doesn't have time to take your blood sample or passport or you can structure the system in such a way that the user cannot prove the provenance of their funds beyond the last transaction." [188] (Emphasis added)

Snowden argued that the dollar is used more often than Bitcoin as payment for illicit goods and services. When he said that, the crowd roared with approval and applause. I could easily disassemble his assertion using per capita corrections and any number of examples from my own forensic experience with deciphering white-collar crime—that is NOT the critical point. The point that should be at the center of everyone's analysis is this: Which currency, OR or VR, provides the best protection against Big

[188] Edward Snowden speaking to the 2019 Bitcoin Conference in San Francisco, CA.

Brother and globalism? Permit me another point of order to add rational color and contour to the term "globalism" as we continue investigating this whodunit.

CHAPTER XXI

GLOBALISM: It may include the planet Mars

The problem with globalism is not global trade or the people of earth developing a feeling of oneness with one another. The problem with globalism is that vested interests are intent upon exercising ultimate control over the entire planet. If that sounds dramatic, it is—and it is well within the realm of possibility due to human psychopathology and the rise of virtual reality. Long ago, psychoanalysts identified certain personality types that crave control, love exercising it over others and make control their life's passion. Colloquially, these people are referred to as "control freaks." The missing critical factor that shackled this particular controlling personality type is the technological means to erase boundaries using currencies that provides to them ultimate control, i.e., an instant audit of everything people do with money.

Global control over currency and taxation will make it impossible for you to escape an environment where your fundamental privacy rights and other freedoms have been violated, because there will be no place where you can escape, as money and taxation will be under the control of the people and institutions that have always had control over money and taxation—but to a limited degree, thanks to technological limitations and OR world currencies. The ONLY way for globalists to achieve their goals is to create a universal V the Reality money. I may be literally discussing globalism, but I am fundamentally discussing virtual reality and human behavior.

Here is just ONE example of how crypto and globalism are two sides of the same coin, and together represent the greatest threat to personal freedom since feudal lords were invented. On April 5, 2021, Secretary of the Treasury of the United States Janet Yellen proposed a universal GLOBAL corporate tax. Taken to its logical extension, that means if you operate a business, no matter where you go on earth, you will be under the strong-arm control of the Federal Reserve—don't forget that Janet Yellen was the former head of the Federal Reserve under President Obama. A little over a month later, on May 20, 2021, Secretary Yellen said a 15 percent UNIVERSAL corporate tax is in the works with members of the G7.

The Treasury Department said it proposed a global minimum corporate tax rate of at least 15% during international tax negotiations on Thursday

- The Treasury Department said it proposed a global minimum corporate tax rate of at least 15% during international tax negotiations on Thursday
- Treasury Secretary Janet Yellen first proposed a 21% global corporate minimum tax as part of President Joe Biden's $2.2 trillion infrastructure spending proposal
- Biden wants to pay for the American Jobs Plan by increasing the corporate tax rate to 28% from the current 21%
- Most countries that have a corporate tax rate below 15% are tax havens such as Bermuda and the Cayman Islands
- All of the G7 nations have a rate higher than 15% and China's rate is 25% [189]

ON THE VERY SAME day Secretary Yellen informed the world she was in the process of instituting a 15 percent globalism corporate tax, she made this point with *uncharacteristic vim and vigor* compared to her usual deadpan delivery style:

---

[189] Daily Mail, May 20, 2021.

The US Treasury wants every crypto transfer larger than $10,000 to be reported to the IRS

- The US Treasury said a proposal to beef up the IRS includes reporting any transfers of at least $10,000 in cryptocurrencies for tax purposes.
- "As with cash transactions, businesses that receive crypto assets with a fair-market value of more than $10,000 would also be reported on," The Treasury Department said.
- Bitcoin sold off by as much as 6% on Thursday following the announcement.
- The Treasury Department detailed plans to have any cryptocurrency transfers of at least $10,000 to be reported to the Internal Revenue Service in a report on Thursday.

  "As with cash transactions, businesses that receive cryptoassets with a fair-market value of more than $10,000 would also be reported on," the Treasury Department said in the report. The report is part of the Biden administration's plans to beef up the IRS in hopes of collecting more tax revenue that otherwise goes unreported. The IRS first began asking individuals if they ever bought or sold virtual currencies in 2020, and now requires individuals to report capital gains realized from any cryptocurrency transactions. [190]

As Edward Snowden addressed at the Bitcoin Convention, the *only* protection against Big Brother or Big Sister is privacy of the Bitcoin transaction. As governments and their acronym agencies have moved parts of their crypto operations onstage, Bitcoin advocates have countered government control using various counterpunch strategies.

One of the strategies Bitcoin users have used in the past to avoid scrutiny is called the "Mixer," also known as a "Tumbler." Essentially, the idea behind this anonymity strategy provides holders of Bitcoin the option to send their coins to a

---

[190] Markets Insider, The US Treasury wants every crypto transfer larger than $10,000 to be reported to the IRS. Story by: Matthew Fox, May 20, 2021.

service which pools customer's Bitcoin, then mixes them up so as to make it difficult for government to track down the source of the digital currency. Consider the timing of this boxing match between Big Brother and Bitcoin users. Just three days BEFORE Janet Yellen laid the law down on a globally coordinated corporate tax AND empowered the tax man to track Bitcoin profiteers, the New York Law Journal published this story:

Prosecutions of Bitcoin Mixers Raise Crypto Privacy Questions

Federal criminal charges filed on April 27, 2021 against the administrator of Bitcoin Fog, a cryptocurrency "mixer," raise questions regarding attempts to require anti-money laundering and "know your customer" regulations for crypto money transmitters, and whether there can be (or is) anonymity or privacy in the purchase or sale of cryptocurrencies.

> *"While some users claim mixers are a legitimate service that allow them to secure their financial privacy, mixers are also reportedly used by* ***criminal enterprises to launder criminal proceeds****, attracting regulatory scrutiny. Cryptocurrency mixers, also known as "tumblers," are not a new part of the cryptocurrency market. In fact, they arguably support the privacy and transactional anonymity that are part of cryptocurrency's appeal. A bitcoin mixer allows a bitcoin holder to send*

bitcoins to a service, which, in turn, pools and scrambles those bitcoins with other bitcoins in a manner that obscures the transaction history and makes it more difficult to identify the original source of the funds. (The transactions that are part of the bitcoin scramble technically remain visible on the blockchain, but become much harder to follow and trace.) While some users claim mixers are a legitimate service that allow them to secure their financial privacy, mixers are also reportedly used by criminal enterprises to launder criminal proceeds, attracting regulatory scrutiny. The Financial Crimes Enforcement Network (FinCEN), the enforcement arm of the ***U.S. Department of Treasury (Janet Yellen in charge),*** *considers anyone that transmits a virtual currency that is not a party to the transaction to be a "money transmitter" for the purposes of regulation. Based on this framework, FinCEN defines cryptocurrency mixers as money transmitters, which subject mixers to FinCEN's anti-money laundering (AML), Bank Secrecy Act (BSA) know-your-customer (KYC) checks, and combating the financing of terrorism (CFT) program requirements that have long been applied to financial entities. A mixer's failure to register with FinCEN makes it an unlicensed money services business (MSB), subject to penalties that include significant fines or imprisonment. (FinCEN has separately made public statements that it does not consider any ICO registered as a securities or derivatives offering to be a transmission of money under their jurisdiction and defers to the U.S. Securities and Exchange Commission (SEC) and Commodities Futures Trading Commission (CFTC) in this regard.)"* [191] (Emphasis added)

---

[191] New York Law Journal: Prosecutions of Bitcoin Mixers Raise Crypto Privacy Questions By Kenneth M. Breen, Phara A. Guberman and Kenneth P. Herzinger | May 17, 2021.

Imagine how complicated it would be—if at all possible—to institute a one-earth monetary system while autonomous nation states had control over their own OR world currency, accompanied by complications such as exchange rates and citizen's control over physically held, i.e., OR world money.

The Euro made great strides toward a global currency, and to declare with certainty that moving toward a global currency wasn't in the back of the Euro developers' minds would be foolishly naive. The Euro may be properly thought of as the missing link between individual nation state OR currency and the Earthcoin. On January 1, 1999, the Euro subsumed the following nation state currencies: Austrian schilling, Belgian franc, Cypriot pound, Deutsche Mark, Dutch guilder, Estonian kroon, Finnish markka, French franc, Greek drachma, Irish pound, Italian lira, Latvian lats, Lithuanian litas, Luxembourg franc, Maltese lira, Monégasque franc, Portuguese escudo, Sammarinese lira, Slovak koruna, Slovenian tolar, Spanish peseta, and the Vatican lira.

From a globalist's point of view, the Euro was a good start, but without digital currencies, citizens maintained physical control over their money and a global ledger would have been impossible. Digital natives in particular have never been educated on the subject of how OR world money is a globalist's nightmare. Perhaps the most damning observation is the fact that even when educated about this subject, digital natives for the most part could not care less. Moreover, without taking too deep of a dive into the social engineering of consent, consider the possibility that by using greed-frenzied trading platforms that allow Gen-Z to gamble with Bitcoin, they have been stampeded into adopting what will sooner or later, whether it is called this or not, become the Earthcoin.

If Bitcoin did not exist, globalists would have to invent it before they could implement their dream currency: Earthcoin.

The globalization/Bitcoin synergy has not been lost on promoters and advocates of BOTH globalization and Bitcoin.

How Cryptocurrencies are Driving Globalization

"With the invention of Bitcoin and the proliferation of other cryptocurrencies, the unrestricted interaction of economies and complete financial inclusion is a possibility for the entire world." [192]

And with globalization using Bitcoin will come international cooperation (euphemism for control) on taxing, international ledgers, and an ultimate dystopian tracking system[193] that even Big Brother could not have imagined, to wit:

Graphic Courtesy of Bitcoin Insider and COINTELEGRAPH

"On the world stage, most of the work on combating cryptocurrency-related crimes is carried out by Interpol and Europol. Organizations at this level not only have access to the entire cryptocurrency market infrastructure but also form relationships with exchanges, brokers, developers and other key industry players. The fact that Interpol deals with international crypto crimes came to light back in 2015, when its representatives first warned of possible threats posed by digital assets and blockchain — in particular, the possibility of embedding malware into the chain. Since then, agencies have taken up cryptocurrency crimes in earnest, establishing the Interpol Global Complex for

[192] Crypto Core Media, June 19, 2018.
[193] During the Roman Empire citizens of Rome referred to their sewers as "the system."

Innovation to explore new techniques that are being increasingly used by cybercriminals. Among them are cryptojacking and ransomware, which have become widespread tools for bad actors and an international concern for governments."[194]

Then we have the United Nations—it functions as a coordinating hub for global cooperation on using TAXATION to enforce social engineering edicts, to wit:

ECOSOC Special Meeting on "International Cooperation in Tax Matters"

"The 2021 ECOSOC[195] *Special Meeting was focus on* ***how countries can use tax policy and administration*** *in* ***tackling*** *some of our most pressing social, economic and environmental challenges – in an increasingly* **digitalized economy** *and in the context of the COVID-19 pandemic. [P]articipants include members and observers of ECOSOC, members of its expert body on tax matters, senior representatives of national tax authorities, relevant international and regional organizations, as well as civil society and academia. Participants contributed to enhancing the impact of expert and intergovernmentally-driven UN policy guidance on tax matters, at the global, regional, national and subnational levels."*[196] (Emphasis added)

Recently I learned of a man by the name of James Daniels at the IRS, who has control of the narrative at the IRS when it comes to Bitcoin and other cryptocurrencies. Mr. Daniels has an exquisite understanding of virtual reality, digitization, and how Bitcoin represents to the IRS not only the mother lode of auditing firepower, but also how crypto can function as a means to an end. What is that end? Crypto

---

[194] Bitcoin Insider, Law Enforcement's Guide to Policing Crypto Cybercrimes.

[195] The United Nations Economic and Social Council (ECOSOC) brings people and issues together to promote *collective* action for a sustainable world. (Emphasis added)

[196] United Nations 75th ECOSOC Special Meeting on "International Cooperation in Tax Matters"

provides the IRS, along with a myriad of other agencies across the globe, the wherewithal to exercise their plenary power to track your every move as a means to enforce social engineering polices. Sound far-fetched? Think again. In fact, investigators at Bitcoin.com have gotten access to Mr. Daniels' PowerPoint presentation made to his colleagues at the IRS and bravely published the following:

> *"The 181-page report is a daunting display of how IRS agents can invade a person's private life in order to prosecute them for tax evasion. James Daniels' slides also show that the IRS is well aware of bitcoin mixers, the use of Tor, and other transaction obfuscation methods. The study gives a detailed analysis of Bitmixer.io and explains that before the site closed down it mixed 65,000 BTC per month since 2014. "In addition to Bitmixer's website on clearnet, the operation also had an official Tor mirror as well on the deep web," the PowerPoint presentation details. The slides also give step-by-step instructions for crypto beginners and explain how agents can easily sign up for Coinbase and other popular exchanges as well as a Bitcoin ATM walkthrough.* ***People will likely be shocked*** *by this display of law enforcement going to great lengths to obtain cryptocurrency information on specific people. Very few crypto users are actively taking steps to protect their privacy 100% of the time. Perhaps this slideshow will urge more people to use mixing applications like Cashshuffle, operate wallets using a VPN and make sure they keep addresses off the clearnet. The recent IRS announcement that* ***virtual*** *currency guidelines are on the way is all but meaningless when agents will investigate or prosecute you anyway if you don't follow the criteria. Pay taxes or wind up in a cage."* [197]

---

[197] Bitcoin.com: IRS Agents Propose Draconian Tactics to Investigate Bitcoin Users. Story by: Jamie Redman, May 22, 2021, updated from July 9, 2019.

Controllers, aka Big Brother/Sister, could have NEVER developed such draconian measures in the OR world, as I will prove to you beyond a reasonable doubt later in this book. The issue is NOT tax evasion, or it should not be. If Bitcoin was developed or is now being used to evade legally owed taxes, then what do you expect? No, the issue is this: V the Reality money is the HUGE gaping hole in any person or group of person's protective wall designed to protect their privacy—it is the epitome of irony that the founders of crypto designed their baby with bulletproof privacy barriers, and to this day that narrative is pushed as if nothing has changed. If members of the Bitcoin church believe the game of Tit for Tat (cryptographers develop new coding privacy protocols, then government, hackers, et al., break into or nullify those safeguards, ad infinitum) will lead to anything but an ever-increasing diminution of what is left of privacy, then perhaps more rational thought and less belief is what the doctor ordered. And if you think the IRS and their kindred spirits all across the globe will limit their attention to V the Reality money legally owed to them, then you are sadly mistaken, to wit:

> *"What's more alarming is that Daniels' slide advocates agents* ***investigate the financial habits of individuals*** *who are using crypto to evade taxes (when using crypto the IRS, et al. find you to be guilty unless proven innocent). This includes, but is not limited to, conducting interviews with "bank tellers, family, and friends of the subject (if feasible), and establishments the subject frequents that may accept bitcoins. [Investigating] Facebook, Twitter, and other social media outlets." The IRS slide suggests searching the subject's financial accounts, including bank, credit card, and PayPal records. "[Automated clearing house] ACHs and wire transfers should be identified to see if any of them are related to bitcoin," Daniels' slide suggests. The "Getting Information" section in the slide states: <u>Transfers to and from a subject's PayPal account should be analyzed in much the same way, verifying the parties involved with each transaction — Vendors who accept bitcoin,</u>*

such as Amazon Payments, can also be considered for subpoena. However, this method may not reliably yield results." [198]

[198] Ibid.

CHAPTER XXII

BACK TO THE FUTURE: Where we're going, we don't need roads

The solution to the diminution and eventual dissolution of your privacy and other spirit-giving freedoms is to be found in the OR world. This is not because it is familiar to me, or that it is a place that holds a special place in my heart. Quite to the contrary, my work in forensics documents that I was an early adopter in applying the science of metadata analysis (VR data) in order to track down and bring to justice individuals and organizations, including governmental organizations. I adopted and mastered the VR world early on, in both my personal and professional life. I take great pride in the fact that I developed a digital interface used in court that stymied the geniuses at the "Genius Bar" —but I digress. Perhaps it is that competency and familiarity with VR that informs my angst over what is in the works when it comes to dark forces usurping crypto, even within the church, aka crypto congregation.

Upon careful and informed reflection, I find it virtually impossible to accept the Cypherpunks, Crypto Anarchists, et al., were not keenly aware of how their baby would and COULD be corrupted, no matter how clever their workarounds. A few informed people who are familiar with the inner workings of the NSA, et al., have made a persuasive case that right from the beginning, this marvelous baby that enthralled all of us who cherish privacy was in reality Rosemary's Baby, and that **the**

fix was in because the threat(s) came from within, i.e., *Et tu, Brute.* [199] To make an earlier made point: My commentary **is pure speculation,** and even if it were true, I could never rationalize it as true, nor would I assert that it is true.

As I have written elsewhere, the root credibility problem with such topics as globalism, central bankers, Big Brother, et al., is these subjects attract a motley crew of people who sense something is amiss, but do not possess the judgment nor the discernment acuity necessary to distinguish their rational fears and suspicions from their paranoid-laced projections. My approach to counter such paranoia-laced projections is to be as empirically oriented as scholarship permits. But just as important is how I "make the case." It is important to not rely upon declarations derivative of "special" knowledge that is hard to document, IF it is real. When it comes to logic, keep in mind that logic can lead to nonsense if the assumptions in the block, to use an analogy, are false or in error. This is why I have labored to document the few assumptions that must be made when dealing with subjects that are purposefully shrouded, for obvious reasons.

Only when whistleblowers come forward is the general public permitted to get a glimpse of these subjects in the light of day, not in a dark alley on a moonless night—now consider the following as you keep Edward Snowden and William Binney's revelations and warnings in mind. My observations are backed up by every chapter in this book that can serve as your primer for what is to follow.

I would be remiss if I did not mention the cavalier and snide attitude held by Bitcoin church members who dismiss the fact that crypto is used by felons as their preferred method of payment. "We didn't outlaw dollars because Pablo Escobar used dollars as a method of exchange." Let me clue you in—if Mr. Escobar had used Bitcoin, he would now probably own the world and would not be in jail, or he would have been in business with the creators of crypto. Here is yet another dismissive attitude repartee often expressed by church members: "Criticizing Bitcoin's energy consumption is just another stone to throw at the crypto community." That is a

---

[199] Et tu Brute appears in Act 3 Scene 1 of William Shakespeare's play Julius Caesar.

pretty big stone, and it is not being thrown at the church—it is falling on our collective heads. Let's take an objective look at these and other important Bitcoin issues absent confirmation bias.

The dollar in *your* pocket is not traceable per se, nor will it make you look suspicious, as Mr. Snowden pointed out is the case should you be asked to trace the provenance of Bitcoin in your crypto wallet or wherever you "keep" your cryptocurrency. The dollars in *your* pocket may have been used in the PAST (including the day before you put them in your wallet/purse) to buy illicit drugs, sexual services, or stolen goods, but they are now *your* dollars and will **not** *hem you up,* as we say in forensics, if you use one of those same dollars when you pay for, let's say, a new car. Those dollars in your pocket will NOT expose you to the scenario laid out by Mr. Snowden in his presentation before a Bitcoin convention, i.e.:

> *"[T]he thing is that coin could have been spent 25 times by then but now you're being asked questions and you're going to have to defend this and going to have to go through and where did you get this and where did you get it from that person and eventually you're going to have to say 'I don't know' and that's going to be suspicious."* [200]

At the coding level, artifacts of the block/blockchain protect against the problem of double spending, and the collective accounting protocol of miners keeps you and your money private. On the other hand, Bitcoins are always linked to you by crypto exchanges for the same reasons your credit card company and bank keep records. The chasm between ultimate anonymity and currency functionality is not resolvable in the crypto world. But that chasm has been narrowed, and sometimes reduced to nil, in the OR world of money. In other words, OR world money has solved these problems better than anything that could replace them—which is one of the fundamental motivations behind the move to replace dollars with crypto by those who are after ultimate control over you and the world you live in!

---

[200] Ibid 120.

Dollars, themselves, retain autonomy from ledgers, the IRS, and law enforcement. Yet, stolen dollars can still be traced to or associated with the person or persons who have committed a crime—a unique combination of privacy and targeted probable cause criminal traceability not possible in the crypto world absent exchanges—and in the crypto world, exchanges are four-letter words.
Here are a few examples of how OR world money provides a functional combination of privacy, targeted probable cause criminal traceability, and egalitarianism.

Consider the functionality and privacy value of OR world money simply because it must adhere to the laws of physics, unlike VR world money. Rob a bank, and on your way back to your safe house you hear an explosion. You open your bag of stolen cash and find you have in your possession handfuls of bright red dollar bills. Dye packs have been around since 1965. They are radio-controlled devices made by ICI Security Systems that call their product the SecurityPac. They are in use in over 75 percent of all banks in the USA.

Back in the day when mob hits were paid for with a suitcase filled with cash, it took cooperating witnesses to swear under oath in a court of law that $50,000 was handed to me in a brown briefcase on such-and-such a date at such-and-such address. Consider the sting operation. When murder for hire stings are arranged, they must have gone through an oversight system called due process that includes a judge who was persuaded to mark a specific number of bills denoted by their unique serial numbers, totaling an exact dollar amount. The reader should consider what this means with regard to *your* OR world money. Not EVERY bill, including the one in *your* pocket, was marked—only those bills earmarked for a specific purpose and specific time were part of the sting. Those same marked bills could be traced back to the targets of the investigation **without affecting you or the OR world monetary system.**

The same cannot be said for Bitcoin—in fact, the opposite is true, because the block/blockchain's claim to fame is anonymity yet verifiable. Crypto marking by its very nature means every single miner's block denoting "your" money *must be marked,* unless a tier system is imposed on the "collective" to track down killers.

> **Compromise anonymity to catch one crook, and you compromise anonymity for the entire system by definition. If coders decide to solve this problem by attaching markers that identify just you and what you buy or spend, then we have defeated a fundamental virtue of Bitcoin.**

When an OR world being interacts with OR world money, the exchange rate is 1:1. When an OR world being interacts with VR world money, the relationship includes an algorithm intermediary as opposed to a literal Central Bank and/or U.S. Treasury intermediary. Bitcoin's algorithmic intermediary is one of the key reasons The People's Bank of China (PBOC) issued the following statement on May 18, 2021:

> *"**Virtual** currencies should not and cannot be used in the market because **they're not real currencies**. [F]inancial and payments institutions are not allowed to price products or services with **virtual** currency."* (Emphasis Added)

One of the reasons the PBOC made this declaration is related to any number of algorithmic intermediaries over whom it would have no control, that can change the value of goods and services—like almost everything in the virtual world—with a few swipes or clicks of an input device. A man named Elon Musk has exercised his power as an intermediary to dramatically move the value of Bitcoin, as we have previously described herein—first by declaring that he will accept Bitcoin as payment for his cars, then soon thereafter withdrawing his approval, which resulted in dramatic price swings in the price of Bitcoin.

Whether you *believe* Bitcoin to be a store of value and/or currency matters not. When one man can wildly swing markets based on a whim tweet, and then just as easily reverse course, has profound implications for financial solvency, especially if you assert that Bitcoin is a currency. If you are a gambler, you must feel like you are on an out-of-control roller coaster. Whether you consider this to be currency manipulation will depend upon your confirmation bias filters. Let me ask those who consider Bitcoin a currency: How do you like holding a "currency" whose value can be manipulated by the publication of an emoji on social media?

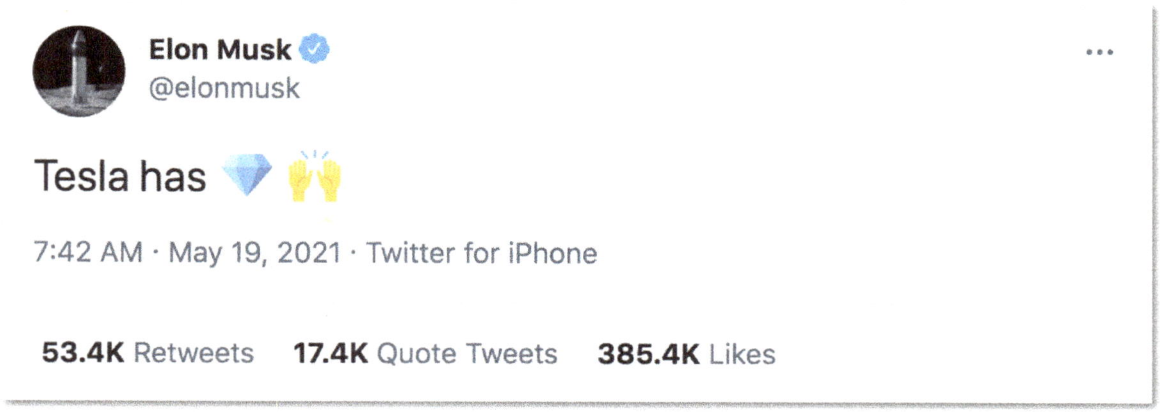

Elon Musk tweeted a 'diamond hands' meme as bitcoin and other cryptocurrencies continue to crash

- Elon Musk tweeted "Tesla has diamond hands" on Wednesday as cryptocurrencies crashed.
- The tweet referenced a meme and indicates Tesla is holding on to its cache of bitcoin.
- The meme has become part of the lingo of Reddit's **Wall Street Bets forum**. Emphasis added) [201]

Bitcoin's price had fallen to approximately $30,000 before Musk published his golden hands tweet, a loss of over 50 percent from its high posted a few weeks earlier ($60,000+), which was itself a spike caused in large measure by Mr. Musk, once again, communicating to his flock using Twitter. Was Mr. Musk's golden hands tweet an overt attempt to put a floor under his $1.5 billion asset? Was it a blatant attempt to communicate to the hapless, greed-frenzied gamers "on" Robinhood and Reddit using insider emoji symbols (gang signs) to provoke them to double down to use a gambling term? In the OR world of money, when countries manipulate their currencies, remedies exist, to wit:

> *"Currency manipulator is a designation applied by United States government authorities, such as the United States Department of the Treasury, to countries that engage in what is called "unfair currency*

---

[201] Business Insider, May 19, 2021.

practices" that give them a trade advantage. Such practices may be currency intervention or monetary policy in which a central bank buys or sells foreign currency in exchange for domestic currency, generally with the intention of influencing the exchange rate and commercial policy."[202]

The PBOC's statement about crypto not being a real currency begs the question, what are REAL currencies? The answer to that pressing question forces us to get to the heart of what it means when V the Reality money is adopted by OR world beings. Before I address this issue, please appreciate that the PBOC has been wary of Bitcoin since it first appeared on the scene, because China understands it could be used by the United States and its allies to either destroy or hobble China's progress as an economic powerhouse. So what if I were to say this: "What Bitcoin needs is a central banker." What? I wouldn't suggest that, because it would be tantamount to recommending that central bankers across the globe should be given even more power and autonomy—not to mention the equivalent of declaring that Mary was not a virgin when she gave birth to the Christ child. But I didn't have to say those words, because backstage crypto dynamics are churning with ideas like that. MacKenzie Sigalos, writing for CNBC (Comcast), wrote this on **May 20, 2021, the exact same day** Secretary of the Treasury Janet Yellen proposed her one world corporate tax rate and increased funding for the IRS to investigate Bitcoin users and traders:

"Bitcoin's volatility is the price it pays for its limited supply ***and its lack of a central bank."*** *(Emphasis added)*

The get-rich-quick crowd can't stop talking about Bitcoin on the net with people they've never met. Today's dilettante crypto anarchists have rationalized their lust to become petite Bill Gates by applauding Tim May and colleagues' dream that "the

---

[202] Bergsten, C. Fred (February 25, 2015). "Currency Manipulation: Why Something Must Be Done. "Forbes.

man" will be erased from earth. All the while, the same crowd, if the truth be told, wants nothing more out of crypto than to have FU money—this is, BE the man.

Perhaps the worst of the worst in this free-for-all are the digital immigrant members of the circa-1980 sewers of Wall Street, who lurk in disguises that are designed to look like the brilliant idealist punk rocker math geniuses who conceived of a way to protect personal freedom using cryptography. You can find out who they really are underneath the disguises they wear in the same way genealogy services tell you where your genomic fingerprint really originated, not where their preened liner notes say they came from. I won't name them, because if readers can't figure out their names, then what would be the point? Fulfilling the prurient interest of readers is of no interest to me.

> **Ironically, the way to fulfill Cypherpunk's and Crypto Anarchist's idealistic dreams is to embrace the OR world and limit VR's access to your brain, your mind and most certainly your money. That is the only way to solve those complex math problems in order to mine privacy and freedom—not digital "coins" which have turned out to be Big Brother's dream come true.**

Again, let us return to the VR versus OR world dynamics to cement the larger point. OR world money can be held in your hand, and you can keep it in a physical location under your *physical* control, if you so desire. If you don't have OR world control, that is, *physical control* over your money, then you really don't *have* the money you think you have. Gold aficionados make this point all the time, and it is not without merit.

> **When controllers literally have to get up off their derrieres and travel to where you are located, search for and then carry your money away to another place, your control is greater than their control.**

I want to interject a classic illustration of the delta between the OR versus VR world on a subject unrelated to money, but which ties to privacy—a form of privacy that gets people's attention: your medical records. Something happened in 2014 that would forever change the way doctors kept medical records. Digital natives may have never laid eyes on the following relatively secure method of keeping patient's records private:

Real World Patient Record Keeping

What happened in 2014? **The VR world was imposed** upon doctors all across the USA:

> **As a part of the American Recovery and Reinvestment Act, all public and private healthcare providers and other eligible professionals (EP) were required to adopt and demonstrate "meaningful use" of electronic medical records (EMR) by January 1, 2014.**

What do you think occurred the very next year? Here is a hint—privacy took a hit because of virtual record-keeping. That means rather than thieves getting up off their derrieres, breaking into your doctor's office, and risking arrest to steal your medical records, they could sit on their amply cushioned behinds while sipping energy drinks and steal some of the most intimate details about your life, to wit:

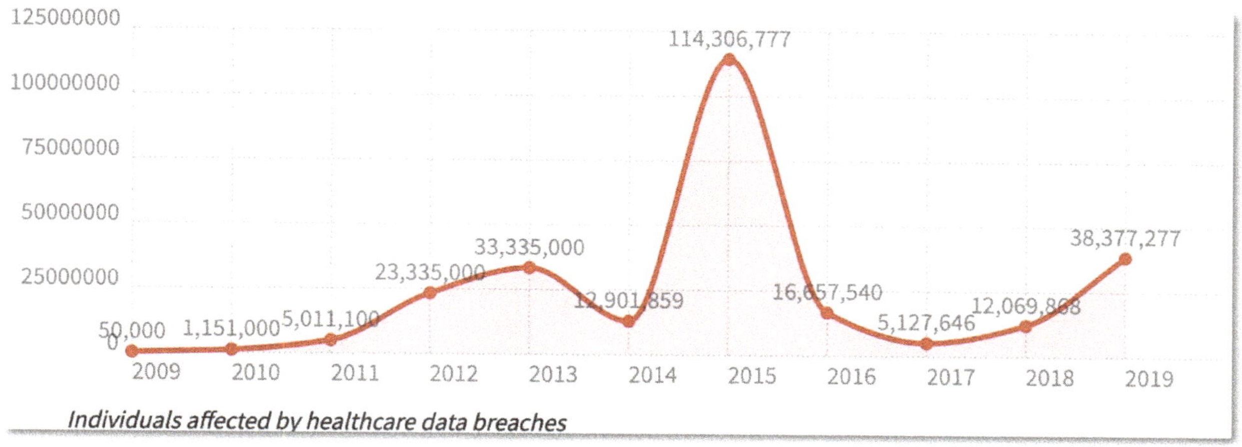

Graphic Courtesy of Privacy Affairs

Now review *hacking activity* related to YOUR health care records, all made possible by virtual reality:

Largest Healthcare Data Breaches (2009-2020)[203]

Rank	Name of Covered Entity	Year	Covered Entity Type	Individuals Affected	Type of Breach
1	Anthem Inc.	2015	Health Plan	78,800,000	Hacking/IT Incident
2	American Medical Collection Agency	2019	Business Associate	26,059,725	Hacking/IT Incident
3	Premera Blue Cross	2015	Health Plan	11,000,000	Hacking/IT Incident
4	Excellus Health Plan, Inc.	2015	Health Plan	10,000,000	Hacking/IT Incident
5	Science Applications International Corporation	2011	Business Associate	4,900,000	Loss
6	University of California, Los Angeles Health	2015	Healthcare Provider	4,500,000	Hacking/IT Incident
7	Community	2014	Business	4,500,000	Hacking/IT Incident

203 HIPPA Journal: Health Care Data Breaches, 2020.

	Health Systems Professional Services Corporations		Associate		
8	Advocate Medical Group	2013	Healthcare Provider	4,029,530	Theft
9	Medical Informatics Engineering	2015	Business Associate	3,900,000	Hacking/IT Incident
10	Banner Health	2016	Healthcare Provider	3,620,000	Hacking/IT Incident
11	Newkirk Products, Inc.	2016	Business Associate	3,466,120	Hacking/IT Incident
12	Trinity Health	2020	Business Associate	3,320,726	Hacking/IT Incident
13	Dominion Dental Services, Inc., Dominion National Insurance Company, and Dominion Dental Services USA, Inc.	2019	Health Plan	2,964,778	Hacking/IT Incident
14	AccuDoc Solutions, Inc.	2018	Business Associate	2,652,537	Hacking/IT Incident
15	21st Century Oncology	2016	Healthcare Provider	2,213,597	Hacking/IT Incident
16	Xerox State Healthcare	2014	Business Associate	2,000,000	Unauthorized Access/Disclosure
17	IBM	2011	Business Associate	1,900,000	Unknown
18	GRM Information Management Services	2011	Business Associate	1,700,000	Theft
19	Inmediata Health Group, Corp.	2019	Healthcare Clearing House	1,565,338	Unauthorized Access/Disclosure
20	UnityPoint Health	2018	Business Associate	1,421,107	Hacking/IT Incident
21	MEDNAX Services, Inc.	2020	Business Associate	1,290,670	Hacking/IT Incident
22	Employees Retirement System of Texas	2018	Health Plan	1,248,263	Unauthorized Access/Disclosure

23	AvMed, Inc.	2010	Health Plan	1,220,000	Theft
24	CareFirst BlueCross BlueShield	2015	Health Plan	1,100,000	Hacking/IT Incident
25	Montana Department of Public Health & Human Services	2014	Health Plan	1,062,509	Hacking/IT Incident

Your healthcare records are valuable because of the monetary value of the costs of your healthcare. Imagine how valuable money itself is to hackers?

There is something else about OR world money, other than built-in security, that should garner more attention from progressive-minded people everywhere. OR world money is egalitarian money. You could be a ditch-digger, and your dollar has exactly the same buying power as a Wall Street billionaire. The egalitarian quality of OR world currencies around the world is taken for granted, because average people fail to discern what V the Reality money means.

CHAPTER XXIII

COUNT YOUR MONEY? Proof of Stake and Proof of Work

CLOAK provided the following overview of Proof of Work (PoW) and Proof of Stake (PoS)

PROOF OF WORK

"Proof of Work was the pioneer consensus mechanism. Its use as the underlying consensus mechanism for Bitcoin, would significantly influence future cryptocurrencies and blockchain projects to adopt it for their own platforms. Proof of Work involves mining which is solving complex mathematical problems to earn rights to produce a block. Mining is done by nodes which can be any device with recommended computational power. The first node to complete the puzzle gets the right to produce the block and a reward as well for block production. The difficulty of the mathematical problem changes depending on the time required to produce blocks and the number of blocks required by the blockchain. More often than not, PoW ends up becoming a guessing game for nodes. Sometimes the puzzles get too complex that guessing becomes the only logical way of solving it, almost like those hard math tests most of us experienced in school. The hardware makes 'educated guesses' to try and solve the puzzles faster. The disadvantage of

guessing is the enormous amounts of power it consumes. To increase the chance of solving a puzzle, many guesses have to be made which requires increased power. The energy consumption associated with PoW is, therefore, high- being one of its greatest setbacks. The other setback PoW faces is its decentralization. Decentralization is the heart and soul of blockchain that users would want to remain intact; as mining pools become more substantial, it becomes easier for power to concentrate within these pools which, in a way, compromises decentralization. PoW is easy to implement. A simple algorithm and the set up would be complete. However, its energy consumption and possible long-term adverse effect on the environment has made developers seek other options.

How PoW works:

- *Transactions are bundled into blocks.*
- *Verification of transaction within blocks done by miners.*
- *Miners solve the math problem.*
- *The first miners to solve the problem are given a reward, and rights to produce the next block.*
- *Verified transactions are then stored in public blockchain.*

Pros

Simple to implement.

Cons

Expensive hardware required.

Consumes much energy.

PROOF OF STAKE

Proof of Stake is like the younger, fun, non-math brother of PoW. Instead of solving puzzles and using enormous amounts of energy, PoS determine which nodes have the right to produce blocks on the blockchain. The basis of selection is the number of coins a node has and the amount of time they have kept the coins. Older and more coins translate to higher points in the PoS system. There are also rewards for mining. The PoS system logic is that nodes that have more coins and have kept them for a more extended period have vested interest in ensuring the success of the coin. Therefore, they are likely to desire improvement in the performance and value of the coin. The PoS system is a much more energy efficient and environmentally friendly system. Instead of miners, PoS has validators who stake their coins which then gives them the power to produce blocks and also gives them voting rights in the blockchain. Validators can improve their rankings without having to upgrade their computer systems. Validators in the PoS set up remain tied to the blockchain as they have their coins staked there.

Pros

Energy efficient.

Cheaper for validators.

Cons

Can easily become centralized.

There has been a migration from PoW to PoS due to the high energy consumption and inefficiencies resulting from PoW. It only makes sense to shift from a high-power low-efficiency system to a low power highly efficient system especially because most nodes are trying to get as much in net profit from their activities."[204]

Currency egalitarianism is soon to be forfeited if cryptocurrency is widely adopted, because VR money is inherently complex and cannot be literally touched or held. While OR world money involves middlemen and conduits (usually countable), those are choices based upon convenience and choice—not necessity. Crypto, by its very nature, mandates middlemen and conduits, and while you can usually track

[204] CLOAK: What are the differences between PoW and PoS? April 15, 2019.

down OR world middlemen (your bank, credit card company), you will be hard-pressed to ever track down crypto middlemen, that number in the hundreds of thousands if not millions.

Let's assume governments and acronym agencies across the globe want the world to adopt cryptocurrencies for the advantages they provide over OR world money related to tracking, monitoring, and ultimately controlling people. Would their retail arms in the crypto business find a solution? Is there a crypto solution to please environmentally oriented digital natives? How about libertarians? How will these battles play out? When the battle first manifests, what will it look like? Like everything sold to the demos, it will be an absolutely delightful solution to a pressing problem we all care about: Enter "Proof of Stake," and one Vitalik Buterin.

> *"Users and developers of the world's most-used blockchain have been wrangling with its carbon-footprint problem for as long as it's been around. Now, they say, several recent breakthroughs will finally enable them to drastically cut energy use in a year or less. Ethereum and better-known-rival Bitcoin both operate using a proof-of-work system that requires a global network of computers running around the clock. Software developers at Ethereum have been working for years to transition the blockchain to what's known as a proof-of-stake system -- which uses a totally different approach to secure the network that also eliminates the carbon emissions issue. The change -- delayed by complicated technical setbacks -- couldn't come soon enough for the cryptocurrency world, which weathered one of its biggest bouts of volatility ever this month after Elon Musk announced that Tesla Inc. would stop accepting Bitcoin as payment for cars because of the surging energy use. Bitcoin's network currently uses more power per year than Pakistan or the United Arab Emirates, according to the Cambridge Bitcoin Electricity Consumption Index. The compilers of the index don't measure Ethereum energy use. 'Switching to proof of stake has become more urgent for us because of how crypto and Ethereum have grown over the last year,' Vitalik Buterin, the inventor of Ethereum, said in an*

> *interview. He's hoping the change is made by year end, while others say it will be in place by the first half of 2022. That's about a year earlier than was expected in December."*[205]

What could possibly be the problem here? This is a book about alternative realities and their biopsychosocial impact upon life itself. Should I get into the details of every corner of the crypto world, our subject matter would be diverted from the overarching to the nuanced esoteric—and because the people who need to discern this content have been literally bioengineered to have the attention span of a fruit fly, the entire proposition would be an exercise in futility. Nevertheless, just be aware that in the VR world, all bets are off. That said, and ONLY in keeping with the focus of our subject matter, a question an intelligence specialist might ask if charged with protecting one nation state against its adversarial colleagues is what, if any, vulnerabilities do Proof of Stake versus Proof of Work (the way it is done now, e.g., Bitcoin uses Proof of Work) expose for the agency and its clients?

> *"Hacking and theft is one of the main real dangers to PoS,* ***especially from aggressive nation states.*** *This is a problem for all cryptocurrencies, but* ***isn't as dangerous*** *for PoW chains. Stolen PoS tokens can keep growing in perpetuity, increasing one's ownership of the network over time (since not everyone will stake). This is different from PoW chains like Bitcoin in that if you steal BTC, it will appreciate, but you won't get more BTC out of it. The other bit is that once stolen, PoS tokens can be kept forever and won't lose their use. You don't even have to let the hacked party know they've been hacked until you've accumulated enough for an attack (e.g., zero-day vulnerability against a popular crypto library)."*[206]

---

[205] Bloomberg Green, Ethereum Closes In on Long-Sought Fix to Cut Energy Use Over 99%. Story by: Matthew Leising, May 23, 2021.

[206] Viktor Bunin, Protocol Specialist at Bison Trails. ex-ETHDenver, ConsenSys, EY.

What if that same intelligence analyst no longer had to concern himself with aggressive nation states, because no nation states existed? Proof of Stake would not matter to the most powerful crypto army, but it would please the green digital natives who care about everything, it seems, but their freedom and privacy. What if everything was run centrally using a single currency, ethos, and zeitgeist? If anyone dared to challenge the Earthcoin, a "Department of Global Monetary Enforcement" would spring into action. Why, that is the stuff of a dystopian nightmare—yes, it is, and a few very smart and caring people tried/are trying to warn good people about this reality. Are you listening yet?

If economists worry about currency manipulation involving nation states, imagine if the unit of exchange became what I envision as the Earthcoin. Exchanging currency manipulation for a monopolistic global coin that NO ONE truly understands, save for a few math savants who will undoubtedly morph into crypto-oligarchs, is not a good bargain. What helped to bring us to a point where 1984 can actually become a reality?

Digital natives have been conditioned, if not deluded into thinking VR money or analogs of it *is* OR world money. Casinos in Las Vegas were aware of and tapped into this cognitive distortion a long time ago. When you play with *real* money, you will risk less of it compared to colorful markers that represent money. Without a credit card, you will buy less compared to handing over cash to make the exact same purchase. These examples go right to the heart of how OR world humans become confused, deluded, empowered, and ultimately led astray by VR money—just ask Ricardo Sanchez about the VR versus OR world.

This is one of the reasons digital natives find themselves in debt more often compared to "cash only people," and appear to be unable to distinguish between other people's money and their own money.

> **The sociopolitical and cultural implications of such delusions empowered, if not made possible, by VR are profound. Will socialism and then communism *necessarily* arise out of the ashes of OR world money?**

To be sure, political ideology forces itself upon almost everything, and crypto is not an exception. To think that an Earthcoin would be void of a political ideology is a delusion born of ignorance about who and what would implement a central currency in the first place, to wit:

> *"Hacktivist Bitcoin developer Amir Taaki took aim at Ethereum co-founder Vitalik Buterin on Twitter recently for essentially writing off smart contracts inventor Nick Szabo as a right-wing crank. Taaki wrote that this sort of attitude was typical of an "Eth[ereum] culture which is about sparkling burner parties, privileged digital nomads, microdosing LSD, sex orgies and 'social-justice' / vague doing-good." Pretty much everyone had the same initial thought: "Why aren't I getting invited to these parties?" But Taaki's comments also highlighted the political divisions between Ethereum and Bitcoin. Is it really as simple as Bitcoiners lean to the right and Ethereans lean to the left? You can make up your own mind about Nick Szabo's views, thanks to this obsessively curated list of his tweets. Buterin characterizes Szabo's utterances as bad faith arguing and "incholate yelling." He appears to regret naming a denomination of Ethereum after Szabo. But Taaki, who is British-Iranian, took exception to "white-leftypol" Ethereans canceling Szabo because "he doesn't fit their worldview" and wrote in a tweet that they reminded him of "white left (fake socialists) on an anti-racist crusade." "It's neo-colonialist white savior attitude," he wrote. "Eth is exactly this."* [207]

Mr. Nakamoto was confronted with a probing statement reminding him that cryptography cannot solve political and ideological problems. The Q&A went like this:

---

[207] MAGAZINE, by COINTELEGRAPH, Is Ethereum left and Bitcoin right? Story by: Andrew Fenton, August 31, 2020.

Anonymous: "You will not find a solution to political problems in cryptography."

Satoshi's answer: "Yes, but we can win a major battle in the arms race and gain a new territory of freedom for several years. Governments are good at cutting off the heads of a centrally controlled networks like Napster, but pure P2P networks like Gnutella and Tor seem to be holding their own."

In fact, here is an actual image of this exchange that took place in 2008 on the Cryptography Mailing List:

```
>You will not find a solution to political problems in cryptography.

Yes, but we can win a major battle in the arms race and gain a new territory of
freedom for several years.

Governments are good at cutting off the heads of a centrally controlled
networks like Napster, but pure P2P networks like Gnutella and Tor seem to be
holding their own.

Satoshi
```

Bitcoin and other cryptocurrencies are wrapped in multiple layers of ideological overlays, whether Satoshi wanted it or not. Collective mindsets are tailor-made for people who cannot make the "mine versus your" money distinction, and digital currencies make that riddle harder to solve than a fourth-year graduate school exam in quantum mechanics.

The rise of socialism and other collectivist ideologies and V the Reality money is consequential, not coincidental. The very nature of VR money makes it impossible to "have" your money without involving countless people (the collective) you've never met to ledger and legitimize it; that is, BLESS your transactions. Perhaps this is why Nick Szabo has been obsessively focused upon solving the "mine versus your" money conundrum in crypto. It also just so happens that Mr. Szabo is an articulate anti-collectivist firebrand voice in the crypto community.

Can you imagine challenging Bitcoin miners' accuracy? Is questioning the collective or block chain tantamount to blasphemy? Is the Siren song of crypto so alluring that you can't imagine a virtual system corrupted, given what you have learned about the NSA and Unit 8200's Pegasus, et al.?[208] Would you like to challenge crypto miners' ledgers if you DO NOT have *paper, i.e., OR world* proof that someone, somewhere short-changed you, used your name, your money? Have you ever heard someone assert, "I have been framed?" Permit me to share some forensic insights about OR versus VR world crime.

[208] Readers would do well to appreciate that what has been shared with you is limited in scope because of the nature of the subjects covered.

CHAPTER XXIV

FORT KNOX: It is hard to steal gold bullion because it is heavy

Thieves are remarkably practical and self-protective people. They are repelled by "jobs" that can result in physical harm, or their face on a wanted poster at the post office. Jewel thieves have told me one of the perks of their job is that diamonds and rubies are easy to pocket (carry). As a generalization, thieves are lazy and are dismissive of nine-to-five workers. To describe them as cunning and manipulative doesn't do them justice—no pun intended. Criminals don't like to do heavy lifting, to use a metaphor. So, let me ask my readers a question in keeping with that last metaphor: do you have any idea how much an electron weighs? Do you know how much space it occupies?

The actual weight of an electron is 9.05 x 10-28 grams—that's right, 9.05 times ten to the minus twenty eighth grams, an incredibly small mass. Multiply 34.1328 x 1023 times 9.05 x 10-28 and we get 308.9 grams times ten to minus 5, or in other words, 3.089 milligrams of electrons. A typical gold bullion bar measuring 7 inches x 3 and 5/8 inches x 1 and 3/4 inches weighs 27.5 pounds. Hmm, how many electrons are in one ounce of gold? I'll let you do the calculation. Here is how you do it:

1. Convert 1.01 ounces to grams

2. Look up the atomic weight and atomic number of gold in your chemistry book. You will want the atomic weight in units of grams per mole.

3. Divide the number of grams of gold by the atomic weight of gold. That gives you the number of moles of gold.

4. Multiply the number of moles of gold by Avogadro's number. That gives you the number of atoms of gold.

5. Multiply the number of atoms of gold by the atomic number of gold. That gives you the number of electrons.

Why am I telling you all of this? It has everything to do with virtual reality's ability to thumb its nose at the objective world, where staples in fingers can land you in the ER.

Bank heists are messy onstage affairs—just ask John Dillinger or Bonnie and Clyde. Infamous bank robber Willie Sutton provided his personal physician an autographed handwritten answer to the question "Why do you rob banks?" "Because that's where the money is." If you think the Willie Suttons of today are out of luck because of your Bitcoin not being in a bank, but spread out among the collective server farms mining crypto, then you may wish to reconsider that belief.

Bitcoin heists are clean backstage affairs—no sirens, no bullet-ridden getaway cars, i.e., just the way crooks like it.

That is the good news, but that is about it.

Bitcoin.com

See the immediately preceding image? No, the thief did not physically carry out digital code over his shoulder, nor is Bitcoin an actual coin. Even the most sophisticated among you probably have no idea how crypto heists are carried out—except you might have guessed that you do not have to get off your derriere to pull one off. I'm not talking about some vague description or something you read after you conducted a Google IQ search. I'm referring to a detailed explanation of how crypto can be stolen, corrupted, and manipulated without fear of imminent physical reprisal. And for the one person out there who may be able to explain it—you are probably an acronym agency agent in the business of thwarting digital thievery, or one of the trusted brain trusts of crypto technology in a disguise that would make Frank Abagnale proud.

Frank Abagnale (Character inspiration for the movie, Catch Me if You Can)

By the way, if you were to explain in detail how crypto theft is carried out, no one among the general public would understand a word you said. On the other hand, the vast majority of bank robberies are intuitive and solvable. Most are so simple that even a grammar school child can explain them with ease: "Man went into a bank with a mask on, pulled a gun and said to the teller, 'give me a bag of cash.' He left the bank and got into a getaway car." Oh, the FDIC protects your money held in a bank, up to $250,000 for an individual and double that amount for a couple with survivorship rights. The day after the bank robbery, you can access the bank's ATM and withdraw the maximum allowable amount without the FBI questioning you about the dollar bills in your pocket. The advantages of OR world money don't stop there when it comes to protecting your money from the bad guys.

Money takes up physical space, which is ostensibly the reason that the largest USD denomination is $100. Fort Knox has one of the world's largest gold reserves. If you want to steal what is inside of Fort Knox, you will have to get up from behind your computer and expose your physical body to armed guards. You then have to transport, that is carry the loot, and then find a place to keep it. If you can steal millions of Bitcoin without getting up off your derriere, and that is literally true, then that is what we call in forensics an "invite." Have the paranoids, psychopaths, and SOBs answered the RSVP? You bet they have.

Let me stress at the outset for the confirmation bias readers and members of the church of crypto, including the Bitcoin, Etherium, et al. denominations, the following listing of crypto thefts (growing everyday) are not problems of the past, e.g.:

- *"Hacker stole around $1.7 billion in Crypto in 2018 alone."*
- *"Hackers Stole Over $4 Billion From Crypto Crimes In 2019 So Far, Up From $1.7 Billion In All of 2018."*
- *"Cryptocurrency Hackers Steal $3.8 Billion in 2020."* [209]

1. **Coincheck**

Japanese crypto exchange Coincheck was hacked to the tune of 500 million NEM (or about 532 million USD) in January 2018.

2. **Mt. Gox**

The Mt. Gox hack reverberated throughout global crypto communities, and for good reason. It is still not entirely clear how many attackers were able to steal exactly how much, but we do know that a vulnerability that allowed users to withdraw more Bitcoin than they owned persisted for quite some time.

---

[209] Organized Crime and Corruption Reporting Project (OCCRP): *Cryptocurrency Hackers Steal $3.8 Billion in 2020. Written by: Will Neal, January 14, 2021.*

3. **Bitfinex**

The Bitfinex hack was first announced in August 2016 and involved a total of about 120,000 Bitcoin, representing a fiat equivalent of 72 million USD at the time. Unlike with Mt. Gox, the coins were stolen in a single attack out of the company's wallets, despite them having set up some precautions to prevent such failure. It is still unclear how and which mechanisms failed and allowed the attackers to get away with such a heist.

4. **NiceHash**

Occupying a place on our list is NiceHash, which was defrauded of 4,700 Bitcoin (or about 64 million USD) in December 2017. NiceHash was a Slovenian cryptocurrency mining marketplace, where independent miners could rent out hash power to users who didn't have their own mining machines. NiceHash operated a number of hot and cold wallets to distribute mining rewards among its members. It was these wallets that were targeted, but despite the large number of funds lost, NiceHash has been able to reimburse over 75% of all losses.

5. **Zaif**

Zaif was plundered of various cryptocurrencies, including Bitcoin, Bitcoin Cash, and Monacoin, losing about 62 million USD in fiat equivalent in September 2018.

It took the exchange three days to realize that funds were missing from its hot wallets, but it promptly announced that company funds would be used to compensate all customers.

6. **Binance**

Hackers swiped 7,000 Bitcoin from Binance, one of the world's most popular crypto exchanges, in May 2019. The amount totaled about 40 million USD in equivalent fiat. Binance was able to reimburse its users with a dedicated 'insurance fund' set up for this purpose. Withdrawals, however, were suspended for a few days as the exchange tried to figure out what went wrong. The CEO, Zhao Changpeng, wrote a comprehensive blog post outlining the attack and engaged in a Twitter exchange to allay user concerns, pre-empting concerns raised especially during the Mt. Gox and Bitfinex crises. [210]

A couple of observations for those church members who would point out that in some cases, some crypto was returned to its owners—and you think that is a positive? How were YOU and YOUR crypto linked? Bitcoin's inherent and unresolvable Achilles' heel is the fact that it is auditioning as V the Reality money, and nothing can change that. Here is just one example of how forensic investigations in the virtual world are eerily similar to the work of the Mario brothers in the sewers of New York City:

£3.5 billion Bitcoin stolen; recoverable. Hope for thousands of others

"Legal proceedings have begun against a number of ***Bitcoin developers****. The action will, for the first time, examine the nature and extent of legal duties conferred upon and owed by developers resulting from the control they exercise over their respective blockchains. Litigation law firm Ontier LLP has begun legal proceedings against Bitcoin developers for the BTC, BCH, BCH ABC, and BSV protocols after a substantial theft of Bitcoin occurred in 2020. The firm is acting on behalf of Tulip Trading Limited (TTL), a Seychelles company whose*

[210] Express VPN, 6 Of The Biggest Crypto Heists Of All Time. May 21 2021.

primary beneficial owner and CEO is Dr. Craig Wright. Dr. Wright claims to be the inventor of Bitcoin who set out his vision for the digital currency in his White Paper under the pseudonym Satoshi Nakamoto. In May 2016 he publicly identified himself as Satoshi Nakamoto, revealing his identity to three media organisations—the BBC, the Economist, and GQ. At the meeting with the BBC, Mr. Wright digitally signed messages using cryptographic keys created during the early days of Bitcoin's development. Although several people believe he is the person who invented Bitcoin, his many detractors dispute that he is actually Nakamoto. They claim he is a fraudster claiming to be Satoshi with no evidence, and claims to own a Bitcoin address stolen from Mt Gox. [211]

V the Reality money and all that goes along with it, including manipulation and theft, will always be more similar to Shigeru Miyamoto and Gunpei Yokoi's vision of New York City's sewer system than the real-world sewers maintained by New York City's Department of Environmental Services.

VR World

[211] ZDNet: Blockchain, Story by: Eileen Brown for Social Business | February 24, 2021.

OR World

Moon Rising Over Mount Sinai (OR)

Moon Rising Over Mount Sinai (VR)

> **Virtual reality will always be a fertile point of entry for control freaks, crooks, greed merchants, and their ilk, until the point in time when it is not vulnerable—and at that point, Bitcoin will have been completely compromised and taken over by the adversaries of the Cypherpunks and Crypto Anarchists, or existent central banks across the globe will have been eradicated and replaced with their VR version—"meet the new boss, same as the old boss," except the new boss will have exponentially more power over you.**

Approximately 82 percent of crypto heists are unsolvable. [212] What about unsolvable bank robberies—and let's include in the mix armored transport vehicles? Permit me to quote Scientific American's analysis on this very subject,

> **Moot Loot: Stats Show Crime Doesn't Pay--for Most Bank Robbers**

---

[212] Traders of Crypto: METHODOLOGY: We combined multiple sources to find the biggest online attacks against financial institutions that resulted in money being directly stolen by the hackers. We looked at the last 10 years of data to find how much was stolen, who it was stolen by and exactly who the targets were.*Some funds can be blocked from being transferred, and in some cases the money can be recovered.**Mt.Gox had continual heists from 2011 to 2014, but the grand total is displayed.

> *"Statistical evidence argues that holding up banks is a dangerous and unlucrative career that nets the average bank robber the annual salary of a cafe barista—and at the peril of getting caught or shot."*

Tellers are typically allowed to keep only $5,000 in their cash drawer. In-bank surveillance and the often-overlooked parking area surveillance systems, which include license plate readers, makes the entire proposition—well, to be gracious——stupid. But why is it stupid? For one primary reason: OR world behaviors are governed by real world physics, and as we noted in the opening section in this book when we defined OR:

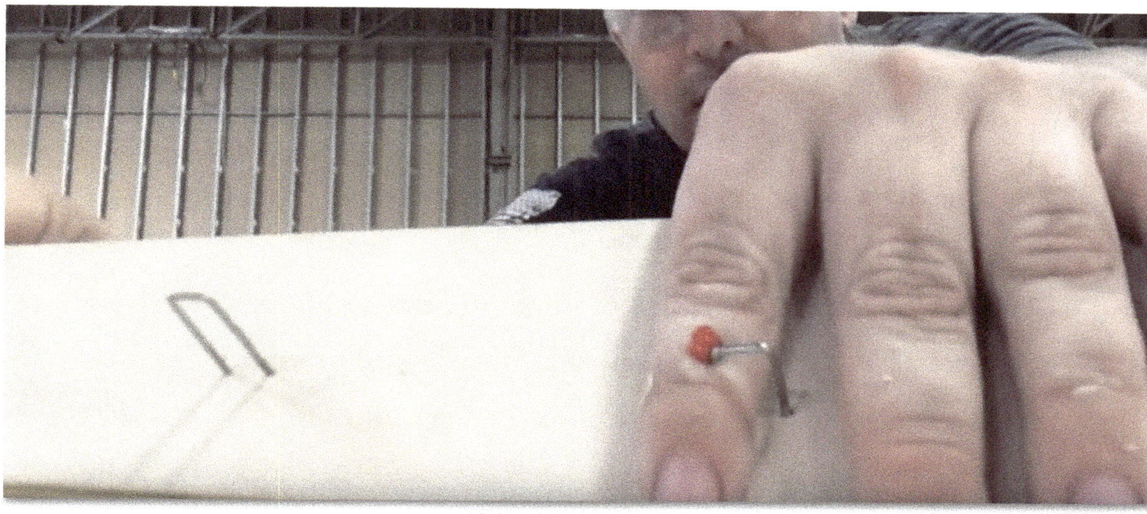

Objective Reality

It is the same fundamental precept that implored globalists to find their dream scenarios in the virtual world, and not the real world.

Virtual reality is a make-believe world where you can violate the natural laws that govern the earth and the people in it. As long as you, an OR world being, and your money do not live in a virtual world, then *you have a chance* of winning the battle for privacy and personal freedom—but *only* if you fight. Never forget this about the battle for freedom and privacy—**at least in the OR world, you have a chance of winning**. Why is that? Aleksandr Solzhenitsyn explained the psychodynamic in his masterpiece *The Gulag Archipelago*:

> *"And how we burned in the camps later, thinking: What would things have been like if every Security I operative, when he went out at night to make an arrest, had been uncertain whether he would return alive and*

> *had to say good-bye to his family? Or if, during periods of mass arrests, as for example in Leningrad, when they arrested a quarter of the entire city, people had not simply sat there in their lairs, paling with terror at every bang of the downstairs door and at every step on the staircase, but had understood they had nothing left to lose and had boldly set up in the downstairs hall an ambush of half a dozen people with axes, hammers, pokers, or whatever else was at hand?... The Organs would very quickly have suffered a shortage of officers and transport and, notwithstanding all of Stalin's thirst, the cursed machine would have ground to a halt! If...if...We didn't love freedom enough. And even more—we had no awareness of the real situation.... We purely and simply deserved everything that happened afterward."*[213]

The self-protective/defense psychodynamics described by Solzhenitsyn in the face of government thugs *only* exist in the OR world.

> **Those who would strip you of your privacy and freedom can do things to you in the VR world that they would or could never do in the OR world. Two of the most potent inhibitory forces that protect privacy, and ultimately your freedom, are missing in the virtual world—immediate physical reprisal and/or the seemingly simple act of identification. In my abiding attempt to keep it real—in the VR world, you do NOT have to face this guy, and that is a gigantic RSVP.**

[213] Part I The Prison Industry, Ch. 1 "Arrest" (p13, The Gulag Archipelago, Collins 1974)

Actor Clint Eastwood as Dirty Harry

CHAPTER XXV

SPACE INVADERS: So you want to play in the matrix

People within the cryptography and coding community spend a disproportionately large amount of their lives planted behind digital devices, manipulating virtual reality that will eventually seep into the real world. These people have made BOTH violating AND protecting your privacy and constitutional freedoms into an international multiplayer videogame competition.

> *"Multiplayer video game competitions involve professional players and teams of pros competing against one another in countries across the globe. Organized competitions have long been a part of video game culture but did not evolve to include paid pros until the late 21st century. The population boom of digital natives fueled professional competition. Digital natives coming of age were willing to pay to watch video gamers compete. By 2010 professional video gaming had come of age which meant game developers were willing to fund tournaments and other events. [By] 2010 the total audience of esports had grown to 454 million viewers, with revenue increasing to more than $1 billion. Those numbers have only increased with each passing year."* [214]

---

214 a. Hamari, Juho, Sjöblom, Max (2016). "What is eSports and why do people watch it?" 10.1108/IntR-04-2016-0085. SSRN 2686182.

To give the reader a historical flavor of the cryptographic/video gaming culture, below is a photo of the 1981 USA *Space Invaders* championship, sponsored by the game's maker, Atari. The event drew over 10,000 participants from across the country.

Gamers Competing in the 1981 USA Space Invaders Championship in Chicago, Illinois Sponsored by Game Maker Atari

While these particular video gamers were enthralled with the nascent world of virtual reality, the likes of Tim May were taking virtual reality to the next level. The following is a photo of Tim May from roughly the same time period as the *Space Invaders* national championship competition:

b. Reuters: Global esports revenues to top $1 billion in 2019, February 12, 2019.

Tim May Wrapped in the American Flag Carrying an Early Iteration of a Guy Fawkes Mask

If you pay close attention to the national security battle between the heirs of the *Space Invaders* contest players, Cypherpunks, Crypto Anarchists, and the PoW versus PoS virtual world writers who either work for "the man" or against "the man," you will soon learn something of importance that was only made possible by—in fact it could have never happened without—mankind's obsession with virtual reality.

For all of the marvelous, enticing analogs of the 1849 California gold rush promised by crypto gamblers and the naïve dream of killing "the man" with crypto, the reality is a recipe for disaster– a conclusion that when written or voiced, will garner the same degree of hatred experienced by the late Madeline Murray O'Hare by the Pentecostal Church in its heyday.

> **Human beings in the collective have turned over their most precious civil rights, psychological well being, psychosexual life's meaning, and financial health to a group of backstage dwellers who properly belong to a small cult that has always lived in the abstract castles in their mind. Those castles are made up of many entertaining, functional, and life-changing technological wonders, but they also contain factories that created death stars.**

Cult members speak a language only they can understand and manipulate variables that can only be seen in the OR world with an electron microscope—if then. Cult members have moved their inherently isolated, esoteric, and rebellious internal psychological world to the real world, where they now define war, the terrain upon which battles are fought, and when and if peace should be declared. To say they will cause the final war is probably going too far, but I don't trust Atlas no matter how eloquently Mr. Schmidt assures me he is like a big puppy dog and we, the original killer robots, will control him.

The virtual world is ego-fulfilling, fun, functional and intoxicatingly addictive—and not merely psychologically addictive, but biochemically addictive. Digital natives, converts, and especially people whose ambition far outstrips their talents, are reluctant to arise from their simulator cockpit and enter the real world where they would have to compete with the likes of Chuck Yeager, or before him the Red Barron. Instead of winning the national championship *Space Invaders* tournament, gamers would come face-to-face with their shortcomings, inadequacies and inability, to socially relate in a conscientious and positive manner.

Put aside flight simulators, which are immaterial for our discussion here. Remove from our scrutiny enticing sex cyborgs and all the open-season social media venues where you can harass others at will without being knocked on your proverbial derriere, as would undoubtedly occur in the real world—those venues are all minor league—positive or negative:

You have no idea who or what you are dealing with when you work or play in the VR world. The military industrial complex and oligarch-controlled VR world provide a universal gateway or access point for sociopaths to enter the minds of anyone and everyone that has allowed parts of themselves to play, work, or transact business in the virtual world. The problem is not virtual reality, per se; it is V is THE reality that is the problem and it is irresolvable by definition.

What can YOU do? Edward Snowden's commentaries have a common thread that runs through them and provides a starting point. His thoughts are mirrored by each and every person who has been backstage: Disconnect, or at the very least, step into the virtual world gingerly and with your eyes wide open. Edward does not use a cell phone. He has explained in the past that even burner phones catch up with you sooner or later, and that goes with the territory of digital communication. It is fascinating that in a moment of reflection, Edward said, "If you want to communicate something private to another person, go for a long walk in the woods and make sure no one follows you, and of course have nothing that runs on electricity on or even near your person." It would also go a very long way for people to develop a deep and abiding humbleness.

Humility is lacking among members of the Gen Z generation and, to a lesser but still pathological level, those who preceded them—it is not their fault, but it is their responsibility to take stock of this issue, or by the time they collectively figure it out, it will be too late. Virtual lives have a way of creating a false sense of your power and influence in life—almost always the false sense error manifests as an overestimation of who and what you are. Is it any wonder that the very moment reality confronts us with its natural selection power, we are repelled and run back to our virtual world where we feel great? But in that bargain to feel good, we give away the only thing that matters when all is said and done—freedom from the paranoids, psychopaths, and SOBs who run roughshod over the virtual world. NOT one, not a SINGLE meaningful revolution that conveyed freedom from oppression, elevation of the human spirit, and certainly not economic justice, could have EVER succeeded if the battleground looked like this:

Minecraft Cinema 4D

The original Cypherpunks and Crypto Anarchists, as well as many of the current crop of true believers, were/are intent upon bridling oppressive power structures and the people who animate them: "The road to hell is paved with good intentions." But instead of putting legacy power structures out of business, or at the very least controlling them, crypto money makers have released the most oppressive institutions, and the people who man them from their brick-and-mortar jail cell, home detention, or curfews, thanks to V the Reality money. To say it another way:

> **For the first time in human history, Big Brother can see the light at the end of the tunnel—and no, it is not an oncoming train. It is you in the collective, with your screens glowing bright and reflecting off your faces as you tune out the real world for a make-believe world you think you control. Those people at the beach held by the tractor beam of VR, with their faces basking in the glow of OLED screens, represent an existential threat to life on earth.**

Consumers of VR would do well to pay attention to the following peek behind the curtain. Eavesdrop as a consigliore to the math savants recreating your world attempted to change their minds if not their hearts.

> "I get it that because you were math savants coming of age in a technological golden era, you came to believe you were literally a nom du guerre *Deathwing*. It doesn't matter what clever code you write, another *Deathwing* impostor will thwart you, then you him, so on and so forth ad infinitum. Locksmiths became a "thing" after the invention of the chastity belt—but neither the inventor of the chastity belt or the locksmiths who learned to hack them changed neural tissue, thoughts, feelings and behaviors like you have done. What did you think the paranoids, psychopaths and SOBs would do with your creation(s)? Am I to believe that you honestly believe **your special group didn't have from the very beginning moles, double agents and betrayal artists?** The existent power structures will either subsume your creations or have one of their own take it over, aka create their own crypto. But when they do, and it is only a matter of time, they will have grown exponentially more powerful."

Some of the crypto-gamblers have and will become rich, in the same way a few GME[215] gamers got rich—hooray! Now you, too, can buy happiness. Don't expect ANY on-air financial guru or commentator to chastise you or your fellow gamblers or dare criticize Robinhood-mediated price action. From their perspective, price IS truth—and besides, they make their living off retail investors' notorious and predictable irrational exuberance, interrupted from time to time with abject panic attacks. We all know financial "channels" log their highest ratings when the SH*T hits the fan. To analysts' and financial network hosts' credit, they know better than to call out the Reddit and Robinhood crowd for doing what Wall Street insiders (the

[215] GME is not an isolated publicly traded company. AMC, Dogecoin and I could list one hundred stock symbols right now that are ripe for the pickings of VR gamblers.

subjects of their reportage if they are competent) have been doing since the proverbial first "power-lunch" insiders' sit-down was had. Besides, NFTs, Robinhood, and Reddit digital cowboys represent new blood and the next generation. Financial reporters and analysts appear to be almost unanimous in their opinion that if the new way is to throw fundamentals into the garbage bin of history for the prestidigitation of flash mobs trading stock, then in their need to be youthful and hip, they'll join in—at least until the music stops, and then you can be sure they'll rediscover what was wrong all along with the new crop of gamblers: "it was all in their head." When that does occur, at least they would be correct for once in their lives.

Only people who really care about you will tell you in no uncertain terms that you are playing the role of a patsy. In the intelligence business, OR world dealings have a Machiavellian flavor to them almost by definition. The real-world men and women who served as agents may not have been or be *Deathwing,* but they were mostly honorable, and their collateral damage didn't *intentionally* involve you. Agents in the VR world are not exactly ladies' men, rugged, or charming, but they are prolific causal agents of collateral damage—civilians beware! No bomb shelters work in the VR world. However, readers should not despair, unless you refuse to rethink your relationship with VR, et al.

During the closing argument scene of the classic movie *The Verdict*, Paul Newman's character, Frank Galvin, is a sole practitioner lawyer and recovering alcoholic who discovers the love of his life has been secretly working for the Catholic hospital defendant, in a case where his vibrant and healthy client had been made an invalid by an act of medical malpractice at the hands of a world-famous doctor. The best lawyers money can buy represent the hospital and the doctor. Galvin's star witness is a whistleblower who kept a copy of a damning intake form. She, like the whistleblowers of today, was found living in exile having been forced to give up the only thing she ever wanted to do-help people in her role as an RN. The press and the general public are convinced that Frank has no hope of winning the case. His closing argument is a reminder to readers that when you possess a desire to do the right thing, and have the courage to do something IN THE OR world, you are not powerless in the face of seemingly insurmountable odds,

> ***"Judge Hoyle**: Summation....summation?*
>
> ***Galvin**: Well...You know, so much of the time we're just lost. We say, "Please, God, tell us what is right. Tell us what is true." I mean there is no justice. The rich win; the poor are powerless. We become tired of hearing people lie. And after a time we become dead, a little dead. We think of ourselves as victims—and we become victims. We become weak; we doubt ourselves; we doubt our beliefs; we doubt our institutions; and we doubt the law –*
>
> *But today you are the law. You are the law, not some book, not the lawyers, not a marble statue, or the trappings of the court. See, those are just symbols of our desire to be just. They are, in fact, a prayer. I mean, a fervent and a frightened prayer. In my religion, they say, "Act as if you had faith; faith will be given to you." If we are to have faith in justice, we need only to believe in ourselves and act with justice. See, I believe there is justice in our hearts."*

Paul Newman Closing Argument Scene from the Movie THE VERDICT

I have only one remaining question for the collective. To be candid, most of you do NOT appreciate the importance of the following question or its answer at this point in time. But I will ask it nonetheless, while you gaze at the following photograph, in hopes that someday you will:

fe63971522de43971f742ed3d409554f5bb7377df9a1d4bf005272b70fb68856

Princeton Prospect House, March 2014 (photo credit: Matt Green)

"Goldfinger

He's the man, the man with the Midas touch

A spider's touch

Such a cold finger

Beckons you to enter his web of sin

But don't go in

Golden words he will pour in your ear

But his lies can't disguise what you fear

For a golden girl knows when he's kissed her

It's the kiss of death from

Mister Goldfinger

Pretty girl beware of this heart of gold

This heart is cold

He loves only gold

Only gold

Golden words he will pour in your ear

But his lies can't disguise what you fear

For a golden girl knows..."[216]

217

Actor Karl Gerhart "Gert" Fröbe as Goldfinger from the Movie GOLDFINGER (1964 MGM)

The Movie *Goldfinger* Plot: While investigating a gold magnate's smuggling, James Bond uncovers **a plot to contaminate the Fort Knox gold reserve.**

Director: Guy Hamilton

Writers: Richard Maibaum (screenplay by), Paul Dehn (screenplay by)

Stars: Sean Connery, Gert Fröbe, Honor Blackman.

James Bond: "Fifteen billion dollars in gold bullion weighs ten-thousand five hundred tons. Sixteen men would take twelve days to load it onto two hundred trucks. Now at the most you're going to have two hours before the Army, Navy, Air Force, Marines move in and make you put it back."

Goldfinger: "Who mentioned anything about removing it?"

---

[216] Goldfinger, Writer/s: ANTHONY NEWLEY, JOHN BARRY, LESLIE BRICUSSE, Publisher: Sony/ATV Music Publishing LLC.
[217] DoYouRemember, by: Fabrizio Nava.

James Bond: "You plan to break into the world's largest bank and not steal anything. Why?

Goldfinger: "Go on, Mr. Bond."

It is then revealed that Goldfinger's devious and brilliant plan is to devalue OR world gold by making it undesirable—that is, radioactive—which will then make Goldfinger's assets in his world increase tenfold. In 1965, crypto had not been invented, but if it had been, Goldfinger would have been named Bitfinger and the movie script would have been a Doppelgänger for what is happening right at this very moment in time. Who says reality doesn't imitate the virtual world?

THE END?

EPILOGUE

In the VR world YOU are the mouse

To a Mouse

BY ROBERT BURNS

On Turning her up in her Nest, with the Plough, November 1785.

Wee, sleeket, cowran, tim'rous beastie,
O, what a panic's in thy breastie!
Thou need na start awa sae hasty,
Wi' bickerin brattle!
I wad be laith to rin an' chase thee
Wi' murd'ring pattle!

I'm truly sorry Man's dominion
Has broken Nature's social union,
An' justifies that ill opinion,
Which makes thee startle,
At me, thy poor, earth-born companion,
An' fellow-mortal!

I doubt na, whyles, but thou may thieve;
What then? poor beastie, thou maun live!
A daimen-icker in a thrave
'S a sma' request:

I'll get a blessin wi' the lave,
An' never miss 't!

Thy wee-bit housie, too, in ruin!
It's silly wa's the win's are strewin!
An' naething, now, to big a new ane,
O' foggage green!
An' bleak December's winds ensuin,
Baith snell an' keen!

Thou saw the fields laid bare an' waste,
An' weary Winter comin fast,
An' cozie here, beneath the blast,
Thou thought to dwell,
Till crash! the cruel coulter past
Out thro' thy cell.

That wee-bit heap o' leaves an' stibble
Has cost thee monie a weary nibble!
Now thou's turn'd out, for a' thy trouble,
But house or hald,
To thole the Winter's sleety dribble,
An' cranreuch cauld!

But Mousie, thou art no thy-lane,
In proving foresight may be vain:
The best laid schemes o' Mice an' Men
Gang aft agley,
An' lea'e us nought but grief an' pain,
For promis'd joy!

Still, thou art blest, compar'd wi' me!
The present only toucheth thee:
But Och! I backward cast my e'e,
On prospects drear!
An' forward tho' I canna see,
I guess an' fear!

My efforts to help good people that are found in the contents of this book will hopefully be as helpful as the following translation of Robert Burns' tale of a kind, sweet, and feeling farmer who unearthed a mouse with his plough. Warm and kind people must find the gumption to knock back the forces of evil onto their heels, lest you find yourself knocked onto your back and living in their world that is as cold as the coming winter.

To a Mouse
By
Robert Burns

The current author's translation and revision to a more perfect world:

Preface: A farmer, able to feel for and with his fellow sentient beings, was tilling his soil when he unearthed a little field mouse that had tried his best to shield himself from the harsh world by burying himself in the untilled soil of the farmer's field.

Small, crafty and cowering scared to death little creature.
You are so panicked and frightened.
You need not run for your life with your little mouth chattering in fear! I would be loathe to run and chase you with a murdering plough to do you harm.
I'm truly sorry man's false sense of his dominion over you destroyed nature's social union between all living things.

You are sadly correct—you need to be afraid of the monsters that roam the earth and no doubt look just like me. I know I am nothing but your poor, earth born companion and fellow mortal!
Oh I hear the monsters justify their murderous intent with their chattering tongues – "That mouse is a thief," they say. – I don't doubt you may steal some grain now and then – so what? "If I do not cull them they will die of overpopulation." Yes, killing has always been a very effective way to destroy life and the men who do it ALWAYS justify it in a million and one ways.
Poor little friend you must live, too! For heaven's sake an odd ear of corn in twenty-four sheaves is a small request for a hungry friend.
I will get a blessing with what is left and I will never miss it.
Your small house is now in ruin thanks to me of no ill will!
Its feeble walls the winds are scattering! And nothing now to build a new one for no grass is left.
And bleak December's winds are coming and they will be bitter and harsh.
You poor dear, you saw the fields laid bare and wasted, and winter coming fast and it looked so cozy here you thought to seek refuge.
Then your peace was crashed! The cruel plough unearthed your home and only by the grace of all that is good you were spared.
That small heap of leaves and stubble has cost you not helped you.
Now you are turned out, for all your trouble, without house or holding to endure the winter's sleety dribble, and bone chilling cold.
But little Mouse, you are not alone,
in proving foresight may be vain:
The best laid schemes of mice and men go often awry,
And leave us nothing but grief and pain despite what we were told and believed. We were promised joy if only we did this or that.

Still you are blessed when compared with me! The present only touches you. But I am one who the monsters told their secrets and backward I cast my eye to prospects dreary and wasted opportunities. Moving forward, I know what I cannot see. I guess and fear but I know this, I will take you into my home and give you a home and at least the two of us will commiserate together.

………………………………………………………………………………………

And finally, for readers still confused about the delta between objective and virtual reality…

"I believe in everything until it's disproved. So I believe in fairies, the myths, dragons. It all exists, even if it's in your mind. Who's to say that dreams and nightmares aren't as real as the here and now?"…. **John Lennon**

"At the time my thinking was he has all of this money, lives in this beautiful apartment and he is into music representing a more cautious lifestyle, a more giving lifestyle," Chapman told parole commissioners. "It made me angry and jealous compared to the way I was living at the time. There was jealousy in there."… **Mark David Chapman**

As of 2021, Mr. Chapman is alive and Mr. Lennon is dead, but John's music lives on in the minds of people who hear it.

INDEX

CPSIA information can be obtained
at www.ICGtesting.com
Printed in the USA
LVHW072032220921
698440LV00009B/267

9 781638 68023